ANDREW
HEYWOOD

POLITICAL IDEOLOGIES

AN INTRODUCTION

4TH EDITION

4TH EDITION

palgrave
macmillan

First edition 1992
Second edition 1998
Third edition 2003
Fourth edition 2007
PALGRAVE MACMILLAN
Houndmills, Basingstoke, Hampshire RG21 6XS and
175 Fifth Avenue, New York, NY 10010
Companies and representatives throughout the world

PALGRAVE MACMILLAN is the global academic imprint of the Palgrave Macmillan
division of St. Martin's Press, LLC and of Palgrave Macmillan Ltd. Macmillan® is a
registered trademark in the United States, United Kingdom and other countries.
Palgrave is a registered trademark in the European Union and other countries.

ISBN-13: 978–0–230–52179–7   hardback
ISBN-10: 0–230–52179–7   hardback
ISBN-13: 978–0–230–52180–3   paperback
ISBN-10: 0–230–52180–0   paperback

This book is printed on paper suitable for recycling and made from fully
managed and sustained forest sources. Logging, pulping and manufacturing
processes are expected to conform to the environmental regulations of the
country of origin.

A catalogue record for this book is available from the British Library.

A catalog record for this book is available from the Library of Congress.

10   9   8   7   6   5
14   13 12 11 10 09

Printed and bound in China

To Jean

SUMMARY OF

CONTENTS

CONTENTS

FIGURES

BOXES

PERSPECTIVES ON . . .

TENSIONS WITHIN . . .

FOREWORD

Ideology has had a strange history. It is inseparable from the political experience of the modern world, yet few major theorists of politics have a good word for it. Figures as diverse as Karl Marx, Michael Oakeshott and Talcott Parsons all condemned it, for different reasons. To its opponents ideology is the opposite of such wholesome things as truth, science, rationality, objectivity and philosophy. It signifies beliefs and doctrines that are either dogmas beyond the reach of criticism or cloaks for individual and group interests.

It is hardly surprising, given the influence of this negative conception, that it should at times have been fashionable to bury ideology and declare it at an end. But like similar efforts to bury history and politics, ideology has a habit of coming back. The politics of the modern world have been shaped by the key ideological traditions. Ideologies are a crucial resource for ordering, defining and evaluating political reality and establishing political identities.

The great merit of Andrew Heywood's book is that he takes ideology seriously, and explores patiently and with admirable clarity the different characteristics of the classic western ideologies, as well as the new themes and directions of recent ideological thought. He has produced one of the best available introductions to the subject anywhere in print.

The western ideological tradition, which originated in the French and American revolutions of the eighteenth century, does not exhaust ways of understanding politics, nor does it eclipse many non-western traditions of political thought. But it is an indispensable tradition nonetheless, and an ability to understand its key terms and internal development is a basic requirement for citizenship in the modern world. Andrew Heywood is the ideal guide.

ANDREW GAMBLE

PREFACE TO THE FOURTH EDITION

The first edition of *Political Ideologies* was written against the backdrop of the east European revolutions of 1989–91. In retrospect, the 'collapse of communism' was both a manifestation of and a catalyst for a series of profoundly significant, and in many cases interconnected, politico-historical developments. Among the most important of these have been the growth of a global capitalist economy, the rise of ethnic nationalism and religious fundamentalism, the advent of postmodern or 'information' societies, the emergence of a US-dominated unipolar world order, and the birth of global terrorism. In dizzying ways, history appears to have speeded up. The certainties and solidities of old are now doubted or, in some cases, have been discarded altogether. These processes have had major implications for political ideologies. Socialism is commonly declared to be dead; some proclaim the final triumph of western liberalism while others point out that it is in crisis; nationalism is adapting to the challenges of supranationalism and multiculturalism; and so forth.

Some commentators regard such shifts as but symptoms of a deeper process: the demise of ideology itself (and, with it, of the programmatic political party). Political ideology simply has no place in a postmodern, globalized world that is characterized by social fragmentation and dominated by personal consumption. However, what we are witnessing is not so much the end of ideology (always a dangerous thing to proclaim) as the fact that the major ideological traditions have, in effect, been out-paced by history. New ideological thinking has struggled to make sense of the world as it is, and, frankly, has little idea where the world is going. Nevertheless, as the principal source of meaning and idealism in politics, ideology, in whatever shape or form it may take, is destined to survive. Ultimately, de-ideologized or consumerist politics is doomed because it does not give people a reason to believe in something larger than material self-interest and because people's personal narratives only make sense when situated within broader historical narratives.

This fourth edition attempts to take account of how the major ideological traditions, and ideology itself, have adapted to these challenges. There is a new chapter on multiculturalism (Chapter 11). Although multiculturalism may not be an ideology in the same sense as, say, liberalism and socialism (a question that is, needless to say, discussed in the text itself), the issues that have arisen from the increasingly multi-ethnic, multi-religious and multi-cultural nature of many modern societies are now so important that they deserve to be addressed separately, and not as sub-debates within liberalism and conservatism. Another issue that receives greater attention is the nature and significance of the transition from so-called 'classical' ideologies to what have been described as 'new' ideologies. Why have these ideologies emerged? In what sense are they 'new'? And how do they differ from 'old' ideologies? The text has been revised and updated throughout, with account being taken both of changes within ideologies themselves and their changing significance. As a result, for instance, the coverage of orthodox communism has been reduced, while the discussions of Islamism and the foreign policy aspects of neoconservatism have been expanded.

In addition to the existing features of the books – in particular, 'thinker', 'isms', 'perspectives on' and 'tensions within' boxes – this edition has a range of new features. These include the following. Each chapter starts with a boxed introductory section, which outlines the overall nature of the ideology and its key themes. Diagrams are more frequently used to illustrate important ideas or theories. Each chapter concludes with a list of 'questions for discussion'. Definitions of key terms, highlighted in **bold** in the text, appear on the page where they are first used, instead in a separate glossary at the end. Finally, as a navigational aid, index entries for 'thinker' , '-isms' and 'perspective' boxes are in **bold**, and those for on-page definitions of key terms are in *italics*.

I would like to thank all those who commented on or gave me feedback on earlier editions of the book, and hope that the fourth edition goes some way to addressing the matters and suggestions they raised.

ANDREW HEYWOOD

CHAPTER 1

INTRODUCTION: UNDERSTANDING IDEOLOGY

PREVIEW

All people are political thinkers. Whether they know it or not, people use political ideas and concepts whenever they express their opinions or speak their mind. Everyday language is littered with terms such as 'freedom', 'fairness', 'equality', 'justice' and 'rights'. In the same way, words such as 'conservative', 'liberal', 'socialist', 'communist' and 'fascist' are regularly employed by people either to describe their own views, or those of others. However, even though such terms are familiar, even commonplace, they are seldom used with any precision or a clear grasp of their meaning. What, for instance, is 'equality'? What does it mean to say that all people are equal? Are people born equal, should they be treated by society as if they are equal? Should people have equal rights, equal opportunities, equal political influence, equal wages? Similarly, words such as 'socialist' or 'fascist' are commonly misused. What does it mean to call someone a 'fascist'? What values or beliefs do fascists hold, and why do they hold them? How do socialist views differ from those of, say, liberals, conservatives or anarchists? This book examines the substantive ideas and beliefs of the major political ideologies. This introductory chapter considers the role of ideas in politics, the life and (sometimes convoluted) times of the concept of ideology, the nature and structure of ideological thought, and the changing landscape of political ideologies.

The role of ideas

Not all political thinkers have accepted that ideas and ideologies are of much importance. Politics has sometimes been thought to be little more than a naked struggle for power. If this is true, political ideas are mere propaganda, a form of words or collection of slogans designed to win votes or attract popular support. Ideas and ideologies are therefore simply 'window dressing', used to conceal the deeper realities of political life. This is certainly a position supported by behaviourism, the school of psychology that holds that human beings are little more than biological machines, conditioned to act (or, more correctly, react) to external stimuli. The thinking subject, together with their ideas, values, feelings and intentions, is simply an irrelevance. A very similar view also informed 'dialectical materialism', the crude form of Marxism that dominated intellectual enquiry in the Soviet Union and other orthodox communist states. This held that political ideas could only be understood in the light of the economic or class interests of those who express them. Ideas have a 'material basis', they have no meaning or significance on their own.

The opposite argument has also been put. The UK economist John Maynard Keynes (1883–1946), for example, argued that the world is ruled by little other than the ideas of economic theorists and political philosophers. As he put it in the closing pages of his *General Theory*:

> Practical men, who believe themselves to be quite exempt from any intellectual influences, are usually the slaves of some defunct economist. Madmen in authority, who hear voices in the air, are distilling their frenzy from some academic scribbler of a few years back. (Keynes [1936] 1963, p. 383)

Far from dismissing ideas as being conditioned responses to practical circumstances, this position highlights the degree to which beliefs and theories provide the wellspring of human action. The world is ultimately ruled by 'academic scribblers'. Such a view suggests, for instance, that modern capitalism, in important respects, developed out of the classical economics of Adam Smith (see p. 50) and David Ricardo (1772–1823), that Soviet communism was significantly shaped by the writing of Karl Marx (see p. 121) and V. I. Lenin (see p. 125), and that the history of Nazi Germany can only be understood by reference to the doctrines advanced in Hitler's *Mein Kampf*.

In reality, both these accounts of political life are one-sided and inadequate. Political ideas are not merely a passive reflection of vested interests or personal ambition, but have the capacity to inspire and guide political action itself and so can shape material life. At the same time, political ideas do not emerge in a vacuum: they do not drop from the sky like rain. All political ideas are moulded by the social and historical circumstances in which they develop and by the political ambitions they serve. Quite simply, political theory and political practice are inseparably linked. Any balanced and persuasive account of political life must therefore acknowledge the constant interplay between ideas and ideologies on the one hand, and historical and social forces on the other.

Ideas and ideologies influence political life in a number of ways. In the first place, they provide a perspective through which the world is understood and explained. People do not see the world as it is, but only as they expect it to be: in other words, they see it through a veil of ingrained beliefs, opinions and assumptions. Whether consciously or subconsciously, everyone subscribes to a set of political beliefs and values that guide their behaviour and influence their conduct. Political ideas and ideologies thus set goals that inspire political action. In this respect, politicians are subject to two very different influ- · ences. Without doubt, all politicians want power. This forces them to be

Pragmatism:
Behaviour shaped in accordance with practical circumstances and goals rather than ideological objectives.

pragmatic, to adopt those policies and ideas that are electorally popular or win favour with powerful groups such as business or the army. However, politicians seldom seek power simply for its own sake. They also possess beliefs, values and convictions about what to do with power when it is achieved. Nevertheless, the balance between pragmatic and ideological considerations varies from politician to politician, and also, in some cases, at different stages in their career.

Political ideas also help to shape the nature of political systems. Systems of government vary considerably throughout the world and are always associated with particular values or principles. Absolute monarchies were based upon deeply established religious ideas, notably the divine right of kings. The political systems in most contemporary western countries are founded on a set of liberal-democratic principles. Western states typically respect the ideas of limited and constitutional government, and also believe that government should be representative, based on regular and competitive elections. In the same way, traditional communist political systems conformed to the principles of Marxism–Leninism. Even the fact that the world is divided into a collection of nation-states and that government power is usually located at the national level reflects the impact of political ideas, in this case of nationalism and, more specifically, the principle of national self-determination.

Finally, political ideas and ideologies can act as a form of social cement, providing social groups, and indeed whole societies, with a set of unifying beliefs and values. Political ideologies have commonly been associated with particular social classes – for example, liberalism with the middle classes, conservatism with the landed aristocracy, socialism with the working class and so forth. These ideas reflect the life experiences, interests and aspirations of a social class, and therefore help to foster a sense of belonging and solidarity. However, ideas and ideologies can also succeed in binding together divergent groups and classes within a society. For instance, there is unifying bedrock of liberal-democratic values in most western states, while in Muslim countries Islam has established a common set of moral principles and beliefs. In providing society with a unified political culture, political ideas help to promote order and social stability. Nevertheless, a unifying set of political ideas and values can develop naturally within a society, or it can be enforced from above in an attempt to manufacture obedience and exercise control. The clearest examples of such 'official' ideologies have been found in fascist and communist regimes.

Views of ideology

This book is primarily a study of political ideologies, rather than an analysis of the nature of ideology. Much confusion stems from the fact that, though obviously related, 'ideology' and 'ideologies' are quite different things to study. To examine 'ideology' is to consider a particular *type* of political thought, distinct from, say, political science or political philosophy. The study of political ideology thus involves reflection on questions about the nature, role and significance of this category of thought, and about which sets of political ideas and arguments should be classified as ideologies. For instance, is ideology true or false, liberating or oppressive, or inevitable or merely transitory? Similarly, are nationalism and multiculturalism ideologies in the same sense as liberalism and socialism? On the other hand, to study 'ideologies' is to be concerned with analysing the *content* of political thought, to be interested in the ideas, doctrines and theories that have been advanced by and within the various ideological traditions. For example, what can liberalism tell us about freedom? Why have socialists traditionally supported equality? How do anarchists defend the idea of a stateless society? Why have fascists regarded struggle and war as healthy? In order to examine such 'content' issues, however, it is necessary to consider the 'type' of political thought we are dealing with. Before discussing the characteristic ideas and doctrines of the so-called ideologies, we need to reflect on why these sets of ideas have been categorized as ideologies. More importantly, what does the categorization tell us? What can we learn about, for example, liberalism, socialism, feminism and fascism from the fact that they are classified as ideologies?

The first problem confronting any discussion of the nature of ideology is the fact that there is no settled or agreed definition of the term, only a collection of rival definitions. As David McLellan (1995) put it, 'Ideology is the most elusive concept in the whole of the social sciences.' Few political terms have been the subject of such deep and impassioned controversy. This has occurred for two reasons. In the first place, as all concepts of ideology acknowledge a link between theory and practice, the term uncovers highly contentious debates, considered in the previous section, about the role of ideas in politics and the relationship between beliefs and theories on the one hand, and material life or political conduct on the other. Second, the concept of ideology has not been able to stand apart from the ongoing struggle between and amongst political ideologies. For much of its history, the term 'ideology' has been used as a political weapon, a device with which to condemn or criticize rival sets of ideas or belief systems. Not until the second half of the twentieth century was a neutral and apparently objective concept of ideology widely employed, and even then disagreements persisted over the social role and political significance of ideology. Among the meanings that have been attached to ideology are the following:

- a political belief system
- an action-orientated set of political ideas
- the ideas of the ruling class
- the world view of a particular social class or social group
- political ideas that embody or articulate class or social interests
- ideas that propagate false consciousness amongst the exploited or oppressed
- ideas that situate the individual within a social context and generate a sense of collective belonging
- an officially sanctioned set of ideas used to legitimize a political system or regime
- an all-embracing political doctrine that claims a monopoly of truth
- an abstract and highly systematic set of political ideas.

The origins of the term are nevertheless clear. The word *ideology* was coined during the French Revolution by Antoine Destutt de Tracy (1754–1836), and was first used in public in 1796. For de Tracy, *idéologie* referred to a new 'science of ideas', literally an *idea*-ology. With a rationalist zeal typical of the Enlightenment, he believed that it was possible objectively to uncover the origins of ideas, and proclaimed that this new science would come to enjoy the same status as established sciences such as biology and zoology. More boldly, since all forms of enquiry are based on ideas, de Tracy suggested that ideology would eventually come to be recognized as the

queen of the sciences. However, despite these high expectations, this original meaning of the term has had little impact on later usage.

The career of ideology as a key political term stems from the use made of
it in the writings of Karl Marx. Marx's use of the term, and the interest
shown in it by later generations of Marxist thinkers, largely explains the
prominence ideology enjoys in modern social and political thought. Yet the
meaning Marx ascribed to the concept is very different from the one usually
accorded it in mainstream political analysis. Marx used the term in the title
of his early work *The German Ideology* ([1846] 1970), written with his life-
long collaborator Friedrich Engels (1820–95). This also contains Marx's
clearest description of his view of ideology:

> The ideas of the ruling class are in every epoch the ruling ideas, i.e. the
> class which is the ruling material force of society, is at the same time
> the ruling intellectual force. The class which has the means of material
> production at its disposal, has control at the same time over the means
> of mental production, so that thereby, generally speaking, the ideas of
> those who lack the means of mental production are subject to it.
> (Marx and Engels, 1970, p. 64)

False consciousness:
A Marxist term
denoting the delusion
and mystification that
prevents subordinate
classes from recog-
nizing the fact of their
own exploitation.

Marx's concept of ideology has a number of crucial
features. First, ideology is about delusion and mystification: it perpetrates a false or mistaken view of the world,
what Engels later referred to as '**false consciousness**'.
Marx used ideology as a critical concept, whose purpose
is to unmask a process of systematic mystification. His
own ideas he classified as scientific, because they were
designed accurately to uncover the workings of history and society. The
contrast between ideology and science, between falsehood and truth, was
thus vital to Marx's use of the term. Second, ideology is linked to the class
system. Marx believed that the distortion implicit in ideology stems from the
fact that it reflects the interests and perspective on society of the ruling class.
The ruling class is unwilling to recognize itself as an oppressor and, equally,
is anxious to reconcile the oppressed to their oppression. The class system is
thus presented upside down, a notion Marx conveyed through the image of
the camera obscura, the inverted picture that is produced by a camera lens or
the human eye. Liberalism, which portrays rights that can only be exercised
by the propertied and privileged as universal entitlements, is therefore the
classic example of ideology. Third, ideology is a manifestation of power. In
concealing the contradictions upon which capitalism, in common with all
class societies, is based, ideology serves to disguise from the exploited
proletariat the fact of its own exploitation, thereby upholding a system of

unequal class power. Ideology literally constitutes the 'ruling' ideas of the age. Finally, Marx treated ideology as a temporary phenomenon. Ideology will only continue so long as the class system that generates it survives. The proletariat – in Marx's view, the 'grave digger' of capitalism – is destined not to establish another form of class society, but rather to abolish class inequality altogether by bringing about the collective ownership of wealth. The interests of the proletariat thus coincide with those of society as a whole. The proletariat, in short, does not need ideology because it is the only class that needs no illusions.

Later generations of Marxists, if anything, showed greater interest in ideology than Marx did himself. This largely reflects the fact that Marx's confident prediction of capitalism's doom proved to be highly optimistic, encouraging later Marxists to focus on ideology as one of the factors explaining the unexpected resilience of the capitalist mode of production. However, important shifts in the meaning of the term also took place. In particular, all classes came to be seen to possess ideologies. In *What is to be Done?* ([1902] 1988) Lenin thus described the ideas of the proletariat as 'socialist ideology' or 'Marxist ideology', phrases that would have been absurd for Marx. For Lenin and most later Marxists, ideology referred to the distinctive ideas of a particular social class, ideas that advance its interests regardless of its class position. However, as all classes, the proletariat as well as the bourgeoisie, have an ideology, the term was robbed of its negative or pejorative connotations. Ideology no longer implied necessary falsehood and mystification, and no longer stood in contrast to science; indeed, 'scientific socialism' (Marxism) was recognized as form of proletarian ideology.

The Marxist theory of ideology was perhaps developed furthest by Antonio Gramsci. Gramsci ([1935] 1971) argued that the capitalist class system is upheld not simply by unequal economic and political power, but by what he termed the '**hegemony**' of bourgeois ideas and theories. Hegemony means leadership or domination and, in the sense of ideological hegemony, it refers to the capacity of bourgeois ideas to displace rival views and become, in effect, the common sense of the age. Gramsci highlighted the degree to which ideology is embedded at every level in society; in its art and literature, in its education system and mass media, in everyday language and popular culture. This bourgeois hegemony, Gramsci insisted, could only be challenged at the political and intellectual level, which means through the establishment of a rival 'proletarian hegemony', based on socialist principles, values and theories. The capacity of capitalism to achieve stability by manufacturing legitimacy was also a particular concern of the Frankfurt

Hegemony: The ascendency or domination of one element of a system over others; for Marxists, hegemony implies ideological domination.

Antonio Gramsci
(1891–1937)

Italian Marxist and social theorist. The son of a minor public official, Gramsci joined the Socialist Party in 1913, becoming in 1921 the general secretary of the newly formed Italian Communist Party. He was elected to the Italian Parliament in 1924, but was imprisoned by Mussolini in 1926. He remained incarcerated until his death.

In *Prison Notebooks* (Gramsci, 1971), written between 1929 and 1935, Gramsci tried to redress the emphasis within orthodox Marxism upon economic or material factors. He rejected any form of 'scientific' determinism by stressing, through the theory of hegemony, the importance of the political and intellectual struggle. Gramsci remained throughout his life a Leninist and a revolutionary. His stress on revolutionary commitment and 'optimism of the will' also endeared him to the new left. Gramsci's concept of hegemony has been a key concept.

School, a group of mainly German neo-Marxists who fled the Nazis and later settled in the USA. Its most widely known member, Herbert Marcuse (see p. 129), argued in *One-Dimensional Man* (1964) that advanced industrial society has developed a 'totalitarian' character in the capacity of its ideology to manipulate thought and deny expression to oppositional views.

By manufacturing false needs and turning humans into voracious consumers, modern societies are able to paralyse criticism through the spread of widespread and stultifying affluence. According to Marcuse, even the apparent tolerance of liberal capitalism serves a repressive purpose in that it creates the impression of free debate and argument, thereby concealing the extent to which indoctrination and ideological control take place.

One of the earliest attempts to construct a non-Marxist concept of ideology was undertaken by the German sociologist Karl Mannheim (1893–1947). Like Marx, he acknowledged that people's ideas are shaped by their social circumstances, but, in contrast to Marx, he strove to rid ideology of its negative implications. In *Ideology and Utopia* ([1929] 1960), Mannheim portrayed ideologies as thought systems that serve to defend a particular social order, and that broadly express the interests of its dominant or ruling group. Utopias, on the other hand, are idealized representations of the future that imply the need for radical social change, invariably serving the interests of oppressed or subordinate groups. He further distinguished between 'particular' and 'total' conceptions of ideology. 'Particular' ideologies are the ideas and beliefs of specific individuals, groups or parties, while

PERSPECTIVES

IDEOLOGY

LIBERALS, particularly during the Cold War period, have viewed ideology as an officially sanctioned belief system that claims a monopoly of truth, often through a spurious claim to be scientific. Ideology is therefore inherently repressive, even totalitarian; its prime examples are communism and fascism.

CONSERVATIVES have traditionally regarded ideology as a manifestation of the arrogance of rationalism. Ideologies are elaborate systems of thought that are dangerous or unreliable because, being abstracted from reality, they establish principles and goals that lead to repression or are simply unachievable. In this light, socialism and liberalism are clearly ideological.

SOCIALISTS, following Marx, have seen ideology as a body of ideas that conceal the contradictions of class society, thereby promoting false consciousness and political passivity amongst subordinate classes. Liberalism is the classic ruling-class ideology. Later Marxists adopted a neutral concept of ideology, regarding it as the distinctive ideas of any social class, including the working class.

FASCISTS are often dismissive of ideology as an over-systematic, dry and intellectualized form of political understanding that is based on mere reason rather than passion and the will. The Nazis preferred to portray their own ideas as a *Weltanschauung* or 'world view', not as a systematic philosophy.

ECOLOGISTS have tended to regard all conventional political doctrines as part of a super-ideology of **industrialism**. Ideology is thus tainted by its association with arrogant humanism and growth-orientated economics – liberalism and socialism being its most obvious examples.

Industrialism:
An economic theory or system based on large-scale factory production and the relentless accumulation of capital (see p. 276).

RELIGIOUS FUNDAMENTALISTS have treated key religious texts as ideology, on the grounds that, by expressing the revealed word of God, they provide a programme for comprehensive social reconstruction. Secular ideologies are therefore rejected because they are not founded on religious principles and so lack moral substance.

'total' ideologies encompass the entire *Weltanschauung*, or 'world view', of a social class, society or even historical period. In this sense, Marxism, liberal capitalism and Islamic fundamentalism can each be regarded as 'total' ideologies. Mannheim nevertheless held that all ideological systems, including utopias, are distorted, because each offers a partial, and necessarily self-interested, view of social reality. However, he argued that the attempt to uncover objective truth need not be abandoned altogether. According to Mannheim, objectivity is strictly the preserve of the 'socially unattached intelligentsia', a class of intellectuals who alone can engage in disciplined and dispassionate enquiry because they have no economic interests of their own.

The subsequent career of the concept was deeply marked by the emergence of totalitarian dictatorships in the inter-war period, and by the heightened ideological tensions of the Cold War of the 1950s and 1960s. Liberal theorists in particular portrayed the regimes that developed in Fascist Italy, Nazi Germany and Stalinist Russia as historically new and uniquely oppressive systems of rule, and highlighted the role played by 'official' ideologies in suppressing debate and criticism and promoting regimented obedience. Writers as different as Karl Popper (1945), Hannah Arendt (1951), J. L. Talmon (1952) and Bernard Crick (1962) and the 'end of ideology' theorists examined in Chapter 12, came to use the term 'ideology' in a highly restrictive manner, seeing fascism and communism as its prime examples. According to this usage, ideologies are 'closed' systems of thought, which, by claiming a monopoly of truth, refuse to tolerate opposing ideas and rival beliefs. Ideologies are thus 'secular religions'; they possess a 'totalizing' character and serve as instruments of social control, ensuring compliance and subordination. However, not all political creeds are ideologies by this standard. For instance, liberalism, based as it is on a fundamental commitment to freedom, tolerance and diversity, is the clearest example of an 'open' system of thought (Popper, 1945).

A distinctively conservative concept of ideology can also be identified. This is based upon a long-standing conservative distrust of abstract principles and philosophies, born out of a sceptical attitude towards rationalism and progress. The world is viewed as infinitely complex and largely beyond the capacity of the human mind to fathom. The foremost modern exponent of this view was the UK political philosopher Michael Oakeshott (1901–90). 'In political activity', Oakeshott argued in *Rationalism in Politics* (1962), 'men sail a boundless and bottomless sea.' From this perspective, ideologies are seen as abstract systems of thought, sets of ideas that are destined to simplify and distort social reality because they claim to explain what is, frankly, incomprehensible. Ideology is thus equated with dogmatism: fixed or doctrinaire beliefs that are divorced from the complexities of the real world. Conservatives have therefore rejected the 'ideological' style of politics, based on attempts to reshape the world in accordance with a set of abstract principles or pre-established theories. Until infected by the highly ideological politics of the new right, conservatives had preferred to adopt what Oakeshott called a 'traditionalist stance', which spurns ideology in favour of pragmatism, and looks to experience and history as the surest guides to human conduct.

Since the 1960s, however, the term 'ideology' has gained a wider currency through being refashioned according to the needs of conventional social and political analysis. This has established ideology as a neutral and objective concept, the political baggage once attached to it having been removed. Martin Seliger (1976), for example, defined an ideology as 'a set of ideas by which men posit, explain and justify the ends and means of organized social action, irrespective of whether such action aims to preserve, amend, uproot or rebuild a given social order'. An ideology is therefore an action-orientated system of thought. So defined, ideologies are neither good nor bad, true nor false, open nor closed, liberating nor oppressive – they can be all these things.

The clear merit of this social-scientific concept is that it is inclusive, in the sense that it can be applied to all 'isms', to liberalism as well as Marxism, to conservatism as well as fascism, and so on. The drawback of any negative concept of ideology is that it is highly restrictive. Marx saw liberal and conservative ideas as ideological but regarded his own as scientific; liberals classify communism and fascism as ideologies but refuse to accept that liberalism is one as well; traditional conservatives condemn liberalism, Marxism and fascism as ideological but portray conservatism as merely a 'disposition'. However, any neutral concept of ideology also has its dangers. In particular, in offloading its political baggage the term may be rendered so bland and generalized that it loses its critical edge altogether. If ideology is interchangeable with terms such as 'belief system', 'world view', 'doctrine' or 'political philosophy', what is the point of continuing to pretend that it has a separate and distinctive meaning? Two questions are especially important in this respect: what is the relationship between ideology and truth, and in what sense can ideology be seen as a form of power?

Contours of ideology

Any short or single-sentence definition of ideology is likely to stimulate more questions than it answers. Nevertheless, it provides a useful and necessary starting point. In this book, ideology is understood as the following:

> An ideology is a more or less coherent set of ideas that provides the basis for organized political action, whether this is intended to preserve, modify or overthrow the existing system of power. All ideologies therefore have the following features:
>
> (a) They offer an account of the existing order, usually in the form of a 'world view'.

(b) They advance a model of a desired future, a vision of the 'good society'.

(c) They explain how political change can and should be brought about – how to get from (a) to (b). (See Figure 1.1.)

This definition is neither original nor novel, and it is entirely in line with the social-scientific usage of the term. It nevertheless draws attention to some of the important and distinctive features of the phenomenon of ideology. In particular, it emphasizes that the complexity of ideology derives from the fact that it straddles the conventional boundaries between descriptive and normative thought, and between political theory and political practice. Ideology, in short, brings about two kinds of synthesis: between understanding and commitment, and between thought and action.

In relation to the first synthesis, the fusion of understanding and commitment, ideology blurs the distinction between what 'is' and what 'should be'. Ideologies are descriptive in that, in effect, they provide individuals and groups with an intellectual map of how their society works and, more broadly, with a general view of the world. This, for instance, helps to explain the important integrative capacity of ideology, its ability to 'situate' people within a particular social environment. However, such descriptive understanding is deeply embedded within a set of normative or prescriptive beliefs, both about the adequacy of present social arrangements and about the nature of any alternative or future society. Ideology therefore has a powerful emotional or affective character: it is a means of expressing hopes and fears, sympathies and hatreds, as well as of articulating beliefs and understanding.

As (a) and (b) above are linked, 'facts' in ideologies inevitably tend to merge into and become confused with 'values'. One of the implications of

Figure 1.1
Features of
Ideology

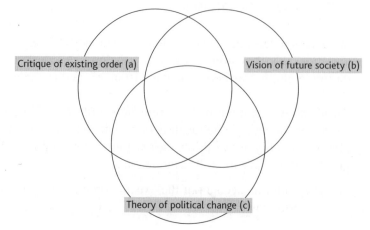

Critique of existing order (a)

Vision of future society (b)

Theory of political change (c)

this is that no clear distinction can be made between ideology and science. In this light, it is helpful to treat ideologies as paradigms, in the sense employed by Thomas Kuhn in *The Structure of Scientific Revolutions* (1962). An ideology, then, can be seen as a set of principles, doctrines and theories that help to structure the process of intellectual enquiry. In effect, it constitutes a framework within which the search for political knowledge takes place, a language of political discourse. For instance, much of academic political science and, still more clearly, mainstream economics, draws upon individualist and rationalist assumptions that have an unmistakable liberal heritage. The notion of ideology as an intellectual framework, or political language, is also important because it highlights the depth at which ideology structures human understanding. The tendency to deny that one's own beliefs are ideological (often while condemning other people for committing precisely this sin) can be explained by the fact that, in providing the very concepts through which the world becomes intelligible, our ideology is effectively invisible. We fail or refuse to recognize that we look at the world through a veil of theories, presuppositions and assumptions that shape what we see and thereby impose meaning on the world. As Gramsci pointed out, ideology comes to assume the status of 'common sense'.

The second synthesis, the fusion of thought and action, reflected in the linkage between (b) and (c) above, is no less significant. Seliger (1976) drew attention to this when referring to what he called the 'fundamental' and 'operative' levels of ideology. At a fundamental level, ideologies resemble political philosophies in that they deal with abstract ideas and theories, and their proponents may at times seem to be engaged in dispassionate enquiry. Although the term 'ideologue' is often reserved for crude or self-conscious supporters of particular ideologies, respected political philosophers such as John Locke (see p. 37), John Stuart Mill (see p. 29) and Friedrich Hayek (see p. 90) each worked within and contributed to ideological traditions. At an operative level, however, ideologies take the form of broad political movements, engaged in popular mobilization and the struggle for power. Ideology in this guise may be expressed in sloganizing, political rhetoric, party manifestos and government policies. While ideologies must, strictly speaking, be both idea-orientated and action-orientated, certain ideologies are undoubtedly stronger on one level than the other. For instance, fascism has always emphasized operative goals and, if you like, the politics of the deed. Anarchism, on the other hand, especially since the mid-twentieth century, has largely survived at a fundamental or philosophical level.

Nevertheless, ideologies invariably lack the clear shape and internal consistency of political philosophies: they are only *more* or *less* coherent. This apparent shapelessness stems in part from the fact that ideologies are not hermetically sealed systems of thought; rather, they are, typically, fluid sets of ideas that overlap with other ideologies and shade into one another. This not only fosters ideological development but also leads to the emergence of hybrid ideological forms, such as liberal conservatism, socialist feminism and conservative nationalism. Moreover, each ideology contains a range of divergent, even rival, traditions and viewpoints. Not uncommonly, disputes between supporters of the same ideology are more passionate and bitter than arguments between supporters of rival ideologies, because what is at stake is the true nature of the ideology in question – what is 'true' socialism, 'true' liberalism or 'true' anarchism? Such conflicts, both between and within ideological traditions, are made more confusing by the fact that they are often played out with the use of the same political vocabulary, each side investing terms such as 'freedom', 'democracy', 'justice' and 'equality' with their own meanings. This highlights the problem of what W. B. Gallie (1955–6) termed 'essentially contested concepts'. These are concepts about which there is such deep controversy that no settled or agreed definition can ever be developed. In this sense, the concept of ideology is certainly 'essentially contested', as indeed are the other terms examined in the 'Perspectives on . . .' boxes.

Clearly, however, there must be a limit to the incoherence or shapelessness of ideologies. There must be a point at which, by abandoning a particularly cherished principle or embracing a previously derided theory, an ideology loses its identity or, perhaps, is absorbed into a rival ideology. Could liberalism remain liberalism if it abandoned its commitment to liberty? Would socialism any longer be socialism if it developed an appetite for violence and war? One way of dealing with this problem, following Michael Freeden (1996), is to highlight the morphology, the form and structure, of an ideology in terms of its key concepts, in the same way that the arrangement of furniture in a room helps us to distinguish between a kitchen, a bedroom, a lounge, and so on. Each ideology is therefore characterized by a cluster of core, adjacent and peripheral concepts, not all of which need be present for a theory or a doctrine to be recognized as belonging to that ideology. A kitchen, for instance, does not cease to be a kitchen simply because the sink or the cooker is removed. Similarly a kitchen remains a kitchen over time despite the arrival of new inventions such as dishwashers and microwave ovens. However, ideologies may be 'thick' or 'thin', in terms of the extent of their conceptual furniture. Whereas liberalism, conservatism and socialism are based on a broad and distinctive set of values, doctrines and beliefs, others such as anarchism and feminism, are more thin-centred, often having a 'cross-cutting' character, in that they incorporate elements from 'thicker' ideological traditions. This also explains why there is (perhaps unresolvable) debate and confusion about whether nationalism and multi-

culturalism in particular are ideologies in their own right or merely embell-
ishments to other, 'host', ideologies.

What does this tell us about the relationship between ideology and truth?
For Marx, as we have seen, ideology was the implacable enemy of truth.
Falsehood is implicit in ideology because, being the creation of the ruling
class, its purpose is to disguise exploitation and oppression. Nevertheless, as
Mannheim recognized, to follow Marx in believing that the proletariat needs
no illusion or ideology is to accept a highly romanticized view of the
working masses as the emancipators of humankind. However, Mannheim's
own solution to this problem, a faith in free-floating intellectuals, does not
get us much further. All people's views are shaped, consciously or subconsciously, by broader social and cultural factors, and while education may
enable them to defend these views more fluently and persuasively, there is
little evidence that it makes those views any less subjective or any more
dispassionate. This implies that there exists no objective standard of truth
against which ideologies can be judged. Indeed, to suggest that ideologies
can be deemed to be either true or false is to miss the vital point that they
embody values, dreams and aspirations that are, by their very nature, not
susceptible to scientific analysis. No one can 'prove' that one theory of
justice is preferable to any other, any more than rival conceptions of human
nature can be tested by surgical intervention to demonstrate once and for all
that human beings possess rights, are entitled to freedom, or are naturally
selfish or naturally sociable. Ideologies are embraced less because they
stand up to scrutiny and logical analysis, and more because they help individuals, groups and societies to make sense of the world in which they live.
As Andrew Vincent (1995) put it, 'We examine ideology as fellow travellers,
not as neutral observers.'

Nevertheless, ideologies undoubtedly embody a claim to uncover truth; in
this sense, they can be seen as 'regimes of truth'. By providing us with a
language of political discourse, a set of assumptions and presuppositions
about how society does and should work, ideology structures both what we
think and how we act. As a 'regime of truth', ideology is always linked to
power. In a world of competing truths, values and theories, ideologies seek
to prioritize certain values over others, and to invest legitimacy in particular
theories or sets of meanings. Furthermore, as ideologies provide intellectual
maps of the social world, they help to establish the relationship between
individuals and groups on the one hand, and the larger structure of power on
the other. Ideologies therefore play a crucial role in either upholding the
prevailing power structure (by portraying it as fair, natural, rightful or whatever) or in weakening or challenging it, by highlighting its iniquities or
injustices and by drawing attention to the attractions of alternative power
structures.

New ideologies for old?

Ideology may have been an inseparable feature of politics since the late eighteenth century (it is often traced back to the 1789 French Revolution), but its content has changed significantly over time, with the rate of ideological transformation having accelerated since the 1960s. New ideologies have emerged, some once-potent ideologies have faded in significance, and all ideologies have gone through a process of sometimes radical redefinition and renewal. Political ideology arose out of a transition from feudalism to industrial capitalism. In simple terms, the earliest, or 'classical', ideological traditions – liberalism, conservatism and socialism – developed as contrasting attempts to shape emergent industrial society. While liberalism championed the cause of individualism, the market and, initially at least, minimal government, conservatism stood in defence of an increasingly embattled *ancien régime*, and socialism advanced the quite different vision of a society based on community, equality and cooperation.

As the nineteenth century progressed, each of these ideologies acquired a clearer doctrinal character, and came to be associated with a particular social class or stratum of society. Simply put, liberalism was the ideology of the rising middle class, conservatism was the ideology of the aristocracy or nobility, and socialism was the ideology of the growing working class. In turn, political parties developed to articulate the interests of these classes and to give 'operative' expression to the various ideologies. These parties therefore typically had a programmatic character. The central theme that emerged from ideological argument and debate during this period was the battle between two rival economic philosophies: capitalism and socialism. Political ideology thus had a strong economic focus. This was captured by the left/right divide and expressed through the linear political spectrum, as depicted in Figure 1.2. The terms '**left**' and '**right**', which dated back to the French Revolution and the seating arrangements adopted by the different groups at the first meeting of the Estates-General in 1789, came to be associated with the preference for equality and common ownership on the one hand, and support for meritocracy and private ownership on the other hand.

Left: A broad ideological disposition that is characterized by sympathy for principles such as liberty, equality, fraternity and progress.

Right: A broad ideological disposition that is characterized by sympathy for principles such as authority, order, hierarchy and duty.

Figure 1.2
Linear spectrum

Left				Right
Communism	Socialism	Liberalism	Conservation	Fascism

The battle lines between capitalism and socialism were significantly sharpened by the 1917 Russian Revolution, which created the world's first socialist state. Indeed, throughout what is sometimes called the 'short' twentieth century (from the outbreak of the First World War in 1914 to the collapse of communism in 1989–91), and particularly during the Cold War period (1945–90), international politics was structured along ideological lines, as the capitalist West confronted the communist East. More generally, left-wing political ideas reflected a distaste for capitalism, ranging from a 'hard left' (communism and anarchism) desire to abolish and replace capitalism to a 'soft left' (socialism and modern liberalism) wish to reform or 'humanize' capitalism. Right-wing ideas (classical liberalism and conservatism), by contrast, were defined by the desire to defend or extend capitalism.

These ideological battle lines were nevertheless made more complicated by the rise of fascism in the 1920s and 1930s. On the face of it, fascism was clearly a 'far right' ideology: it was fiercely anti-communist and shared with conservatism, albeit in a more extreme form, a sympathy for hierarchy and elitism. However, radical elements within fascist movements sometimes expressed 'leftist' views in criticizing capitalism and big business, and fascism also gave expression to ideologically new ideas such as anti-westernism and politico-spiritual renewal, which were later to resurface in certain forms of religious fundamentalism. A further complication was that communist and fascist regimes exhibited certain similarities, both developing repressive, authoritarian forms of political rule, which some described as 'totalitarian'. This brought the value of the left/right divide, and the linear political spectrum, into question. During the 1950s and 1960s, it became increasingly common to use an alternative, horseshoe-shaped political spectrum, which indicated that the extreme points on the left and the right tended to converge, distinguishing both from the 'democratic' beliefs of liberalism, socialism and conservatism. This is depicted in Figure 1.3.

However, since around the 1960s, the ideological landscape has been transformed. Not only have major changes occurred to established or 'classical' ideologies (for instance, in the rise of the new left, the new right and, most dramatically, with the collapse of orthodox communism), but a series

Figure 1.3
Horseshoe
spectrum

of 'new' ideological traditions have also emerged. The most significant of these can be set out as follows:

'Classical' ideologies	'New' ideologies
Liberalism	Feminism
Conservatism	Ecologism
Socialism	Religious fundamentalism
Nationalism	Multiculturalism
Anarchism	
Fascism (?)	

The designation of these ideologies as 'new' can be misleading, as each of them has roots that stretch back to the nineteenth century, if not beyond. Moreover, they also tended to draw heavily from existing, mainstream ideologies, giving them, typically, a hybrid or cross-cutting character. Nevertheless, these ideologies are 'new' in the sense that they have given particular areas of ideological debate a prominence they never previously enjoyed and, in the process, they have fostered the emergence of fresh and challenging ideological perspectives. Why has this process of ideological transformation occurred? The three main factors are the following:

- the transition from industrial societies to postindustrial societies;
- the collapse of communism and the changing world order;
- globalization and transnationalism.

The structure and nature of modern societies have undergone a profound process of change since about the 1950s. Social thinkers have heralded this change in a variety of ways. For example, Beck (1992) proclaimed the transition from the 'first' to the 'second' modernity, Giddens (1994) analysed the shift from 'simple' to 'reflexive' modernity, whilst Baumann (2000) discussed the change from 'solid' to 'liquid' modernity. At the heart of these changes, however, is the transition from industrial societies to postindustrial ones. Industrial societies tended to be solidaristic, in that they were based on relatively clear class divisions (crudely, those between capital and labour), which, in turn, helped to structure the political process, including the party system, interest-group competition and ideological debate. Postindustrial societies are different in a number of ways. They tend, in the first place, to be more affluent societies, in which the struggle for material subsistence has become less pressing for a growing proportion of people. In conditions of wider prosperity, individuals express more interest in 'quality of life' or 'postmaterial' issues. These are typically concerned with morality, political justice and personal fulfilment, and include issues such as gender equality, world peace, racial harmony, environmental protection and animal rights. Second, the structure of society and the nature of social connectedness have altered. Whereas industrial societies tended to generate 'thick' social bonds, based on social class and nationality in particular, postindustrial societies tend to be characterized by growing individualization and 'thinner' and more fluid social bonds. Although this may mean that people have a less clear sense of who they are and where they stand on moral and social issues in particular, the advent of postindustrial societies has 'liberated' people from their class-based ideological identities, and allowed – even encouraged – them to seek new identities.

The ideological ramifications of the collapse of communism have been profound and wide-ranging, and, in many ways, continue to unfold. The ideology most clearly affected has been socialism. Revolutionary socialism, especially in its Soviet-style, Marxist–Leninist guise, was revealed as a spent force, both because of the economic failings of central planning and because of the system's association with state authoritarianism. However, democratic socialism has also been affected; some argue that it has been fatally compromised. In particular, democratic socialists have lost faith in 'top-down' state control, and have come to accept the market as the only reliable means of generating wealth. The collapse of communism, and the general retreat from socialism, has provided opportunities for new ideological forces. Chief amongst these have been nationalism, particularly ethnic nationalism, which has displaced Marxist–Leninism as the leading ideology in many postcommunist states, and religious fundamentalism, which, in its various forms, has had growing influence in the developing world. The advent of global terrorism, through the devastating attacks on New York and Washington on 11 September 2001, and the initiation of the so-called 'war on terror' have had further consequences for political ideologies. The 'war on terror' highlights the emergence of new ideological battle lines that, some believe, may define global politics in the twenty-first century. In the widely discussed if highly controversial thesis of Samuel Huntingdon (1993), the ideological battle between capitalism and communism has been displaced by a 'clash of civilizations', in which the most significant division is between the West and Islam.

Globalization:
A complex web of interconnectedness through which life is increasingly shaped by decisions or events taken at a distance; globalization reflects the increasing permeability of the nation-state.

Globalization, in its economic, cultural and political forms, has influenced the development of political ideologies in a number of ways. First, it contributed to the collapse of communism. It did this both through the tendency of economic globalization to bolster growth rates in the capitalist West from the 1970s onwards, thereby widening material differentials between capitalism and communism, and through growing media penetration of eastern Europe, spreading pro-western and pro-capitalist values and appetites. Second, political nationalism, linked to the doctrine of national self-determination, has been compromised by the fact that nation-states now operate in 'post-sovereign' conditions. As the state in a global era has a declining capacity to generate political allegiance and civic loyalty, 'particularist' ideological identities, based around culture, ethnicity and religion, have been strengthened. Third, globalization has strengthened trends towards multiculturalism by increasing levels of international migration, giving more and more societies a multi-religious and multi-ethnic character. Finally, globalization, and in particular the spread of a global capitalist economy, has generated a range of oppositional forces. These include a strengthening of religious fundamentalism in the developing world, leading, as Benjamin Barber (1995) put it, to a confrontation between 'Jihad' and 'MacWorld', and an anti-globalization or anti-capitalist movement in the developed world that has recast, and sometimes strengthened, the ideas of anarchism, feminism and ecologism.

The 'new' ideologies are not only new, but also differ from 'classical' ideologies in a number of other ways. This has altered the focus and sometimes the terms of ideological debate. Three broad differences can be identified. In the first place, there has been a shift away from economics and towards culture. Liberalism, conservatism and socialism were primarily concerned with issues of economic organization, or at least their moral vision was grounded in a particular economic model. By contrast, and in their various ways, the 'new' ideologies are more interested in culture than in economics: their primary concerns tend to be orientated around people's values, beliefs and ways of life, rather than economic well-being or even social justice. Second, there has been a shift from social class to identity. Identity links the personal to the social, in seeing the individual as 'embedded' in a particular cultural, social, institutional and ideological context, but it also highlights the scope for personal choice and self-definition, reflecting a general social trend towards individualization. In this sense, the 'new' ideologies offer individuals not worked-out sets of political solutions that 'fit' their social position, but, rather, provide them with a range of ideological options. This means that political activism has become, in effect, a lifestyle choice. Finally, there has been a shift from **universalism** to

Universalism: The belief that it is possible to uncover certain values and principles that are applicable to all people and all societies, regardless of historical, cultural and other differences.

Particularism: The belief that historical, cultural and other differences between people and societies are more significant than what they have in common.

particularism. Whereas, most clearly, liberalism and socialism shared an Enlightenment faith in reason and progress, reflecting the belief that there is a common core to human identity shared by people everywhere, the 'new' ideologies, such as feminism, ethnic nationalism, multiculturalism and religious fundamentalism, stress the importance of factors such as gender, locality, culture and ethnicity. In that sense, they practise the 'politics of difference' rather than the politics of universal emancipation.

Structure of the book

This book examines each ideology or ideological tradition in turn. They are organized, roughly, in chronological terms, so that the larger process of ideological development, whereby one ideology influences others and so forth, can be mapped out. Each chapter has the same general structure. Following a brief overview, which highlights the broad nature of the ideology, its origins and historical development are examined. The next main section explains and analyses the core themes of the ideology, the values, doctrines and theories that, taken together, define the shape or morphology of the ideology. This section highlights what is distinctive about each ideological tradition, but also notes overlaps between ideologies. The following sections deal with the sub-traditions which characterize each and every political ideology. The focus here is not only on the distinctive features of each sub-tradition, many of which are, anyway, hybrid ideological constructs (conservative nationalism, socialist feminism, liberal multiculturalism and so on), but also on the internal coherence, or lack of coherence, of the ideology as a whole. This therefore focuses on areas of disagreement between supporters of the same ideology. The final main section examines contemporary developments within the ideological tradition in question and reflects on its prospects in the twenty-first century. Each chapter concludes with a list of questions for discussion, and suggestions for further reading. A full bibliography appears at the end of the book. Boxed material can be found in each chapter, providing more information about key thinkers in each tradition, 'isms' other than the main ideologies, rival perspectives on important political themes (such as authority, equality, freedom, the state), and highlighting points of tension within each ideology.

Questions for discussion

→ Are 'practical men' really the slaves of 'academic scribblers' (Keynes)?

→ How does the Marxist concept of ideology differ from the mainstream concept?

→ Is ideology necessarily false? If so, why?

→ Can 'socially unattached' intellectuals rise above ideology?

→ Are all sets of political ideas ideologies, or only some?

→ What is new about the 'new' ideologies'?

→ To what extent has ideological commitment become a lifestyle choice?

→ Does the rise of 'new' ideologies mean that the old ones are now defunct?

Further reading

Eagleton, T., *Ideology: An Introduction* (London and New York: Verso, 1991). An examination of the different definitions of ideology that considers the ideas of key Marxist thinkers through to the various poststructuralists.

Festenstein, M. and M. Kenny, *Political Ideologies: A Reader and Guide* (Oxford): Oxford University Press, 2005). A very useful collection of extracts from key texts on ideology and ideologies, supported by lucid commentaries.

Freeden, M., *Ideology: A Very Short Introduction* (Oxford: Oxford University Press, 2004). An accessible and lively introduction to the concept: an excellent starting place.

McLellan, D., *Ideology* (Milton Keynes: Open University Press, 2nd edn, 1995). A clear and short yet comprehensive introduction to the elusive concept of ideology.

Schwartzmantel, J., *The Age of Ideology: Political Ideologies from the American Revolution to Post-Modern Times* (Basingstoke: Palgrave Macmillan, 1998). A broad-ranging analysis of how the major ideological traditions are coping with the challenge of postmodern society.

Seliger, M., *Ideology and Politics* (London: Allen & Unwin, 1976). A very thorough account of ideology, considered by some to be the classic treatment of the subject.

CHAPTER 2
LIBERALISM

The term 'liberal' has been in use since the fourteenth century but has had a wide variety of meanings. The Latin *liber* referred to a class of free men; in other words, men who were neither serfs nor slaves. It has meant generous, as in 'liberal' helpings of food and drink; or, in reference to social attitudes, it has implied openness or open-mindedness. It also came to be increasingly associated with ideas of freedom and choice. The term 'liberalism' to denote a political allegiance made its appearance much later: it was not used until the early part of the nineteenth century, being first employed in Spain in 1812. By the 1840s, the term was widely recognized throughout Europe as a reference to a distinctive set of political ideas. However, it was taken up more slowly in the UK: although the Whigs started to call themselves Liberals during the 1830s, the first distinctly Liberal government was not formed until Gladstone took office in 1868.

The central theme of liberal ideology is a commitment to the individual and the desire to construct a society in which people can satisfy their interests and achieve fulfilment. Liberals believe that human beings are, first and foremost, individuals, endowed with reason. This implies that each individual should enjoy the maximum possible freedom consistent with a like freedom for all. However, although individuals are entitled to equal legal and political rights, they should be rewarded in line with their talents and their willingness to work. Liberal societies are organized politically around the twin principles of constitutionalism and consent, designed to protect citizens from the danger of government tyranny. Nevertheless, there are significant differences between classical liberalism and modern liberalism. *Classical liberalism* is characterized by a belief in a 'minimal' state, whose function is limited to the maintenance of domestic order and personal security. *Modern liberalism*, in contrast, accepts that the state should help people to help themselves.

Origins and development

As a systematic political creed, liberalism may not have existed before the nineteenth century, but it was based on ideas and theories that had developed during the previous three hundred years. Indeed, as Paul Seabright (2004) argued, the origins of liberalism can perhaps be traced back as far as to early agricultural societies, when people started living in settled communities and were forced, for the first time, to find ways of trading and living with strangers. Nevertheless, liberalism as a developed ideology was a product of the breakdown of **feudalism** in Europe, and the growth, in its place, of a market or capitalist society. In many respects, liberalism reflected the aspirations of the rising middle classes, whose interests conflicted with the established power of absolute monarchs and the landed aristocracy. Liberal ideas were radical: they sought fundamental reform and even, at times, revolutionary change. The English Revolution of the seventeenth century and the American and French Revolutions of the late eighteenth century each embodied elements that were distinctively liberal, even though the word 'liberal' was not at the time used in a political sense. Liberals challenged the absolute power of the monarchy, supposedly based on the doctrine of the '**divine right** of kings'. In place of **absolutism**, they advocated constitutional and, later, representative government. Liberals criticized the political and economic privileges of the landed aristocracy and the unfairness of a feudal system in which social position was determined by the 'accident of birth'. They also supported the movement towards freedom of conscience in religion and questioned the authority of the established church.

Feudalism: A system of agrarian-based production that is characterized by fixed social hierarchies and a rigid pattern of obligations.

Divine right: The doctrine that earthly rulers are chosen by God and thus wield unchallengeable authority; divine right is a defence for monarchical absolutism.

Absolutism: A form of government in which political power is concentrated in the hands of a single individual or small group, in particular, an absolute monarchy.

The nineteenth century was in many way the liberal century. As industrialization spread throughout western countries, liberal ideas triumphed. Liberals advocated an industrialized and market economic order 'free' from government interference, in which businesses would be allowed to pursue profit and nations encouraged to trade freely with one another. Such a system of industrial capitalism developed first in the UK, from the mid-eighteenth century onwards, and was well established by the early nineteenth century. It subsequently spread to North America and throughout Europe, initially into western Europe and then, more gradually, into eastern Europe. From the twentieth century onwards industrial capitalism exerted a powerful appeal for developing states in Africa, Asia and Latin America, especially when social and political development was defined in essentially western terms. However, developing-world states have sometimes been resistant to the attractions of liberal capitalism because their political cultures have emphasized community rather than the individual. In such cases, they have provided more fertile ground for the growth of socialism, nationalism or religious fundamentalism, rather than western liberalism. Where capitalism has been successfully established, as in Japan, it has tended to assume a corporate rather than an individualistic character. Japanese industry, for example, is motivated more by traditional ideas of group loyalty and duty than by the pursuit of individual self-interest.

Liberalism has undoubtedly been the most powerful ideological force shaping the western political tradition. Indeed, some portray liberalism as the ideology of the industrialized West and identify it with western civilization itself. Nevertheless, historical developments since the nineteenth century have clearly influenced the nature and substance of liberal ideology. The character of liberalism changed as the 'rising middle classes' succeeded in establishing their economic and political dominance. The radical, even revolutionary edge of liberalism faded with each liberal success. Liberalism thus became increasingly conservative, standing less for change and reform, and more for the maintenance of existing – largely liberal – institutions. Liberal ideas, too, could not stand still. From the late nineteenth century onwards, the progress of industrialization led liberals to question, and in some ways to revise, the ideas of early liberalism. Whereas early liberals had wanted government to interfere as little as possible in the lives of its citizens, modern liberals came to believe that government should be responsible for delivering welfare services such as health, housing, pensions and education, as well as for managing, or at least regulating, the economy. This led to the development of two traditions of thought within liberalism, commonly called **classical liberalism** and **modern liberalism**. As a result, some commentators have argued that liberalism is an incoherent ideology, embracing contradictory beliefs, notably about the desirable role of the state.

Classical liberalism: A tradition within liberalism that seeks to maximize the realm of unconstrained individual action, typically by establishing a minimal state and a reliance on market economics.

Modern liberalism: A tradition within liberalism that provides (in contrast to classical liberalism) a qualified endorsement for social and economic intervention as a means of promoting personal development.

The twentieth century appeared to culminate in the worldwide triumph of liberalism, as the liberal model of representative government combined with market-based economics that had dominated political and social development in the West since the nineteenth century spread remorselessly throughout the globe. In the context of the collapse of communism, the US social theorist Francis Fukuyama (1989, 1992) memorably proclaimed that: 'We are witnessing the end of history as such: that is, the endpoint of mankind's ideological evolution and the universalization of Western liberal democracy as the final form of human government.' Philip Bobbitt (2002) articulated a similar idea in arguing that the 'long war' between liberal parliamentarianism, communism and fascism to define the constitutional structure of the nation-state, which had dominated world politics between 1914 and 1990, had ended in the victory of liberalism over its rivals. This was demonstrated, moreover, by the process of 'democratization' that was underway in Africa, Asia and Latin America, which involved the spread of competitive party systems and a growing enthusiasm for market reforms. By 2000, about two-thirds of the states in the world had political systems that exhibited significant liberal-democratic features. However, as discussed in the final section of the chapter, at the very point of its 'triumph' liberalism was confronted with the rise of markedly illiberal forces, most notably religious fundamentalism, both in the developing world and in its western homeland.

Core themes – the primacy of the individual

Liberalism is, in a sense, the ideology of the industrialized West. So deeply have liberal ideas permeated political, economic and cultural life that their influence can become hard to discern, liberalism appearing to be indistinguishable from 'western civilization' in general. Liberal thinkers in the eighteenth and nineteenth centuries, influenced by an **Enlightenment** belief in

Enlightenment, the:
An intellectual movement that reached its height in the eighteenth century and challenged traditional beliefs in religion, politics and learning in general in the name of reason and progress.

universal reason, tended to subscribe to an explicitly foundationist form of liberalism, which sought to establish fundamental values and championed a particular vision of human flourishing or excellence, usually linked to personal autonomy. This form of liberalism was boldly universalist, in that it implied that human history would be marked by the gradual but inevitable triumph of liberal principles and institutions. Progress, in short, was understood in strictly liberal terms.

During the twentieth century, however, it became fashionable to portray liberalism as morally neutral. This is reflected in the belief that liberalism gives priority to 'the right' over 'the good'. In other words, liberalism strives to establish the conditions in which people and groups can pursue the good life as each defines it, but it does not prescribe or try to promote any particular notion of what is good. From this perspective, liberalism is not simply an ideology but a 'meta-ideology'; that is, a body of rules that lays down the grounds on which political and ideological debate can take place. However, this does not mean that liberalism is simply a philosophy of 'do your own thing'. While liberalism undoubtedly favours openness, debate and self-determination, it is also characterized by a powerful moral thrust. The moral and ideological stance of liberalism is embodied in a commitment to a distinctive set of values and beliefs. The most important of these are the following:

- the individual
- freedom
- reason
- justice
- toleration.

The individual

In the modern world, the concept of the individual is so familiar that its political significance is often overlooked. In the feudal period, there was little idea of individuals having their own interests or possessing personal and unique identities. Rather, people were seen as members of the social groups to which they belonged: their family, village, local community or social class. Their lives and identities were largely determined by the character of these groups in a process that changed little from one generation to the next. However, as feudalism was displaced by increasingly market-orientated societies, individuals were confronted by a broader range of choices and social possibilities. They were encouraged, perhaps for the first time, to think *for* themselves, and to think *of* themselves in personal terms. A serf, for example, whose family may always have lived and worked on the same piece of land, became a 'free man' and acquired some ability to choose who to work for, or maybe the opportunity to leave the land altogether and look for work in the growing towns or cities.

As the certainties of feudal life broke down, a new intellectual climate emerged. Rational and scientific explanations gradually displaced traditional religious theories, and society was increasingly understood from the viewpoint of the human individual. Individuals were thought to possess personal and distinctive qualities: each was of special value. This was evident in the growth of natural rights theories in the seventeenth and eighteenth centuries, which are discussed later, in relation to classical liberalism. The German philosopher Immanuel Kant (1724–1804) expressed a similar belief in the dignity and equal worth of human beings in his conception of individuals as 'ends in themselves' and not merely as means for the achievement of the

INDIVIDUALISM

Individualism is the belief in the supreme importance of the individual over any social group or collective body. In the form of methodological individualism, this suggests that the individual is central to any political theory or social explanation – all statements about society should be made in terms of the individuals who compose it. Ethical individualism, on the other hand, implies that society should be constructed so as to benefit the individual, giving moral priority to individual rights, needs or interests. Classical liberals and the new right subscribe to *egoistical* individualism, which places emphasis on self-interestedness and self-reliance. Modern liberals, in contrast, have advanced a *developmental* form of individualism that prioritizes human flourishing over the quest for interest satisfaction.

ends of others. However, emphasizing the importance of the individual has two contrasting implications. First, it draws attention to the uniqueness of each human being: individuals are primarily defined by inner qualities and attributes specific to themselves. Second, they nevertheless each share the same status in that they are all, first and foremost, individuals. Many of the tensions within liberal ideology can, indeed, be traced back to these rival ideas of uniqueness and equality.

A belief in the primacy of the individual is the characteristic theme of liberal ideology, but it has influenced liberal thought in different ways. It has led some liberals to view society as simply a collection of individuals, each seeking to satisfy his or her own needs and interests.

Atomism: A belief that society is made up of a collection of self-interested and largely self-sufficient individuals, or atoms, rather than social groups.

Such a view has been equated with **atomism**; indeed, it can lead to the belief that 'society' itself does not exist, but is merely a collection of self-sufficient individuals. Such extreme individualism is based on the assumption that the individual is egoistical, essentially self-seeking, and largely self-reliant. C. B. Macpherson (1973) characterized early liberalism as 'possessive individualism',

Human nature: The essential and innate character of all human beings: what they owe to nature rather than to society.

in that it regarded the individual as 'the proprietor of his own person or capacities, owing nothing to society for them'. In contrast, later liberals have held a more optimistic view of **human nature**, and have been more prepared to believe that egoism is tempered by a sense of social responsibility, especially a responsibility for those who are unable to look after themselves. Whether egoism is unrestrained or is qualified by a sense of social responsibility, liberals are united in their desire to create a

John Stuart Mill (1806–73)

UK philosopher, economist and politician. Mill was subjected to an intense and austere regime of education by his father, the utilitarian theorist James Mill, resulting in a mental collapse at the age of 20. He went on to found and edit the *London Review* and was MP for Westminster from 1865 to 1881.

Mill's varied and complex work was crucial to the development of liberalism because, in many ways, it straddled the divide between classical and modern theories. His opposition to collectivist tendencies and traditions was firmly rooted in nineteenth-century principles, but his emphasis on the quality of individual life, reflected in a commitment to 'individuality', as well as his sympathy for causes such as female suffrage and, later, workers' cooperatives, looked forward to twentieth-century developments. Mill's major writings include *On Liberty* (1859), *Considerations on Representative Government* (1861) and *The Subjection of Women* (1869).

society in which each person is capable of developing and flourishing to the fullness of his or her potential.

Freedom

A belief in the supreme importance of the individual leads naturally to a commitment to individual **freedom**. Individual liberty (liberty and freedom being interchangeable) is for liberals the supreme political value and, in many ways, the unifying principle within liberal ideology. For early liberals, liberty was a natural right, an essential requirement for leading a truly human existence. It also gave individuals the opportunity to pursue their own interests by exercising choice: the choice of where to live, who to work for, what to buy and so forth. Later liberals have seen liberty as the only condition in which people are able to develop their skills and talents and fulfil their potential. Nevertheless, liberals do not accept that individuals have an absolute entitlement to freedom. If liberty is unlimited it can become 'licence', the right to abuse others. In *On Liberty* ([1859] 1972, p. 73) John Stuart Mill argued that 'the only purpose for which power can be rightfully exercised over any

Freedom (or liberty): The ability to think or act as one wishes, a capacity that can be associated with the individual, a social group or a nation.

PERSPECTIVES

FREEDOM

LIBERALS give priority to freedom as the supreme individualist value. While classical liberals support negative freedom, understood as the absence of constraints – or freedom of choice – modern liberals advocate positive freedom in the sense of personal development and human flourishing.

CONSERVATIVES have traditionally endorsed a weak view of freedom as the willing recognition of duties and responsibilities, negative freedom posing a threat to the fabric of society. The new right, however, endorses negative freedom in the economic sphere, freedom of choice in the marketplace.

SOCIALISTS have generally understood freedom in positive terms to refer to self-fulfilment achieved through either free creative labour or cooperative social interaction. Social democrats have drawn close to modern liberalism in treating freedom as the realization of individual potential.

ANARCHISTS regard freedom as an absolute value, believing it to be irreconcilable with any form of political authority. Freedom is understood to mean the achievement of personal autonomy, not merely being 'left alone' but being rationally self-willed and self-directed.

FASCISTS reject any form of individual liberty as a nonsense. 'True' freedom, in contrast, means unquestioning submission to the will of the leader and the absorption of the individual into the national community.

ECOLOGISTS, particularly deep ecologists, treat freedom as the achievement of oneness, self-realization through the absorption of the personal ego into the ecosphere or universe. In contrast with political freedom, this is sometimes seen as 'inner' freedom, freedom as self-actualization.

RELIGIOUS FUNDAMENTALISTS see freedom as essentially an inner or spiritual quality. Freedom means conformity to the revealed will of God, spiritual fulfilment being associated with submission to religious authority.

member of a civilized community, against his will, is to prevent harm to others'. Mill's position is libertarian (see p. 86) in that it accepts only the most minimal restrictions on individual freedom, and then only in order to prevent 'harm to others'. He distinguished clearly between actions that are 'self-regarding', over which individuals should exercise absolute freedom, and those that are 'other-regarding', which can restrict the freedom of others or do them damage. Mill did not accept any restrictions on the individual that are designed to prevent a person from damaging himself or herself, either physically or morally. Such a view suggests, for example, that laws forcing car drivers to put on seat belts or motor cyclists to wear crash helmets are as unacceptable as any form of censorship that limits what an individual may read or listen to. Radical libertarians may defend the right of people to use addictive drugs such as heroin and cocaine on the same grounds. Although the individual may be sovereign over his or her body and mind, each must respect the fact that every other individual enjoys an equal right to liberty. This has been expressed by John Rawls (see p. 58) in the principle that everyone is entitled to the widest possible liberty consistent with a like liberty for all.

Although liberals agree about the value of liberty, they have not always agreed about what it means for an individual to be 'free'. In his 'Two Concepts of Liberty' ([1958] 1969), the UK historian of ideas Isaiah Berlin (1909–97) distinguished between a 'negative' theory of liberty and a 'positive' one. Early or classical liberals have believed in **negative freedom**, in that freedom consists in each person being left alone, free from interference and able to act in whatever way they may choose (negative freedom). This conception of freedom is 'negative' in that it is based on the absence of external restrictions or constraints on the individual. Modern liberals, on the other hand, have been attracted to a more 'positive' conception of liberty – **positive freedom** – defined by Berlin as the ability to be one's own master, to be autonomous. Self-mastery requires that the individual is able to develop skills and talents, broaden his or her understanding, and gain fulfilment. This led to an emphasis on the capacity of human beings to develop and ultimately achieve self-realization. These rival conception of liberty have not merely stimulated academic debate within liberalism, but have encouraged liberals to hold very different views about the desirable relationship between the individual and the state.

Negative freedom: The absence of external restrictions or constraints on the individual, allowing freedom of choice.

Positive freedom: Self-mastery or self-realization; the achievement of autonomy and the development of human capacities.

Reason

The liberal case for freedom is closely linked to a faith in reason. Liberalism is, and remains, very much part of the Enlightenment project. The central theme of the Enlightenment was the desire to release humankind from its bondage to superstition and ignorance, and unleash an 'age of reason'. Key Enlightenment thinkers included Jean-Jacques Rousseau (see p. 153), Immanuel Kant, Adam Smith (see p. 50) and Jeremy Bentham (see p. 49).

RATIONALISM

Rationalism is the belief that the world has a rational structure, and that this can be disclosed through the exercise of human reason and critical enquiry. As a philosophical theory, rationalism is the belief that knowledge flows from reason rather than experience, and thus contrasts with empiricism. As a general principle, however, rationalism places a heavy emphasis on the capacity of human beings to understand and explain their world, and to find solutions to problems. While rationalism does not dictate the ends of human conduct, it certainly suggests how these ends should be pursued. It is associated with an emphasis on principle and reason-governed behaviour, as opposed to a reliance on custom or tradition, or on non-rational drives and impulses.

Enlightenment rationalism influenced liberalism in a number of ways. In the first place, it strengthened its faith in both the individual and liberty. To the extent that human beings are rational, thinking creatures, they are capable of defining and pursuing their own best interests. By no means do liberals believe that individuals are infallible in this respect, but the belief in reason builds into liberalism a strong bias against **paternalism**. Not only does paternalism prevent individuals from making their own moral choices and, if necessary, from learning from their own mistakes, but it also creates the prospect that those invested with responsibility for others will abuse their position for their own ends.

Paternalism: Authority exercised from above for the guidance and support of those below, modelled on the relationship between fathers and children.

A further legacy of rationalism is that liberals are inclined to view human history in terms of progress. Progress literally means advance, a movement forward. In the liberal view, the expansion of knowledge, particularly through the scientific revolution, enabled people not only to understand and explain their world but also to help shape it for the better. In short, the power of reason gives human beings the capacity to take charge of their own lives and fashion their own destinies. Reason thus emancipates humankind from the grip of the past and from the weight of custom and tradition. Each generation is able to advance beyond the last as the stock of human knowledge and understanding progressively increases. This also explains the characteristic liberal emphasis on education. People can better or improve themselves through the acquisition of knowledge and the abandonment of prejudice and superstition. Education, particularly in the modern liberal view, is thus a good in itself. It is a vital mean of promoting personal self-development and, if extended widely, of achieving historical and social advancement.

Reason, moreover, is significant in highlighting the importance of discussion, debate and argument. While liberals are generally optimistic about human nature, seeing people as reason-guided creatures, they have seldom subscribed to the utopian creed of human perfectibility because they recognize the power of self-interest and egoism. The inevitable result of this is rivalry and conflict. Individuals battle for scarce resources, businesses compete to increase profits, nations struggle for security or strategic advantage, and so forth. The liberal preference is clearly that such conflicts be settled through debate and negotiation. The great advantage of reason is that it provides a basis on which rival claims and demands can be evaluated – do they 'stand up' to analysis, are they 'reasonable'? Furthermore, it highlights the cost of not resolving disputes peacefully: namely, violence, bloodshed and death. Liberals therefore typically deplore the use of force and aggression; for example, war is invariably seen as an option of the very last resort. From the liberal perspective, the use of force is justified either on the grounds of self-defence or as a means of countering oppression, but always and only after reason and argument have been exhausted.

Justice

Justice denotes a particular kind of moral judgement, in particular one about the distribution of rewards and punishment. In short, justice is about giving each person what he or she is 'due'. The narrower idea of social justice refers to the distribution of material rewards and benefits in society, such as wages, profits, housing, medical care, welfare benefits and so on. The liberal theory of justice is based on a belief in equality of various kinds. In the first place, individualism implies a commitment to foundational **equality**. Human beings are seen to be 'born' equal in the sense that each individual is of equal moral worth, an idea embodied in the notion of natural rights or human rights. Second, foundational equality implies a belief in formal equality, the idea that individuals should enjoy the same formal status in society, particularly in terms of the distribution of rights and entitlements. Consequently, liberals fiercely disapprove of any social privileges or advantages that are enjoyed by some but denied to others on the basis of factors such as gender, race, colour, creed, religion or social background. Rights should not be reserved for any particular class of person, such as men, whites, Christians or the wealthy. This is the sense in which liberalism is 'difference blind'. The most important forms

Justice: A moral standard of fairness and impartiality; social justice is the notion of a fair or justifiable distribution of wealth and rewards in society.

Equality: The principle that human beings are of identical worth or are entitled to be treated in the same way; equality can have widely differing applications.

of formal equality are legal equality and political equality. The former emphasizes 'equality before the law' and insists that all non-legal factors be strictly irrelevant to the process of legal decision-making. The latter is embodied in the idea of 'one person, one vote; one vote, one value', and underpins the liberal commitment to democracy.

Third, liberals subscribe to a belief in equality of opportunity. Each and every individual should have the same chance to rise or fall in society. The game of life, in that sense, must be played on an even playing field. This is not to say that there should be equality of outcome or reward, that living conditions and social circumstances should be the same for all. Liberals believe social equality to be undesirable because people are not born the same. They possess different talents and skills, and some are prepared to work much harder than others. Liberals believe that it is right to reward merit, ability and the willingness to work – indeed, they think it essential to do so if people are to have an incentive to realize their potential and develop the talents they were born with. Equality, for a liberal, means that individuals should have an equal opportunity to develop their unequal skills and abilities.

This leads to a belief in '**meritocracy**'. A meritocratic society is one in which inequalities of wealth and social position solely reflect the unequal

Meritocracy: Literally, rule by those with merit, merit being intelligence plus effort; a society in which social position is determined exclusively by ability and hard work.

distribution of merit or skills amongst human beings, or are based on factors beyond human control: for example, luck or chance. Such a society is socially just because individuals are judged not by their gender, the colour of their skin or their religion, but according to their talents and willingness to work, or on what Martin Luther King called 'the content of their character'. By extension, social equality is unjust because it treats unlike individuals alike.

However, liberal thinkers have disagreed about how these broad principles of justice should be applied in practice. Classical liberals have endorsed strict meritocracy on both economic and moral grounds. Economically, they place heavy stress on the need for incentives. Morally, justice requires that unequal individuals are not treated equally. Modern liberals, on the other hand, have taken social justice to imply a belief in some measure of social equality. For example, in *A Theory of Justice* (1970), John Rawls argued that economic inequality is only justifiable if it works to the benefit of the poorest in society.

Toleration

The liberal social ethic is very much characterized by a willingness to accept and, in some cases, celebrate moral, cultural and political diversity. Indeed, an acceptance of **pluralism** can be said to be rooted in the principle of indi-

Pluralism: A belief in diversity or choice, or the theory that political power is or should be widely and evenly dispersed (see p. 325).

Toleration: Forbearance; a willingness to accept views or action with which one is in disagreement.

vidualism, and the assumption that human beings are separate and unique creatures. However, the liberal preference for diversity has more commonly been associated with **toleration**. This commitment to toleration, attributed to the French writer Voltaire (1694–1778), is memorably expressed in the declaration that, 'I detest what you say but will defend to the death your right to say it'. Toleration is both an ethical ideal and a social principle. On the one hand, it represents the goal of personal autonomy; on the other, it establishes a set of rules about how human beings should behave towards one another. The liberal case for toleration first emerged in the seventeenth century in the attempt by writers such as John Milton (1608–74) and John Locke to defend religious freedom. Locke argued that since the proper function of government is to protect life, liberty and property, it has no right to meddle in 'the care of men's souls'. Toleration should be extended to all matters regarded as 'private' on the grounds that, like religion, they concern moral questions that should be left to the individual.

In *On Liberty* ([1859] 1972), J. S. Mill developed a wider justification for toleration that highlighted its importance to society as well as the individual. From the individual's point of view, toleration is primarily a guarantee of personal autonomy and is thus a condition for moral self-development. Nevertheless, toleration is also necessary to ensure the vigour and health of society as a whole. Only within a free market of ideas will 'truth' emerge, as good ideas displace bad ones and ignorance is progressively banished. Contest, debate and argument, the fruit of diversity or multiplicity, are therefore the motor of social progress. For Mill, this was particularly threatened by democracy and the spread of 'dull conformism', linked to the belief that the majority must always be right. Mill ([1859] 1972) was thus able to argue as follows:

> If all mankind minus one, were of one opinion, and only one person were of the contrary opinion, mankind would be no more justified in silencing that one person, than he, if he had the power, would be justified in silencing mankind.

Sympathy for toleration and diversity is also linked to the liberal belief in a balanced society, one not riven by fundamental conflict. Although individuals and social groups pursue very different interests, liberals hold that there is a deeper harmony or balance amongst these competing interests. For example, the interests of workers and employers differ: workers want better pay, shorter hours and improved working conditions; employers wish to increase their profits by keeping their production costs – including wages – as low as possible. Nevertheless, these competing interests also complement one another: workers need jobs, and employers need labour. In other words, each group is essential to the achievement of the other group's goals. Individuals and groups may pursue self-interest but a natural equilibrium will tend to assert itself. The relationship between liberalism and social harmony in a diverse society is examined further in Chapter 11, in connection with multiculturalism.

Liberalism, government and democracy

The liberal state

Law: Established and public rules of social conduct, backed up by the machinery of the state: the police, courts and prisons.

Government: The machinery through which collective decisions are made on behalf of the state, usually comprising a legislature, executive and judiciary.

State: An association that establishes sovereign power within a defined territorial area, usually possessing a monopoly of coercive power.

Social contract: A (hypothetical) agreement amongst individuals through which they form a state in order to escape from the disorder and chaos of the 'state of nature'.

Liberals do not believe that a balanced and tolerant society will develop naturally out of the free actions of individuals and voluntary associations. This is where liberals disagree with anarchists, who believe that both **law** and **government** are unnecessary. Liberals fear that free individuals may wish to exploit others, steal their property or even turn them into slaves if it is in their interests to do so. They may also break or ignore their contracts when it is to their advantage. The liberty of one person is always, therefore, in danger of becoming a licence to abuse another; each person can be said to be both a threat to and under threat from every other member of society. Our liberty requires that they are restrained from encroaching on our freedom and, in turn, their liberty requires that they are safeguarded from us. Liberals have traditionally believed that such protection can only be provided by a sovereign **state**, capable of restraining all individuals and groups within society. Freedom can therefore only exist 'under the law'; as John Locke put it, 'where there is no law there is no freedom'.

This argument is the basis of the **social contract** theories, developed by seventeenth-century writers such as Thomas Hobbes (see p. 72) and John Locke, which, for liberals, explains the individual's political obligations towards the state. Hobbes and Locke constructed a picture of what life had been like before government was

John Locke
(1632–1704)

English philosopher and politician. Born in Somerset, Locke studied medicine at Oxford before becoming secretary to Anthony Ashley Cooper, first Earl of Shaftesbury. His political views were developed against the background of, and were shaped by, the English Revolution.

A consistent opponent of absolutism and often portrayed as the philosopher of the 'Glorious Revolution' of 1688, which established a constitutional monarchy, Locke is usually seen as a key thinker of early liberalism. Although he accepted that by nature humans are free and equal, the priority he accorded property rights prevented him from endorsing political equality or democracy in the modern sense. Locke 's most important political works are *A Letter Concerning Toleration* (1689) and *Two Treatises of Government* (1690).

State of nature:
A pre-political society characterized by unrestrained freedom and the absence of established authority.

formed, in a stateless society or what they called a '**state of nature**'. As individuals are selfish, greedy and power-seeking, the state of nature would be characterized by an unending civil war of each against all, in which, in Hobbes' words, human life would be 'solitary, poor, nasty, brutish and short'. As a result, they argued, rational individuals would enter into an agreement, or 'social contract', to establish a sovereign government, without which orderly and stable life would be impossible. All individuals would recognize that it is in their interests to sacrifice a portion of their liberty in order to set up a system of law; otherwise their rights, and indeed their lives, would constantly be under threat. Hobbes and Locke were aware that this 'contract' is a historical fiction. The purpose of the social contract argument, however, is to highlight the value of the sovereign state to the individual. In other words, Hobbes and Locke wished individuals to behave as if the historical fiction were true, by respecting and obeying government and law, in gratitude for the safety and security that only a sovereign state can provide.

The social contract argument embodies two important liberal attitudes towards the state in particular, and political authority in general. In the first place, it suggests that, in a sense, political authority comes 'from below'. The state is created *by* individuals and *for* individuals; it exists in order to serve their needs and interests. Government arises out of the agreement, or consent, of the governed. This implies that citizens do not have an absolute obligation to obey all laws or accept any form of government. If government is based on a contract, made by the governed, government itself may break the terms of this contract. When the legitimacy of government evaporates, the people have the right of rebellion.

Second, social contract theory portrays the state as an umpire or neutral referee in society. The state is not created by a privileged elite, wishing to exploit the masses, but out of an agreement amongst all the people. The state therefore embodies the interests of all its citizens and acts as a neutral arbiter when individuals or groups come into conflict with one another. For instance, if individuals break contracts made with others, the state applies the 'rules of the game' and enforces the terms of the contract, provided, of course, each party had entered into the contract voluntarily and in full knowledge. The essential characteristic of any such umpire is that its actions are, and are seen to be, impartial. Liberals thus regard the state as a neutral arbiter amongst the competing individuals and groups within society.

Constitutional government

Although liberals are convinced of the need for government, they are also acutely aware of the dangers that government embodies. In their view, all governments are potential tyrannies against the individual. On the one hand, this is based on the fact that government exercises sovereign power and so poses a constant threat to individual liberty. On the other hand, it reflects a distinctively liberal fear of power. As human beings are self-seeking creatures, if they have power – the ability to influence the behaviour of others – they will naturally use it for their own benefit and at the expense of others. Simply put, the liberal position is that egoism plus power equals corruption. This was expressed in Lord Acton's famous warning: 'Power tends to corrupt, and absolute power corrupts absolutely', and in his conclusion: 'Great men are almost always bad men'. Liberals therefore fear arbitrary government and uphold the principle of limited government. Government can be limited, or 'tamed', through the establishment of constitutional constraints and, as discussed in the next section, by **democracy**.

Democracy: Rule by the people; democracy implies both popular participation and government in the public interest, and can take a wide variety of forms.

A constitution is a set of rules that seeks to allocate duties, powers and functions amongst the various institutions of government. It therefore constitutes the rules that govern the government itself. As such, it both defines the extent of government power and limits its exercise. Support for constitutionalism can take two forms. In the first place, the powers of government bodies and politicians can be limited by the introduction of

CONSTITUTIONALISM

Constitutionalism, in a narrow sense, is the practice of limited government brought about by the existence of a constitution. Constitutionalism in this sense can be said to exist when government institutions and political processes are effectively constrained by constitutional rules. More broadly, constitutionalism refers to a set of political values and aspirations that reflect the desire to protect liberty through the establishment of internal and external checks on government power. It is typically expressed in support for constitutional provisions that establish this goal; notably, a codified constitution, a bill of rights, separation of powers, bicameralism and federalism or decentralization. Constitutionalism is thus a species of political liberalism.

external and, usually, legal constraints. The most important of these is a so-called written constitution, which codifies the major powers and responsibilities of government institutions within a single authoritative document. A written constitution thus constitutes 'higher' law. The first such document was the US Constitution, written in 1787, but during the nineteenth and twentieth centuries written constitutions were adopted in all liberal democracies, with the exception of the UK, Israel and New Zealand. In many cases, bills of rights also exist, which entrench individual rights by providing a legal definition of the relationship between the individual and the state. The first ten amendments of the US Constitution, for example, list individual rights and are collectively called the 'Bill of Rights'. A similar 'Declaration of the Rights of Man' (1789) was adopted during the French Revolution. Where neither written constitutions nor bills of rights exist, as in the UK, liberals have stressed the importance of statute law in checking government power through the principle of the rule of law. This was most clearly expressed in nineteenth-century Germany in the concept of the *Rechtsstaat*, a state ruled by law.

Second, constitutionalism can be established by the introduction of internal constraints which disperse political power among a number of institutions and create a network of 'checks and balances'. As the French political philosopher Montesquieu (1689–1775) put it, 'power should be a check to power'. All liberal political systems exhibit some measure of internal fragmentation. This can be achieved by applying the doctrine of the separation of powers, proposed by Montesquieu himself. This holds that the legislative, executive and judicial powers of government should be exercised by three independent institutions, thus preventing any individual or small group from gaining dictatorial power. The US presidential system of government, for example, is based on a strict separation of powers between Congress, the presidency and the Supreme Court. The principle of judicial independence is respected in all liberal democracies. As the judiciary interprets the meaning of law, both constitutional and statutory, and therefore reviews the powers of government itself, it must enjoy formal independence and political neutrality if it is to protect the individual from the state. Other device for fragmenting government power include cabinet government (which checks the power of the prime minister), parliamentary government (which check the power of the executive), bicameralism (which check the power of each legislative chamber) and territorial divisions such as federalism, **devolution** and local government (which check the power of central government).

Devolution: The transfer of power from central government to subordinate regional bodies, without (unlike federalism) leading to shared sovereignty.

Liberal democracy

Liberal democracy is the dominant political force in the developed world, and increasingly in the developing world. Indeed, the collapse of communism and the advance of 'democratization' (usually understood to imply the introduction of liberal-democratic reforms; that is, electoral democracy and economic liberalization) in Asia, Latin America and Africa, especially since the 1980s, led 'end of history' theorists to proclaim the worldwide triumph of western liberal democracy. However, what is liberal democracy?

Liberal democracy: A form of democracy that incorporates both limited government and a system of regular and competitive elections; liberal democracy is also used as a regime type.

Liberal democracy is a form of political rule that balances the principle of limited government against the ideal of popular consent. Its 'liberal' features are reflected in a network of internal and external checks on government that are designed to guarantee liberty and afford citizens protection against the state. These goals are essentially achieved through constitutional government, as previously discussed. The 'democratic' character of liberal democracy is based on a system of regular and competitive elections, conforming to the principles of universal suffrage and political equality. Although it may be used to describe a political principle, the term 'liberal democracy' more commonly describes a particular type of regime.

The core features of a liberal-democratic regime are the following:

- constitutional government based on formal, usually legal, rules;
- guaranteed **civil liberties** and individual rights;

- institutional fragmentation and a system of checks and balances;
- regular elections respecting the principle of universal suffrage and 'one person, one vote';
- political pluralism, in the form of electoral choice and party competition;
- a healthy **civil society** in which organized groups and interests enjoy independence from government;
- a capitalist or private-enterprise economy organized along market lines.

Civil liberty:
The private sphere of existence, belonging to the citizen not to the state; freedom from government.

Civil society: A realm of autonomous associations and groups, formed by private citizens and enjoying independence from the government; civil society includes businesses, clubs, families and so on.

The hybrid nature of liberal democracy reflects a basic ambivalence within liberalism towards democracy. In many ways, this is rooted in the competing implications of individualism, which both embodies a fear of collective power and leads to a belief in political equality. In the nineteenth century, liberals often saw democracy as threatening or dangerous. In this respect, they echoed the ideas of earlier political theorists such as Plato and Aristotle, who viewed democracy as a system of rule by the masses at the expense of wisdom and property. The central liberal concern has been that democracy can become the enemy of individual liberty. This arises from the fact that 'the people' are not a single entity but rather a collection of individuals and groups, possessing different opinions and opposing interests. The 'democratic solution' to conflict is a recourse to numbers and the application of majority rule: the principle that the will of the majority or greatest number should prevail over that of the minority. Democracy thus comes down to the rule of

Majoritarianism:
A belief in majority rule; majoritarianism implies either that the majority dominates the minority, or that the minority should defer to the judgement of the majority.

the 51 per cent, a prospect that the French politician and social commentator Alexis de Tocqueville (1805–59) famously described as 'the tyranny of the majority'. Individual liberty and minority rights can thus be crushed in the name of the people. James Madison articulated similar views at the US Constitutional Convention in Philadelphia in 1787. Madison argued that the best defence against **majoritarianism** is a network of checks and balances that would make government responsive to competing minorities and also safeguard the propertied few from the propertyless masses.

Liberals have expressed particular reservations about democracy not merely because of the danger of majority rule, but also because of the make-up of the majority in modern, industrial societies. As far as J. S. Mill was concerned, for instance, political wisdom is unequally distributed and is

James Madison
(1751–1836)

US statesman and political theorist. Madison was a Virginian who was a keen advocate of American nationalism at the Continental Congress, 1774 and 1775. He helped to set up the Constitutional Convention in 1778, and played a major role in writing the Constitution. Madison served as Jefferson's Secretary of State, 1801–9, and was the fourth President of the United States, 1809–17.

Madison was a leading proponent of pluralism and divided government, urging the adoption of federalism, bicameralism and the separation of powers as the basis of US government. Madisonianism thus implies a strong emphasis upon checks and balances as the principal means of resisting tyranny. Nevertheless, when in office, Madison was prepared to strengthen the powers of national government. His best-known political writings are his contributions to *The Federalist* (1787–8), which campaigned for Constitutional ratification.

largely related to education. The uneducated are more liable to act according to narrow class interests, whereas the educated are able to use their wisdom and experience for the good of others. He therefore insisted that elected politicians should speak for themselves rather than reflect the views of their electors, and he proposed a system of plural voting that would disenfranchise the illiterate and allocate one, two, three or four votes to people depending on their level of education or social position.

Ortega y Gasset (1883–1955), the Spanish social thinker, expressed such fears more dramatically in *The Revolt of the Masses* ([1930] 1972). Gasset warned that the arrival of mass democracy had led to the overthrow of civilized society and the moral order, paving the way for authoritarian rulers to come to power by appealing to the basest instincts of the masses. By the twentieth century, however, a large proportion of liberals had come to see democracy as a virtue, although this was based on a number of arguments and doctrines. The earliest liberal justification for democracy was founded on consent, and the idea that citizens must have a means of protecting themselves from the encroachment of government. In the seventeenth century, John Locke developed a limited theory of protective democracy by arguing that voting rights should be extended to the propertied, who could then defend their natural rights against government. If government, through taxation, possesses the power to expropriate property, citizens are entitled to protect themselves by controlling the composition of the tax-making body – the legis-

Utilitarianism:
A moral and political philosophy that evaluates 'goodness' in terms of pleasure and pain, and ultimately seeks to achieve 'the greatest happiness for the greatest number' (see p. 48).

lature. During the American Revolution, this idea was taken up in the slogan: 'No taxation without representation'. Utilitarian theorists such as Jeremy Bentham and James Mill (1773–1836) developed the notion of democracy as a form of protection for the individual into a case for universal suffrage. **Utilitarianism** implies that individuals will vote so as to advance or defend their interests as they define them. Bentham came to believe that universal suffrage (conceived in his day as manhood suffrage) is the only way of promoting 'the greatest happiness for the greatest number'.

A more radical endorsement of democracy is linked to the virtues of political participation. This has been associated with the ideas of J.-J. Rousseau but received a liberal interpretation in the writings of J. S. Mill. In a sense, J. S. Mill encapsulates the ambivalence of the liberal attitude towards democracy. In its unrestrained form, democracy leads to tyranny, but, in the absence of democracy, ignorance and brutality will prevail. For Mill, the central virtue of democracy is that it promotes the 'highest and most harmonious' development of human capacities. By participating in political life, citizens enhance their understanding, strengthen their sensibilities and achieve a higher level of personal development. This form of developmental democracy holds democracy to be, primarily, an educational experience. As a result, although he rejected political equality, Mill believed that the franchise should be extended to all but those who are illiterate and, in the process, suggested (radically for his time) that suffrage should also be extended to women. However, since the twentieth century, liberal theories about democracy have tended to focus less on consent and participation and more on the need for consensus in society. This can be seen in the writings of pluralist theorists, who have argued that organized groups, not individuals, have become the primary political actors and portrayed modern industrial societies as increasing complex, characterized by competition between and amongst rival interests. From this point of view, the attraction of democracy is that it is the only system of rule capable of maintaining equilibrium within complex and fluid modern societies. As democracy gives competing groups a political voice it binds them to the political system and so maintains political stability.

Classical liberalism

Classical liberalism was the earliest liberal tradition. Classical liberal ideas developed during the transition from feudalism to capitalism, and reached their high point during the early industrialization of the nineteenth century.

DEMOCRACY

PERSPECTIVES

LIBERALS understand democracy in individualist terms as consent expressed through the ballot box, democracy being equated with regular and competitive elections. Whilst democracy constrains abuses of power, it must always be conducted within a constitutional framework in order to prevent majoritarian tyranny.

CONSERVATIVES endorse liberal-democratic rule but with qualifications about the need to protect property and traditional institutions from the untutored will of 'the many'. The new right, however, has linked electoral democracy to the problems of over-government and economic stagnation.

SOCIALISTS traditionally endorsed a form of radical democracy based on popular participation and the desire to bring economic life under public control, dismissing liberal democracy as simply capitalist democracy. Nevertheless, modern social democrats are now firmly committed to liberal-democratic structures.

ANARCHISTS endorse direct democracy and call for continuous popular participation and radical decentralization. Electoral or representative democracy is merely a façade that attempts to conceal elite domination and reconcile the masses to their oppression.

FASCISTS embrace the ideas of totalitarian democracy, holding that a genuine democracy is an absolute dictatorship, as the leader monopolizes ideological wisdom and is alone able to articulate the 'true' interests of the people. Party and electoral competition are thus corrupt and degenerate.

ECOLOGISTS have often supported radical or participatory democracy. 'Dark' greens have developed a particular critique of electoral democracy that portrays it as a means of imposing the interests of the present generation of humans on (unenfranchised) later generations, other species and nature as a whole.

As a result, classical liberalism has sometimes been called 'nineteenth-century liberalism'. The cradle of classical liberalism was the UK, where the capitalist and industrial revolutions were most advanced. Its ideas have always been more deeply rooted in Anglo-Saxon countries, particularly the UK and the USA, than in other parts of the world. However, classical liberalism is not merely a nineteenth-century form of liberalism, whose ideas are now only of historical interest. Its principles and theories, in fact, have had growing appeal from the second half of the twentieth century onwards. Although what is called neoclassical liberalism, or neoliberalism, initially had greatest impact in the UK and the USA, its influence has spread much wider, in large part fuelled by the advance of globalization.

Classical liberal ideas have taken a variety of forms but they have a number of common characteristics. First, classical liberals subscribe to egoistical individualism. They view human beings as rationally self-interested creatures, who have a pronounced capacity for self-reliance. Society is therefore seen to be atomistic, composed of a collection of largely self-sufficient individuals, meaning that the characteristics of society can be traced back to the more fundamental features of human nature. Second, classical liberals believe in negative freedom. The individual is free insofar as he or she is left alone, not interfered with or coerced by others. As stated earlier, freedom in this sense is the absence of external constraints on the individual. Third, the state is regarded at best as, in Thomas Paine's words, a 'necessary evil'. It is necessary in that, at the very least, it lays down the conditions for orderly existence; and it is evil in that it imposes a collective will on society, thereby limiting the freedom and responsibilities of the individual. Classical liberals thus believe in a minimal state, which acts, using Locke's metaphor, as a 'nightwatchman'. In this view, the state's proper role is restricted to the maintenance of domestic order, the enforcement of contracts, and the protection of society against external attack. Finally, classical liberals have a broadly positive view of civil society. Civil society is not only deemed to be a 'realm of freedom' – by comparison to the state, which is a 'realm of coercion' – but it is also seen to reflect the principle of balance or equilibrium. This is most clearly expressed in the classical liberal belief in a self-regulating market economy. Classical liberalism nevertheless draws on a variety of doctrines and theories. The most important of these are the following:

- natural rights
- utilitarianism
- economic liberalism
- social Darwinism
- neoliberalism

Natural rights

The natural rights theorists of the seventeenth and eighteenth centuries, such as John Locke in England and Thomas Jefferson in America, had a considerable influence on the development of liberal ideology. Modern political debate is littered with references to 'rights' and claims to possess 'rights'. A right, most simply, is an entitlement to act or be treated in a particular way.

Natural rights:
God-given rights that are fundamental to human beings and are therefore inalienable (they cannot be taken away).

Human rights: Rights to which people are entitled by virtue of being human; universal and fundamental rights.

Such entitlements may be either moral or legal in character. For Locke and Jefferson, rights are 'natural' in that they are invested in human beings by nature or God. **Natural rights** are now more commonly called **human rights**. They are, in Jefferson's words, 'inalienable' because human beings are entitled to them by virtue of being human: they cannot, in that sense, be taken away. Natural rights are thus thought to establish the essential conditions for leading a truly human existence. For Locke, there were three such rights: 'life, liberty and property'. Jefferson did not accept that property was a natural or God-given right, but rather one that had developed for human convenience. In the American Declaration of Independence he therefore described inalienable rights as those of 'life, liberty and the pursuit of happiness'.

The idea of natural or human rights has affected liberal thought in a number of ways. For example, the weight given to such rights distinguishes authoritarian thinkers such as Thomas Hobbes from early liberals such as John Locke. As explained earlier, both Hobbes and Locke believed that government was formed through a 'social contract'. However, Hobbes ([1651] 1968) argued that only a strong government, preferably a monarchy, would be able to establish order and security in society. He was prepared to invest the king with sovereign or absolute power, rather than risk a descent into a 'state of nature'. The citizen should therefore accept *any* form of government because even repressive government is better than no government at all. Locke, on the other hand, argued against arbitrary or unlimited government. Government is established in order to protect natural rights. When these are protected by the state, citizens should respect government and obey the law. However, if government violates the rights of its citizens, they in turn have the right of rebellion. Locke thus approved of the English Revolution of the seventeenth century, and applauded the establishment of a constitutional monarchy in 1688.

For Locke, moreover, the contract between state and citizen is a specific and limited one: its purpose is to protect a set of defined natural rights. As a result, Locke believed in limited government. The legitimate role of government is limited to the protection of 'life, liberty and property'. Therefore, the functions of government should not extend beyond the 'minimal' function of preserving public order and protecting property, providing defence against external attack and ensuring that contract are enforced. Other issues and responsibilities are properly the concern of private individuals. Thomas Jefferson expressed the same sentiment a century later when he declared: 'That government is best which governs least'.

Thomas Jefferson (1743–1826)

US political philosopher and statesman. Jefferson was a wealthy Virginian planter who was a delegate to the Second Continental Congress, 1775, and Governor of Virginia, 1779–81. He served as the first Secretary of State, 1789–94, and was the third President of the United States, 1801–9. Jefferson was the principal author of the Declaration of Independence and wrote a vast number of addresses and letters.

Jefferson developed a democratic form of agrarianism that sought to blend a belief in rule by a natural aristocracy with a commitment to limited government and *laissez-faire*. He also exhibited sympathy for social reform, favouring the extension of public education, the abolition of slavery (despite being a slave-owner) and greater economic equality. In the USA, Jeffersonianism stands for resistance to strong central government and a stress on individual freedom and responsibility, and states' rights.

Utilitarianism

Natural rights theories were not the only basis of early liberalism. An alternative and highly influential theory of human nature was put forward in the early nineteenth century by the utilitarians, notably Jeremy Bentham and James Mill. Bentham regarded the idea of rights as 'nonsense' and called natural rights 'nonsense on stilts'. In their place, he proposed what he believed to be the more scientific and objective idea that individuals are motivated by self-interest and that these interests can be defined as the desire for pleasure, or happiness, and the wish to avoid pain, both calculated in terms of **utility**. The principle of utility is, furthermore, a moral principle in that it suggests that the 'rightness' of an action, policy or institution can be established by its tendency to promote happiness. Just as each individual can calculate what is morally good by the quantity of pleasure an action will produce, so the principle of 'the greatest happiness for the greatest number' can be used to establish which policies or institutions will benefit society at large.

Utility: Use-value; in economics, utility describes the satisfaction that is gained from the consumption of material goods and services.

Utilitarian ideas have had a considerable impact on classical liberalism. In particular, they have provided a moral philosophy that explains how and

UTILITARIANISM

Utilitarianism is a moral philosophy that was developed by Jeremy Bentham and James Mill. It equates 'good' with pleasure or happiness, and 'evil' with pain or unhappiness. Individuals are therefore assumed to act so as to maximize pleasure and minimize pain, these being calculated in terms of utility or use-value, usually seen as satisfaction derived from material consumption. The 'greatest happiness' principle can be used to evaluate laws, institutions and even political systems. *Act* utilitarianism judges an act to be right if it produces at least as much pleasure-over-pain as any other act. *Rule* utilitarianism judges an act to be right if it conforms to a rule which, if generally followed, produces good consequences.

why individuals act as they do. The utilitarian conception of human beings as rationally self-interested creatures was adopted by later generations of liberal thinkers. Moreover, each individual is thought to be able to perceive his or her own best interests. This cannot be done on their behalf by some paternal authority, such as the state. Bentham argued that individuals act so as to gain pleasure or happiness in whatever way they choose. No one else can judge the quality or degree of their happiness. If each individual is the sole judge of what will give him or her pleasure, then the individual alone can determine what is morally right. On the other hand, utilitarian ideas can also have illiberal implications. Bentham held that the principle of utility could be applied to society at large and not merely to individual human behaviour. Institutions and legislation can be judged by the yardstick of 'the greatest happiness'. However, this formula has majoritarian implications because it uses the happiness of 'the greatest number' as a standard of what is morally correct, and therefore allows that the interests of the majority outweigh those of the minority or the rights of the individual.

Economic liberalism

The late eighteenth and early nineteenth centuries witnessed the development of classical economic theory in the work of political economists such as Adam Smith and David Ricardo (1770–1823). Smith's *The Wealth of Nations* ([1776] 1976) was in many respects the first economics text book. His ideas drew heavily on liberal and rationalist assumptions about human nature and made a powerful contribution to the debate about the desirable

Jeremy Bentham
(1748–1832)

BENTHAM

UK philosopher, legal reformer and founder of utilitarianism. Bentham's ideas formed the basis of philosophical radicalism, which was responsible for many of the reforms in social administration, law, government and economics in Victorian Britain.

Bentham developed a supposedly scientific alternative to natural rights theory, in the form of a moral and philosophical system based upon the belief that human beings are rationally self-interested creatures, or utility maximizers. Using the principle of general utility – 'the greatest happiness for the greatest number' – he developed a justification for *laissez-faire* economics, constitutional reform and, in later life, political democracy. Bentham's utilitarian creed was developed in *Fragments on Government* (1776) and more fully in *Principles of Morals and Legislation* (1789).

Mercantilism: A school of economic thought that emphasizes the state's role in managing international trade and delivering prosperity.

role of government within civil society. Smith wrote at a time of wide-ranging government restrictions upon economic activity. **Mercantilism**, the dominant economic idea of the sixteenth and seventeenth centuries, had encouraged governments to intervene in economic life in an attempt to encourage the export of goods and restrict imports. Smith's economic writings were designed to attack mercantilism, arguing instead for the principle that the economy works best when it is left alone by government.

Smith thought of the economy as a **market**, indeed as a series of interrelated markets. He believed that the market operates according to the wishes and decisions of free individuals. Freedom within the market means freedom of choice: the ability of the businesses to choose what goods to make, the ability of workers to choose an employer, and the ability of consumers to choose what goods or services to buy.

Market: A system of commercial exchange between buyers and sellers, controlled by impersonal economic forces: 'market forces'.

Relationships within such a market – between employers and employees, and between buyers and sellers – are therefore voluntary and contractual, made by self-interested individuals for whom pleasure is equated with the acquisition and consumption of wealth. Economic theory therefore drew on utilitarianism, in constructing the idea of 'economic man', the notion that human beings are essentially egoistical and bent on material acquisition.

The attraction of classical economics was that, although each individual is

Adam Smith
(1723–90)

SMITH

Scottish economist and philosopher, usually seen as the founder of the 'dismal science'. After holding the chair of logic and then moral philosophy at Glasgow University, Smith became tutor to the Duke of Buccleuch, which enabled him to visit France and Geneva and develop his economic theories.

In *The Theory of Moral Sentiments* (1759), Smith developed a theory of motivation that tried to reconcile human self-interestedness with unregulated social order. His most famous work, *The Wealth of Nations* (1776), was the first systematic attempt to explain the workings of the economy in market terms, emphasizing the importance of a division of labour. Though often seen as a free-market theorist, Smith was nevertheless aware of the limitations of *laissez-faire*.

materially self-interested, the economy itself is thought to operate according to a set of impersonal pressures – market forces – that tend naturally to promote economic prosperity and well-being. For instance, no single producer can set the price of a commodity – prices are set by the market, by the number of goods offered for sale and the number consumers who are willing to buy. These are the forces of supply and demand. The market is a self-regulating mechanism: it needs no guidance from outside. The market should be 'free' from government interference because it is managed by what Smith referred to as an 'invisible hand'. This idea of a self-regulating market reflects the liberal belief in a naturally existing harmony amongst the conflicting interests within society. Smith ([1776] 1976) expressed the economic version of this idea as follows:

> It is not from the benevolence of the butcher, the brewer or the baker that we expect our dinner, but from their regard to their own interests.

Free-market ideas became economic orthodoxy in the UK and the USA during the nineteenth century. The high point of free-market beliefs was reached with the doctrine of **laissez-faire**, meaning 'let [them] act'. This is the idea that the state should have no economic role, but should simply leave the economy alone and allow businesspeople to act however they please. *Laissez-faire* ideas opposed all forms of factory legislation, including restrictions on the employment of

Free market:
The principle or policy of unfettered market competition, free from government interference.

Laissez-faire: The doctrine that economic activity should be entirely free from government interference, an extreme belief in the free market.

children, limits to the number of hours worked and any regulation of working conditions. Such economic individualism is usually based on a belief that the unrestrained pursuit of profit will ultimately lead to general benefit. *Laissez-faire* theories remained strong in the UK throughout much of the nineteenth century, and in the USA they were not seriously challenged until the 1930s. Since the late twentieth century, faith in the free market has been revived through the rise of neoliberalism and its assault on the 'dead hand' of government, examined later in this section. The other manifestation of economic liberalism, a commitment to free trade, is discussed in Chapter 5 in relation to liberal internationalism.

Social Darwinism

One of the distinctive features of classical liberalism is its attitude to poverty and social equality. An individualistic political creed will tend to explain social circumstances in terms of the talents and hard work of each individual human being. Individuals make what they want, and what they can, of their own lives. Those with ability and a willingness to work will prosper, while the incompetent or the lazy will not. This idea was memorably expressed in the title of Samuel Smiles' book *Self-Help* ([1859] 1986) which begins by reiterating the well-tried maxim that 'Heaven helps those who help themselves'. Such ideas of individual responsibility were widely employed by supporters of *laissez-faire* in the nineteenth century. For instance, Richard Cobden (1804–65), the UK economist and politician, advocated an improvement of the conditions of the working classes, but argued that it should come about through 'their own efforts and self-reliance, rather than from law'. He advised them to 'look not to Parliament, look only to yourselves'.

Ideas of individual self-reliance reached their boldest expression in Herbert Spencer's *The Man versus the State* ([1884] 1940). Spencer (1820–1904), the UK philosopher and social theorist, developed a vigorous defence of the doctrine of *laissez-faire*, drawing on ideas that the UK scientist Charles Darwin (1809–82) had developed in *The Origin of Species* ([1859] 1972). Darwin presented a theory of evolution that explained the diversity of species found on Earth. He proposed that each species undergoes a series of random physical and mental changes, or mutations. Some of these changes enable a species to survive and prosper: they are pro-survival. Other mutations are less favourable and make survival more difficult or even impossible. A process of 'natural selection' therefore decides which species are fitted to survive by nature, and which are not. By the end of the nineteenth century, these ideas had extended beyond biology and were increasingly affecting social and political theory.

Spencer, for example, used the theory of natural selection to develop the social principle of 'the survival of the fittest'. People who are best suited by nature to survive, rise to the top, while the less fit fall to the bottom. Inequalities of wealth, social position and political power are therefore natural and inevitable, and no attempt should be made by government to interfere with them. Spencer's US disciple William Sumner (1840–1910) stated this principle boldly in 1884, when he asserted that 'the drunkard in the gutter is just where he ought to be'.

Neoliberalism

Neoliberalism, sometimes called neoclassical liberalism, refers to a revival of economic liberalism that has taken place since the 1970s. Neoliberalism is counter-revolutionary: its aim is to halt, and if possible reverse, the trend towards 'big' government and state intervention that had characterized much of the twentieth century. Neoliberalism had its greatest initial impact in the two states in which free-market economic principles had been most firmly established in the nineteenth century, the UK and the USA. However, in the case of both 'Thatcherism' in the UK and 'Reaganism' in the USA, neoliberalism formed part of a larger, new right ideological project that sought to fuse *laissez-faire* economics with an essentially conservative social philosophy. This project is examined in Chapter 3. Neoliberalism, nevertheless, is not merely an arm of the new right. It has been shaped by wider forces, notably those of economic globalization, and it has had an effect on liberal and socialist parties as well as conservative ones, and has been influential well beyond its Anglo-American homeland.

Neoliberalism amounts to a form of **market fundamentalism**. The market is seen to be morally and practically superior to government and any form of political control. In that sense, neoliberalism goes beyond classical economic theory. For instance, although Adam Smith is rightfully viewed as the father of market economics, he also recognized the limitations of the market and certainly did not subscribe to a crude utility-maximizing model of human nature. From the neoliberal perspective, the defects of government are many and various. Free-market economists, such as Friedrich von Hayek (see p. 90) and the US economist Milton Friedman (1912–2006), attacked the economic role of government. Hayek (1944)

Market fundamentalism: An absolute faith in the market, reflecting the belief that the market mechanism offers solutions to all economic and social problems.

Keynesianism:
A theory (developed by J. M. Keynes) or policy of economic management, associated with regulating aggregate demand to achieve full employment (see p. 59).

advanced a damning economic and political critique of central planning in particular and economic intervention in general. He argued that planning in any form is bound to be economically inefficient because state bureaucrats, however competent they might be, are confronted by a range and complexity of information that is simply beyond their capacity to handle. Friedman criticized **Keynesianism** on the grounds that 'tax and spend' policies fuel inflation by encouraging governments to increase borrowing without, in the process, affecting the 'natural rate' of unemployment.

In contrast, the market has near-miraculous qualities. First and foremost, because they tend towards long-term equilibrium, markets are self-regulating. Re-stating Smith's idea of the 'invisible hand', Hayek likened the market to a vast nervous system that is capable of regulating the economy because it can convey an almost infinite number of messages simultaneously via the price mechanism. Second, markets are naturally efficient and productive. Market economies are efficient at a macroeconomic level because resources are drawn inexorably to their most profitable use, and because rich and poor alike have an incentive to work. At a microeconomic level, private businesses are inherently more efficient than public bodies because they are disciplined by the profit motive, forcing them to keep costs low, while the taxpayer will always pick up the bill for public losses. Third, markets are responsive, even democratic, mechanisms. Competition guarantees that producers produce only what consumers are willing to buy, and at a price they can afford; the consumer, in short, is king. Finally, markets deliver fairness and economic justice. The market gives all people the opportunity to rise or fall on the basis of talent and hard work. Material inequality thus simply reflects a natural inequality amongst humankind.

Modern liberalism

Modern liberalism is sometimes described as 'twentieth-century liberalism'. Just as the development of classical liberalism was closely linked to the emergence of industrial capitalism in the nineteenth century, so modern liberal ideas were related to the further development of industrialization. Industrialization had brought about a massive expansion of wealth for some, but was also accompanied by the spread of slums, poverty, ignorance and disease. Moreover, social inequality became more difficult to ignore as a growing industrial working class was seen to be disadvantaged by low pay, unemployment and degrading living and working conditions. These development had an impact on UK liberalism from the late nineteenth century onwards, but in other countries they did not take effect until much later; for example, US liberalism was not affected until the depression of the 1930s. In these changing historical circumstances, liberals found it progressively more difficult to maintain the belief that the arrival of industrial capitalism had brought with it general prosperity and liberty for all. Consequently, many came to revise the early liberal expectation that the unrestrained pursuit of self-interest produced a socially just society. As the idea of economic individualism came increasingly under attack, liberals rethought their attitude towards the state. The minimal state of classical theory was quite incapable of rectifying the injustices and inequalities of civil society. Modern liberals were therefore prepared to advocate the development of an interventionist or enabling state.

However, modern liberalism has been viewed in two, quite different, ways. Classical liberals in particular have argued that it effectively broke with the principles and doctrines that had previously defined liberalism, notably that it had abandoned individualism and embraced collectivism (see p. 104). Modern liberals, however, have been at pains to point out that they built on, rather than betrayed, classical liberalism. In this view, whereas classical liberalism is characterized by clear theoretical consistency, modern liberalism represents a marriage between new and old liberalism, and thus embodies ideological and theoretical tensions, notably over the proper role of the state. The distinctive ideas of modern liberalism include the following:

- individuality
- positive freedom
- social liberalism
- economic management.

Individuality

John Stuart Mill's ideas have been described as 'the heart of liberalism'. This is because he provided a 'bridge' between classical and modern liberalism: his ideas look both back to the early nineteenth century and forward to the twentieth century. Mill's interests ranged from political economy to the campaign for female suffrage, but it was the ideas developed in *On Liberty* ([1859] 1972) that most clearly show Mill as a contributor to modern liberal thought. This work contains some of the boldest liberal statements in favour of individual freedom. Mill suggested that 'Over himself, over his own body and mind, the individual is sovereign' (1972, p. 73), a conception of liberty that is essentially negative for it portrays freedom as the absence of restrictions on an individual's 'self-regarding' actions. Mill believed this to be a necessary condition for liberty, but not in itself a sufficient one. He thought that liberty was a positive and constructive force. It gave individuals the ability to take control of their own lives, to gain autonomy or achieve self-realization.

Mill was strongly influenced by European romanticism and found the notion of human beings as utility maximizers both shallow and unconvincing. He believed passionately in **individuality**. The value of liberty is that it enables individuals to develop, to gain talents, skills and knowledge and to refine their sensibilities. Mill disagreed with Bentham's utilitarianism insofar as Bentham believed that actions could only be distinguished by the quantity of pleasure or pain they generated. For Mill, there were 'higher' and 'lower' pleasures. Mill was concerned to promote those pleasure that develop an individual's intellectual, moral or aesthetic sensibilities. He was clearly not concerned with simple pleasure-seeking, but with personal self-development, declaring that he would rather be 'Socrates dissatisfied than a fool satisfied'. As such, he laid the foundations for a developmental model of individualism that placed emphasis on human flourishing rather than the crude satisfaction of interests.

Individuality: Self-fulfilment achieved through the realization of an individual's distinctive or unique identity or qualities; that which distinguishes one person from all others.

Positive freedom

The clearest break with early liberal thought came in the late nineteenth century with the work of the UK philosopher T. H. Green (1836–82), whose writing influenced a generation of so-called 'new liberals' such as L. T. Hobhouse (1864–1929) and J. A. Hobson (1854–1940). Green believed that the unrestrained pursuit of profit, as advocated by classical liberalism, had given rise to new forms of poverty and injustice. The economic liberty of the few had blighted the life chances of the many. Following J. S. Mill, he rejected the early liberal conception of human beings as essentially self-seeking utility maximizers, and suggested a more optimistic view of human nature. Individuals, according to Green, have sympathy for one another; they are capable of **altruism**. The individual possesses social responsibilities and not merely individual responsibilities, and is therefore linked to other individuals by ties of caring and empathy. Such a conception of human nature was clearly influenced by socialist ideas that emphasized the sociable and cooperative nature of

Altruism: Concern for the interests and welfare of others, based either upon enlightened self-interest or a belief in a common humanity.

humankind. As a result, Green's ideas have been described as 'socialist liberalism'.

Green also challenged the classical liberal notion of liberty. Negative liberty merely removes external constraints on the individual, giving the individual freedom of choice. In the case of the businesses that wish to maximize profits, negative freedom justifies their ability to hire the cheapest labour possible; for example, to employ children rather than adults, or women rather than men. Economic freedom can therefore lead to exploitation or the 'freedom to starve'. Freedom of choice in the marketplace is therefore an inadequate conception of individual freedom.

In the place of negative freedom, Green proposed the idea of positive freedom. Freedom is the ability of the individual to develop and attain individuality; it involves the ability of the individual to realize his or her potential, attain skills and knowledge, and achieve fulfilment. Thus, whereas negative freedom acknowledges only legal and physical constraints on liberty, positive freedom recognizes that liberty may also be threatened by social disadvantage and inequality. This, in turn, implied a revised view of the state. By protecting individuals from the social evils that threaten to cripple their lives, the state can expand freedom, and not merely diminish it. In place of the minimal state of old, modern liberals have therefore endorsed an enabling state, exercising an increasingly wide range of social and economic responsibilities.

Although such ideas undoubtedly involved a revision of classical liberal theories, it did not amount to the abandonment of core liberal beliefs. Modern liberalism drew closer to socialism, but it did not place society before the individual. For T. H. Green, for example, freedom ultimately consisted in individuals acting morally. The state could not force people to be good; it could only provide conditions in which they can make more responsible moral decisions. The balance between the state and the individual has been altered, but the underlying commitment to the needs and interests of the individual remains. Modern liberals share the classical liberal preference for self-reliant individuals who take responsibility for their own lives; the essential difference is the recognition that this can only occur if social conditions are conducive to it. The central thrust of modern liberalism is therefore to help individuals to help themselves.

Social liberalism

The twentieth century witnessed the growth of state intervention in most western states and in many developing ones. Much of this intervention took the form of social welfare: attempts by government to provide welfare

Welfare State: A state that takes primary responsibility for the social welfare of its citizens, discharged through a range of social-security, health, education and other services.

support for its citizens by overcoming poverty, disease and ignorance. If the minimal state was typical of the nineteenth century, during the twentieth century modern states became **welfare states**. This occurred as a consequence of a variety of historical and ideological factors. Governments, for example, sought to achieve national efficiency, more healthy work forces and stronger armies. They also came under electoral pressure for social reform from newly enfranchised industrial workers and, in some cases, the peasantry. The political argument for welfarism has not been the prerogative of any single ideology. It has been put, in different ways, by socialists, liberals, conservatives, feminists and even at times by fascists. Within liberalism, the case for social welfare is made by modern liberals, in marked contrast to classical liberals, who extol the virtues of self-help and individual responsibility.

Modern liberals defend welfarism on the basis of equality of opportunity. If particular individuals or groups are disadvantaged by their social circumstances, then the state possesses a social responsibility to reduce or remove these disadvantages to create equal, or at least more equal, life chances. Citizens have thus acquired a range of welfare or social rights, such as the right to work, the right to education and the right to decent housing. Welfare rights are positive rights because they can only be satisfied by the positive actions of government, through the provision of state pensions, benefits and, perhaps, publicly funded health and education services. During the twentieth century, liberal parties and liberal governments were therefore converted to the cause of social welfare. For example, the expanded welfare state in the UK was based on the Beveridge Report (1942), which set out to attack the so-called 'five giants' – want, disease, ignorance, squalor and idleness. It memorably promised to protect citizens 'from the cradle to the grave'. In the USA, liberal welfarism developed in the 1930 during the administration of F. D. Roosevelt, but reached its height in the 1960s with the 'New Frontier' policies of John F. Kennedy and Lyndon Johnson's 'Great Society' programme. Social liberalism was further developed in the second half of the twentieth century with the emergence of so-called social-democratic liberalism, especially in the writings of John Rawls. Social-democratic liberalism is distinguished by its support for relative social equality, usually seen as the defining value of socialism. In *A Theory of Justice* (1970), Rawl developed a defence of redistribution and welfare based on the idea of 'equality as fairness'. He argued that, if people were unaware of their social position and circumstances, they would view an egalitarian society as 'fairer' than an inegalitarian one, on the grounds that the desire to avoid poverty is greater than the attraction of riches. He therefore proposed the 'difference principle':

John Rawls
(1921–2002)

US academic and political philosopher. Rawls' major work, *A Theory of Justice* (1970), is regarded as the most important work of political philosophy written in English since the Second World War, and it has had a crucial influence on both modern liberal and social democratic thought.

Rawls used a form of social contract theory to reconcile liberal individualism with the principles of redistribution and social justice. His notion of 'justice as fairness' is based upon the belief that behind a 'veil of ignorance' (that is, not knowing our own social position and circumstances) most people would favour two basic principles: (a) that the liberty of each person should be compatible with a like liberty for all, and (b) that social inequality should only exist if it works to the benefit of the poorest in society. The universalist presumptions of his early work were somewhat modified in *Political Liberalism* (1993).

that social and economic inequalities should be arranged so as to benefit the least well-off, recognizing the need for some measure of inequality to provide an incentive to work. Nevertheless, such a theory of justice remains liberal rather than socialist, as it is rooted in assumptions about egoism and self-interest, rather than a belief in social solidarity.

Economic management

In addition to providing social welfare, twentieth-century western governments also sought to deliver prosperity by 'managing' their economies. This once again involved rejecting classical liberal thinking, in particular its belief in a self-regulating free market and the doctrine *of laissez-faire*. The abandonment of *laissez-faire* came about because of the increasing complexity of industrial capitalist economies and their apparent inability to guarantee general prosperity if left to their own devices. The Great Depression of the 1930s, sparked off by the Wall Street Crash of 1929, led to high levels of unemployment throughout the industrialized world and in much of the developing world. This was the most dramatic demonstration of the failure of the free market. After the Second World War, virtually all western states adopted policies of economic intervention in an attempt to prevent a return to the pre-war levels of unemployment. To a large extent these interventionist policies were guided by the work of the UK economist John Maynard Keynes (1883–1946).

In *The General Theory of Employment, Interest and Money* ([1936] 1963), Keynes challenged classical economic thinking and rejected its belief in a self-regulating market. Classical economists had argued that there was a 'market solution' to the problem of unemployment and, indeed, all other economic problems. Keynes argued, however, that the level of economic activity, and therefore of employment, is determined by the total amount of demand – aggregate demand – in the economy. He suggested that governments could 'manage' their economies by influencing the level of aggregate demand. Government spending is, in this sense, an 'injection' of demand into the economy. Taxation, on the other hand, is a 'withdrawal' from the economy: it reduces aggregate demand and dampens down economic activity. At time of high unemployment, Keynes recommended that governments should 'reflate' their economies by either increasing public spending or cutting taxes. Unemployment could therefore be solved, not by the invisible hand of capitalism, but by government intervention, in this case by running a budget deficit, meaning that the government literally 'overspends'.

Keynesian demand management thus promised to give governments the ability to manipulate employment and growth levels, and hence to secure general prosperity. As with the provision of social welfare, modern liberals have seen economic management as constructive in promoting prosperity

KEYNESIANISM

Keynesianism refers, narrowly, to the economic theories of J. M. Keynes (1883–1946) and, more broadly, to a range of economic policies that have been influenced by these theories. Keynesianism provides an alternative to neoclassical economics and, in particular, advances a critique of the 'economic anarchy' of *laissez-faire* capitalism.

Keynes argued that growth and employment levels are largely determined by the level of 'aggregate demand' in the economy, and that government can regulate demand, primarily through adjustments to fiscal policy, so as to deliver full employment. Keynesianism came to be associated with a narrow obsession with 'tax and spend' policies, but this

ignores the complexity and sophistication of Keynes' economic writings. Influenced by economic globalization, a form of *neo-Keynesianism* has emerged that rejects 'top-down' economic management but still acknowledges that market are hampered by uncertainty, inequality and differential levels of knowledge.

and harmony in civil society. Keynes was not opposed to capitalism; indeed, in many ways, he was its saviour. He simply argued that unrestrained private enterprise is unworkable within complex industrial societies. The first, if limited, attempt to apply Keynes' ideas was undertaken in the USA during Roosevelt's 'New Deal'. By the end of the Second World War, Keynesianism was widely established as an economic orthodoxy in the West, displacing the older belief in *laissez-faire*. Keynesian policies were credited with being the key to the 'long boom', the historically unprecedented economic growth of the 1950s and 1960s, which witnessed the achievement of widespread affluence, at least in western countries. However, the re-emergence of economic difficulties in the 1970s generated renewed sympathy for the theories of classical political economy, and led to a shift away from Keynesian priorities. Nevertheless, the failure of the free-market revolution of the 1980s and 1990s to ensure sustained economic growth resulted in the emergence of the 'new' political economy, or neo-Keynesianism. Although this recognized that the 'crude' Keynesianism of the 1950s and 1960s had been rendered redundant by globalization, it also marks a renewed awareness of the fact that unregulated capitalism tends to bring low investment, short-termism and social fragmentation.

TENSIONS WITHIN
LIBERALISM

CLASSICAL LIBERALISM	v.	MODERN LIBERALISM
economic liberalism	←→	social liberalism
egoistical individualism	←→	developmental individualism
maximize utility	←→	personal growth
negative freedom	←→	positive freedom
minimal state	←→	enabling state
free-market economy	←→	managed economy
rights-based justice	←→	justice as fairness
strict meritocracy	←→	concern for the poor
individual responsibility	←→	social responsibility
safety-net welfare	←→	cradle-to-grave welfare

Liberalism in the twenty-first century

The high point of liberal optimism came in the aftermath of the collapse of communism. A new world order appeared to have come into effect in which, as 'end of history' theorists proclaimed, liberal democracy was revealed as the final solution to the problem of political organization. This was confirmed both by a further wave of democratization in developing and postcommunist states, and by the 'liberal peace' that appeared to reign in international affairs once the Cold War was over. There are two main reasons for believing that these trends, despite, perhaps, temporary setbacks, will continue through the twenty-first century, making it the century of global liberalism. First, as societies become increasingly complex and diverse, the task of maintaining political stability requires the existence of sophisticated channels of communication between government and the people that only a liberal polity can provide. Rule-based governance, regular and competitive elections and freedom of association allow the political process to be responsive to societal pressures coming from various directions. This suggests that political systems around the world will, sooner or later, be reconfigured on the basis of liberal-democratic principles. Second, the advance of liberalism is closely linked to the seemingly remorseless construction of a global capitalist system. Economic globalization has been driven by market forces that liberal theorists have long believed are both irresistible and bent on delivering general prosperity. A globalized twenty-first century will therefore coincide with the establishment of global liberalism, in both its economic and political forms.

However, liberal triumphalism needs to be tempered by the recognition of new challenges and threats to liberalism. One of these comes from the nature of capitalism and the implications of a global capitalist system. Although the socialist challenge appears to have been defeated, is this defeat, or the defeat of other forms of anti-capitalism, permanent? The tendency within capitalism towards inequality, an inevitable feature of private enterprise and market economics, suggests that oppositional forces to liberal capitalism may always arise. Indeed, the basis for this may already have been laid by the contemporary anti-globalization or anti-capitalist movement. A second challenge to liberalism comes from a recognition of the growing importance of difference or diversity. This challenges the universalist assumptions of liberalism, highlighting the fact that it is increasingly difficult to root values and identity in the abstract notion of the individual, as 'the particular' gains credibility over 'the universal'. The earliest such attack on liberalism was launched by communitarian thinkers, who rejected individualism as facile, on the grounds that it suggests that the self is 'unencumbered'. In this view, identity does not derive from within,

POSTMODERNISM

Postmodernism is a controversial and confusing term that was first used to describe experimental movements in western arts, architecture and cultural development in general. As a tool of social and political analysis, postmodernism highlights the shift away from societies structured by industrialization and class solidarity to increasingly fragmented and pluralistic 'information societies', in which individuals are transformed from producers to consumers, and individualism replaces class, religious and ethnic loyalties. Postmodernists argue that there is no such thing as certainty; the idea of absolute and universal truth must be discarded as an arrogant pretence. Emphasis is placed instead on discourse, debate and democracy.

but rather from the social, historical or cultural context in which people live. Such a view has also been advanced by multiculturalists, who advance a collective notion of identity based on culture, ethnicity, language or religion. At best, such ideas may only be accommodated within a 'post-liberal' framework (Gray, 1995b), and many believe that liberalism and multiculturalism are opposing forces.

Finally, in this respect, the very foundations of liberalism have been questioned by postmodernism, which has proclaimed the effective collapse of the Enlightenment project. This project was based on the assumption that a set of universally applicable rational principles can lay down conditions that allow individuals to pursue incommensurable ends. However, postmodern thinkers, such as Richard Rorty (1989), have questioned the idea of objective truth and argued that liberalism, like other ideologies and indeed all belief systems, is merely a 'vocabulary' that cannot be viewed as any more 'accurate' than other 'vocabularies'.

Challenges to liberalism also come from outside its western homeland. There is as much evidence that the end of the bipolar world order, dominated as it was by the clash between a capitalist West and the communist East, has unleashed non-liberal political forces, as there is evidence of the 'triumph' of liberal democracy. In eastern Europe and parts of the developing world, resurgent nationalism, whose popular appeal is based on strength, certainty and security, has often proved more potent than equivocal liberalism. Moreover, this nationalism is more commonly associated with ethnic purity and authoritarianism than with liberal ideals such as self-determination and civic pride. Various forms of fundamentalism (see p. 288), quite at odds with liberal culture, have also arisen in the Middle East and parts of Africa and Asia. Indeed, political Islam may prevail over liberalism in much of the developing world precisely because of its capacity to offer a non-western, even anti-western, stance. Furthermore, where successful market economies have been established they have not always been founded on the basis of liberal values and institutions. For instance, the political regimes of East Asia may owe more to Confucianism's ability to maintain social stability than to the influence of liberal ideas such as competition and self-striving. Far from moving towards a unified, liberal world, political development in the twenty-first century may be characterized by growing ideological diversity. Political Islam, Confucianism and even authoritarian nationalism may yet prove to be enduring rivals to western liberalism.

Questions for discussion

→ Why do liberals reject unlimited freedom?

→ How convincing is the liberal notion that human beings are reason-guided creatures?

→ Which forms of equality do liberals support, and which do they reject?

→ Why do liberals believe that power tends to corrupt, and how do they think it can be 'tamed'?

→ Why have liberals sometimes questioned the benefits of democracy?

→ How do classical liberals defend unregulated capitalism?

→ How far are modern liberals willing to go in endorsing social and economic intervention?

→ Do modern liberals have a coherent view of the state?

→ Is liberal democracy the final solution to the problem of political organization?

Further reading

Arblaster, A., *The Rise and Decline of Western Liberalism* (Oxford: Basil Blackwell, 1984). A wide-ranging and very stylish account of liberal doctrines, emphasizing their individualist character.

Bellamy, R., *Liberalism and Modern Society: An Historical Argument* (Cambridge: Polity Press, 1992). An analysis of the development of liberalism that focuses on the adaptations necessary to apply liberal values to new social realities.

Gray, J., *Two Faces of Liberalism* (Cambridge: Polity Press, 2000). An account of liberalism that emphasizes the divide between its universalist and pluralist forms.

Gray, J., *Liberalism*, 2nd edn (Milton Keynes: Open University Press, 1995). A short and not uncritical introduction to liberalism as the political theory of modernity; contains a discussion of postliberalism.

Harvey, D., *A Brief History of Neoliberalism* (Oxford and New York: Oxford University Press, 2005). A concise but comprehensive guide to the nature, origins and implications of neoliberalism, looking at the developing world, including China, as well as the developed world.

Holden, B., *Understanding Liberal Democracy*, 2nd edn (Hemel Hempstead: Harvester Wheatsheaf, 1993). An accessible introduction to the concept and nature of liberal democracy, which looks at criticisms and justifications.

Ramsay, M., *What's Wrong with Liberalism? A Radical Critique of Liberal Political Philosophy* (London: Leicester University Press, 1997). A thoughtful and accessible account of liberal theory and practice from a variety of critical perspectives.

CHAPTER 3

CONSERVATISM

PREVIEW

In everyday language, the term 'conservative' has a variety of meanings. It can refer to moderate or cautious behaviour, a lifestyle that is conventional, even conformist, or a fear of or refusal to change, particularly denoted by the verb 'to conserve'. 'Conservatism' was first used to describe a distinctive political position or ideology in the early nineteenth century. In the USA, it implied a pessimistic view of public affairs. By the 1820s, the term was being used to denote opposition to the principles and spirit of the 1789 Revolution. In the UK, 'Conservative' gradually replaced 'Tory' as a title of the principal opposition party to the Whigs, becoming the party's official name in 1835.

As a political ideology, conservatism is defined by the desire to conserve, reflected in a resistance to, or at least a suspicion of, change. However, although the desire to resist change may be the recurrent theme within conservatism, what distinguishes conservatism from rival political creeds is the distinctive way in which this position is upheld, in particular through support for tradition, a belief in human imperfection, and the attempt to uphold the organic structure of society. Conservatism nevertheless encompasses a range of tendencies and inclinations. The chief distinction within conservatism is between what is called traditional conservatism and the 'new right'. Traditional conservatism defends established institutions and values on the ground that they safeguard the fragile 'fabric of society', giving security-seeking human beings a sense of stability and rootedness. The new right is characterized by a belief in a strong but minimal state, combining economic libertarianism with social authoritarianism.

Origins and development

Conservative ideas arose in reaction to the growing pace of political, social and economic change, which, in many ways, was symbolized by the French Revolution. One of the earliest, and perhaps the classic, statement of conservative principles is contained in Edmund Burke's (see p. 70) *Reflections on the Revolution in France* ([1790] 1968), which deeply regretted the revolutionary challenge to the *ancien régime* that had occurred the previous year. During the nineteenth century, western states were transformed by the pressures unleashed by industrialization and reflected in the growth of liberalism, socialism and nationalism. While these ideologies preached reform, and at times supported revolution, conservatism stood in defence of an increasingly embattled traditional social order.

Conservative thought has varied considerably as it has adapted itself to existing traditions and national cultures. UK conservatism, for instance, has drawn heavily on the ideas of Burke, who advocated not blind resistance to change, but rather a prudent willingness to 'change in order to conserve'. In the nineteenth century, UK conservatives defended a political and social order that had already undergone profound change, in particular the overthrow of the absolute monarchy, as a result of the English Revolution of the seventeenth century. Such pragmatic principles have also influenced the conservative parties established in other Commonwealth countries. The Canadian Conservative Party adopted the title Progressive Conservative precisely to distance itself from reactionary ideas. In continental Europe, where some auto-

Authoritarianism:
A belief that strong central authority, imposed from above, is either desirable or necessary, and therefore demands unquestioning obedience. (see p. 80).

cratic monarchies persisted throughout much of the nineteenth century, a very different and more **authoritarian** form of conservatism developed, which defended monarchy and rigid autocratic values against the rising tide of reform. Only with the formation of Christian democratic parties after the Second World War did continental conservatives, notably in Germany and Italy, fully accept political democracy and social reform. The USA, on the other hand, has been influenced relatively little by conservative ideas. The US system of government and its political culture reflect deeply established liberal and progressive values, and politicians of both major parties – the Republicans and the Democrats – have traditionally resented being labelled 'conservative'. It is only since the 1960s that overtly conservative views have been expressed by elements within both parties, notably by southern Democrats and the wing of the Republican party that was associated in the 1960s with Barry Goldwater, and which supported Ronald Reagan in the 1980s and later George W. Bush.

As conservative ideology arose in reaction against the French Revolution and the process of modernization in the West, it is less easy to identify political conservatism outside Europe and North America. In Africa, Asia and Latin America, political movements have developed that sought to resist change and preserve traditional ways of life, but they have seldom employed specifically conservative arguments and values. An exception to this is perhaps the Japanese Liberal Democratic Party, which has dominated politics in Japan since 1955. The LDP has close links with business interests and is committed to promoting a healthy private sector. At the same time, it has attempted to preserve traditional Japanese values and customs, and has therefore supported distinctively conservative principles such as loyalty, duty and hierarchy. In other countries, conservatism has exhibited a populist-authoritarian character. Perón in Argentina and Khomeini (see p. 298) in Iran, for instance, both established regimes based on strong central authority, but which also mobilized mass popular support on issues such as nationalism, economic progress and the defence of traditional values.

Although conservatism is the most intellectually modest of political ideologies, it has also been remarkably resilient, perhaps because of this fact. Conservatism has prospered because it has been unwilling to be tied down to a fixed system of ideas. A significant revival of conservative fortunes has, in fact, been evident since the 1970s, gaining impetus from growing concerns about the welfare state and economic management. Particularly prominent in this respect were the Thatcher government in the UK (1979–90) and the Reagan administration in the USA (1981–89), both of which practised an unusually radical and ideological brand of conservatism, commonly termed the 'new right'. **New right** ideas have drawn heavily on free-market economics and, in so doing, have exposed deep divisions within conservatism. Indeed, commentators argue that 'Thatcherism' and 'Reaganism', and the new right project in general, do not properly belong within conservative ideology at all, so deeply are they influenced by classical liberal economics. The new right has challenged traditional conservative economic views, but it nevertheless remains part of conservative ideology. In the first place, it has not abandoned traditional conservative social principles such as a belief in order, authority and discipline, and in some respects it has strengthened them. Furthermore, the new right's enthusiasm for the free market has exposed the extent to which conservatism had already been influenced by liberal ideas. As with all political ideologies, conservatism contains a range of traditions. In the nineteenth century, it was closely associated with an authoritarian defence of monarchy and aristocracy, which has survived in the form of authoritarian populist movements in the developing world. In the twentieth century, western conservatives were divided between paternalistic support for state intervention and a libertarian commitment to

New right:
An ideological trend within conservatism that embraces a blend of market individualism and social authoritarianism.

the free market. The significance of the new right is that it sought to revive the electoral fortunes of conservatism by readjusting the balance between these traditions in favour of libertarianism (see p. 86). However, in so doing, it brought such deep ideological tensions to the surface that it may have threatened the very survival of conservatism.

Core themes – the desire to conserve

The character of conservative ideology has been the source of particular argument and debate. For example, it is often suggested that conservatives have a clearer understanding of what they oppose than of what they favour. In that sense, conservatism has been portrayed as a negative philosophy, its purpose being simply to preach resistance to, or at least suspicion of, change. However, if conservatism were to consist of no more than a knee-jerk defence of the *status quo*, it would be merely a political attitude rather than an ideology. In fact, many people or groups can be considered 'conservative' in the sense that they resist change, but certainly cannot be said to subscribe to a conservative political creed. For instance, socialists who campaign in defence of the welfare state or nationalized industries could be classified as conservative in terms of their actions, but certainly not in terms of their political principles. The desire to resist change may be the recurrent theme within conservatism, but what distinguishes conservatives from supporters of rival political creeds is the distinctive way they uphold this position.

A second problem is that to describe conservatism as an ideology is to risk irritating conservatives themselves. They have often preferred to describe their beliefs as an 'attitude of mind' or 'common sense', as opposed to an 'ism' or ideology. Others have argued that what is distinctive about conservatism is its emphasis on history and experience, and its distaste for rational thought. Conservatives have thus typically eschewed the 'politics of principle' and adopted instead a traditionalist political stance. Their opponents have also lighted upon this feature of conservatism, sometimes portraying it as little more than an unprincipled apology for the interests of a ruling class or elite. However, both conservatives and their critics ignore the weight and range of theories that underpin conservative 'common sense'. Conservatism is neither simple pragmatism nor mere opportunism. It is founded on a particular set of political beliefs about human beings, the societies they live in, and the importance of a distinctive set of political values. As such, like liberalism and socialism, it should rightfully be described as an ideology. The most significant of its central beliefs are the following:

- tradition
- human imperfection
- organic society
- hierarchy and authority
- property

Tradition

Conservatives have argued against change on a number of grounds. A central and recurrent theme of conservatism is its defence of **tradition**. Tradition refers to values, practices and institutions that have endured through time and, in particular, been passed down from one generation to the next. For some conservatives, this emphasis on tradition reflects their religious faith. If the world is thought to have been fashioned by God the Creator, traditional customs and practices in society will be regarded as 'God given'. Burke thus believed that society was shaped by 'the law of our Creator', or what he also called 'natural law'. If human beings tamper with the world, they are challenging the will of God, and as a result they are likely to make human affairs worse rather than better. Since the eighteenth century, however, it has become increasingly difficult to maintain that tradition reflects the will of God. As the pace of historical change accelerated, old traditions were replaced by new ones, and these new ones – for example, free elections and universal suffrage – were clearly seen to be man-made rather than in any sense 'God given'. Nevertheless, the religious objection to change has been kept alive by modern fundamentalists, who believe that God's wishes have been revealed to humankind in the literal truth of their religious texts. Such ideas are discussed in Chapter 10.

Tradition: A practice or institution that has endured through time and has therefore been inherited from an earlier period.

Most conservatives, however, support tradition without needing to argue that it has divine origins. Burke, for example, described society as a partnership between 'those who are living, those who are dead and those who are to be born'. G. K. Chesterton (1874–1936), the UK novelist and essayist, expressed this idea as follows:

> Tradition means giving votes to the most obscure of all classes: our ancestors. It is a democracy of the dead. Tradition refuses to submit to the arrogant oligarchy of those who merely happen to be walking around   (see O'Sullivan, 1976).

Tradition, in this sense, reflects the accumulated wisdom of the past. The institutions and practices of the past have been 'tested by time', and should

Edmund Burke
(1729–97)

Dublin-born British statesmen and political theorist, often seen as the father of the Anglo-American conservative tradition. A Whig politician, Burke was sympathetic towards the American Revolution of 1776 but earned his reputation through the staunch criticism of the 1789 French Revolution that he presented in *Reflections on the Revolution in France* (1790).

Burke was deeply opposed to the attempt to recast French politics in accordance with abstract principles such as liberty, equality and fraternity, arguing that wisdom resides largely in experience, tradition and history. Nevertheless, he held that the French monarchy was in part responsible for its own fate, as it had obstinately refused to 'change in order to conserve'. Burke had a gloomy view of government, recognizing that, although it can prevent evil, it rarely promotes good. He also supported the classical economics of Adam Smith (see p. 50) and regarded market forces as 'natural law'.

therefore be preserved for the benefit of the living and for generations to come. This notion of tradition reflects an almost Darwinian belief that those institutions and customs that have survived have only done so because they have worked and been found to be of value. They have been endorsed by a process of 'natural selection' and demonstrated their fitness to survive. Conservatives in the UK, for instance, argue that the institution of monarchy should be preserved because it embodies historical wisdom and experience. In particular, the crown has provided the UK with a focus of national loyalty and respect 'above' party politics; quite simply, it has worked.

Conservatives also venerate tradition because it generates, for both society and the individual, a sense of identity. Established customs and practices are ones that individuals can recognize; they are familiar and reassuring. Tradition thus provides people with a feeling of 'rootedness' and belonging, which is all the stronger because it is historically based. It generates social cohesion by linking people to the past and providing them with a collective sense of who they are. Change, on the other hand, is a journey into the unknown: it creates uncertainty and insecurity, and so endangers our happiness. Tradition, therefore, consists of rather more than political institutions that have stood the test of time. It encompasses all those customs and social practices that are familiar and generate security and belonging, ranging from the judiciary's insistence on wearing traditional robes and wigs to campaigns to preserve, for example, the traditional colour of letter boxes or telephone boxes.

Human imperfection

In many ways, conservatism is a 'philosophy of human imperfection' (O'Sullivan, 1976). Other ideologies assume that human beings are naturally 'good', or that they can be made 'good' if their social circumstances are improved. In their most extreme form, such beliefs are utopian and envisage the perfectibility of humankind in an ideal society. Conservatives dismiss these ideas as, at best, idealistic dreams, and argue instead that human beings are both imperfect and unperfectible.

Human imperfection is understood in several ways. In the first place, human beings are thought to be psychologically limited and dependent creatures. In the view of conservatives, people fear isolation and instability. They are drawn psychologically to the safe and the familiar, and, above all, seek the security of knowing 'their place'. Such a portrait of human nature is very different from the image of the self-reliant, enterprising, 'utility maximizer' proposed by early liberals. The belief that individuals desire security and belonging has led conservatives to emphasize the importance of social order, and to be suspicious of the attractions of liberty. Order ensures that human life is stable and predictable; it provides security in an uncertain world. Liberty, on he other hand, presents individuals with choices and can generate change and uncertainty. Conservatives have often echoed the views of Thomas Hobbes in being prepared to sacrifice liberty in the cause of social order.

Whereas other political philosophies trace the origins of immoral or criminal behaviour to society, conservatives believe it is rooted in the individual. Human beings are thought to be morally imperfect. Conservatives hold a pessimistic, even Hobbesian, view of human nature. Humankind is innately selfish and greedy, anything but perfectible; as Hobbes put it, the desire for 'power after power' is the primary human urge. Some conservatives explain this by reference to the Old Testament doctrine of 'original sin'. Crime is therefore not a product of inequality or social disadvantage, as socialists and modern liberals tend to believe; rather, it is a consequence of base human instincts and appetites. People can only be persuaded to behave in a civilized fashion if they are deterred from expressing their violent and anti-social impulses. And the only effective deterrent is law, backed up by the knowledge that it will be strictly enforced. This explains the conservative prefer-

Thomas Hobbes
(1588–1679)

HOBBES

English political philosopher. Hobbes – the son of a minor clergyman who subsequently abandoned his family – became tutor to the exiled Prince of Wales, Charles Stuart, and lived under the patronage of the Cavendish family. Writing at a time of uncertainty and civil strife, precipitated by the English Revolution, Hobbes was the first since Aristotle to develop a comprehensive theory of nature and human behaviour.

Hobbes' classic work *Leviathan* (1651) defended absolutist government as the only alternative to anarchy and disorder, and proposed that citizens have an unqualified obligation towards their state. In so doing, he provided a rationalist defence for authoritarianism, which nevertheless disappointed supporters of the divine right of kings. Hobbes' individualist methodology, and the use he made of social contract theory, prefigured early liberalism.

ence for strong government and for 'tough' criminal justice regimes, based, often, on long prison sentences and the use of corporal or even capital punishment. For conservatives, the role of law is not to uphold liberty, but to preserve order. The concepts of 'law' and 'order' are so closely related in the conservative mind that they have almost become a single, fused concept.

Humankind's intellectual powers are also thought to be limited. As discussed in Chapter 1, conservatives have traditionally believe that the world is simply too complicated for human reason to grasp fully. The political world, as the UK political philosopher Michael Oakeshott (1901–90) put it, is 'boundless and bottomless'. Conservatives are therefore suspicious of abstract ideas and systems of thought that claim to understand what is, they argue, simply incomprehensible. They prefer to ground their ideas in tradition, experience and history, adopting a cautious, moderate and above all pragmatic approach to the world, and avoiding, if at all possible, doctrinaire or dogmatic beliefs. High-sounding political principles such as the 'rights of man', 'equality' and 'social justice' are fraught with danger because they provide a blueprint for the reform or remodelling of the world. Reform and revolution, conservatives warn, often lead to greater suffering rather than less. For a conservative, to do nothing may be preferable to doing something, and a conservative will always wish to ensure, in Oakeshott's words said, that 'the cure is not worse than the disease'. Nevertheless, conservative support for both traditionalism and pragmatism has weakened as a result of the rise of the new right. In the first place, the new right is

HUMAN NATURE

LIBERALS view human nature as a set of innate qualities intrinsic to the individual, placing little or no emphasis on social or historical conditioning. Humans are self-seeking and largely self-reliant creatures; but they are also governed by reason and are capable of personal development, particularly through education.

CONSERVATIVES believe that human beings are essentially limited and security-seeking creatures, drawn to the known, the familiar, the tried and tested. Human rationality is unreliable, and moral corruption is implicit in each human individual. The new right, nevertheless, embraces a form of self-seeking individualism.

SOCIALISTS regard humans as essentially social creatures, their capacities and behaviour being shaped more by nurture than by nature, and particularly by creative labour. Their propensity for cooperation, sociability and rationality means that the prospects for human development and personal growth are considerable.

ANARCHISTS view human nature in highly optimistic terms. Humans are either seen to have a powerful inclination towards sociable, gregarious and cooperative behaviour, being capable of maintaining order through collective effort alone, or to be basically self-interested but rationally enlightened.

FASCISTS believe that humans are ruled by the will and other non-rational drives, most particularly by a deep sense of social belonging focused on the nation or race. Although the masses are fitted only to serve and obey, elite members of the national community are capable of personal regeneration as 'new men' through dedication to the national or racial cause.

FEMINISTS usually hold that men and women share a common human nature, gender differences being culturally or socially imposed. Separatist feminists, nevertheless, argue that men are genetically disposed to domination and cruelty, while women are naturally sympathetic, creative and peaceful.

ECOLOGISTS, particularly deep ecologists, see human nature as part of the broader ecosystem, even as part of nature itself. Materialism, greed and egoism therefore reflect the extent to which humans have become alienated from the oneness of life and thus from their own true nature. Human fulfilment requires a return to nature.

radical, in that it has sought to advance free-market reforms by dismantling inherited welfarist and interventionist structures. Second, new right radicalism is based on rationalism (see p. 32) and a commitment to abstract theories and principles, notably those of economic liberalism.

Organic society

Conservatives believe, as explained earlier, that human beings are dependent and security-seeking creatures. This implies that they do not, and cannot, exist outside society, but desperately need to belong, to have 'roots' in society. The individual cannot be separated from society, but is part of the social groups that nurture him or her: family, friends or peer group, workmates or colleagues, local community and even the nation. These groups provide individual life with security and meaning. As a result, traditional conservatives are reluctant to understand freedom in terms of 'negative freedom', in which the individual is 'left alone' and suffers, as the French sociologist Durkheim put it, from **anomie**. Freedom is, rather, a willing acceptance of social obligations and ties by individuals who recognize their value. Freedom involves 'doing one's duty'. When, for example, parents instruct children how to behave, they are not constraining their liberty, but providing guidance for their children's benefit. To act as a dutiful son or daughter and conform to parental wishes is to act freely, out of a recognition of one's obligations. Conservatives believe that a society in which individuals know only their rights, and do no acknowledge their duties, would be rootless and atomistic. Indeed, it is the bonds of duty and obligation that hold society together.

Anomie: A weakening of values and normative rules, associated with feelings of isolation, loneliness and meaninglessness.

Such ideas are based on a very particular view of society, sometimes called **organicism**. Conservatives have traditionally thought of society as a living thing, an organism, whose parts work together just as the brain, heart, lungs and liver do within a human organism. Organisms differ from artefacts or machines in two important respects. First, unlike machines, organisms are not simply a collection of individual parts that can be arranged and, indeed, rearranged at will. Within an organism, the whole is more than a collection of its individual parts; the whole is sustained by a fragile set of relationships between and amongst its parts, which, once damaged, can result in the organism's death. Thus, a human body cannot be stripped down and reassembled in the same way as, say, a bicycle. Second, organisms are shaped by 'natural' factors rather than human ingenuity. An organic society

Organicism: A belief that society operates like an organism or living entity, the whole being more than a collection of its individual parts.

SOCIETY

LIBERALS regard society not as an entity in its own right but as a collection of individuals. To the extent that society exists, it is fashioned out of voluntary and contractual agreements made by self-interested human beings. Nevertheless, there is a general balance of interests in society that tends to promote harmony and equilibrium.

CONSERVATIVES see society as an organism, a living entity. Society thus has an existence outside the individual, and in a sense is prior to the individual; it is held together by the bonds of tradition, authority and a common morality. The new right, nevertheless, subscribes to a form of liberal atomism.

SOCIALISTS have traditionally understood society in terms of unequal class power, economic and property divisions being deeper and more genuine than any broader social bonds. Marxists believe that society is characterized by class struggle, and argue that the only stable and cohesive society is a classless one.

ANARCHISTS believe that society is characterized by unregulated and natural harmony, based on the natural human disposition towards cooperation and sociability. Social conflict and disharmony are thus clearly unnatural, a product of political rule and economic inequality.

NATIONALISTS view society in terms of cultural or ethnic distinctiveness. Society is thus characterized by shared values and beliefs, ultimately rooted in a common national identity. This implies that multinational or multicultural societies are inherently unstable.

FASCISTS regard society as a unified organic whole, implying that individual existence is meaningless unless it is dedicated to the common good rather than the private good. Nevertheless, membership of society is strictly restricted on national or racial grounds.

FEMINISTS have understood society in terms of patriarchy and an artificial division between the 'public' and 'private' spheres of life. Society may therefore be seen as an organized hypocrisy designed to routinize and uphold a system of male power.

MULTICULTURALISTS view society as a mosaic of cultural groups, defined by their distinctive ethnic, religious or historical identities. The basis for wider social bonds, cutting across cultural distinctiveness, is thus restricted, perhaps, to civic allegiance.

is fashioned, ultimately, by natural necessity. For example, the family has not been 'invented' by any social thinker or political theorist, but is a product of natural social impulses such as love, caring and responsibility. In no sense do children in a family agree to a 'contract' on joining the family – they simply grow up within it and are nurtured and guided by it.

The use of the 'organic metaphor' for understanding society has some profoundly conservative implications. A mechanical view of society, as adopted by liberals and most socialists, in which society is constructed by rational individuals for their own purposes, suggests that society can be tampered with and improved. This leads to a belief in progress, either in the shape of reform or revolution. If society is organic, its structures and institutions have been shaped by forces beyond human control and, possibly, understanding, which implies that its delicate 'fabric' should be preserved and respected by the individuals who live within it. Organicism also shapes our attitude to particular institutions, society's 'parts'. These are viewed from a functionalist perspective: institutions develop and survive for a reason, and this reason is that they contribute to maintaining the larger social whole. In other words, by virtue of existing, institutions demonstrates they are worthwhile and desirable. Any attempt to reform or, worse, abolish an institution is thus fraught with dangers.

However, the rise of the new right has weakened support within conservatism for organic ideas and theories. In line with the robust individualism (see p. 28) of classical liberalism, libertarian conservatives, including the liberal new right, have held that society is a product of the actions of self-seeking and largely self-reliant individuals. This position was memorably expressed in Margaret Thatcher's assertion, paraphrasing Jeremy Bentham (see p. 49) that, 'There is no such thing as society, only individuals and their families'.

Hierarchy and authority

Conservatives have traditionally believed that society is naturally hierarchical, characterized by fixed or established social gradations. Social equality is therefore rejected as undesirable and unachievable; power, status and property are always unequally distributed. Conservatives agree with liberals in accepting natural inequality amongst individuals: some are born with talents and skills that are denied to others. For liberals, however, this leads to a belief in meritocracy, in which individuals rise or fall according to their abilities and willingness to work. Traditionally, conservatives have believed that inequality is more deep-rooted. Inequality is an inevitable feature of an organic society, not merely a consequence of individual differences. Pre-

Natural aristocracy: The idea that talent and leadership are innate or inbred qualities that cannot be acquired through effort or self-advancement.

democratic conservatives such as Burke were, in this way, able to embrace the idea of a '**natural aristocracy**'. Just as the brain, the heart and the liver all perform very different functions within the body, the various classes and groups that make up society also have their own specific roles. There must be leaders and there must be followers; there must be managers and there must be workers; for that matter, there must be those who go out to work and those who stay at home and bring up children. Genuine social equality is therefore a myth; in reality, there is a natural inequality of wealth and social position, justified by a corresponding inequality of social responsibilities. The working class might not enjoy the same living standards and life chances as their employers, but, at the same time, they do not have the livelihoods and security of many other people resting on their shoulders. **Hierarchy** and organicism have thus invested in traditional conservatism a pronounced tendency towards paternalism (see p. 82).

Hierarchy: A gradation of social positions or status; hierarchy implies structural or fixed inequality in which position is unconnected with individual ability.

The belief in hierarchy is strengthened by the emphasis conservatives place on **authority**. Conservatives do not accept the liberal belief that authority arises out of a contract made by free individuals. In liberal theory, authority is thought to be established by individuals for their own benefit. In contrast, conservatives believe that authority, like society, develops naturally. Parents have authority over children: they control virtually every aspect of their young lives, but without any contract or agreement having been undertaken. Authority develops, once again, from natural necessity, in this case through the need to ensure that children are cared for, kept away from danger, have a healthy diet, go to bed at sensible times and so on. Such authority can only be imposed 'from above', quite simply because children do not know what is good for them. It does not and cannot arise 'from below'; in no sense can children be said to have agreed to be governed. Authority is thought to be rooted in the nature of society and all social institutions. In schools, authority should be exercised by the teacher, in the workplace, by the employer, and in society at large, by government. Conservatives believe that authority is necessary and beneficial as everyone needs the guidance, support and security of knowing 'where they stand' and what is expected of them. Authority thus counters rootlessness and anomie. This has led conservatives to place special emphasis on leadership and discipline. Leadership is a vital ingredient in any society because it is the capacity to give direction and provide inspiration for others. Discipline is not just mindless obedience but a willing and healthy respect

Authority: The right to exert influence over others by virtue of an acknowledged obligation to obey.

for authority. Authoritarian conservatives go further and portray authority as absolute and unquestionable. Most conservatives, however, believe that authority should be exercised within limits and that these limits are imposed not by an artificial contract but by the natural responsibilities that authority entails. Parents should have authority over their children, but not the right to treat them in any way they choose. The authority of a parent reflects an obligation to nurture, guide and, if necessary, punish their children, but it does not empower a parent to abuse a child or, for instance, sell the child into slavery.

Property

Property is an asset that possesses a deep and, at times, almost mystical significance for conservatives. Liberals believe that property reflects merit: those who work hard and possess talent will, and should, acquire wealth. Property, therefore, is 'earned'. This doctrine has an attraction for those conservatives who regard the ability to accumulate wealth as an important economic incentive. Nevertheless, conservatives also hold that property has a range of psychological and social advantages. For example, it provides security. In an uncertain and unpredictable world, property ownership gives people a sense of confidence and assurance, something to 'fall back on'. Property, whether the ownership of a house or savings in the bank, provides individuals with a source of protection. Conservatives therefore believe that thrift – caution in the management of money – is a virtue in itself and have sought to encourage private savings and investment in property. Property ownership also promotes a range of important social values. Those who possess and enjoy their own property are more likely to respect the property of others. They will also be aware that property must be safeguarded from disorder and lawlessness. Property owners therefore have a 'stake' in society; they have an interest, in particular, in maintaining law and order. In this sense, property ownership can promote what can be thought of as the 'conservative values' of respect for law, authority and social order. However, a deeper and more personal reason why conservatives support property ownership is that it can be regarded as an extension of an individual's personality. People 'realize' themselves, even see themselves, in what they own. Possessions are not merely external objects, valued because they are useful – a house to keep us warm and dry, a car to provide transport and so on – but also reflect something of the owner's personality and character. This is why, conservatives point out, burglary is a particularly unpleasant crime: its victims suffer not only the

Property: The ownership of physical goods or wealth, whether by private individuals, groups of people or the state.

loss of, or damage to, their possessions, but also the sense that they have been personally violated. A home is the most personal and intimate of possessions, it is decorated and organized according to the tastes and needs of its owner and therefore reflects his or her personality. The proposal of traditional socialists that property should be 'socialized', owned in common rather than by private individuals, thus strikes conservatives as particularly appalling because it threatens to create a soulless and depersonalized society.

Conservatives, however, are not prepared to go as far as *laissez-faire* liberals in believing that each individual has an absolute right to use their property however they may choose. While libertarian conservatives, and therefore the liberal new right, support an essentially liberal view of property, conservatives have traditionally argued that all rights, including property rights, entail obligations. Property is not an issue for the individual alone, but is also of importance to society. This can be seen, for example, in the social bonds that cut across generations. Property is not merely the creation of the present generation. Much of it – land, houses, works of art – has been passed down from earlier generations. The present generation is, in that sense, the custodian of the wealth of the nation and has a duty to preserve and protect it for the benefit of future generations. Harold Macmillan, the UK Conservative prime minister, 1957–63, expressed just such a position in the 1980s when he objected to the Thatcher government's policy of **privatization**, describing it as 'selling off the family silver'.

Privatization: The transfer of state assets from the public to the private sector, reflecting a contraction of the state's responsibilities.

Authoritarian conservatism

Whereas all conservatives would claim to respect the concept of authority, few modern conservatives would accept that their views are authoritarian. Nevertheless, although contemporary conservatives are keen to demonstrate their commitment to democratic, particularly liberal-democratic, principles, there is a tradition within conservatism that has favoured authoritarian rule, especially in continental Europe. At the time of the French Revolution, the principal defender of autocratic rule was the French political thinker Joseph de Maistre (1753–1821). De Maistre was a fierce critic of the French Revolution, but, in contrast to Burke, he wished to restore absolute power to the hereditary monarchy. He was a reactionary and was quite unprepared to accept any reform of the *ancien régime*, which had been overthrown in 1789. His political philosophy was based on willing and complete subordination to 'the master'. In *Du Pape* ([1817] 1971) de Maistre went further

AUTHORITARIANISM

Authoritarianism is belief in or the practice of government 'from above', in which authority is exercised over a population with or without its consent. Authoritarianism thus differs from authority. The latter rests on legitimacy, and in that sense arises 'from below'. Authoritarian thinkers typically base their views on either a belief in the wisdom of established leaders or the idea that social order can only be maintained by unquestioning obedience. However, authoritarianism is usually distinguished from totalitarianism (see p. 217). The practice of government 'from above', which is associated with monarchical absolutism, traditional dictatorships and most forms of military rule, is concerned with the repression of opposition and political liberty, rather than the more radical goal of obliterating the distinction between the state and civil society.

and argued that above the earthly monarchies a supreme spiritual power should rule in the person of the pope. His central concern was the preservation of order, which alone, he believed, could provide people with safety and security. Revolution, and even reform, would weaken the chains that bind people together and lead to a descent into chaos and oppression.

Throughout the nineteenth century, conservatives in continental Europe remained faithful to the rigid and hierarchical values of autocratic rule, and stood unbending in the face of rising liberal, nationalist and socialist protest. Nowhere was authoritarianism more entrenched than in Russia, where Tsar Nicholas I, (1825–55), proclaimed the principles of 'orthodoxy, autocracy and nationality', in contrast to the values that had inspired the French Revolution: 'liberty, equality and fraternity'. Nicholas's successors stubbornly refused to allow their power to be constrained by constitutions or the development of parliamentary institutions. In Germany, constitutional government did develop, but Bismarck, the imperial chancellor, (1871–90), ensured that it remained a sham. Elsewhere, authoritarianism remained particularly strong in Catholic countries. The papacy suffered not only the loss of its temporal authority with the achievement of Italian unification, which led Pius IX to declare himself a 'prisoner of he Vatican', but also an assault on its doctrines with the rise of secular political ideologies. In 1864, Pope Pius IX condemned all radical or progressive ideas, including those of nationalism, liberalism and socialism, as 'false doctrines of our most unhappy age', and when confronted with the loss of the papal states and Rome, he proclaimed in 1870 the edict of papal infallibility. The unwillingness of continental conservatives to come to terms with reform and democratic government extended well into the twentieth century. For example, conservative elites in Italy and Germany helped to overthrow parliamentary democracy and bring Mussolini (see p. 218) and Hitler (see p. 210) to power by providing support for and giving respectability to rising fascist movements.

In other cases, conservative-authoritarian regimes have looked to the newly enfranchised masses for political support. This happened in nineteenth-century France, where Louis Napoleon succeeded in being elected president, and later establishing himself as Emperor Napoleon III, by appealing to the smallholding peasantry, the largest element of the French electorate. The Napoleonic regime fused authoritarianism with the promise of economic prosperity and social reform in the kind of plebiscitary dictatorship more commonly found in the twentieth century. Bonapartism has parallels with twentieth-century Perónism. Juan Perón was dictator of Argentina (1946–55), and proclaimed the familiar authoritarian themes of obedience, order and national unity. However, he based his political support not on the interests of traditional elites, but on an appeal to the impoverished masses, the 'shirtless ones', as Perón called them. The Perónist regime was **populist** in that it moulded its policies according to the instincts and wishes of the common people, in this case popular resentment against 'Yankee imperialism', and a widespread desire for economic and social progress. Similar regimes have developed in parts of Africa, Asia and the Middle East.

Populism: A belief that popular instincts and wishes are the principal legitimate guide to political action, often reflecting distrust of or hostility towards political elites (see p. 291).

However, although such regimes have tended to consolidate the position of conservative elites, and often embrace a distinctively conservative form of nationalism, authoritarian-populist regimes such as Perón's perhaps exhibit features that are more closely associated with fascism than conservatism.

Paternalistic conservatism

Although continental conservatives adopted an attitude of uncompromising resistance to change, a more flexible and ultimately more successful Anglo-American tradition can be traced back to Edmund Burke. The lesson that Burke drew from the French Revolution was that change can be natural or inevitable, in which case it should not be resisted. 'A state without the means of some change', he suggested, 'is without the means of its conservation' ([1790] 1975, p. 285). The characteristic style of Burkean conservatism is cautious, modest and pragmatic; it reflects a suspicion of fixed principles, whether revolutionary or reactionary. As Ian Gilmour (1978) put it, 'the wise

Conservative travels light'. The values that conservatives hold most dear – tradition, order, authority, property and so on – will be safe only if policy is developed in the light of practical circumstances and experience. Such a position will rarely justify dramatic or radical change, but accepts a prudent willingness to 'change in order to conserve'. Pragmatic conservatives support neither the individual nor the state in principle, but are prepared to support either, or, more frequently, recommend a balance between the two, depending on 'what works'. In practice, the reforming impulse in conservatism has also been closely associated with the survival into the modern period of neo-feudal paternalistic values. There are two main traditions of paternalistic conservatism:

- one-nation conservatism
- Christian democracy.

One-nation conservatism

The Anglo-American paternalistic tradition is often traced back to Benjamin Disraeli (1804–81), UK prime minister in 1868 and again 1874–80. Disraeli developed his political philosophy in two novels, *Sybil* (1845) and *Coningsby* (1844), written before he assumed ministerial responsibilities. These novels emphasized the principle of social obligation, in stark contrast to the extreme individualism then dominant within the political establishment. Disraeli wrote against a background of growing industrialization, economic inequality and, in continental Europe at least, revolutionary upheaval. He tried to draw attention to the danger of Britain

PATERNALISM

Paternalism literally means to act in a fatherly fashion. As a political principle, it refers to power or authority being exercised over others with the intention of conferring benefit or preventing harm. Social welfare and laws such as the compulsory wearing of seat belts in cars are examples of paternalism. 'Soft' paternalism is characterized by broad consent on the part of those subject to paternalism. 'Hard' paternalism operates regardless of consent, and thus overlaps with authoritarianism. The basis for paternalism is that wisdom and experience are unequally distributed in society; those in authority 'know best'. Opponents argue that authority is not to be trusted and that paternalism restricts liberty and contributes to the 'infantalization' of society.

being divided into 'two nations: the Rich and the Poor'. In the best conservative tradition, Disraeli's argument was based on a combination of prudence and principle.

On the one hand, growing social inequality contains the seed of revolution. A poor and oppressed working class, Disraeli feared, would not simply accept its misery. The revolutions that had broken out in Europe in 1830 and 1848 seemed to bear out this belief. Reform would therefore be sensible, because, in stemming the tide of revolution, it would ultimately be in the interests of the rich. On the other hand, Disraeli appealed to moral values. He suggested that wealth and privilege brought with them social obligations, in particular a responsibility for the poor or less well-off. In so doing, Disraeli drew on the organic conservative belief that society is held together by an acceptance of duty and obligations. He believed that society is naturally hierarchical, but also held that inequalities of wealth or social privilege give rise to an inequality of responsibilities. The wealthy and powerful must shoulder the burden of social responsibility, which, in effect, is the price of privilege. These ideas were based on the feudal principle of noblesse oblige, the obligation of the aristocracy to be honourable and generous. For example, the landed nobility claimed to exercise a paternal responsibility for their peasants, as the king did in relation to the nation. Disraeli recommended that these obligations should not be abandoned, but should be expressed, in an increasingly industrialized world, in social reform. Such ideas came to be represented by the slogan 'one nation'. In office, Disraeli was responsible both for the Second Reform Act of 1867, which for the first time extended the right to vote to the working class, and for the social reforms that improved housing conditions and hygiene.

Disraeli's ideas had a considerable impact on conservatism and contributed to a radical and reforming tradition that appeals both to the pragmatic instincts of conservatives and to their sense of social duty. In the UK, these ideas provide the basis of what is called 'one-nation conservatism', whose supporters sometimes style themselves as 'Tories' to denote their commitment to pre-industrial, hierarchic and paternal values. Disraeli's ideas were subsequently taken up in the late nineteenth century by Randolph Churchill in the form of 'Tory democracy'. In an age of widening political democracy, Churchill stressed the need for traditional institutions – for example, the monarchy, the House of Lords and the church – to enjoy a wider base of social support. This could be achieved by winning working-class votes for the Conservative Party by continuing Disraeli's policy of social reform. One-nation conservatism can thus be seen as a form of Tory welfarism.

The high point of the one-nation tradition was reached in the 1950s and 1960s, when conservative governments in the UK and elsewhere came to

TORYISM

'Tory' was used in eighteenth-century Britain to refer to a parliamentary faction that (as opposed to the Whigs) supported monarchical power and the Church of England, and represented the landed gentry; in the USA, it implied loyalty to the British crown. Although in the mid-nineteenth century the British Conservative Party emerged out of the Tories, and in the UK 'Tory' is still widely (but unhelpfully) used as a synonym for Conservative, Toryism is best understood as a distinctive ideological stance within broader conservatism. Its characteristic features are a belief in hierarchy, tradition, duty and organicism. While 'high' Toryism articulates a neo-feudal belief in a ruling class and a pre-democratic faith in established institutions, the Tory tradition is also hospitable to welfarist and reformist ideas, providing these serve the cause of social continuity.

practice a version of Keynesian social democracy, managing the economy in line with the goal of full employment and supporting enlarged welfare provision. This stance was based on the need for a non-ideological, 'middle way' between the extremes of *laissez-faire* liberalism and socialist state planning. Conservatism was therefore the way of moderation, and sought to draw a balance between rampant individualism and overbearing collectivism. In the UK, this idea was most clearly expressed in Harold Macmillan's *The Middle Way* ([1938] 1966). Macmillan, who was to be prime minister from 1957–1963, advocated what he called 'planned capitalism', which he described as 'a mixed system which combines state ownership, regulation or control of certain aspects of economic activity with the drive and initiative of private enterprise'. Such ideas later resurfaced, in the USA and the UK, in the notion of 'compassionate conservatism'. However, paternalist conservatism only provides a qualified basis for social and economic intervention. The purpose of one-nationism, for instance, is to consolidate hierarchy rather than to remove it, and its wish to improve the conditions of the less well-off is limited to the desire to ensure that the poor no longer pose a threat to the established order.

Christian democracy

Interventionist policies were also adopted by the Christian democratic parties that were formed in various parts of continental Europe after 1945. The most important of these were the Christian Democratic Union (CDU) in then-West Germany and the Christian Democratic Party (DC) in Italy. In the aftermath of the Second World War, continental conservatives abandoned their authoritarian beliefs. This new form of conservatism was committed to political democracy and influenced by the paternalistic social traditions of Catholicism. As Protestantism is associated with the idea of salvation through individual effort, its social theory has often been seen to endorse individualism and extol the value of hard work, competition and personal responsibility. Catholic social theory, in contrast, has traditionally focused on the social group rather than the individual, and stressed balance or organic harmony rather than competition. After 1945, Catholic social theory encouraged the newly formed Christian democratic parties to practise a form of democratic corporatism that highlighted the importance of intermediate institutions, such as churches, unions and business groups, bound together by the notion of 'social partnership'. In contrast to the traditional stress on

Christian democracy:
An ideological
tradition within
European conservatism
that is characterized
by a commitment to
the social market and
qualified economic
intervention.

the nation, **Christian democracy**, particularly in Germany, also supported the Catholic principle of subsidiarity, the idea that decisions should be made by the lowest appropriate institution. Sympathy for subsidiarity has allowed Christian democrats to favour decentralization, particularly in the form of federalism, and, in marked contrast to UK conservatives, to support European integration.

The willingness of Christian democratic parties to practise Keynesian-welfarist policies draws more heavily on the flexible and pragmatic ideas of economists such as Friedrich List (1789–1846) than upon the strict market principles of Adam Smith (see p. 50) and David Ricardo (1772–1823). List emphasized the economic importance of politics and political power, for instance, in recognizing the need for government intervention to protect infant industries from the rigours of foreign competition. This led to support from the idea of the 'social market economy', which has been widely influential across much of continental Europe. A social market is an economy that is structured by market principles and largely free from government control, operating in the context of a society in which cohesion is maintained through a comprehensive welfare system and effective public services. The market is thus not so much an end in itself as a means of generating wealth in order to achieve broader social goals. Such thinking has resulted in a particular model of capitalism being adopted across much of continental Europe and, to an extent, within the EU, which is sometimes dubbed Rhine-Alpine capitalism or 'social capitalism', in contrast to Anglo-American capitalism, or 'enterprise capitalism'. Whereas the former stresses partnership and cooperation, the latter is based on the untrammelled workings of market economics.

Libertarian conservatism

Although conservatism draws heavily on pre-industrial ideas such as organicism, hierarchy and obligation, the ideology has also been much influenced by liberal ideas, especially classical liberal ideas. This is sometimes seen as a late-twentieth-century development, the new right having in some way 'hijacked' conservatism in the interests of classical liberalism. Nevertheless, liberal doctrines, especially those concerning the free market, have been advanced by conservatives since the late eighteenth century, and can be said to constitute a rival tradition to conservative paternalism. These ideas are libertarian in that

Economic liberalism: A belief in the market as a self-regulating mechanism that tends naturally to deliver general prosperity and opportunities for all.

they advocate the greatest possible economic liberty and the least possible government regulation of social life. Libertarian conservatives have no simply converted to liberalism, but believe liberal economics to be compatible with a more traditional, conservative social philosophy, based on values such as authority and duty. This is evident in the work of Edmund Burke, in many ways the founder of traditional conservatism, but also a keen supporter of the **economic liberalism** of Adam Smith.

The libertarian tradition has been strongest in those countries where classical liberal ideas have had the greatest impact, once again the UK and the USA. As early as the late eighteenth century, Burke expressed a strong preference for free trade in commercial affairs and a competitive, self-regulating market economy in domestic affairs. The free market is efficient and fair, but it is also, Burke believed, natural and necessary. It is 'natural' in that it reflects a desire for wealth, a 'love of lucre', that is part of human nature.

LIBERTARIANISM

Libertarianism refers to a range of theories that give strict priority to liberty (understood in negative terms) over other values, such as authority, tradition and equality. Libertarians thus seek to maximize the realm of individual freedom and minimize the scope of public authority, typically seeing the state as the principal threat to liberty. The two best-known libertarian traditions are rooted in the idea of individual rights (as with Robert Nozick, see p. 92) and in *laissez-faire* economic doctrines (as with Friedrich von Hayek, see p. 90), although socialists have also embraced libertarianism. Libertarianism is some-times distinguished from liberalism on the ground that the latter, even in its classical form, refuses to give priority to liberty over order. However, it differs from anarchism in that libertarians generally recognize the need for a minimal state, sometimes styling themselves as 'minarchists'.

TENSIONS WITHIN
CONSERVATISM (1)

PATERNALIST CONSERVATISM	v.	LIBERTARIAN CONSERVATISM
pragmatism	← →	principle
traditionalism	← →	radicalism
social duty	← →	egoism
organic society	← →	atomistic individualism
hierarchy	← →	meritocracy
social responsibility	← →	individual responsibility
natural order	← →	market order
'middle way' economics	← →	*laissez-faire* economics
qualified welfarism	← →	anti-welfarism

The laws of the market are therefore 'natural laws'. He accepted that working conditions dictated by the market are, for many, 'degrading, unseemly, unmanly and often most unwholesome', but insisted that they would suffer further if the 'natural course of things' were disturbed. The capitalist free market could thus be defended on the grounds of tradition, just like the monarchy and the church. Libertarian conservatives are not, however, consistent liberals. They believe in economic individualism and 'getting government off the back of business', but they are less prepared to extend this principle of individual liberty to other aspects of social life. Conservatives, even libertarian conservatives, have a more pessimistic view of human nature. A strong state is required to maintain public order and ensure that authority is respected. Indeed, in some respects libertarian conservatives are attracted to free-market theories precisely because they promise to secure social order. Whereas liberals have believed that the market economy preserves individual liberty and freedom of choice, conservatives have at times been attracted to the market as an instrument of social discipline. Market forces regulate and control economic and social activity. For example, they may deter workers from pushing for higher wage increases by threatening them with unemployment. As such, the market can be seen as an instrument that maintains social stability and works alongside the more evident forces of coercion: the police and the courts. While some conservatives have feared that market capitalism leads to endless innovation and restless competition, upsetting social cohesion, others have been attracted to it in the belief that it can establish a 'market order', sustained by impersonal 'natural laws' rather than the guiding hand of political authority.

New right

During the early post-1945 period, pragmatic and paternalistic ideas dominated conservatism throughout much of the western world. The remnants of authoritarian conservatism collapsed with the overthrow of the Portuguese and Spanish dictatorships in he 1970s. Just as conservatives had come to accept political democracy during he nineteenth century, after 1945 they came to accept a qualified form of social democracy. This tendency was confirmed by the rapid and sustained economic growth of the postwar years, the 'long boom', which appeared to bear out the success of 'managed capitalism'. During the 1970s, however, a set of more radical ideas developed within conservatism, directly challenging the Keynesian-welfarist orthodoxy. These new right ideas had their greatest initial impact in the USA and the UK, but they came to be influential in parts of continental Europe, Australia and New Zealand, and had some kind of effect on western states across the globe.

The 'new right' is a broad term and has been used to describe ideas that range from the demand for tax cuts to calls for greater censorship of television and films, and even campaigns against immigration or in favour of repatriation. In essence, the new right is a marriage between two apparently contrasting ideological traditions. The first of these is classical liberal economics, particularly the free-market theories of Adam Smith, which were revived in the second half of the twentieth century as a critique of 'big' government and economic and social intervention. This is called the liberal new right, or **neoliberalism**. The second element in the new right is traditional conservative – and notably pre-Disraelian – social theory, especially its defence of order, authority and discipline. This is called the conservative new right, or **neoconservatism**. The new right thus attempts to fuse economic libertarianism with state and social authoritarianism. As such, it is a blend of radical, reactionary and traditional features. Its radicalism is evident in its robust efforts to dismantle or 'roll back' interventionist government and liberal or permissive social values. This radicalism is clearest in relation

Neoliberalism:
An updated version of classical political economy that is dedicated to market individualism and minimal statism (see pp. 52–3).

Neoconservatism:
A modern version of social conservatism that emphasizes the need to restore order, return to traditional or family values or revitalize nationalism.

to the liberal new right, which draws on rational theories and abstract principles, and so dismisses tradition. New right radicalism is nevertheless reactionary, in that both the liberal and conservative new right hark back to a usually nineteenth-century 'golden age' of supposed economic propriety and moral fortitude. However, the new right also makes an appeal to tradition, particularly though the emphasis neoconservatives place on so-called 'traditional values'.

Liberal new right

The liberal new right was a product of the end of the 'long boom' of the post-1945 period, which shifted economic thinking away from Keynsianism (see p. 59) and reawakened interest in earlier, free-market thinking. The liberal aspects of new right thinking are most definitely drawn from classical rather than modern liberalism, and in particular from neoliberalism. It amounts to a restatement of the case for a minimal state. This has been summed up as 'private, good; public, bad'. The liberal new right is anti-statist. The state is regarded as a realm of coercion and unfreedom: collectivism restricts individual initiative and saps self-respect. Government, however benignly disposed, invariably has a damaging effect on human affairs. Instead, faith is placed in the individual and the market. Individuals should be encouraged to be self-reliant and to make rational choices in their own interests. The market is respected as a mechanism through which the sum of individual choices will lead to progress and general benefit. As such, the liberal new right has attempted to establish the dominance of libertarian ideas over paternalistic ones within conservative ideology.

The dominant theme within this anti-statist doctrine is an ideological commitment to the free market. The new right has resurrected the classical economics of Smith and Ricardo, as it has been presented in the work of more recent economists such as Hayek (see p. 90) and Milton Friedman (1912–2006). Free-market ideas gained renewed credibility during the 1970s as governments experienced increasing difficulty in delivering economic stability and sustained growth. Doubts consequently developed about whether it was in the power of government at all to solve economic problems. Hayek and Friedman, for example, challenged the very idea of a 'managed' or planned' economy. They argued that the task of allocating resources in a complex, industrialized economy was simply too difficult for any set of state bureaucrats to achieve successfully. The virtue of the market, on the other hand, is that it acts as the central nervous system of the economy, reconciling the supply of goods and services with the demand for them. It allocates resources to their most profitable use and thereby ensures

Friedrich von Hayek (1899–1992)

Austrian economist and political philosopher. Hayek, an academic, taught at the London School of Economics and the Universities of Chicago, Freiburg and Salzburg. He was awarded the Nobel Prize for economics in 1974. An exponent of the so-called Austrian School, Hayek was a firm believer in individualism and market order, and an implacable critic of socialism. *The Road to Serfdom* (1944) was a pioneering work that attacked economic interventionism as implicitly totalitarian; later works such as *The Constitution of Liberty* (1960) and *Law, Legislation and Liberty* (1979) supported a modified form of traditionalism and upheld an Anglo-American version of constitutionalism (see p. 39). Hayek's writings had a considerable impact on the emergent new right.

that consumer needs are satisfied. In the light of the re-emergence of unemployment and inflation in the 1970s, Hayek and Friedman argued that government was invariably the cause of economic problems, rather than the cure.

The ideas of Keynesianism were one of the chief targets of new-right criticism. Keynes had argued that capitalist economies were not self-regulating. He placed particular emphasis on the 'demand side' of the economy, believing that the level of economic activity and employment were dictated by 'aggregate demand' in the economy. Milton Friedman, on the other hand, argued that there was a 'natural rate of unemployment', which was beyond the ability of government to influence, and that the attempts of government to eradicate unemployment by employing Keynesian techniques had merely caused other, more damaging, economic problems, notably inflation. Inflation is a rise in the general price level, which leads to a decline in the value of money. Inflation, neoliberals believe, threatens the entire basis of a market economy because in reducing faith in money, the means of exchange, it discourages people from undertaking commercial or economic activity. However, Keynesianism had, in effect, encouraged governments to 'print money', albeit in a well-meaning attempt to create jobs. The free-market solution to inflation is to control the supply of money by cutting public spending, a policy practised by both the Reagan and the Thatcher administrations during the 1980s. Both administrations also allowed unemployment to rise sharply in the belief that only the market could solve the problem.

The new right is also opposed to the mixed economy and public ownership and practised so-called supply-side economics. Starting under Thatcher in the UK in the 1980s but later extending to many other western states, and most aggressively pursued in postcommunist states in the 1990s, a policy of privatization has effectively dismantled both mixed economies and collectivized economies by transferring industries from public to private ownership. Nationalized industries were criticized as being inherently inefficient, because, unlike private firms and industries, they are not disciplined by the profit motive.

The new right's emphasis on the 'supply-side' of the economy was reflected in the belief that governments should foster growth by providing conditions that encourage producers to produce, rather than consumers to consume. The main block to the creation of an entrepreneurial, supply-side culture is high taxes. Taxes, in this view, discourage enterprise and infringe property rights. 'Reaganomics' in the 1980s was largely defined by the most dramatic cuts in personal and corporate taxation ever witnessed in the USA. After his election victory in 2000, George W. Bush revived this policy with a sweeping programme of tax cuts. Under Thatcher in the UK, levels of direct taxation were progressively reduced to near US levels.

The liberal new right is not only anti-statist on grounds of economic efficiency and responsiveness, but also because of its political principles, notably its commitment to individual liberty. The new right claims to be defending freedom against 'creeping collectivism'. At the extreme, these ideas lead in the direction of anarcho-capitalism, discussed in Chapter 6, which believes that all goods and services, including the courts and public order, should be delivered by the market. The freedom defended by the liberal, libertarian and even anarchist elements of the new right is negative freedom: the removal of external restrictions on the individual. As the collective power of government is seen as the principal threat to the individual, freedom can only be ensured by 'rolling back the state'. This, in particular, means rolling back social welfare. In addition to economic arguments against welfare – for example, that increased social expenditure pushes up taxes, and that public sector welfare institutions are inherently inefficient – the new right objects to welfare on moral grounds. In the first place, the welfare state is criticized for having created a 'culture of dependency': it saps initiative and enterprise and robs people of dignity and self-respect. Welfare is thus the cause of disadvantage, not its cure. Such a theory resurrects the notion of the 'undeserving poor'. The idea that people owe nothing to society and, in turn, are owed nothing by society was most graphically expressed in Margaret Thatcher's assertion that 'there is no such thing as society'. Charles Murray (1984) also argued that, as welfare relieves women of dependency on 'breadwinning' men, it is a major cause of family break-down, creating an underclass largely composed of single mothers and fatherless children. A further new right argument against welfare is based on a commitment to individual rights. Robert

Robert Nozick
(1938–2002)

US academic and political philosopher. Nozick's major work *Anarchy, State and Utopia* (1974) is widely seen as one of the most important modern works of political philosophy, and it has profoundly influenced new right theories and beliefs.

Nozick developed a form of rights-based libertarianism in response to the ideas of John Rawls (see p. 58). Drawing on Locke and nineteenth-century US individualists such as Lysander Spooner (1808–87) and Benjamin Tucker (1854–1939), he argued that property rights should be strictly upheld, provided the property was justly purchased or justly transferred from one person to another. This position implies support for minimal government and minimal taxation, and undermines the case for welfare and redistribution. In later life, Nozick modified his extreme libertarianism.

Nozick (1974) advanced this most forcefully in condemning all policies of welfare and redistribution as a violation of property rights. In this view, so long as property has been acquired justly, to transfer it, without consent, from one person to another amounts to 'legalized theft'.

Conservative new right

The conservative new right, or neoconservatism, emerged in the USA in the 1970s as a backlash against the ideas and values of the 1960s. It was defined by a fear of social fragmentation or breakdown, which was seen as a product of liberal reform and the spread of '**permissiveness**'. In sharp contrast to the liberal new right, neoconservatives stress the privacy of politics and seek to strengthen leadership and authority in society. This emphasis on authority, allied to a heightened sensitivity to the fragility of society, demonstrates that neoconservatism has its roots in traditional or organic conservatism. However, it differs markedly from paternalistic conservatism, which also draws heavily on organic ideas. Whereas one-nation conservatives, for instance, believe that community is best maintained by social reform and the reduction of poverty, neoconservatives look to strengthen community by restoring authority and imposing social discipline. Neoconservative authoritarianism is, to this

Permissiveness: The willingness to allow people to make their own moral choices; permissiveness suggests that there are no authoritative values.

extent, consistent with neoliberal libertarianism. Both of them accept the rolling back of the state's economic responsibility.

Neoconservatives have developed distinctive views about both domestic policy and foreign policy. The two principal domestic concerns of neoconservatism have been with law and order and public morality. Neoconservatives believe that rising crime, delinquency and anti-social behaviour generally are a consequence of a larger decline of authority that has affected most western societies since the 1960s. People need and want the security of knowing 'where they stand'. This security is provided by the exercise of authority, in the family by the father, at school by the teacher, at work by the employer, and in society at large by a system of 'law and order'. Permissiveness, the cult of the individual and of 'doing one's own thing', undermines the established structures of society by permitting, even encouraging, the questioning of authority. Neoconservatives thus subscribe to a form of social authoritarianism. This can be seen in neoconservative calls for the strengthening of the family. The 'family', however, is naturally hierarchical – children should listen to, respect and obey their parents – and naturally patriarchal. The husband is the provider and the wife the home-maker. This social authoritarianism is matched by state authoritarianism, the desire for a strong state reflected in a 'tough' stance on law and order. This has led, in the USA and the UK in particular, to a greater emphasis on custodial sentences and to longer prison sentences, reflecting the belief that 'prison works'.

The conservative new right's concern about public morality is based on a desire to reassert the moral foundations of politics. A particular target of neoconservative criticism was the 'permissive 1960s' and the growing culture of 'do your own thing'. In the face of this, Thatcher in the UK proclaimed her support for 'Victorian values', and in the USA organizations such as Moral Majority campaigned for a return to 'family values'. Neoconservatives see two dangers in a permissive society. In the first place, the freedom to choose one's own morals or life-style could lead to the choice of immoral or 'evil' views. There is, for instance, a significant religious element in the conservative new right, especially in the USA (which is examined in Chapter 11). The second danger of permissiveness is not so much that people may adopt the *wrong* morals or lifestyles, but may simply choose *different* moral positions. For a liberal, moral pluralism is healthy because it promotes diversity and rational debate, but for a neoconservative it is deeply threatening because it undermines the cohesion of society. A permissive society is a society that lacks ethical norms and unifying moral standards. It is a 'pathless desert', which provides neither guidance nor support for individuals and their families. If individuals merely do as they please, civilized standards of behaviour will be impossible to maintain.

TENSIONS WITHIN
CONSERVATISM (2)

LIBERAL NEW RIGHT	v.	CONSERVATIVE NEW RIGHT
classical liberalism	←→	traditional conservatism
atomism	←→	organicism
radicalism	←→	traditionalism
libertarianism	←→	authoritarianism
economic dynamism	←→	social order
self-interest/enterprise	←→	traditional values
equality of opportunity	←→	natural hierarchy
minimal state	←→	strong state
internationalism	←→	insular nationalism
pro-globalization	←→	anti-globalization

The issue that links the domestic and foreign policy aspects of neoconservative thinking is a concern about the nation and the desire to strengthen national identity in the face of threats from within and without. The value of the nation, from the neoconservative perspective, is that it binds society together giving it a common culture and civic identity, which is all the stronger for being rooted in history and tradition. National patriotism thus strengthens a people's political will. The most significant threat to the nation 'from within' is the growth of multiculturalism, which weakens the bonds of nationhood by threatening political community and creating the spectre of ethnic and racial conflict. Neoconservatives have therefore often been in the forefront of campaigns for stronger controls on immigration and, sometimes, for a privileged status to be granted to the 'host' community's culture. The conservative critique of multiculturalism is discussed in greater detail in Chapter 11. The threats to the nation 'from without' are many and various. In the UK, the main perceived threat has come from the process of European integration; indeed, in the 1990s, UK conservatism almost came to be defined by 'Euroscepticism', a hostility to European integration and, in particular, monetary union, born out of the belief that they posed a fatal threat to national identity. However, the nationalist dimension of neoconservative thinking has also given rise to a distinctive stance on foreign policy, particularly in the USA.

The core themes of neoconservative, or 'neocon', foreign policy have been an emphasis on the pursuit of the national interest, particularly US national interests, and a tendency to view international politics in terms of an ongoing struggle between good and evil. The principal intellectual influence on neocon foreign policy thinking is usually identified as the German-Jewish US political theorist Leo Strauss (1899–1973), who linked the 'crisis of the West' to the loss of the wisdom of ancient philosophers such as Plato and Aristotle. During its earliest phase, neocon foreign policy was defined by its robust anti-communism. This was reflected in Ronald Reagan's description of the Soviet Union as an 'evil empire', and in the launch in the 1980s of the 'second' Cold War, through a US military buildup that would ultimately put the Soviet economy under an impossible strain. The end of the Cold War and the advent in the early 1990s of a 'liberal peace' appeared to make neocon thinking irrelevant.

However, influenced by Samuel Huntington's (1996) theory about an emerging 'clash of civilization', and concerned to preserve or reinforce the USA's 'benevolent global hegemony' in a unipolar world, neocon thinking came to have a growing impact on the administration of George W. Bush, becoming, arguably, its dominant influence in the years following the 9/11 terrorist attacks. The neocons argued that US hegemony should be preserved through a kind of 'new' imperialism, which has three key features. First, the USA had to build up its military strength and achieve a position of 'power beyond challenge', both to deter its rivals and to extend its global reach. Second, the neocons aimed to spread US-style democracy throughout the world. This was based on a form of Wilsonian internationalism (see p. 169), which suggests both that democracy is the best antidote to war and expansionism, and that democracy has a universal appeal to people everywhere regardless of their culture and history. Third, the neocons favoured an assertive, interventionist foreign policy that sets out to promote liberal-democratic governance through a process of 'regime change', achieved, if necessary, by pre-emptive military strikes. The US-led attack on Afghanistan in 2001 and the Iraq War of 2003 were clearly guided by neocon assumptions and beliefs. Nevertheless, faith in neocon foreign policy thinking has declined as military intervention in Afghanistan and Iraq has been seen to have dawn the USA and its allies into protracted and profoundly difficult counter-insurgency wars.

Conservatism in the twenty-first century

The late twentieth century seemed to provide fuel for conservative optimism, if not triumphalism. Conservatism appeared to have succeeded in overthrowing the 'pro-state' tendency that has characterized government throughout much of the twentieth century, especially since 1945, and in establishing an alternative 'pro-market' tendency. However, perhaps the major achievement of conservatism has been the vanquishing of its major rival, socialism. Parliamentary socialists, in states ranging from New Zealand and Australia to Spain, Sweden and the UK, have increasingly sought to maintain electoral credibility by embracing the values and philosophy of the market, accepting that there is no economically viable alternative to capitalism. More dramatically, the collapse of communism in eastern Europe and elsewhere produced, at least initially, a flowering of traditionalist political doctrines and free-market economics ones. What is more, conservatism's contribution to this process lay largely in its capacity to recreate itself as an ideological project. Distancing itself from its organicist, hierarchical and non-ideological instincts, conservatism, in the guise of the new right, aligned itself with market individualism and social authoritarianism. Although the 'heroic' phase of new right politics, associated with figures such as Thatcher and Reagan and the battle against 'big government', may have passed and given way to a 'managerial' phase, this should not disguise the fact that market values have come to be accepted across the spectrum of conservative beliefs. Having exposed the twentieth-century 'socialist' mistakes of central planning and welfare capitalism, public policy in the twenty-first century looks set to be dominated by the 'new' conservative blend of the free market and the strong state.

However, conservatism also confronts a number of challenges in the twenty-first century. One of these is that the very collapse of socialism creates problems in itself. As the twentieth century progressed, conservatism increasingly defined itself through its antipathy towards state control, usually associated with the advance of socialism. However, if conservatism has become a critique of central planning and economic management, what role will it have once these have disappeared? A further problem stems from the long-term economic viability of the free-market philosophy. Faith in the free market has been historically and culturally limited. Enthusiasm for unregulated capitalism has been a largely Anglo-American phenomenon that peaked during the nineteenth century in association with classical liberalism, and was revived in the late twentieth century in the form of the new right. 'Rolling back the state' in economic life may sharpen incentives, intensify competition and promote entrepreneurialism, but sooner or later its disadvantages become apparent, notably short-termism, low investment, widening inequality and social exclusion. Just as liberals eventually came to recognize that the free market is an economic dead end, conservatives in the twenty-first century may have to learn the same lesson. This is reflected in a tendency in many states for conservatives to define themselves less in terms of economic freedom but increasingly in terms of community and compassion.

Furthermore, conservatism has, at best, an ambivalent relationship with postmodernity. On the one hand, there is more than an echo of traditional conservative scepticism in the postmodernist rejection of the Enlightenment project. Both traditional conservatism and **postmodernism** hold that truth is essentially partial and local. Moreover, as Giddens (see p. 138) has argued, as risk and uncertainty increase, the attraction of 'philosophic conservatism', viewed as a philosophy of protection, conservation and solidarity, becomes greater. On the other hand, the advent of late modernity or postmodernity threatens to undermine the very basis of traditional or organic conservatism. The increasing complexity of modern society confronts individuals with ever wider choices and opportunities, and makes it increasingly difficult to identify, still less defend, 'established' values or a 'common' culture. Globalization also contributes to this process of 'de-traditionalization' by intensifying social flux and diluting any sense of national identity. Indeed, it can be argued that conservatism, in the form of the liberal new right, has in this sense powerfully contributed to conservatism's undoing. The neoliberal utopia is, after all, a society that is strictly individualist and endlessly dynamic.

Postmodernism: An intellectual movement that rejects the idea of absolute and universal truth, and usually emphasizes discourse, debate and democracy (see p. 62).

Questions for discussion

→ Why, and to what extent, have conservatives supported tradition?

→ Is conservatism a 'disposition' rather than a political ideology?

→ Why has conservatism been described as a philosophy of imperfection?

→ How does the conservative view of property differ from the liberal view?

→ How far do conservatives go in endorsing authority?

→ Is conservatism merely ruling class ideology?

→ What is the link between conservatism and paternalism?

→ How and why have supporters of the new right criticized welfare?

→ To what extent are neoliberalism and neoconservatism compatible?

Further reading

Eatwell, R. and O'Sullivan, N. (eds), *The Nature of the Right: European and American Politics and Political Thought since 1789* (London: Pinter, 1989). An authoritative and thoughtful collection of essays on approaches to right-wing thought and the variety of conservative and rightist traditions.

Gamble, A., *The Free Economy and the Strong State*, 2nd edn (Basingstoke: Macmillan, 1994). An influential examination of the new right project that focuses specifically on Thatcherism in the UK.

Gray, J. and Willetts, D., *Is Conservatism Dead?* (London: Profile Books, 1997). A short and accessible account of both sides of the debate about the future of conservatism.

Honderich, T., *Conservatism* (Harmondsworth: Penguin, 1991). A distinctive and rigorously unsympathetic account of conservative thought; closely argued and interesting.

O'Sullivan, N., *Conservatism* (London: Dent; New York: St Martin's Press, 1976). A classic account of conservatism that lays particular stress upon its character as a 'philosophy of imperfection'.

Scruton, R., *The Meaning of Conservatism*, 3rd edn (Basingstoke and New York: Palgrave Macmillan, 2001). A stylish and openly sympathetic study that develops its own view of the conservative tradition.

Stelzer, I., *Neoconservatism* (London: Atlantic Books, 2004). An insightful collection of articles examining both the domestic and foreign policy idea of neoconservatism.

CHAPTER 4

SOCIALISM

PREVIEW

The term 'socialist' derives from the Latin *sociare*, meaning to combine or to share. Its earliest known usage was in 1827 in the UK, in an issue of the *Co-operative Magazine*. By the early 1830s, the followers of Robert Owen in the UK and Saint-Simon in France had started to refer to their beliefs as 'socialism' and, by the 1840s, the term was familiar in a range of industrialized countries, notably France, Belgium and the German states.

Socialism, as an ideology, has traditionally been defined by its opposition to capitalism and the attempt to provide a more humane and socially worthwhile alternative. At the core of socialism is a vision of human beings as social creatures united by their common humanity. This highlights the degree to which individual identity is fashioned by social interaction and the membership of social groups and collective bodies. Socialists therefore prefer cooperation to competition. The central, and some would say defining, value of socialism is equality, especially social equality. Socialists believe that social equality is the essential guarantee of social stability and cohesion, and that it promotes freedom, in the sense that it satisfies material needs and provides the basis for personal development. Socialism, however, contains a bewildering variety of divisions and rival traditions. These divisions have been about both 'means' (how socialism should be achieved) and 'ends' (the nature of the future socialist society). For example, communists or Marxists have usually supported revolution and sought to abolish capitalism through the creation of a classless society based on the common ownership of wealth. In contrast, democratic socialists or social democrats have embraced gradualism and aimed to reform or 'humanize' the capitalist system through a narrowing of material inequalities and the abolition of poverty.

Origins and development

Although socialists have sometimes claimed an intellectual heritage that goes back to Plato's *Republic* or Thomas More's *Utopia* ([1516] 1965), as with liberalism and conservatism, the origins of socialism lie in the nineteenth century. Socialism arose as a reaction against the social and economic conditions generated in Europe by the growth of industrial **capitalism**. Socialist ideas came quickly to be linked to the development of a new but growing class of industrial workers, who suffered the poverty and degradation that are so often a feature of early industrialization. Although socialism and liberalism have common roots in the Enlightenment, and share a faith in principles such as reason and progress, socialism emerged as a critique of liberal market society and was defined by its attempt to offer an alternative to industrial capitalism.

> **Capitalism**: An economic system in which wealth is owned by private individuals or businesses and goods are produced for exchange, according to the dictates of the market.

The character of early socialism was influenced by the harsh and often inhuman conditions in which the industrial working class lived and worked. Wages were typically low, child and female labour were commonplace, the working day often lasted up to twelve hours and the threat of unemployment was ever-present. In addition, the new working class was disorientated, being largely composed of first-generation urban dwellers, unfamiliar with the conditions of industrial life and work, and possessing few of the social institutions that could give their lives stability or meaning. As a result, early socialists often sought a radical, even revolutionary alternative to industrial capitalism. For instance, Charles Fourier (1772–1837) in France and Robert Owen (1771–1858) in the UK subscribed to **utopianism** in founding experimental communities based on sharing and cooperation. The Germans Karl Marx (see p. 121) and Friedrich Engels (1820–95), developed more complex and systematic theories, which claimed to uncover the 'laws of history' and proclaimed that the revolutionary overthrow of capitalism was inevitable.

> **Utopianism**: A belief in the unlimited possibilities of human development, typically embodied in the vision of a perfect or ideal society, a utopia (see p. 182).

In the late nineteenth century, the character of socialism was transformed by a gradual improvement in working-class living conditions and the advance of political democracy. The growth of trade unions, working-class political parties and sports and social clubs served to provide greater economic security and to integrate the working class into industrial society. In the advanced industrial societies of western Europe, it became increasingly difficult to continue to see the working class as a revolutionary force. Socialist political parties progressively adopted legal and constitutional

Communism:
The principle of the common ownership of wealth, or a system of comprehensive collectivization; communism is often viewed as 'Marxism in practice'.

tactics, encouraged by the gradual extension of the vote to working-class men. By the First World War, the socialist world was clearly divided between those socialist parties that had sought power through the ballot box and preached reform, and those, that proclaimed a continuing need for revolution. The Russian Revolution of 1917 entrenched this split: revolutionary socialists,

following the example of Lenin (see p. 125) and the Bolsheviks, usually adopted the term 'communism', while reformist socialists described their ideas as either 'socialism' or '**social democracy**'.

Social democracy:
A moderate or reformist brand of socialism that favours a balance between the market and the state, rather than the abolition of capitalism.

The twentieth century witnessed the spread of socialist ideas into African, Asian and Latin American countries with little or no experience of industrial capitalism. Socialism in these countries often developed out of the anticolonial struggle, rather than a class struggle. The idea of class exploitation was replaced by that of colonial oppression, creating a potent fusion of socialism and nationalism, which is examined more fully in Chapter 5.

The Bolshevik model of communism was imposed on eastern Europe after 1945; it was adopted in China after the revolution of 1949 and subsequently spread to North Korea, Vietnam, Cambodia and Laos. More moderate forms of socialism were practised elsewhere in the developing world, for example by the Congress Party in India. Distinctive forms of African and Arab socialism also developed, being influenced respectively by the communal values of traditional tribal life and the moral principles of Islam. In Latin America in the 1960s and 1970s, socialist revolutionaries waged war against military dictatorships, often seen to be operating in the interests of US imperialism. The Castro regime, which came to power after the Cuban revolution of 1959, developed close links with the Soviet Union, while the Sandinista guerrillas, who seized power in Nicaragua in 1979, remained non-aligned. In Chile in 1970, Salvador Allende became the world's first democratically elected Marxist head of state, but was overthrown and killed in a CIA-backed coup in 1973.

Since the late twentieth century, socialism has suffered a number of spectacular reverses, leading some to proclaim the 'death of socialism'. The most dramatic of these reverses was, of course, the collapse of communism in the eastern European revolutions of 1989–91. However, rather than socialists uniting around the principles of western social democracy, these principles were thrown into doubt as parliamentary socialist parties in many parts of the world embraced ideas and policies that are more commonly associated with liberalism or even conservatism. The final section of this chapter looks at whether socialism any longer has a future as a distinctive ideology.

Core themes – no man is an island

One of the difficulties of analyzing socialism is that the term has been understood in at least three distinctive ways. From one point of view, socialism is seen as an economic model, usually linked to some form of collectivization and planning. Socialism, in this sense, stands as an alternative to capitalism, the choice between these two qualitatively different productive systems traditionally being seen as the most crucial of all economic questions. However, the choice between 'pure' socialism and 'pure' capitalism was always an illusion, as all economic forms have, in different ways, blended features of both systems. Indeed, modern socialists tend to view socialism not so much as an alternative to capitalism, but as a means of harnessing capitalism to broader social ends. The second approach treats socialism as an instrument of the labour movement.

Labourism: A tendency exhibited by socialist parties to serve the interests of the organized labour movement rather than pursue broader ideological goals.

Socialism, in this view, represents the interests of the working class and offers a programme through which the workers can acquire political or economic power. Socialism is thus really a form of '**labourism**', a vehicle for advancing the interest of organized labour. From this perspective, the significance of socialism fluctuates with the fortunes of the working-class movement worldwide. Nevertheless, although the historical link between socialism and organized labour cannot be doubted, socialist ideas have also been associated with skilled craftsmen, the peasantry and, for that matter, with political and bureaucratic elites. That is why, in this book, socialism is understood in a third and broader sense as a political creed or ideology, characterized by a particular cluster of ideas, values and theories. The most significant of these are the following:

- community
- cooperation
- equality
- class politics
- common ownership.

Community

At its heart, socialism offers a unifying vision of human beings as social creatures, capable of overcoming social and economic problems by drawing on the power of the community rather than simply individual effort. This is a collectivist vision because it stresses the capacity of human beings for collective action, their willingness and ability to pursue goals by working together, as opposed to striving for personal self-interest. Most socialists, for instance, would be prepared to echo the words of the English metaphysical poet, John Donne (1571–1631):

No man is an Island entire of itself;
every man is a piece of the Continent, a part of the main; . . .
any man's death diminishes me, because I am involved in Mankind;
and therefore never send to know for whom the bell tolls;
it tolls for thee.

Human beings are therefore 'comrades', 'brothers' or 'sisters', tied to one another by the bonds of a common humanity. This is expressed in the principle of **fraternity**.

Fraternity: Literally, brotherhood; bonds of sympathy and comradeship between and amongst human beings.

Socialists are far less willing than either liberals or conservatives to believe that human nature is unchanging and fixed at birth. Rather, they believe that human nature is 'plastic', moulded by the experiences and circumstances of social life. In the long-standing philosophical debate about whether 'nurture' or 'nature' determines human behaviour, socialists side resolutely with nurture. From birth – perhaps even while in the womb – each individual is subjected to experiences that shape and condition his or her personality. All human skills and attributes are learnt from society, from the fact that we stand upright to the language we speak. Whereas liberals draw a clear distinction between the 'individual' and 'society', socialists believe that the individual is inseparable from society. Human beings are neither self-sufficient nor self-contained; to think of them as separate or atomized 'individuals' is absurd. Individuals can only be understood, and understand themselves, through the social groups to which they belong. The behaviour of human beings therefore tells us more about the society in which they live and have been brought up, than it does about any abiding or immutable human nature.

The radical edge of socialism derives not from its concern with what people are like, but with what they have the capacity to become. This has led socialists to develop utopian visions of a better society in which human beings can achieve genuine emancipation and fulfilment as members of a community. African and Asian socialists have often stressed that their traditional, preindustrial societies already emphasize the importance of social life and the value of community. In these circumstances, socialism has sought to preserve traditional social values in the face of the challenge from western individualism. As Julius Nyerere, president of Tanzania, 1964–85, pointed out, 'We, in Africa, have no more real need to be "converted" to socialism,

COLLECTIVISM

Collectivism is, broadly, the belief that collective human endeavour is of greater practical and moral value than individual self-striving. It thus reflects the idea that human nature has a social core, and implies that social groups, whether 'classes', 'nations', 'races' or whatever, are meaningful political entities. However, the term is used with little consistency. Bakunin (see p. 185) and other anarchists used collectivism to refer to self-governing associations of free individuals. Others have treated collectivism as strictly the opposite of individualism (see p. 28), holding that it implies that collective interests should prevail over individual ones. It is also sometimes linked to the state as the mechanism through which collective interests are upheld, suggesting that the growth of state responsibilities marks the advance of collectivism.

than we have of being "taught" democracy.' He therefore described his own views as 'tribal socialism'.

In the West, however, the social dimension of life has had to be 'reclaimed' after generations of industrial capitalism. This was the goal of nineteenth-century utopian socialists such as Fourier and Owen, who organized experiments in communal living. Charles Fourier encouraged the founding of model communities, each containing about 1800 members, which he called 'phalansteries'. Robert Owen also set up a number of experimental communities, the best known being New Harmony in Indiana, 1824–9. The most enduring communitarian experiment has been the *kibbutz* system in Israel, which consists of a system of cooperative, usually rural, settlements that are collectively owned and run by their members. However, the communitarian emphasis of the *kibbutz* system had been diluted since the 1960s by, for instance, the abandonment of collective childrearing.

Cooperation

If human beings are social animals, socialists believe that the natural relationship amongst them is one of **cooperation** rather than competition.

Cooperation: Working together; collective effort intended to achieve mutual benefit.

Socialists believe that competition pits one individual against another, encouraging each of them to deny or ignore their social nature rather than embrace it. As a result, competition fosters only a limited range of social attributes and, instead, promotes selfishness and aggression. Cooperation, on the other hand, makes moral and economic sense. Individuals who work together rather than against each other develop bonds of sympathy, caring and affection. Furthermore, the energies of the community rather than those of the single individual can be harnessed. The Russian anarchist Peter Kropotkin (see p. 191), for example, suggested that the principal reason why the human species had survived and prospered was because of its capacity for 'mutual aid'. Socialists believe that human beings can be motivated by moral incentives and not merely by material incentives. In theory, capitalism rewards individuals for the work they do: the harder they work, or the more abundant their skills, the greater their rewards will be. The moral incentive to work hard, however, is the desire to contribute to the common good, which develops out of a sympathy, or sense of responsibility, for fellow human beings, especially those in need. Although few modern social democrats would contemplate the outright abolition of material incentives, they nevertheless insist on the need for a balance of some kind between material and moral incentives. For instance, socialists would argue that an important incentive for achieving economic growth is that it helps to finance the provision of welfare support for the poorest and most vulnerable elements in society.

The socialist commitment to cooperation has stimulated the growth of cooperative enterprises, designed to replace the competitive and hierarchic businesses that have proliferated under capitalism. Both producers' and consumers' cooperatives have attempted to harness the energies of groups of people working for mutual benefit. In the UK, cooperative societies sprang up in the early nineteenth century. These societies bought goods in bulk and sold them cheaply to their working-class members. The 'Rochdale Pioneers' set up a grocery shop in 1844 and their example was soon taken up throughout industrial England and Scotland. Producer cooperatives, owned and run by their workforce, are common in parts of northern Spain and the former Yugoslavia, where industry is organized according to the principle of workers' self-management. Collective farms in the Soviet Union were also designed to be cooperative and self-managing, though in practice they operated within a rigid planning system and were usually controlled by local party bosses.

Equality

A commitment to equality is in many respects the defining feature of socialist ideology, equality being the political value that most clearly distinguishes socialism from its rivals, notably liberalism and conser-

Egalitarianism:
A theory or practice based on the desire to promote equality; egalitarianism is sometimes seen as the belief that equality is the primary political value.

vatism. Socialist **egalitarianism** is characterized by a belief in social equality, or equality of outcome. Socialists have advanced at least three arguments in favour of this form of equality. First, social equality upholds justice or fairness. Socialists are reluctant to explain the inequality of wealth in terms of innate differences of ability amongst individuals. Socialists believe that just as capitalism has fostered competitive and selfish behaviour, human inequality very largely reflects the unequal structure of society. They do not hold the naive belief that all people are born identical, possessing precisely the same capacities and skills. An egalitarian society would not, for instance, be one in which all students gained the same mark in their mathematics examinations. Nevertheless, socialists believe that the most significant forms of human inequality are a result of unequal treatment by society, rather than unequal endowment by nature. Justice, from a socialist perspective, therefore demands that people are treated equally, or at least more equally, by society in terms of their rewards and material circumstances. Formal equality, in its legal and political senses, is clearly inadequate in itself because it disregards the structural inequalities of the capitalist system. Equality of opportunity, for its part, legitimizes inequality by perpetuating the myth of innate inequality.

Second, social equality underpins community and cooperation. If people live in equal social circumstances, they will be more likely to identify with one another and work together for common benefit. Equal outcomes therefore strengthen social solidarity. Social inequality, by the same token, leads to conflict and instability. This also explains why socialists have criticized equality of opportunity for breeding a 'survival of the fittest' mentality. The UK social philosopher R. H. Tawney (1880–1962), for example, dismissed it as a 'tadpole philosophy', highlighting the struggle for survival amongst tadpoles as they develop into frogs. Third, socialists support social equality because they hold that need-satisfaction is the basis for human fulfilment and self-realization. A 'need' is a necessity: it *demands* satisfaction; it is not simply a frivolous wish or a passing fancy. Basic needs, such as the need for food, water, shelter, companionship and so on, are fundamental to the human condition, which means that, for socialists, their satisfaction is the very stuff of freedom. Marx expressed this in his communist theory of distribution: 'From each according to his ability, to each according to his needs'. Since all people have broadly similar needs, distributing wealth on the basis of need-satisfaction has clearly egalitarian implications. Nevertheless, need-satisfaction can also have inegalitarian implications, as in the case of so-called 'special' needs, arising, for instance, from physical or mental disability.

PERSPECTIVES

EQUALITY

LIBERALS believe that people are 'born' equal in the sense that they are of equal moral worth. This implies formal equality, notably legal and political equality, as well as equality of opportunity; but social equality is likely to threaten freedom and penalize talent. Whereas classical liberals emphasize the need for strict meritocracy and economic incentives, modern liberals argue that genuine equal opportunities require relative social equality.

CONSERVATIVES have traditionally viewed society as naturally hierarchical and have thus dismissed equality as an abstract and unachievable goal. Nevertheless, the new right evinces a strongly individualist belief in equality of opportunity while emphasizing the economic benefits of material inequality.

SOCIALISTS regard equality as a fundamental value and, in particular, endorse social equality. Despite shifts within social democracy towards a liberal belief in equality of opportunity, social equality, whether in its relative (social democratic) or absolute (communist) sense, has been seen as essential to ensuring social cohesion and fraternity, establishing justice or equity, and enlarging freedom in a positive sense.

ANARCHISTS place a particular stress on political equality, understood as an equal and absolute right to personal autonomy, implying that all forms of political inequality amount to oppression. Anarcho-communists believe in absolute social equality achieved through the collective ownership of productive wealth.

FASCISTS believe that humankind is marked by radical inequality, both between leaders and followers and between the various nations or races of the world. Nevertheless, the emphasis on the nation or race implies that all members are equal, at least in terms of their core social identity.

FEMINISTS take equality to mean sexual equality, in the sense of equal rights and equal opportunities (liberal feminism) or equal social or economic power (socialist feminism) irrespective of gender. However, some radical feminists have argued that the demand for equality may simply lead to women being 'male-identified'.

ECOLOGISTS advance the notion of biocentric equality, which emphasizes that all life forms have an equal right to 'live and blossom'. Conventional notions of equality are therefore seen as anthropocentric, in that they exclude the interests of all organisms and entities other than humankind.

Collectivization: The abolition of private property and the establishment of a comprehensive system of common or public ownership, usually through the mechanisms of the state.

Although socialists agree about the virtue of social and economic equality, they disagree about the extent to which this can and should be brought about. Marxists and communists believe in absolute social equality, brought about by the abolition of private property and **collectivization** of productive wealth. Social democrats, however, believe in relative social equality, achieved through the redistribution of wealth through the welfare state and a system of progressive taxation. The social-democratic desire to tame capitalism rather than abolish it, reflects an acceptance of a continuing role for material incentives, and the fact that the significance of need-satisfaction is largely confined to the eradication of poverty. This, in turn, blurs the distinction between social equality and equality of opportunity.

Class Politics

Socialists have traditionally viewed **social class** as the deepest and most politically significant of social divisions. Socialist class politics have been

Social class: A social division based on economic or social factors; a social class is a group of people who share a similar socio-economic position.

expressed in two ways, however. In the first, social class is an analytical tool. In pre-socialist societies at least, socialists have believed that human beings tend to think and act together with others with whom they share a common economic position or interest. In other words, social classes, rather than individuals, are the principal actors in history and therefore provide the key to under-standing social and political change. This is most clearly demonstrated in the Marxist belief that historical change is the product of class conflict. The second form of socialist class politics focuses specifically on the working class, and is concerned with political struggle and emancipation. Socialism has often been viewed as an expression of the interests of the working class, and the working class has been seen as the vehicle through which socialism will be achieved. Nevertheless, social class has not been accepted as a necessary or permanent feature of society: socialist societies have either been seen as classless or as societies in which class inequalities have been substantially reduced. In emancipating itself from capitalist exploitation, the working class thus also emancipates itself from its own class identity, becoming, in the process, fully developed human beings.

Socialists have nevertheless been divided about the nature and importance of social class. In the Marxist tradition, class is linked to economic power, as defined by the individual's relationship to the means of production. From

Bourgeoisie: A Marxist term denoting the ruling class of a capitalist society, the owners of productive wealth.

Proletariat: A Marxist term denoting a class that subsists through the sale of its labour power; strictly speaking, the proletariat is not equivalent to the manual working class

this perspective, class divisions are divisions between 'capital' and 'labour' or the **bourgeoisie** and the **proletariat**; that is, between the owners of productive wealth (the bourgeoisie) and those who live off the sale of their labour power (the proletariat). This Marxist two-class model is characterized by irreconcilable conflict between the bourgeoisie and the proletariat, leading, inevitably, to the overthrow of capitalism through a proletarian revolution. Social democrats, on the other hand, have tended to define social class in terms of income and status differences between 'white collar' or non-manual workers (the middle class) and 'blue collar' or manual workers (the working class). From this perspective, the advance of socialism is associated with the narrowing of divisions between the middle class and the working class brought about through economic and social intervention. Social democrats have therefore believed in social amelioration and class harmony rather than social polarization and class war.

However, the link between socialism and class politics has declined since the mid-twentieth century. This has largely been a consequence of declining levels of class solidarity and, in particular, the shrinkage of the traditional working class or urban proletariat. The waning in class politics is a consequence of deindustrialization, reflected in the decline of traditional labour-intensive industries such as coal, steel, shipbuilding and so on. Not only has this forced traditional socialist parties to revise their policies in order to appeal to middle-class voters, but it has also encouraged them to define their radicalism less in terms of class emancipation and more in relation to issues such as feminism, environmentalism, peace and international development.

Common ownership

Socialists have often traced the origins of competition and inequality to the institution of private property, by which they usually mean productive wealth or 'capital', rather than personal belongings such as clothes, furniture or houses. This attitude to property sets socialism apart from liberalism and conservatism, which both regard property ownership as natural and proper. Socialists criticize private property for a number of reasons. In the first place, property is unjust: wealth is produced by the collective effort of human labour and should therefore be owned by the community, not by private individuals. Second, socialists believe that property breeds acquisitiveness and so is morally corrupting. Private property encourages people to

ECONOMY

LIBERALS see the economy as a vital part of civil society and have a strong preference for a market or capitalist economic order based on property, competition and material incentives. However, while classical liberals favour *laissez-faire* capitalism, modern liberals recognize the limitations of the market and accept limited economic management.

CONSERVATIVES show clear support for private enterprise but have traditionally favoured pragmatic if limited intervention, fearing the free-for-all of *laissez-faire* and the attendant risks of social instability. The new right, however, endorses unregulated capitalism.

SOCIALISTS in the Marxist tradition have expressed a preference for common ownership and absolute social equality, which in orthodox communism was expressed in state collectivization and central planning. Social democrats, though, support welfare or regulated capitalism, believing that the market is a good servant but a bad master.

ANARCHISTS reject any form of economic control or management. However, while anarcho-communists endorse common ownership and small-scale self-management, anarcho-capitalists advocate an entirely unregulated market economy.

FASCISTS have sought a 'third way' between capitalism and communism, often expressed through the ideas of corporatism, supposedly drawing labour and capital together into an organic whole. Planning and nationalization are supported as attempts to subordinate profit to the (alleged) needs of the nation or race.

ECOLOGISTS condemn both market capitalism and state collectivism for being growth-obsessed and environmentally unsustainable. Economics, therefore, must be subordinate to ecology, and the drive for profit at any cost must be replaced by a concern with long-term sustainability and harmony between humankind and nature.

be materialistic, to believe that human happiness or fulfilment can be gained through the pursuit of wealth. Those who own property wish to accumulate more, while those who have little or no wealth long to acquire it. Finally, property is divisive: it fosters conflict in society, for example, between owners and workers, employers and employees, or simply the rich and the poor. Socialists have therefore proposed that the institution of private property either be abolished and replaced by the common ownership of productive wealth, or, more modestly, that the right to property be balanced against the interests of the community.

Fundamentalist socialists, such as Marx and Engels, envisaged the abolition of private property, and hence the creation of a classless, communist society in place of capitalism. They clearly believed that property should be owned collectively and used for the benefit of humanity. However, they said little about how this goal could be achieved in practice. When Lenin and the Bolsheviks seized power in Russia in 1917, they believed that socialism could be built through **nationalization**. This process was not completed until the 1930s, when Stalin's 'second revolution' witnessed the construction of a centrally planned economy, a system of state collectivization. 'Common ownership' came to mean 'state ownership', or what the Soviet constitution described as 'socialist state property'. The Soviet Union thus developed a form of **state socialism**.

Nationalization:
The extension of state or public ownership over private assets or industries, either individual enterprises or the entire economy (often called collectivization).

State socialism:
A form of socialism in which the state controls and directs economic life, acting, in theory, in the interests of the people.

Social democrats have also been attracted to the state as an instrument through which wealth can be collectively owned and the economy rationally planned. However, in the West, nationalization has been applied more selectively, its objective not being full state collectivization but the construction of a mixed economy, in which some industries would remain in private hands while others would be publicly owned. In the UK, for example, the Attlee Labour government, (1945–51) nationalized what it called the 'commanding heights' of the economy: major industries such as coal, steel, electricity and gas. Through these industries, the government hoped to regulate the entire economy without the need for comprehensive collectivization. However, since the 1950s, parliamentary socialist parties have gradually distanced themselves from the 'politics of ownership', preferring to define socialism in term of the pursuit of equality and social justice rather than the advance of public ownership.

Roads to socialism

Two major issues have divided competing traditions and tendencies within socialism. The first is the goals, or 'ends', for which socialists should strive. Socialists have held very different conceptions of what a socialist society should look like; in effect, they have developed competing definitions of 'socialism'. The principal disagreement here is between **fundamentalist**

Fundamentalist socialism: A form of socialism that seeks to abolish capitalism and replace it with a qualitatively different kind of society.

Revisionist socialism: A form of socialism that has revised its critique of capitalism and seeks to reconcile greater social justice with surviving capitalist forms.

socialism and **revisionist socialism**, represented, respectively, by the communist and the social demo-cratic traditions. These traditions are examined in the next two sections of this chapter. This section discusses the second issue that has divided socialists: the 'means' they should use to achieve socialist ends, sometimes seen as the 'roads to socialism'. This concern with means follows from the fact that socialism has always had an oppositional character: it is a force for change, for the transformation of the capitalist or colonial societies in which it emerged. The 'road' that socialists have adopted is not merely a matter of strategic significance alone; it both determines the character of the socialist movement and influences the form of socialism eventu-ally achieved. In other words, means and ends within socialism are often interconnected.

Revolutionary socialism

Many early socialists believed that socialism could only be introduced by the revolutionary overthrow of the existing political system, and accepted that violence would be an inevitable feature of such a **revolution**. One of the earliest advocates of revolution was the French socialist

Revolution: A fundamental and irreversible change, often a brief but dramatic period of upheaval; systemic change.

Auguste Blanqui (1805–81), who proposed the forma-tion of a small band of dedicated conspirators to plan and carry out a revolutionary seizure of power. Marx and Engels, on the other hand, envisaged a 'proletarian revo-lution', in which the class-conscious working masses would rise up to overthrow capitalism. The first success-ful socialist revolution did not, however, take place until 1917, when a dedi-cated and disciplined group of revolutionaries, led by Lenin and the Bolsheviks, seized power in Russia in what was more a *coup d'état* than a popular insurrection. In many ways, the Bolshevik Revolution served as a model for subsequent generations of socialist revolutionaries.

During the nineteenth century, revolutionary tactics were attractive to socialists for two reasons. First, the early stages of industrialization produced stark injustice as the working masses were afflicted by grinding poverty and widespread unemployment. Capitalism was viewed as a system of naked oppression and exploitation, and the working class was thought to be on the brink of revolution. When Marx and Engels wrote in 1848 that 'A spectre is haunting Europe – the spectre of Communism', they were writing against a background of revolt and revolution in many parts of the continent. Second, the working classes had few alternative means of political influence; indeed, almost everywhere they were excluded from political life. Where autocratic monarchies persisted throughout the nineteenth century, as in Russia, these were dominated by the landed aristocracy. Where constitutional and representative government had developed, the right to vote was usually restricted by a property qualification to the middle classes.

Revolution has, however, not merely been a tactical consideration for socialists; it also reflects their analysis of the state and of the nature of the state power. Whereas liberals believe the state to be a neutral body, responding to the interests of all citizens and acting in the common good, revolutionary socialists have viewed the state as an agent of class oppression, acting in the interests of 'capital' and against those of 'labour'. Marxists, for example, believe that political power reflects class interests, and that the state is a 'bourgeois state', inevitably biased in favour of capital. Political reform and gradual change are clearly pointless. Universal suffrage and regular and competitive elections are at best a façade, their purpose being to conceal the reality of unequal class and to misdirect the political energies of the working class. A class-conscious proletariat thus has no alternative: in order to build socialism, it has first to overthrow the bourgeois state through political revolution.

In the second half of the twentieth century, faith in revolution was most evident amongst socialists in the developing world. In the post-1945 period, many national liberation movements embraced the 'armed struggle' in the belief that colonial rule could neither be negotiated nor voted out of existence. In Asia, the Chinese Revolution of 1949, led by Mao Zedong, was the culmination of a long military campaign against both Japan and the Chinese Nationalists, the Kuomintang. Vietnamese national unity was achieved in 1975 after a prolonged war fought first against France, and subsequently against the USA. Until his death in 1967, Che Guevara, the Argentine revolutionary, led guerrilla forces in various parts of South America and commanded troops during the Cuban revolution of 1959, which brought Fidel Castro to power. Similar revolutionary struggles took place in Africa: for example, the bitter war through which Algeria eventually gained independence from France in 1962.

The choice of revolutionary or insurrectionary political means had profound consequences for socialism. For instance, the use of revolution usually led to the pursuit of fundamentalist ends. Revolution had the advantage that it allowed the remnants of the old order to be overthrown and an entirely new social system to be constructed. Thus when the Khmer Rouge, led by Pol Pot, seized power in Cambodia in 1975, they declared 'Year Zero'. Capitalism could be abolished and a qualitatively different socialist society established in its place. Socialism, in this context, usually took the form of state collectivization, modelled on the Soviet Union during the Stalinist period. The revolutionary 'road' was also associated with a drift towards dictatorship and the use of political repression. This occurred for a number of reasons. First, the use of force accustomed the new rulers to regard violence as a legitimate instrument of policy; as Mao put it, 'power resides in the barrel of a gun'. Second, revolutionary parties typically adopted military-style structures, based on strong leadership and strict discipline, that were merely consolidated once power was achieved. Third, in rooting out the vestiges of the old order, all oppositional forces were also removed, effectively preparing the way for the construction of totalitarian dictatorships. The revolutionary socialist tradition, nevertheless, was fatally undermined by the collapse of communism, in what were, effectively, the counter-revolutions of 1989–91. This finally ended the divide that had opened up in socialist politics in 1917, and completed the conversion of socialism to constitutional and democratic politics. Where revolutionary socialism survives, it is only in pockets such as continuing Maoist insurgency in Peru and Nepal.

Evolutionary socialism

Although early socialists often supported the idea of revolution, as the nineteenth century progressed enthusiasm for popular revolt waned, at least in the advanced capitalist states of western and central Europe. Capitalism itself had matured and, by the late nineteenth century, the urban working class had lost its revolutionary character and was being integrated into society. Wages and living standards had started to rise, and the working class had begun to develop a range of institutions (working men's clubs, trade unions, political parties and so on) that both protected their interests and nurtured a sense of belonging within industrial society. Furthermore, the gradual advance of political democracy led to the extension of the franchise (the right to vote) to the working classes. By the end of the First World War, a large majority of western states had introduced universal manhood suffrage, with a growing number extending voting rights also to women. The combined effect of these factors was to shift the attention of socialists away from violent insurrection and to persuade them that there was an alternative evolutionary, 'democratic' or 'parliamentary' road to socialism.

The Fabian Society, formed in 1884, took up the cause of parliamentary socialism in the UK. The Fabians, led by Beatrice Webb (1858–1943) and Sidney Webb (1859–1947), and including noted intellectuals such as George Bernard Shaw and H. G. Wells, took their name from the Roman General

Fabius Maximus, who was noted for the patient and defensive tactics he had employed in defeating Hannibal's invading armies. In their view, socialism would develop naturally and peacefully out of liberal capitalism via a very similar process. This would occur through a combination of political action and education. Political action required the formation of a socialist party, which would compete for power against established parliamentary parties rather than prepare for violent revolution. They therefore accepted the liberal theory of the state as a neutral arbiter, rather than the Marxist belief that it is an agent of class oppression. The Webbs were actively involved in the formation of the UK Labour Party, and helped to write its 1918 constitution. The Fabians also believed that elite groups, such as politicians of all parties, civil servants, scientists and academics, could be converted to socialism through education. These elite groups would be 'permeated' by socialist ideas as they recognized that socialism is morally superior to capitalism, being based, for example, on Biblical principles, and is also more rational and efficient.

Fabian ideas also had an impact on the German Socialist Democratic Party (SDP), formed in 1875. The SPD quickly became the largest socialist party in Europe and, in 1912, the largest party in the German Reichstag. Although committed in theory to a Marxist strategy, in practice it adopted a reformist approach, influenced by the ideas of Ferdinand Lassalle (1825–64). Lassalle had argued that the extension of political democracy could enable the state to respond to working-class interests, and he envisaged socialism being established through a gradual process of social reform, introduced by a benign state.

Gradualism: Progress brought about by gradual, piecemeal improvements, rather than dramatic upheaval; change through legal and peaceful reform.

Such ideas were developed more thoroughly by Eduard Bernstein (see p. 132), whose *Evolutionary Socialism* ([1898] 1962) developed ideas that paralleled the Fabian belief in **gradualism**. Bernstein was particularly impressed by the development of the democratic state, which he believed made the Marxist call for revolution redundant. The working class could use the ballot box to introduce socialism, which would therefore develop as an evolutionary outgrowth of capitalism. Such principles dominated the working-class political parties that sprang up around the turn of the century: the Australian Labour Party was founded in 1891, the UK Labour Party in 1900, the Italian Socialist Party in 1892, its French counterpart in 1905, and so on. They came, in the 1970s, to be adopted also by western communist parties, led by the Spanish, Italian and French communist parties. The resulting **Eurocommunism** was committed to pursuing a democratic road to communism and maintaining an open, competitive political system.

Eurocommunism: A form of deradicalized communism, most influential in the 1970s, which attempted to blend Marxism with liberal-democratic principles.

The inevitability of gradualism?

The advent of political democracy in the late nineteenth and early twentieth centuries caused a wave of optimism to spread throughout the socialist movement, as reflected, for example, in the Fabian prophecy of 'the inevitability of gradualism'. The idea that the victory of socialism was inevitable was not new. For instance, Marx had predicted the inevitable overthrow of capitalist society in a proletarian revolution. However, whereas Marx believed that history was driven forward by the irresistible forces of class conflict, evolutionary socialists highlighted the logic of the democratic process itself.

Their optimism was founded on a number of assumptions. First, the progressive extension of the franchise would eventually lead to the establishment of universal adult suffrage, and therefore of political equality. Second, political equality would, in practice, work in the interests of the majority; that is, those who decide the outcome of elections. Socialists thus believed that political democracy would invest power in the hands of the working class, easily the most numerous class in any industrial society. Third, socialism was thought to be the natural 'home' of the working class. As capitalism was seen as a system of class exploitation, oppressed workers would naturally be drawn to socialist parties, which offered them the prospect of social justice and emancipation. The electoral success of socialist parties would therefore be guaranteed by the numerical strength of the working class. Fourth, once in power, socialist parties would be able to carry out a fundamental transformation of society through a process of social reform. In this way, political democracy not only opened up the possibility of achieving socialism peacefully, it made this process inevitable.

Such optimistic expectations have, however, not been borne out in reality. Some have even argued that democratic socialism is founded on a contradiction: in order to respond successfully to electoral pressures, socialists have been forced to revise or 'water down' their ideological beliefs. Socialist parties have enjoyed periods of power in virtually all liberal democracies, with the exception of North America. However, they have certainly not been guaranteed power. The Swedish Social Democratic Labour Party (SAP) has been the most successful in this respect, having been in power alone, or as the senior partner in a coalition, for most of the period since 1951. Nevertheless, even the SAP has only once achieved 50 per cent of the popular vote (in 1968). The UK Labour Party gained its greatest support (49 per cent) in 1951, equalled by the Spanish Socialist Workers' Party in 1982. The SPD in Germany got 46 per cent of the vote in 1972, and the combined socialist and communist vote in Italy in 1976 amounted to 44 per cent. Moreover, although these parties have undoubtedly introduced significant social reforms when in power (usually involving the expansion of welfare provision and economic management) they have certainly not presided over any fundamental social transformation. At best, capitalism has been reformed, not abolished.

Democratic socialism has, in fact, encountered a number of problems not envisaged by its founding figures. In the first place, does the working class any longer constitute the majority of the electorate in advanced industrial societies? Socialist parties have traditionally focused their electoral appeal on urban manual workers, the 'factory fodder' of capitalist societies. Modern capitalism, however, has become increasingly technological, demanding a skilled workforce often engaged in technical rather than manual tasks. The 'traditional' working class, composed of manual labourers working in established 'heavy' industries, has thus declined in size, giving rise to the idea of so-called 'two-thirds, one-third' societies, in which poverty and disadvantage are concentrated in the 'underclass'. In *The Culture of Contentment* (1992), J. K. Galbraith drew attention to the emergence in modern societies, or at least amongst the politically active, of a 'contented majority' whose material affluence and economic security encourage them to be politically conservative. If working-class support no longer offers socialist parties the prospect of an electoral majority, they are either forced to appeal more broadly for support to other social classes, or to share power as a coalition partner with middle-class parties. Both options require socialist parties to modify their ideological commitments, either in order to appeal to electors who have little or no interest in socialism, or to work with parties that seek to uphold capitalism.

Furthermore, is the working class socialist at heart? Is socialism genuinely in the interests of the working class? Socialist parties have been forced to acknowledge the ability of capitalism to 'deliver the goods', especially since the Second World War. During the 1950s socialist parties, once committed to fundamental change, revised their policies in an attempt to appeal to an increasingly affluent working class. A similar process has taken place since the 1980s, as socialist parties have struggled to come to terms with the changing class structure of capitalism as well as the pressures generated by economic globalization. In effect, socialism has come to be associated with attempts to make the market economy work, rather than with the attempt to re-engineer the social structure of capitalism. Such shifts are examined in more detail later, in connection with social democracy.

However, left-wing socialists have a different explanation for the declining socialist character of the working class. Rather than highlighting the benefits of capitalism or its changing class structure, they have emphasized the role of ideological manipulation. Marxists thus argue that '**bourgeois ideology**' pervades society, preventing the working class from perceiving

Bourgeois ideology: A Marxist term denoting ideas and theories that serve the interests of the bourgeoisie by disguising the contradictions of capitalist society.

Class consciousness: A Marxist term denoting an accurate awareness of class interests and a willingness to pursue them; a class-conscious class is a class-for-itself.

the reality of its own exploitation. For example, Lenin proclaimed that without the leadership of a revolutionary party, the working class would only be able to gain 'trade union consciousness', a desire for material improvement within the capitalist system, but not full revolutionary '**class consciousness**'. Gramsci (see p. 8) emphasized that capitalism survives not through its economic power alone, but also through a process of 'ideological hegemony'.

Finally, can socialist parties, even if elected to power, carry out socialist reforms? Socialist parties have formed single-party governments in a number of western countries, including France, Sweden, Spain, the UK, Australia and New Zealand. Once elected, however, they have been confronted with entrenched interests in both the state and society. As early as 1902, the SPD leader Karl Kautsky (1854–1938) pointed out that 'the capitalist class rules but it does not govern, it contents itself with ruling the government'. This is made easier by the fact that political elites in the administration, courts and the military share the same social background as business elites. Moreover, elected governments, of whatever ideological inclination, must respect the power of big business, which is the major employer and investor in the economy as well as the wealthiest contributor to party funds. In other words, although democratic socialist parties may succeed in forming elected governments, there is the danger that they will merely win office without necessarily acquiring power.

Marxism

Strictly speaking, 'Marxism' as a codified body of thought only came into existence after Marx's death in 1883. It was the product of the attempt, notably by Marx's lifelong collaborator, Engels, Kautsky and the Russian theoretician Georgi Plekhanov (1857–1918), to condense Marx's ideas and theories into a systematic and comprehensive world view that suited the

Dialectical materialism: The crude and deterministic form of Marxism that dominated intellectual life in orthodox communist states.

needs of the growing socialist movement. Engels' *Anti-Dühring*, written in 1876, while Marx was still alive, is sometimes seen as the first work of Marxist orthodoxy, emphasizing the need for adherence to an authoritative interpretation of Marx's work. This orthodox Marxism, which is often portrayed as '**dialectical materialism**' (a term coined by Plekhanov and not used by Marx), later formed the basis of Soviet communism. Some see Marx as an economic determinist, while others proclaim him to be a humanist socialist. Moreover, distinctions have also been drawn between his early and later writings, sometimes presented as the distinction between the 'young Marx' and the 'mature Marx'. It is, nevertheless, clear that Marx himself believed that he had developed a new brand of socialism that was scientific in the sense that it was primarily concerned with disclosing the nature of social and historical development, rather than with advancing an essentially ethical critique of capitalism.

At least three forms of Marxism can be identified. These are as follows:

- classical Marxism
- orthodox communism
- modern Marxism.

Classical Marxism

Philosophy

The core of classical Marxism – the Marxism of Marx – is a philosophy of history that outlines why capitalism is doomed and why socialism is destined to replace it, based on supposedly scientific analysis. But in what sense did Marx believe his work to be scientific? Marx criticized earlier socialist thinkers such as the French social reformer Saint-Simon (1760–1825), Fourier and Owen as 'utopians' on the basis that their social-ism was grounded in a desire for total social transformation unconnected with the necessity of class struggle and revolution. Marx, in contrast, under-took a laborious empirical analysis of history and society, hoping thereby to gain insight into the nature of future developments. However, whether with Marx's help or not, Marxism as the attempt to gain historical understanding through the application of scientific methods, later developed into Marxism as a body of scientific truths, gaining a status more akin to that of a religion. Engels' declaration that Marx had uncovered the 'laws' of historical and social development was a clear indication of this transition.

Historical materialism: A Marxist theory that holds that material or economic conditions ultimately structure law, politics, culture and other aspects of social existence.

What made Marx's approach different from that of other social thinkers was that he subscribed to what Engels called the 'materialist conception of history', or **historical materialism** (see Figure 4.1). Rejecting the idealism of the German philosopher Hegel (1770–1831), who believed that history amounted to the unfolding of the so-called 'world spirit', Marx held material circum-stances to be fundamental to all forms of social and

Figure 4.1
Historical
materialism

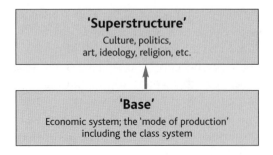

'Superstructure'
Culture, politics,
art, ideology, religion, etc.

'Base'
Economic system; the 'mode of production'
including the class system

historical development. This reflected the belief that the production of the means of subsistence is the most crucial of all human activities. Since humans cannot survive without food, water, shelter and so on, the way in which these are produced conditions all other aspects of life; in short, 'social being determines consciousness'. In the preface to *A Contribution to the Critique of Political Economy*, written in 1859, Marx gave this theory its most succinct expression, by suggesting that social consciousness and the 'legal and political superstructure' arise from the 'economic base', the real foundation of society. This 'base' consists essentially of the 'mode of production' or economic system – feudalism, capitalism, socialism and so on. This led Marx to conclude that political, legal, cultural, religious, artistic and other aspects of life could primarily be explained by reference to economic factors.

Although in other respects a critic of Hegel, Marx nevertheless embraced his belief that the driving force of historical change was the **dialectic**, In effect, progress is the consequence of internal conflict.

Dialectic: A process of development in which interaction between two opposing forces leads to a further or higher stage; historical change resulting from internal contradictions within a society.

For Hegel, this explained the movement of the 'world spirit' towards self-realization through conflict between a thesis and its opposing force, an antithesis, producing a higher level, a synthesis, which in turn constitutes a new thesis. Marx, as Engels put it, 'turned Hegel on his head', by investing this Hegelian dialectic with a materialistic interpretation. Marx thus explained historical change by reference to internal contradictions within each mode of production, arising from the existence of private property. Capitalism is thus doomed because it embodies its own antithesis, the proletariat, seen by Marx as the 'grave digger of capitalism'. Conflict between capitalism and the proletariat will therefore lead to a higher stage of development in the establishment of a socialist, and eventually a communist, society.

Marx's theory of history is therefore teleological, in the sense that it invests history with meaning or a purpose, reflected in its goal: classless communism. This goal would nevertheless only be achieved once history had developed through a series of stages or epochs, each characterized by its own economic structure and class system. In *The German Ideology* ([1846]

Karl Marx
(1818–83)

German philosopher, economist and political thinker, usually portrayed as the father of twentieth-century communism. After a brief career as a teacher and journalist, Marx spent the rest of his life as an active revolutionary and writer, living mainly in London and supported by his friend and life-long collaborator Friedrich Engels.

Marx's work was derived from a synthesis of Hegelian philosophy, British political economy and French socialism. Its centrepiece was a critique of capitalism that highlights its transitional nature by drawing attention to systemic inequality and instability. Marx subscribed to a teleological theory of history that held that social development would inevitably culminate in the establishment of communism. His classic work is the three-volume *Capital* (1867, 1885 and 1894); his best-known and most accessible work, with Engels, is the *Communist Manifesto* (1848).

1970) Marx identified four such stages: (1) primitive communism or tribal society, in which material scarcity provided the principal source of conflict; (2) slavery, covering classical or ancient societies and characterized by conflict between master and slave; (3) feudalism, marked by antagonism between land owners and serfs; and (4) capitalism, dominated by the struggle between the bourgeoisie and the proletariat. Human history had therefore been a long struggle between the oppressed and the oppressor, the exploited and the exploiter. However, following Hegel, Marx envisaged an end of history, which would occur when a society was constructed that embodied no internal contradictions or antagonisms. This, for Marx, meant communism, a classless society based on the common ownership of productive wealth. With the establishment of communism, what Marx called the 'pre-history of mankind' would come to an end.

Economics

In Marx's early writings much of his critique of capitalism rests on the notion of **alienation**. Since capitalism is a system of production for exchange, it alienates humans from the product of their labour: they work to produce not what they need or what is useful, but 'commodities' to be sold for profit. They are also alienated from the process of labour, because most are forced to work under the supervision of foremen or managers. In addition, work is not social: individuals are encouraged to be self-interested and

Alienation: To be separated from one's genuine or essential nature; used by Marxists to describe the process whereby, under capitalism, labour is reduced to being a mere commodity.

are therefore alienated from fellow human beings. Finally, workers are alienated from themselves. Labour itself is reduced to a mere commodity and work becomes a depersonalized activity instead of a creative and fulfilling one.

However, in his later work, Marx analysed capitalism more in terms of class conflict and exploitation. Marx defined class in terms of economic power, specifically where people stand in relation to the ownership of the 'means of production', or productive wealth. He believed that capitalist society was increasingly being divided into 'two great classes facing one another: Bourgeoisie and Proletariat'. For Marx and later Marxists, the analysis of the class system provides the key to historical understanding and enables predictions to be made about the future development of capitalism: in the words of the *Communist Manifesto*, 'The history of all hitherto existing societies is the history of class struggle.' Classes, rather than individuals, parties or other movements, are the chief agents of historical change.

Crucially, Marx believed that the relationship between classes is one of irreconcilable antagonism, the subordinate class being necessarily and systematically exploited by the 'ruling class'. This he explained by reference

Surplus value: A Marxist term denoting the value that is extracted from the labour of the proletariat by the mechanism of capitalist exploitation.

to the idea of '**surplus value**'. Capitalism's quest for profit can only be satisfied through the extraction of surplus value from its workers, by paying them less than the value their labour generates. Economic exploitation is therefore an essential feature of the capitalist mode of production, and it operates regardless of the meanness or generosity of particular employers. Marx was concerned not only to highlight the inherent instability of capitalism, based on irreconcilable class conflict, but also to analyse the nature of capitalist development. In particular, he drew attention to its tendency to experience deepening economic crises. These stemmed, in the main, from cyclical crises of overproduction, plunging the economy into stagnation and bringing unemployment and immiseration to the working class. Each crisis would be more severe than the last, because, Marx calculated, in the long term the rate of profit would fall. This would eventually, and inevitably, produce conditions in which the proletariat, the vast majority of society, would rise up in revolution.

Politics

Marx's most important prediction was that capitalism was destined to be overthrown by a proletarian revolution. This would be not merely a political revolution that would remove the governing elite or overthrow the state machine, but a **social revolution** that would establish a new mode of

Social revolution:
A qualitative change in the structure of society; for Marxists a social revolution involves a change in the mode of production and the system of ownership.

production and culminate in the achievement of full communism. Such a revolution, he anticipated, would occur in the most mature capitalist countries – for example, Germany, Belgium, France or the UK – where the forces of production had expanded to their limit within the constraints of the capitalist system. Nevertheless, revolution would not simply be determined by objective conditions alone. The subjective element would be supplied by a 'class-conscious' proletariat, meaning that revolution would occur when both objective and subjective conditions were 'ripe'. As class antagonisms intensified, the proletariat would recognize the fact of its own exploitation and become a revolutionary force: a class-for-itself. In this sense, revolution would be a spontaneous act, carried out by the proletarian class that, in effect, would lead or guide itself.

The initial target of this revolution was to be the bourgeois state. The state, in this view, is an instrument of oppression wielded by the economically dominant class. As Marx put it in the *Communist Manifesto*: 'The executive of the modern state is the committee for managing the common affairs of the bourgeoisie.' However, Marx recognized that there could be no immediate transition from capitalism to communism. A transitionary 'socialist' stage of development would last as long as class antagonisms

Dictatorship of the proletariat: A Marxist term denoting the transitionary phase between the collapse of capitalism and the establishment of full communism, characterized by the establishment of a proletarian state.

persisted. This would be characterized by what Marx called the **dictatorship of the proletariat**. The purpose of this proletarian state was to safeguard the gains of the revolution by preventing counter-revolution carried out by the dispossessed bourgeoisie. However, as class antagonisms began to fade with the emergence of full communism, the state would 'wither away' – once the class system had been abolished, the state would lose its reason for existence. The resulting communist society would therefore be stateless as well as classless, and would allow a system of commodity production to give way to one geared to the satisfaction of human needs. In Marx's words, 'the free development of each is the precondition of the free development of all'.

Orthodox communism

The Russian Revolution and its consequences dominated the image of communism in the twentieth century. The Bolshevik party, led by V. I. Lenin, seized power in a *coup d'état* in October 1917, and the following year adopted the name 'Communist Party'. As the first successful communist revolutionaries, the Bolshevik leaders enjoyed unquestionable authority within the communist world, at least until the 1950s. Communist parties set up elsewhere accepted the ideological leadership of Moscow and joined the Communist International, or 'Comintern', founded in 1919. The communist regimes established in eastern Europe after 1945, in China in 1949, in Cuba in 1959 and elsewhere were consciously modelled on the structure of the Soviet Union. Thus, Soviet communism became the dominant model of communist rule, and the ideas of Marxism-Leninism became the ruling ideology of the communist world.

However, twentieth-century communism differed significantly from the ideas and expectations of Marx and Engels. In the first place, although the communist parties that developed in the twentieth century were founded on the theories of classical Marxism, they were forced to adapt these to the tasks of winning and retaining political power. Twentieth-century communist leaders had, in particular, to give greater attention to issues such as leadership, political organization and economic management than Marx had done. Second, the communist regimes were shaped by the historical circumstances in which they developed. Communist parties did not achieve power, as Marx had anticipated, in the developed capitalist states of western Europe, but in backward, largely rural countries such as Russia and China. In consequence, the urban proletariat was invariably small and unsophisticated, quite incapable of carrying out a genuine class revolution. Communist rule thus became the rule of a communist elite, and of communist leaders. Soviet communism, furthermore, was crucially shaped by the decisive personal contribution of the first two Bolshevik leaders, Lenin and Stalin (1879–1953).

Lenin was both a political leader and a major political thinker. Lenin's theories reflected his overriding concern with the problems of winning power and establishing communist rule. The central feature of **Leninism** was a belief in the need for a new kind of political party, a revolutionary party or vanguard party. Unlike Marx, Lenin did not believe that the proletariat would spontaneously develop revolutionary class consciousness, as the working class was deluded by bourgeois ideas and beliefs. He suggested that only a 'revolutionary party' could lead the working class from 'trade union consciousness' to revolutionary class consciousness. Such a party should be composed of professional and dedicated revolutionaries. Its claim to leadership would lie in its ideological wisdom, specifically its understanding of Marxist theory. This party could therefore act as the 'vanguard of the proletariat' because, armed with Marxism, it would be able to perceive the genuine interests of the proletariat and be dedicated to awakening the proletarian class to its revolutionary potential. Lenin further proposed that the

Leninism:
Lenin's theoretical contributions to Marxism, notably his belief in the need for a revolutionary or vanguard party to raise the proletariat to class consciousness.

Vladimir Ilich Lenin
(1870–1924)

LENIN

Russian Marxist theorist and revolutionary. Lenin was drawn into active politics by the execution of his brother in 1887, and became a Marxist in 1889. In 1903, he founded the Bolshevik Party, later masterminding the 1917 October Revolution. Lenin remained leader of the Soviet state until his death, although he effectively retired in late 1922 after a series of strokes.

Undoubtedly the most influential Marxist theorist of the twentieth century, Lenin was primarily concerned with the issues of organization and revolution. *What is to be Done?* (1902) emphasized the central importance of a tightly organized 'vanguard' party to lead and guide the proletarian class. In *Imperialism, the Highest Stage of Capitalism* (1916), he analysed colonialism as an economic phenomenon and highlighted the possibility of turning world war into class war. *The State and Revolution* (1917) outlined Lenin's firm commitment to the 'insurrectionary road' and rejected electoral democracy as 'bourgeois parliamentarianism'.

Democratic centralism: The Leninist principle of party organization, based on a supposed balance between freedom of discussion and strict unity of action.

vanguard party should be organized according to the principles of **democratic centralism**.

When the Bolsheviks seized power in 1917 they did so as a vanguard party, and therefore in the name of the proletariat. If the Bolshevik Party was acting in the interests of the working class, it followed that opposition parties must represent the interests of classes hostile to the proletariat, in particular the bourgeoisie. The dictatorship of the proletariat required that the revolution be protected against its class enemies, which effectively meant the suppression of all parties other than the Communist Party. By 1920, Russia had become a one-party state. Leninist theory therefore implied the existence of a monopolistic party, which enjoys sole responsibility for articulating the interests of the proletariat and guiding the revolution toward its ultimate goal, that of 'building communism'.

Soviet communism was no less deeply influenced by the rule of Joseph Stalin, 1924–53, than that of Lenin. Indeed more so, as the Soviet Union was more profoundly affected by Stalin's 'second revolution' in the 1930s than it had been by the October Revolution. Stalin's most important ideological shift was to embrace the doctrine of 'Socialism in One Country', initially developed by Bukharin. Announced in 1924, this proclaimed that the Soviet

Union could succeed in 'building socialism' without the need for international revolution. After consolidating himself in power, however, Stalin oversaw a dramatic economic and political upheaval, commencing with the announcement of the first Five Year Plan in 1928. Stalin's Five Year Plans brought about rapid industrialization as well as the swift and total eradication of private enterprise. From 1929, agriculture was collectivized, and

Stalinism: A centrally planned economy supported by systematic and brutal political oppression, based on the structures of Stalin 's Russia.

Soviet peasants were forced at the cost of literally millions of lives to give up their land and join state or collective farms. Economic **Stalinism**, therefore, took the form of state collectivization or 'state socialism'. The capitalist market was entirely removed and replaced by a system of central planning, dominated by the State Planning Committee, 'Gosplan', and administered by a collection of powerful economic ministries based in Moscow.

Major political changes accompanied this 'second revolution'. During the 1930s, Stalin used his power to brutal effect, removing anyone suspected of disloyalty or criticism in an increasingly violent series of purges carried out by the secret police, the NKVD. The membership of the Communist Party was almost halved, over a million people lost their lives, including all the surviving members of Lenin's Politburo, and many millions were imprisoned in labour camps, or gulags. Political Stalinism was therefore a form of totalitarian dictatorship, operating through a monolithic ruling party, in which all forms of debate or criticism were eradicated by terror in what amounted to a civil war conducted against the party itself.

Modern Marxism

While Marxism – or, more usually, Marxism-Leninism – was turned into a

Orthodoxy: Adherence to an established or conventional view, usually enjoying 'official' sanction or support.

secular religion by the **orthodox** communist regimes of eastern Europe and elsewhere, a more subtle and complex form of Marxism developed in western Europe. Referred to as modern Marxism, western Marxism or **neo-Marxism**, this amounted to an attempt to revise or recast the classical ideas of Marx while remaining faithful to certain Marxist principles or aspects of Marxist methodology.

Neo-Marxism: An updated and revised form of Marxism that rejects determinism, the primacy of economics and the privileged status of the proletariat.

Two principal factors shaped the character of modern Marxism. First, when Marx's prediction about the imminent collapse of capitalism failed to materialize, modern Marxists were forced to re-examine conventional class analysis. In particular, they took greater interest in

Hegelian ideas and in the stress on 'Man the creator' found in Marx's early writings. Modern Marxists were thus able to break free from the rigid 'base/superstructure' straightjacket. In short, the class struggle was no longer treated as the beginning and end of social analysis. Second, modern Marxists were usually at odds with, and sometimes profoundly repelled by, the Bolshevik model of orthodox communism.

The Hungarian Marxist Georg Lukács (1885–1971) was one of the first to present Marxism as a humanistic philosophy, emphasizing the process of 'reification', through which capitalism dehumanizes workers by reducing them to passive objects or marketable commodities. Antonio Gramsci drew attention to the degree to which the class system is upheld not simply by unequal economic and political power, but also by bourgeois 'hegemony', the spiritual and cultural supremacy of the ruling class, brought about through the spread of bourgeois values and beliefs via civil society – the media, churches, youth movements, trade unions and so on. A more overtly Hegelian brand of Marxism was developed by the so-called Frankfurt School, whose leading members were Theodor Adorno (1903–69), Max Horkheimer (1895–1973) and Herbert Marcuse (see p. 128). Frankfurt theorists developed what was called 'critical theory', a blend of Marxist political economy, Hegelian philosophy and Freudian psychology, that came to have a considerable impact on the so-called 'new left'. In contrast, a form of structural Marxism emerged from the writings of the French communist Louis Althusser (1918–90). This was based on the assumption that Marx viewed individuals as simply bearers of functions that arise from their structural location. A very different approach has been adopted by analytical Marxists such as John Roemer (1986), who has tried to fuse Marxism with a methodological individualism that is more commonly associated with liberalism.

New left: An ideological movement that sought to revitalize socialist thought by developing a radical critique of advanced industrial society, stressing the need for decentralization, participation and personal liberation.

The death of Marxism?

The year 1989 marked a dramatic watershed in the history of communism and in ideological history generally. Commencing in April with student-led 'democracy movement' demonstrations in Tiananmen Square in Beijing and culminating in November in the fall of the Berlin Wall, the division of Europe into a capitalist West and a communist East was brought to an end. By 1991 the Soviet Union, the model of orthodox communism, had ceased to exist. Where communist regimes continue, as in China, Cuba, Vietnam, North Korea and elsewhere, they have either blended political Stalinism with market-orientated economic reform (most clearly in the case of China) or suffered increasing isolation (as in the case of North Korea). These developments were a result of a number of structural flaws from which orthodox communism suffered. Chief amongst these were that although central planning proved effective in bringing about early industrialization, it could not cope with the complexities of modern industrial societies and, in particular, failed to deliver the levels of prosperity enjoyed in the capitalist West from the 1950s onwards.

There is, nevertheless, considerable debate about the implications of the collapse of communism for Marxism. On the one hand, there are those who, like the 'end of history' theorist, Francis Fukuyama (1989, 1992), argue that the 'collapse of communism' is certain proof of the demise of Marxism as a world-historical force. On the other hand, there are those who argue that the Soviet-style communism that was rejected in the revolutions of 1989–91 differed markedly from the 'Marxism of Marx'. However, to point out that it was not Marxism but a Stalinist version of Marxism–Leninism that collapsed in 1989–91 is very far from demonstrating the continuing relevance of Marxism. A far more serious problem for Marxism is the failure of Marx's predictions (about the inevitable collapse of capitalism and its replacement by communism) to be realized. Quite simply, advanced industrial societies have not been haunted by the 'spectre of communism'. Even

Herbert Marcuse (1898–1979)

German political philosopher and social theorist, cofounder of the Frankfurt School. A refugee from Hitler's Germany, Marcuse lived in the USA and developed a form of neo-Marxism that drew heavily on Hegel and Freud. He came to prominence in the 1960s as a leading new left thinker and 'guru' of the student movement.

Central to Marcuse's work was the portrayal of advanced industrial society as an all-encompassing system of repression, subduing argument and debate and absorbing all forms of opposition – 'repressive tolerance'. Against this 'one-dimensional society', he held up the unashamedly utopian prospect of personal and sexual liberation, looking not to the conventional working class as a revolutionary force but to groups such as students, ethnic minorities, women and workers in the Third World. Marcuse's most important works include *Reason and Revolution* (1941), *Eros and Civilization* (1958) and *One-Dimensional Man* (1964).

those who believe that Marx's views on matters such as alienation and exploitation continue to be relevant, have to accept that classical Marxism failed to recognize the remarkable resilience of capitalism and its capacity to recreate itself. This can certainly be seen in capitalism's seemingly inexorable appetite for technological innovation, meaning that instead of experiencing deepening crises, bringing the proletariat to revolutionary class consciousness, capitalism's crises have become less severe and class consciousness has been diluted by rising living standards.

Some Marxists have responded to these problems by advancing 'post-Marxist' ideas and theories. Post-Marxism, nevertheless, has two implications. The first is that the Marxist project, and the historical materialism on which it is based, should be abandoned in favour of alternative ideas. This is evident in the writings of the one-time Marxist Jean-François Lyotard (1984), who suggested that Marxism as a totalizing theory of history, and for that matter all other 'grand narratives', had been made redundant by the emergence of postmodernity. In its alternative version, post-Marxism consists of an attempt to salvage certain key Marxist insights by attempting to reconcile Marxism with aspects of postmodernism (see p. 62) and post-structuralism. Ernesto Laclau and Chantal Mouffe (1985) accepted that the priority traditionally accorded social class, and the central position of the working class in bringing about social change, were no longer sustainable. In so doing, they opened up space within Marxism for a wide range of other 'moments' of struggle, usually linked to so-called new social movements such as the women's movement, the ecological movement, the gay and lesbian movement, the peace movement, and so on.

Social democracy

As an ideological stance, social democracy took shape around the mid-twentieth century, resulting from the tendency among western socialist parties not only to adopt parliamentary strategies, but also to revise their socialist goals. In particular, they abandoned the goal of abolishing capitalism and sought instead to reform or 'humanize' it. Social democracy therefore came to stand for a broad balance between the market economy, on the one hand, and state intervention, on the other. The major features of the social-democratic stance are the following:

- Social democracy endorses liberal-democratic principles and accepts that political change can and should be brought about peacefully and constitutionally.

- Capitalism is accepted as the only reliable means of generating wealth; socialism, therefore, is not qualitatively different from capitalism.
- Capitalism is nevertheless viewed as morally defective, particularly as a means for distributing wealth; capitalism is associated with structural inequality and poverty.
- The defects of the capitalist system can be rectified by the state through a process of economic and social engineering; the state is the custodian of public or common interest.
- The nation-state is a meaningful unit of political rule, in the sense that states have a significant capacity to regulate economic and social life within their own borders.

Social democracy was most fully developed in the early post-1945 period, during which enthusiasm for social-democratic ideas and theories extended well beyond its socialist homeland, creating, in many western states, a social-democratic consensus. However, since the 1970s and 1980s social democracy has struggled to retain its electoral and political relevance in the face of the advance of neoliberalism and changed economic and social circumstances. The final decades of the twentieth century therefore witnessed a process of ideological retreat on the part of reformist socialist parties across the globe.

Ethical socialism

The theoretical basis for social democracy has been provided more by moral or religious beliefs, rather than by scientific analysis. Social democrats have not accepted the materialist and highly systematic ideas of Marx and Engels, but rather advanced an essentially moral critique of capitalism. In short, socialism is portrayed as morally superior to capitalism because human beings are ethical creatures, bound to one another by the ties of love, sympathy and compassion. Such ideas have often given socialism a markedly utopian character. The moral vision that underlies ethical socialism has been

Humanism:
A philosophy that gives moral priority to the satisfaction of human needs and aspirations.

based on both humanistic and religious principles. Socialism in France, the UK and other Commonwealth countries has been more strongly influenced by the **humanist** ideas of Fourier, Owen and William Morris (1854–96) than by the 'scientific' creed of Karl Marx. However ethical socialism has also drawn heavily on Christianity. For example, there is a long-established tradition of Christian socialism in the UK, reflected in the twentieth century in the work of R. H.

Tawney. The Christian ethic that has inspired UK socialism is that of univer-sal brotherhood, the respect that should be accorded all individuals as creations of God, a principle embodied in the commandment 'Thou shalt love thy neighbour as thyself'. In *The Acquisitive Society* (1921), Tawney condemned unregulated capitalism because it is driven by the 'sin of avarice' rather than faith in a 'common humanity'.

Such religious inspiration has also been evident in the ideas of liberation theology, which has influenced many Catholic developing-world states, especially in Latin America. After years of providing support for repressive regimes in Latin America, Roman Catholic bishops meeting at Medellin, Colombia, in 1968 declared a 'preferential option for the poor'. The reli-gious responsibilities of the clergy were seen to extend beyond the narrowly spiritual and to embrace the social and political struggles of ordinary people. Despite the condemnation of Pope John Paul II and the Vatican, radical priests in many parts of Latin America campaigned against poverty and political oppression and, at times, even backed socialist revolutionary move-ments. Similarly, socialist movements in the predominantly Muslim coun-tries of North Africa, the Middle East and Asia have been inspired by religion. Islam is linked to socialism in that it exhorts the principles of social justice, charity and cooperation, and specifically prohibits usury or profi-teering.

In abandoning scientific analysis in favour of moral or religious princi-ples, however, social democracy weakened the theoretical basis of social-ism. Social democracy has been primarily concerned with the notion of a just or fair distribution of wealth in society. This is embodied in the overriding principle of social democ-racy: **social justice**. Social democracy consequently came to stand for a broad range of views, extending from a left-wing commitment to extending equality and expanding the collective ownership of wealth, to a more right-wing acceptance of the need for market efficiency and individual self-reliance that may be indistinguishable from certain forms of liberalism or conservatism. Attempts have nevertheless been made to give social democ-racy a theoretical basis, usually involving re-examining capitalism itself and redefining the goal of socialism.

Social justice:
A morally justifiable distribution of wealth, usually implying a commitment to greater equality

Revisionist socialism

The original, fundamentalist goal of socialism was that productive wealth should be owned in common by all, and therefore used for the common benefit. This required the abolition of private property and the transition

Eduard Bernstein (1850–1932)

German socialist politician and theorist. An early member of the German Social Democratic Party, Bernstein became one of its leading intellectuals, deeply embroiled in the revisionist controversy. He left the party because of his opposition to the First World War, though he subsequently returned.

Influenced by British Fabianism and the philosophy of Kant (1724–1804), Bernstein attempted to revise and modernize orthodox Marxism. In *Evolutionary Socialism* (1898), he argued that economic crises were becoming less, not more acute, and drew attention to the 'steady advance of the working class'. He therefore called for alliances with the liberal middle class and the peasantry, and emphasized the possibility of a gradual and peaceful transition to socialism. In his later writings, he abandoned all semblance of Marxism and developed a form of ethical socialism based on neo-Kantianism.

from a capitalist mode of production to a socialist one, usually through a process of revolutionary change. Capitalism, in this view, is unredeemable: it is a system of class exploitation and oppression that deserves to be abolished altogether, not merely reformed. However, by the end of the nineteenth century, some socialists had come to believe that analysis of capitalism was defective. The clearest theoretical expression of this belief was found in Eduard Bernstein's *Evolutionary Socialism* ([1898] 1962), which undertook a comprehensive criticism of Marx and the first major attempt at Marxist **revisionism**.

Revisionism: The revision or reworking of a political theory that departs from earlier interpretations in an attempt to present a 'corrected' view.

Bernstein's theoretical approach was largely empirical; he rejected Marx's method of analysis – historical materialism – because the predictions Marx had made had proved to be incorrect. Capitalism had shown itself to be both stable and flexible. Rather than class conflict intensifying, dividing capitalist society into 'two great classes' (the bourgeoisie and the proletariat), Bernstein suggested that capitalism was becoming increasingly complex and differentiated. In particular, the ownership of wealth had widened as a result of the introduction of joint stock companies, owned by a number of shareholders, instead of a single powerful industrialist. The ranks of the middle classes had also swollen by the growing number of salaried employees, technicians, government officials and professional workers, who were neither capitalists nor proletarians. In Bernstein's view, capitalism was no longer a system of naked class oppression. Capitalism could therefore be reformed by the nationalization of major industries and the extension of legal protection and welfare benefits to the working class, a process which Bernstein was confident could be achieved peacefully and democratically.

Western socialist parties have been revisionist in practice, if not always in theory, intent on 'taming' capitalism rather than abolishing it. In some cases they long retained a formal commitment to fundamentalist goals, as in the UK Labour Party's belief in 'the common ownership of the means of production, distribution and exchange', expressed in clause IV of its 1918 constitution. Nevertheless, as the twentieth century progressed, social democrats dropped their commitment to planning as they recognized the efficiency and vigour of the capitalist market. The Swedish Social Democratic Labour Party formally abandoned planning in the 1930s, as did the West German Social Democrats at the Bad Godesberg Congress of 1959, which accepted the principle 'competition when possible; planning when necessary'. In the UK, a similar bid formally to embrace revisionism in the late 1950s ended in failure when the Labour Party conference rejected the then leader Hugh Gaitskell's attempt to abolish clause IV. Nevertheless, when in power, the Labour Party never revealed any appetite for wholesale nationalization.

The abandonment of planning and comprehensive nationalization left social democracy with three more modest objectives. The first of these was the mixed economy, a blend of public and private ownership that stands between free-market capitalism and state collectivism. Nationalization, when advocated by social democrats, is invariably selective and reserved for the 'commanding heights' of the economy, or industries that are thought to be 'natural monopolies'. The 1945–51 Attlee Labour government, for instance, nationalized the major utilities – electricity, gas, coal, steel, the railways and so on – but left most of UK industry in private hands. Second, social democrats sought to regulate or manage capitalist economies in order to maintain economic growth and keep unemployment low. After 1945, most social democratic parties were converted to Keynesianism (see p. 59) as a device for controlling the economy and delivering full employment. Third, socialists were attracted to the welfare state as the principal means of reforming or humanizing capitalism. The welfare state was seen as a redistributive mechanism that would help to promote social equality and eradicate poverty. Capitalism no longer needed to be abolished, only modified through the establishment of reformed or welfare capitalism.

An attempt to give theoretical substance to these developments, and in effect update Bernstein, was made by the UK politician and social theorist Anthony Crosland (1918–77) in *The Future of Socialism* (1956). He

TENSIONS WITHIN
SOCIALISM (1)

SOCIAL DEMOCRACY	v.	COMMUNISM
ethical socialism	←→	scientific socialism
revisionism	←→	fundamentalism
reformism	←→	utopianism
evolution/gradualism	←→	revolution
'humanize' capitalism	←→	abolish capitalism
redistribution	←→	common ownership
ameliorate class conflict	←→	classless society
relative equality	←→	absolute equality
mixed economy	←→	state collectivization
economic management	←→	central planning
parliamentary party	←→	vanguard party
political pluralism	←→	dictatorship of proletariat
liberal-democratic state	←→	proletarian/people's state

Managerialism: The theory that a governing class of managers, technocrats and state officials – those who possess technical and administrative skills – dominates both capitalist and communist societies.

subscribed to **managerialism**, in believing that modern capitalism bore little resemblance to the nineteenth-century model that Marx had had in mind. Crosland suggested that a new class of managers, experts and technocrats had supplanted the old capitalist class and come to dominate all advanced industrial societies, both capitalist and communist. Crosland believed that the ownership of wealth had become divorced from its control. Whereas shareholders, who own businesses, were principally concerned with profit, salaried managers, who make day-to-day business decisions, have a broader range of goals, including the maintenance of industrial harmony as well as the public image of their company. Marxism had therefore become irrelevant: if capitalism could no longer be viewed as a system of class exploitation, the fundamentalist goals of nationalization and planning were simply outdated. Crosland thus recast socialism in terms of politics of social justice, rather than the politics of ownership. Wealth need not be owned in common, but it could be redistributed through a welfare state, financed by progressive taxation. However, Crosland recognized that economic growth plays a crucial role in the achievement of socialism. A growing economy is essential to generate the tax revenues needed to finance more generous social expenditure, and the prosperous will only be prepared to finance the needy if their own living standards are underwritten by economic growth.

The crisis of social democracy

During the early post-1945 period, Keynesian social democracy – or traditional social democracy – appeared to have triumphed. Its strength was that it harnessed the dynamism of the market without succumbing to the levels of inequality and instability that Marx believed would doom capitalism. Nevertheless, Keynesian social democracy was based on an (arguably) inherently unstable compromise. On the one hand, there was a pragmatic acceptance of the market as the only reliable means of generating wealth. This reluctant conversion to the market meant that social democrats accepted that there was no viable socialist alternative to the market, meaning that the socialist project was reborn as an attempt to reform, not replace, capitalism. On the other hand, the socialist ethic survived in the form of a commitment to social justice. This, in turn, was linked to a weak notion of equality: distributive equality, the idea that poverty should be reduced and inequality narrowed through the redistribution of wealth from rich to poor.

At the heart of Keynesian social democracy there lay a conflict between its commitment to both economic efficiency and egalitarianism. During the 'long boom' of the postwar period, social democrats were not forced to confront this conflict because sustained growth, low unemployment and low inflation improved the living standards of all social groups and helped to finance more generous welfare provision. However, as Crosland had anticipated, recession in the 1970s and 1980s created strains within social democracy, polarizing socialist thought into more clearly defined left-wing and right-wing positions. Recession precipitated a 'fiscal crisis of the welfare state', simultaneously increasing demand for welfare support as unemployment re-emerged, and squeezing the tax revenues that financed welfare spending, because fewer people were at work and businesses were less profitable. A difficult question had to be answered: should social democrats attempt to restore efficiency to the market economy, which might mean cutting inflation and possibly taxes, or should they defend the poor and the lower paid by maintaining or even expanding welfare provision?

This crisis of social democracy was intensified in the 1980s and 1990s by a combination of further factors. In the first place, the electoral viability of social democracy was undermined by deindustrialization and the shrinkage of the traditional working class, the social base of Keynesian social democracy. Whereas in the early post-1945 period the tide of democracy had flowed with progressive politics, since the 1980s it has increasingly been orientated around the interests of what J. K. Galbraith (1992) called the 'contented majority'. Social democratic parties paid a high price for these social and electoral shifts. For instance, the UK Labour Party lost four successive general elections between 1979 and 1992; the SPD in Germany was out of power between 1982 and 1998; and the French Socialist Party suffered crushing defeats, notably in 1993 and 2002, when the Socialist candidate, Lionel Jospin, failed to get through to the run-off stage of the presidential election. Second, the economic viability of social democracy has been undermined by the advance of economic globalization. The integration of national economies into a larger, global capitalist system not only rendered Keynesianism unworkable, because Keynesian policies require that governments manage discrete national economies, but also intensified international competition, creating pressure to reduce tax and spending levels, particularly by reforming the welfare state, and to promote labour flexibility. Third, the intellectual credibility of social democracy was badly damaged by the collapse of communism. Not only did this create a world without any significant non-capitalist economic forms, but it also undermined faith in what Anthony Giddens (see p. 138) called the 'cybernetic model' of socialism, in which the state, acting as the brain within society, serves as the principal agent of economic and social reform. In this light, Keynesian social democracy could be viewed as only a more modest version of the 'top-down' state socialism that had been so abruptly discarded in the revolutions of 1989–91.

Neo-revisionism and the 'third way'

Since the 1980s, reformist socialist parties across the globe have undergone a further bout of revisionism, sometimes termed neo-revisionism, in which they have distanced themselves, to a greater or lesser extent, from the principles and commitments of traditional social democracy. The resulting ideological stance has been described in various ways, including 'new' social democracy, the '**third way**', the 'radical centre', the 'active centre' and the '*Neue Mitte*' (new middle). However, the ideological significance of neo-revisionism, and its relationship to traditional social democracy in particular and to socialism in general, are shrouded in debate and confusion. This is partly because neo-revisionism has taken different forms in different

Third way: The notion of an alternative form of economics to both state socialism and free-market capitalism, sought at different times by conservatives, socialists and fascists.

countries. There are therefore a number of contrasting neo-revisionist projects, including those associated with Bill Clinton and the 'new' Democrats in the USA and Tony Blair and 'new' Labour in the UK, as well as those that have emerged in states such as Germany, the Netherlands, Italy and New Zealand. In some cases, these projects are nonsocialist or post-socialist in character, while in others an explicit attempt has been made to salvage socialist or at least social-democratic values.

The central thrust of neo-revisionism has been the attempt to develop a so-called 'third way'. The third way broadly encapsulates the idea of an alternative to both capitalism and socialism. In its modern form, the third way represents, more specifically, an alternative to old-style social democracy and neoliberalism. Although the third way is (perhaps inherently) imprecise and subject to a number of interpretations, certain characteristic third-way themes can nevertheless be identified. The first of these is the belief that socialism, at least in the form of 'top-down' state intervention, is dead: there is no alternative to what the revised clause IV of the UK Labour Party's 1995 constitution refers to as 'a dynamic market economy'. With this goes a general acceptance of globalization and the belief that capitalism has mutated into an 'information society' or 'knowledge economy', which places a premium on information technology, individual skills and both labour and business flexibility. This general acceptance of the market over the state, and the adoption of a pro-business and pro-enterprise stance, means that the third way attempts to build on, rather than reverse, the neoliberal revolution of the 1980s and 1990s.

The second key third-way belief is its emphasis on community and moral responsibility. Community, of course, has a long socialist heritage, drawing as it does, like fraternity and cooperation, on the idea of a social essence. Although the third way accepts many of the economic theories of neoliberalism, it firmly rejects its philosophical basis and its moral and social implications. The danger of market fundamentalism is that it generates a free-for-all that undermines the moral foundations of society. Some versions of the third way, notably the so-called 'Blair project' in the UK, nevertheless attempt to

Communitarianism:
A belief that the self or person is constituted through the community in the sense that there are no 'unencumbered selves' (see p. 316).

fuse **communitarian** ideas with liberal ones, creating a form of communitarian liberalism, which in many ways resembles the 'New Liberalism' of the late nineteenth century. The cornerstone belief of communitarian liberalism is that rights and responsibilities are intrinsically bound together: all rights must be balanced against responsibilities and vice versa. This view is based on a so-called 'new' individualism, which endorses autonomy but stresses that individuals operate within a context of interdependence and reciprocity.

Third, supporters of the third way tend to adopt a consensus view of society, in contrast to socialism's conflict view of society. This is evident, for

Anthony Giddens
(born 1938)

GIDDENS

UK social and political theorist. Giddens was director of the London School of Economics, 1997–2003. Frequently referred to as 'Tony Blair's guru', he has had a strong impact on the development of a new social-democratic agenda in the UK and elsewhere.

Giddens' importance as a social theorist was established by his theory of structuration, developed in works such as *New Rules of Sociological Method* (1976) and *The Constitution of Society* (1984), which set out to transcend the conventional dualism of structure and agency. In his later work, including *Beyond Left and Right* (1994), *The Third Way* (1998), *The Runaway World* (1999) and *The Third Way and Its Critics* (2000), he has sought to remodel social democracy in the light of the advent of late modernity, taking account of developments such as globalization, de-traditionalization and the increase in social reflexivity (reciprocity and interdependence).

example, in the tendency of community to highlight ties that bind all members of society, and thus to ignore, or conceal, class differences and economic inequalities. Similarly, the idea of a 'knowledge-driven economy' suggests that material rewards are no longer distributed on the basis of structural inequalities but now correspond more closely to the fluid distribution of work-related skills across society. A faith in consensus and social harmony is also reflected in the value framework of the third way, which rejects the either/or approach of conventional moral and ideological thinking, and offers what almost amounts to a non-dualistic world-view. Third-way politicians thus typically endorse enterprise *and* fairness, opportunity *and* security, self-reliance *and* interdependence, and so on.

Fourth, the third way has substituted a concern with social inclusion for the traditional socialist commitment to equality. This is evident in the stress placed on liberal ideas such as opportunity, and even meritocracy. Egalitarianism is therefore scaled down to a belief in equality of opportunities or 'asset-based egalitarianism', the right of access to assets and opportunities that enable individuals to realise their potential. Third-way proposals for welfare reform therefore typically reject both the neoliberal emphasis on 'standing on your own two feet' and the social democratic belief in 'cradle to grave' welfare. Instead, welfare should be targeted on the 'socially excluded' and should follow the modern liberal approach of 'helping people to help themselves', or as Clinton put it, giving people 'a hand up, not a hand out'. Welfare policies

TENSIONS WITHIN
SOCIALISM (2)

SOCIAL DEMOCRACY	v.	THIRD WAY
ideological	←→	pragmatic
nation-state	←→	globalization
industrial society	←→	information society
class politics	←→	community
mixed economy	←→	market economy
full employment	←→	full employability
equality of outcome	←→	equality of opportunity
concern for underdog	←→	meritocracy
social justice	←→	opportunity for all
irradicate poverty	←→	promote inclusion
social rights	←→	rights and responsibilities
cradle-to-grave welfare	←→	welfare-to-work
social-reformist state	←→	competition/market state

should, in particular, aim to widen access to work, in line with the US idea of 'workfare', the belief that welfare support should be conditional on an individual's willingness to seek work and become self-reliant.

Finally, the third way is characterized by new thinking about the proper role of the state. The third way embraces the idea of a competition state or market state. A competition state is a state whose principal role is to pursue strategies for national prosperity in conditions of intensifying global competition. The state should therefore concentrate on social investment, which means improving the infrastructure of the economy and, most importantly, strengthening the skills and knowledge of the country's workforce. Education rather than social security should therefore be the government's priority, with education being valued not in its own right, because it furthers personal development (the modern liberal view), but because it promotes employability and benefits the economy (the utilitarian or classical liberal view). From this perspective, the government is essentially a cultural actor, whose purpose is to shape or reshape the population's attitudes, values, skills, beliefs and knowledge, rather than to carry out a programme of economic and social engineering.

Socialism in the twenty-first century

Some would regard a discussion of socialism in the twenty-first century as pointless. Socialism is dead and the obituaries have been written. The evidence to sustain this view is all too familiar. The eastern European revolutions of 1989–91 removed the last vestiges of 'actually existing socialism', and where nominally socialist regimes survive, as in China and Cuba, it is only because of the willingness of communist parties to introduce market reforms. Elsewhere, parliamentary socialist parties have been in flight from traditional principles, attempting to maintain electoral credibility by demonstrating growing sympathy for market-orientated economics. The only serious debate has been about the cause of socialism's death. End-of-history theorists such as Francis Fukuyama (1992) have put it down to the inherent flaws in all socialist models and the manifest superiority of liberal capitalism. Others have highlighted the tendency of a globalized economy irresistibly to draw all nations into a global capitalist system. Still others have emphasized the shrinkage of socialism's political base from the mass ranks of the working class to an isolated and depoliticized underclass. Whatever the explanation, the world has shifted dramatically and permanently to the right, consigning socialism to what Leon Trotsky (see p. 171), in very different circumstances, called the 'dustbin of history'.

However, socialists with a longer sense of history are unlikely to succumb to this despond. Just as predictions at the beginning of the twentieth century about the inevitable victory of socialism proved to be flawed, so proclamations about the death of socialism made at the beginning of the twenty-first century are likely to be unreliable. Indeed, as recently as the 1960s it was free-market liberalism that was considered to be redundant, while socialism appeared to be making irresistible progress. Hopes for the survival of socialism largely rest on the enduring, and perhaps intrinsic, imperfections of the capitalist system. As Ralph Miliband put it in his final work, *Socialism for a Sceptical Age* (1995), 'the notion that capitalism has been thoroughly transformed and represents the best that humankind can ever hope to achieve is a dreadful slur on the human race'. In that sense, socialism is destined to survive if only because it serves as a reminder that human development can extend beyond market individualism. Moreover, globalization may bring opportunities for socialism as well as challenges. Just as capitalism is being transformed by the growing significance of the supranational dimension of economic life, socialism may be in the process of being transformed into a critique of global exploitation and inequality. Although it is as yet theoretically unsophisticated, this, after all, is the thrust of the emergent anti-capitalist or anti-globalization movement. In other words, socialism in the twenty-first century may be reborn as global anti-capitalism.

If socialism survives, what kind of socialism will it be? What seems clear is that it is unlikely to draw inspiration from the bureaucratic authoritarianism of the Soviet era. Marxism–Leninism may indeed be dead, and few socialist tears would be shed at its passing. One of the consequences of this may be a re-examination of Marx's legacy, now disentangled from the experience of Leninism and Stalinism. However, this is more likely to be Marx the humanist socialist rather than the more familiar twentieth-century image of Marx the economic **determinist**. As far as parliamentary socialism is concerned, an important task remains. Keynesian social democracy, at least in its post-1945 guise, may have been discarded, but a politically and electorally viable alternative to market capitalism has yet to emerge. Interest in the third way and in other neo-revisionist projects undoubtedly provides evidence of the desire for 'new thinking' within socialism, and particularly of the need to resist fundamentalist neoliberalism, but it is difficult to see it as proof of socialism's rebirth. Meanwhile, the search for the new socialist paradigm continues.

Determinism: A belief that human actions and choices are entirely conditioned by external factors; determinism implies that free will is a myth.

Questions for discussion

→ What is distinctive about the socialist view of equality?

→ Why do socialists favour collectivism, and how have they tried to promote it?

→ What are the implications of trying to achieve socialism through revolutionary means?

→ What are the implications of trying to achieve socialism through democratic means?

→ On what grounds have Marxists predicted the inevitable collapse of capitalism?

→ How closely did orthodox communism reflect the classical idea of Marx?

→ Is social democracy really a form of socialism?

→ Was the social-democratic 'compromise' inherently unstable?

→ Can there be a 'third way' between capitalism and socialism?

Further reading

Giddens, A., *The Third Way: The Renewal of Social Democracy* (Cambridge: Polity Press, 1998). Widely regarded as the key text of third-way politics.

Harrington, M., *Socialism: Past and Future* (London: Pluto Press, 1993). A committed, passionate and insightful discussion of where socialism has been and where it is going.

Martell, L. (ed.), *Social Democracy: Global and National Perspectives* (Basingstoke and New York: Palgrave Macmillan, 2001). A collection of articles that analyse developments within social democracy in the light of globalization, Europeanization and different national traditions.

McLellan, D., *The Thought of Karl Marx*, 2nd edn (London: Macmillan, 1980). A thorough and helpful introduction to Marx's work, supported by selective texts.

Moschonas, G., *In the Name of Social Democracy – The Great Transformation: 1945 to the Present* (London and New York: Verso, 2002). An impressive and thorough account of the nature, history and impact of social democracy that focuses on the emergence of 'new social democracy'.

Sassoon, D., *One Hundred Years of Socialism* (London: Fontana, 1997). A very stylish and detailed account of the life and times of democratic socialist ideas and movements.

Wright, A., *Socialisms: Theories and Practices* (Oxford and New York: Oxford University Press, 1996). A good, brief and accessible introduction to the basic themes of socialism, highlighting the causes of disagreement within the socialist family.

CHAPTER 5

NATIONALISM

The word 'nation' has been used since the thirteenth century and derives from the Latin *nasci*, meaning to be born. In the form of *natio*, it referred to a group of people united by birth or birthplace. In its original usage, nation thus implied a breed of people or a racial group, but possessed no political significance. It was not until the late eighteenth century that the term acquired political overtones, as individuals and groups started to be classified as 'nationalists'. The term 'nationalism' was first used in print in 1789 by the anti-Jacobin French priest Augustin Barruel. By the mid-nineteenth century, nationalism was widely recognized as a political doctrine or movement; for example, as a major ingredient of the revolutions that swept across Europe in 1848.

Nationalism can broadly be defined as the belief that the nation is the central principle of political organization. As such, it is based on two core assumptions. First, humankind is naturally divided into distinct nations and, second, the nation is the most appropriate, and perhaps only legitimate, unit of political rule. Classical political nationalism therefore set out to bring the borders of the state into line with the boundaries of the nation. Within so-called nation-states, nationality and citizenship would therefore coincide. However, nationalism is a complex and highly diverse ideological phenomenon. Not only are there distinctive political, cultural and ethnic forms of nationalism, but the political implications of nationalism have been wide-ranging and sometimes contradictory. Although nationalism has been associated with a principled belief in national self-determination, based on the assumption that all nations are equal, it has also been used to defend traditional institutions and the established social order, as well as to fuel programmes of war, conquest and imperialism. Nationalism has been linked to widely contrasting ideological traditions, ranging from liberalism to fascism.

Origins and development

The idea of nationalism was born during the French Revolution. Previously, countries had been thought of as 'realms', 'principalities' or 'kingdoms'. The inhabitants of a country were 'subjects', their political identity being formed by an allegiance to a ruler or ruling dynasty, rather than any sense of national identity or **patriotism**. However, the revolutionaries in France who rose up against Louis XVI in 1789 did so in the name of the people, and understood the people to be the 'French nation'. Their ideas were influenced by the writings of Jean-Jacques Rousseau (see p. 153) and the new doctrine of popular self-government. Nationalism was therefore a revolutionary and democratic creed, reflecting the idea that 'subjects of the crown' should become 'citizens of France'. The **nation** should be its own master. However, such ideas were not the exclusive property of the French. During the Revolutionary and Napoleonic Wars (1792–1815), much of continental Europe was invaded by France, giving rise to both resentment against France and a desire for independence. In Italy and Germany, long divided into a collection of states, the experience of conquest helped to forge, for the first time, a consciousness of national unity, expressed in a new language of nationalism, inherited from France. Nationalist ideas also spread to Latin America in the early nineteenth century, where Simon Bolivar (1783–1830), 'the Liberator', led revolutions against Spanish rule in what was then New Grenada, now the countries of Colombia, Venezuela and Ecuador, as well as in Peru and Bolivia.

Patriotism: Literally, love of one 's fatherland; a psychological attachment and loyalty to one's nation or country (see p. 155).

Nation: A collection of people bound together by shared values and traditions, a common language, religion and history, and usually occupying the same geographical area (see pp. 148–51).

In many respects, nationalism developed into the most successful and compelling of political creeds, helping to shape and reshape history in many parts of the world for over two hundred years. The rising tide of nationalism redrew the map of Europe in the nineteenth century as the autocratic and multinational empires of Turkey, Austria and Russia started to crumble in the face of liberal and nationalist pressure. In 1848, nationalist uprisings broke out in the Italian states, amongst the Czechs and the Hungarians, and in Germany, where the desire for national unity was expressed in the creation of the short-lived Frankfurt parliament. The nineteenth century was a period of nation building. Italy, once dismissed by the Austrian Chancellor Metternich as a 'mere geographical expression', became a united state in 1861, the process of unification being completed with the acquisition of Rome in 1870. Germany, formerly a collection of 39 states, was unified in 1871, following the Franco-Prussian War.

Nevertheless, it would be a mistake to assume that nationalism was either an irresistible or a genuinely popular movement during this period. Enthusiasm for nationalism was largely restricted to the rising middle classes, who were attracted to the ideas of national unity and constitutional government. Although middle-class nationalist movements kept the dream of national unity or independence alive, they were nowhere strong enough to accomplish the process of nation building on their own. Where nationalist goals were realized, as in Italy and Germany, it was because nationalism coincided with the ambition of rising states such as Piedmont and Prussia. For example, German unification owed more to the Prussian army, which defeated Austria in 1866 and France in 1870–71, than it did to the liberal nationalist movement.

However, by the end of the nineteenth century nationalism had become a truly popular movement, with the spread of flags, national anthems, patriotic poetry and literature, public ceremonies and national holidays. Nationalism became the language of mass politics, made possible by the growth of primary education, mass literacy and the spread of popular newspapers. The character of nationalism also changed. Nationalism had previously been associated with liberal and progressive movements, but was increasingly taken up by conservative and reactionary politicians. Nationalism came to stand for social cohesion, order and stability, particularly in the face of the growing challenge of socialism, which embodied the ideas of social revolution and international working-class solidarity. Nationalism sought to integrate the increasingly powerful working class into the nation, and so to preserve the established social structure. Patriotic fervour was no longer aroused by the prospect of political liberty or democracy, but by the commemoration of past national glories and military victories. Such nationalism became increasingly **chauvinistic** and **xenophobic**. Each nation claimed its own unique or superior qualities, while other nations were regarded as alien, untrustworthy, even menacing. This new climate of popular nationalism helped to fuel policies of colonial expansion that intensified dramatically in the 1870s and 1880s, and, by the end of the century, had brought most of the world's population under European control. It also contributed to a mood of international rivalry and suspicion, which led to world war in 1914.

Chauvinism: Uncritical and unreasoned dedication to a cause or group, typically based on a belief in its superiority, as in 'national chauvinism' or 'male chauvinism'.

Xenophobia: A fear or hatred of foreigners; pathological ethnocentrism.

The end of the First World War saw the completion of the process of nation building in central and eastern Europe. At the Paris Peace Conference, US President Woodrow Wilson advocated the principle of national self-determination. The German, Austro-Hungarian and Russian empires were broken up and eight new states created, including Finland, Hungary, Czechoslovakia, Poland and Yugoslavia. These new countries were designed to be nation-states that conformed to the geography of existing national or ethnic groups. However, the First World War failed to resolve the serious national tensions that had precipitated conflict in the first place. Indeed, the experience of defeat and disappointment with the terms of the peace treaties left an inheritance of frustrated ambition and bitterness. This was most evident in Germany, Italy and Japan, where fascist or authoritarian movements came to power in the inter-war period by promising to restore national pride through policies of expansion and empire. Nationalism was therefore a powerful factor leading to war in both 1914 and 1939.

During the twentieth century the doctrine of nationalism, which had been born in Europe, spread throughout the globe as the peoples of Asia and Africa rose in opposition to colonial rule. The process of **colonialism** had involved not only the establishment of political control and economic dominance, but also the importation of western ideas, including nationalism, which began to be used against the colonial masters themselves. Nationalist uprisings took place in Egypt in 1919 and quickly spread throughout the Middle East. The Anglo-Afghan war also broke out in 1919, and rebellions took place in India, the Dutch East Indies and Indochina. After 1945, the map of Africa and Asia was redrawn as the British, French, Dutch and Portuguese empires each disintegrated in the face of nationalist movements that either succeeded in negotiating independence or winning wars of 'national liberation'.

Colonialism: The theory or practice of establishing control over a foreign territory, usually by settlement or economic domination.

Anti-colonialism not only witnessed the spread of western-style nationalism to the developing world, but also generated new forms of nationalism. Nationalism in the developing world has embraced a wide range of movements. In China, Vietnam and parts of Africa, nationalism has been fused with Marxism, and national liberation has been regarded not simply as a political goal but as part of a social revolution. Elsewhere, developing-world nationalism has been anti-western, rejecting both liberal democratic and revolutionary socialist conceptions of nationhood. This has been particularly evident in the rise of forms of religious nationalism and especially in the emergence of religious fundamentalism. The relationship between nationalism and religious fundamentalism is examined in Chapter 10.

Core themes – for the love of country

To treat nationalism as an ideology in its own right is to encounter at least three problems. The first is that nationalism is sometimes classified as a political doctrine rather than a fully fledged ideology. Whereas, for instance, liberalism, conservatism and socialism constitute complex sets of interrelated ideas and values, nationalism, the argument goes, is at heart the simple belief that the nation is the natural and proper unit of government. The drawback of this view is that it focuses only on what might be regarded as 'classical' political nationalism, and ignores the many other, and in some respects no less significant, manifestations of nationalism, such as cultural nationalism and ethnic nationalism. The core feature of nationalism is therefore not its narrow association with self-government and the nation-state, but its broader link to movements and ideas that in whatever way acknowledge the central importance to political life of the nation. Second, nationalism is sometimes portrayed as an essentially psychological phenomenon – usually as loyalty towards one's nation or dislike of other nations – instead of as a theoretical construct. Undoubtedly, one of the key features of nationalism is the potency of its affective or emotional appeal, but to understand it in these terms alone is to mistake the ideology of nationalism for the sentiment of patriotism.

Third, nationalism has a schizophrenic political character. At different times, nationalism has been progressive and reactionary, democratic and authoritarian, rational and irrational, and left-wing and right-wing. It has also been associated with almost all the major ideological traditions. In their different ways, liberals, conservatives, socialists, fascists and even communists have been attracted to nationalism; perhaps only anarchism, by virtue of its outright rejection of the state, is fundamentally at odds with nationalism. Nevertheless, although nationalist doctrines have been used by a bewildering variety of political movements and associated with sometimes diametrically opposed political causes, a bedrock of nationalist ideas and theories can be identified. The most important of these are the following:

- the nation
- organic community
- self-determination
- identity politics.

The nation

The basic belief of nationalism is that the nation is, or should be, the central principle of political organization. However, much confusion surrounds what nations are and how they can be defined. In everyday language, words such as 'nation', 'state', 'country' and even 'race' are often confused or used as if they are interchangeable. Many political disputes, moreover, are really disputes about whether a particular group of people should be regarded as a nation, and should therefore enjoy the rights and status associated with nationhood. This applies, for instance, to the Tibetans, the Kurds, the Palestinians, the Basques, the Tamils, and so on. On the most basic level, nations are cultural entities, collections of people bound together by shared values and traditions, in particular a common language, religion and history, and usually occupying the same geographical area. From this point of view, the nation can be defined by 'objective' factors: people who satisfy a requisite set of cultural criteria can be said to belong to a nation; those who do not can be classified as non-nationals or members of foreign nations. However, to define a nation simply as a group of people bound together by a common culture and traditions raises some very difficult questions. Although particular cultural features are commonly associated with nationhood, notably language, religion, ethnicity, history and tradition, there is no blueprint nor any objective criteria that can establish where and when a nation exists.

Language is often taken to be the clearest symbol of nationhood. A language embodies distinctive attitudes, values and forms of expression that produce a sense of familiarity and belonging. German nationalism, for instance, has traditionally been founded on a sense of cultural unity, reflected in the purity and survival of the German language. Nevertheless, at the same time, there are peoples who share the same language without having any conception of a common national identity: Americans, Australians and New Zealanders may speak English as a first language, but certainly do not think of themselves as members of an 'English nation'. Other nations have enjoyed a substantial measure of national unity without possessing a national language, as is the case in Switzerland where, in the absence of a Swiss language, three major languages are spoken: French, German and Italian.

Religion is another major component of nationhood. Religion expresses common moral values and spiritual beliefs. In Northern Ireland, people who speak the same language are divided along religious lines: most Protestants regard themselves as Unionists and wish to preserve their links with the UK, while many in the Catholic community favour a united Ireland. Islam has been a major factor in forming national consciousness in much of North Africa and the Middle East. On the other hand, religious beliefs do not always coincide with a sense of nationhood. Divisions between Catholics and Protestants in mainland UK do not inspire rival nationalisms, nor has the remarkable religious diversity found in the USA threatened to divide the country into a collection of distinct nations. At the same time, countries such as Poland, Italy, Brazil and the Philippines share a common Catholic faith but do not feel that they belong to a unified 'Catholic nation'.

Nations have also been based on a sense of ethnic or racial unity. This was particularly evident in Germany during the Nazi period. However, nationalism usually has a cultural rather than a biological basis; it reflects an ethnic unity that may be based on race, but more usually draws from shared values and common cultural beliefs. The nationalism of US blacks, for example, is based less on colour than on their distinctive history and culture. Nations thus usually share a common history and traditions. Not uncommonly, national identity is preserved by recalling past glories, national independence, the birthdays of national leaders or important military victories. The USA celebrates Independence Day and Thanksgiving; Bastille Day is commemorated in France; in the UK, ceremonies continue to mark Armistice Day. However, nationalist feelings may be based more on future expectations than on shared memories or a common past. This applies in the case of immigrants who have been 'naturalized', and is most evident in the USA, a 'land of immigrants'. The journey of the Mayflower and the War of Independence have no direct relevance for most Americans, whose families arrived centuries after these events occurred.

The cultural unity that supposedly expresses itself in nationhood is therefore very difficult to pin down. It reflects a varying combination of cultural factors, rather than any precise formula. Ultimately, therefore, nations can only be defined 'subjectively', by their members, not by any set of external factors. In this sense, the nation is a psycho-political entity, a group of people who regard themselves as a natural political community and are distinguished by shared loyalty or affection in the form of patriotism. Objective difficulties such as the absence of land, small population or lack of economic resources are of little significance if a group of people insists on demanding what it sees as 'national rights'. Latvia, for example, became an independent nation in 1991 despite having a population of only 2. 6 million (barely half of whom are ethnic Lats), no source of fuel and very few natural resources. Likewise, Kurdish peoples of the Middle East have nationalist aspirations, even though the Kurds have never enjoyed formal political unity and are presently spread over parts of Turkey, Iraq, Iran and Syria.

The fact that nations are formed through a combination of objective and subjective factors has given rise to rival concepts of the nation. While all nationalists agree that nations are a blend of cultural and psycho-political

THE NATION

LIBERALS subscribe to a 'civic' view of the nation that places as much emphasis on political allegiance as on cultural unity. Nations are moral entities in the sense that they are endowed with rights, notably an equal right to self-determination.

CONSERVATIVES regard the nation as primarily an 'organic' entity, bound together by a common ethnic identity and a shared history. As the source of social cohesion and collective identity, the nation is perhaps the most politically significant of social groups.

SOCIALISTS tend to view the nation as an artificial division of humankind whose purpose is to disguise social injustice and prop up the established order. Political movements and allegiances should therefore have an international, not a national, character.

ANARCHISTS have generally held that the nation is tainted by its association with the state, and therefore with oppression. The nation is thus seen as a myth, designed to promote obedience and subjugation in the interests of the ruling elite.

FASCISTS view the nation as an organically unified social whole, often defined by race, which gives purpose and meaning to individual existence. However, nations are pitted against one another in a struggle for survival in which some are fitted to succeed and others to go to the wall.

FUNDAMENTALISTS regard nations as, in essence, religious entities, communities of 'believers'. Nevertheless, religion is seldom coextensive with conventional nations, hence the idea of transnational religious communities, such as the 'nation of Islam'.

factors, they disagree strongly about where the balance between the two lies. On the one hand, 'exclusive' concepts of the nation stress the importance of ethnic unity and a shared history. By viewing national identity as 'given', unchanging and indeed unchangeable, this implies that nations are characterized by common descent and so blurs the distinction between nations and races. Nations are thus held together by 'primordial bonds', powerful and seemingly innate emotional attachment to a language, religion, traditional

Primordialism: The belief that nations are ancient and deep-rooted, fashioned, variously, out of psychology, culture and biology

way of life or a homeland. To different degrees, conservatives and fascists adopt such a view of the nation. On the other hand, 'inclusive' concepts of the nation highlight the importance of civic consciousness and patriotic loyalty, suggesting that nations may be multi-racial, multi-ethnic, multi-religious and so forth. This, in turn, tends to blur the distinction between the nation and the state, and thus between nationality and **citizenship**. Liberals and socialists tend to adopt an inclusive view of the nation. These different approaches to the nation are illustrated in Figure 5.1.

> **Citizenship**: Membership of a state; a relationship between the individual and the state based on reciprocal rights and responsibilities.

Figure 5.1
Views of the nation

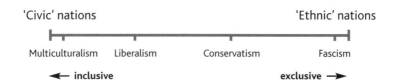

Organic community

Although nationalists may disagree about the defining features of the nation, they are unified by their belief that nations are organic communities. Humankind, in other words, is naturally divided into a collection of nations, each possessing a distinctive character and separate identity. This, nationalists argue, is why a 'higher' loyalty and deeper political significance attaches to the nation than to any other social group or collective body. Whereas, for instance, class, gender, religion and language may be important in particular societies, or may come to prominence in particular circumstances, the bonds of nationhood are more fundamental. National ties and loyalties are found in all societies, they endure over time, and they operate at an instinctual, even primordial, level. Nevertheless, different explanations have been provided for this. 'Primordialist' approaches to nationalism portray national identity as historically embedded: nations are rooted in a common cultural heritage and language that may long predate statehood or the quest for independence, and are characterized by deep emotional attachments that resemble kinship ties. Anthony Smith (1986), for instance, highlighted the continuity between modern nations and pre-modern ethnic communities, which he called 'ethnies'. This implies that there is little difference between **ethnicity** and nationality, modern nations essentially being updated versions of immemorial ethnic

> **Ethnicity**: A sentiment of loyalty towards a particular population, cultural group or territorial area; bonds that are cultural rather than racial.

communities. In contrast, 'situationalist' approaches to nationalism suggests that nation identity is forged in response to changing situations and historical challenges. Ernest Gellner (1983) thus emphasized the degree to which nationalism is linked to modernization, and in particular to the process of industrialization. He stressed that, while pre-modern or 'agro-literate' societies were structured by a network of feudal bonds and loyalties, emerging industrial societies promoted social mobility, self-striving and competition, and so required a new source of cultural cohesion. This was provided by nationalism. Although Gellner's theory suggests that nations coalesced in response to particular social conditions and circumstances, it also implies that the national community is deep-rooted and enduring, as a return to pre-modern loyalties and identities is unthinkable.

The national community is a particular kind of **community**, however. The German sociologist Ferdinand Tonnies (1855–1936) distinguished between

Community:
A principle or sentiment based on the collective identity of a social group; bonds of comradeship, loyalty and duty.

two quite different forms of social relationship. *Gemeinschaft*, or 'community' is typically found in traditional societies and is characterized by natural affection and mutual respect. In contrast, *Gesellschaft*, or 'association' consists of the looser, artificial and contractual relationships that are typically found in urban and industrialized societies. For nationalists, the nation is definitely forged out of *Gemeinschaft*-type relationships. Nevertheless, as Benedict Anderson (1983) pointed out, nations constitute only 'imagined communities'. Anderson argued that nations exist more as mental images than as genuine communities that require a degree of face-to-face interaction to sustain the notion of a common identity. Within nations, individuals only ever meet a tiny proportion of those with whom they supposedly share a national identity. If nations exist, they exist as imagined artifices, constructed for us through education, the mass media and a process of political socialization.

The idea that nations are 'imagined', not organic, communities has been seized on by critics of nationalism. '**Constructivist**' approaches to national-

Constructivism: The theory that meaning is imposed on the external world by the beliefs and assumptions we hold; reality is a social construct

ism regard national identity as very largely an ideological construct, usually serving the interests of powerful groups. The Marxist historian Eric Hobsbawm (1983), for example, highlighted the extent to which nations are based on 'invented traditions'. Hobsbawm argued that a belief in historical continuity and cultural purity is invariably a myth, and, what is more, a myth created by nationalism itself. In this view, nationalism creates nations, not the other way round. A widespread consciousness of nationhood did not, for example, develop until the late nineteenth century, perhaps fashioned by the invention of national anthems and national flags, and the extension of primary education and thus mass literacy.

Self-determination

Nationalism as a political ideology only emerged when the idea of national community encountered the doctrine of popular **sovereignty**. This occurred during the French Revolution and was influenced by the writings of Jean-Jacques Rousseau, sometimes seen as the 'father' of modern nationalism. Although Rousseau did not specifically address the question of the nation, or discuss the phenomenon of nationalism, his stress on popular sovereignty, expressed in the idea of the 'general will', was the seed from which nationalist doctrines sprang. As a result of the Polish struggle for independence from Russia, he came to believe that this is vested in a culturally unified people. The 'general will' is the common or collective interest of society, the will of all provided each acts selflessly. Rousseau argued that government should be based not on the absolute power of a monarch, but on the indivisible collective will of the entire community. During the French Revolution, these beliefs were reflected in the assertion that the French people were 'citizens' possessed of inalienable rights and duties, no longer merely 'subjects' of the crown. Sovereign power thus resided with the 'French nation'. The form of nationalism that emerged from the French Revolution was therefore based on the vision of a people or nation governing itself. In other words, the nation is not merely a natural community: it is a natural political community.

Sovereignty: The principle of absolute or unrestricted power expressed either as unchallengeable legal authority or unquestionable political power.

Jean-Jacques Rousseau (1712–78)

Geneva-born French moral and political philosopher, perhaps the principal intellectual influence on the French Revolution. Rousseau was entirely self-taught. He moved to Paris in 1742 and became an intimate of leading members of the French Enlightenment, especially Diderot (1713–84).

Rousseau's writings range over education, the arts, science, literature and philosophy. His philosophy reflects a deep belief in the goodness of 'natural man' and the corruption of 'social man'. Rousseau's political teaching, summarised in *Émile* (1762) and developed in *The Social Contract* (1762), advocates a radical form of democracy based on the idea of the 'general will'. It is impossible to link Rousseau to any one political tradition; his thought has influenced liberal, socialist, anarchist and, some argue, fascist thought.

Nation-state: A
sovereign political
association within
which citizenship and
nationality overlap;
one nation within a
single state.

Unification: The
process through which
a collection of
separate political
entities, usually
sharing cultural
characteristics, are
integrated into a single
state.

Independence: The
process through which
a nation is liberated
from foreign rule,
usually involving the
establishment of
sovereign statehood.

In this tradition of nationalism, nationhood and state-hood are intrinsically linked. The litmus test of national identity is the desire to attain or maintain political independence, usually expressed in the principle of national self-determination. The goal of nationalism is therefore the founding of a '**nation-state**'. To date, this has been achieved in one of two ways. First, it may involve a process of **unification**. German history, for instance, has repeatedly witnessed unification. This occurred in medieval times under Charlemagne through the Holy Roman Empire; in the nineteenth century under Bismarck; and when the 'two Germanies' (East Germany and West Germany) were reunited in 1990. Second, nation-states can be created through the achievement of **independence**. For example, much of Polish history has witnessed successive attempts to achieve independence from the control of various foreign powers. Poland ceased to exist in 1793 when the Poles were partitioned by Austria, Russia and Prussia. Recognized by the Treaty of Versailles of 1919, Poland was proclaimed in 1918 and became an independent republic. However, in accordance with the Nazi–Soviet Pact of 1939, Poland was invaded by Germany and repartitioned, this time between Germany and the Soviet Union. Although Poland achieved formal independence in 1945, for much of the postwar period it remained firmly under Soviet control. The election of a non-communist government in 1989 therefore marked a further liberation of the country from foreign control.

For nationalists, the nation-state is the highest and most desirable form of political organization. The great strength of the nation-state is that it offers the prospect of both cultural cohesion and political unity. When a people who share a common cultural or ethnic identity gain the right to self-government, nationality and citizenship coincide. Moreover, nationalism legitimizes the authority of government. Political sovereignty in a nation-state resides with the people or the nation itself. Consequently, nationalism represents the idea of popular self-government, the idea that government is carried out either by the people or for the people, in accordance with their 'national interest'. This is why nationalists believe that the forces that have created a world of independent nation-states are natural and irresistible, and that no other social group could constitute a meaningful political community. The nation-state, in short, is the only viable political unit.

However, it would be misleading to suggest that nationalism is always associated with the nation-state or is necessarily linked to the idea of self-

Separatism:
The quest to secede from a larger political formation with a view to establishing an independent state.

determination. Some nations, for instance, may be satisfied with a measure of political autonomy that stops short of statehood and full independence. This can be seen in the case of Welsh nationalism in the UK and Breton and Basque nationalism in France. Nationalism is thus not always associated with **separatism**, but may instead be expressed through federalism or devolution. Nevertheless, it is unclear whether devolution or even federalism establishes a sufficient measure of self-government to satisfy nationalist demands. The granting of wide-ranging powers to the Basque region of Spain has failed to end ETA's campaign of terrorism. Similarly, the creation of a Scottish Parliament in the UK in 1999 has not ended the SNP's campaign to achieve an independent Scotland within the EU.

Identity politics

All forms of nationalism address the issue of identity. Whatever political causes nationalism may be associated with, it advances these on the basis of a sense of collective identity, usually understood as patriotism. For the political nationalist, 'objective' considerations such as territory, religion and language are no more important than 'subjective' ones such as will, memory and patriotic loyalty. Nationalism, therefore, not only advances political causes but also tells people who they are: it gives people a history, forges social bonds and a collective spirit, and creates a sense of destiny larger than individual existence. Indeed, it may be precisely the strength of national-

PATRIOTISM

Patriotism (from the Latin *patria*, meaning 'fatherland') is a sentiment, a psychological attachment to one's nation, literally a 'love of one's country'. The terms nationalism and patriotism are often confused. Nationalism has a doctrinal character and embodies the belief that the nation is in some way the central principle of political organization. Patriotism provides the affective basis for that belief, and thus underpins all forms of nationalism. It is difficult to conceive of a national group demanding, say, political independence without possessing at least a measure of patriotic loyalty or national consciousness. However, not all patriots are nationalists. Not all of those who identify with, or even love their nation, see it as a means through which political demands can be articulated.

Cultural nationalism:
A form of nationalism
that places primary
emphasis on the
regeneration of the
nation as a distinctive
civilization rather than
on self-government.

Ethnic nationalism: A
form of nationalism
that is fuelled prima-
rily by a keen sense of
ethnic distinctiveness
and the desire to
preserve it.

ism's affective elements and the relative weakness of its doctrinal ones that accounts for the unusual success of nationalism as a political creed.

Certain forms of nationalism, however, are less closely related to overtly political demands than others. This particularly applies in the case of **cultural nationalism** and **ethnic nationalism**. Cultural nationalism is a form of nationalism that emphasises the strengthening or defence of cultural identity over overt political demands. Not uncommonly, cultural nationalists view the state as a peripheral if not an alien entity. Whereas political nationalism is 'rational' and may be principled, cultural nationalism is 'mystical', in that it is based on a roman-tic belief in the nation as a unique historical and organic whole. Typically, cultural nationalism is a 'bottom-up' form of nationalism that draws more on popular rituals, traditions and legends than on elite or 'higher' culture. Though it is often anti-modern in character, cultural nation-alism may also serve as an agent of modernization by enabling a people to 'recreate' itself.

The importance of a distinctive national consciousness was first empha-sized in Germany in the late eighteenth century. Writers such as Herder (1744–1803) and Fichte (1762–1814) highlighted what they believed to be the uniqueness and superiority of Germanic culture, in contrast to the ideas of the French Revolution. Herder believed that each nation possesses a *Volksgeist* or 'national spirit', which provides its peoples with their creative impulse. The role of nationalism is therefore to develop an awareness and appreciation of a nation's culture and traditions. During the nineteenth century, such cultural nationalism was particularly marked in Germany in a revival of folk traditions and the rediscovery of German myths and legends. The Brothers Grimm, for example, collected and published German folk tales, and the composer Richard Wagner based many of his operas on ancient legends and myths. Since the mid-twentieth century, cultural nation-alism has strengthened as peoples, such as the Welsh in the UK and the Bretons and Basques in France, have sought to preserve national cultures that have been threatened by membership of a multinational state. (The rela-tionship between nationalism and multiculturalism is discussed in Chapter 11.) To some extent, this shift from politics to culture, and thus from state to region, within nationalism reflects the declining capacity of nation-states, in a context of economic globalization, to maintain a meaningful sense of loyalty and affection.

In some respects, ethnic nationalism differs from cultural nationalism, even though the terms 'ethnicity' and 'culture' overlap. Ethnicity is loyalty

TENSIONS WITHIN
NATIONALISM (1)

CIVIC NATIONALISM	v.	ETHNOCULTURAL NATIONALISM
political nation	← →	cultural/historical nation
inclusive	← →	exclusive
universalism	← →	particularism
equal nations	← →	unique nations
rational/principled	← →	mystical/emotional
national sovereignty	← →	national 'spirit'
voluntaristic	← →	organic
based on citizenship	← →	based on descent
civic loyalty	← →	ethnic allegiance
cultural diversity	← →	cultural unity

towards a distinctive population, cultural group or territorial area. The term is complex because it has both racial and cultural overtones. Members of ethnic groups are often seen, correctly or incorrectly, to have descended from common ancestors, and the groups are thus thought of as extended kinship groups, united by blood. Even when ethnicity is understood in strictly cultural terms, it operates at a deep emotional level and highlights values, traditions and practices that give a people a sense of distinctiveness. As it is not possible to 'join' an ethnic group (except perhaps through inter-marriage), ethnic nationalism has a clearly exclusive character.

Nationalism and politics

Political nationalism is a highly complex phenomenon, being characterized more by ambiguity and contradictions than by a single set of values and goals. For example, nationalism has been both liberating and oppressive: it has brought about self-government and freedom, and it has led to conquest and subjugation. Nationalism has been both progressive and regressive: it has looked to a future of national independence or national greatness, and it has celebrated past national glories and entrenched established identities.

Nationalism has also been both rational and irrational: it has appealed to principled beliefs, such as national self-determination, and it has bred from non-rational drives and emotions, including ancient fears and hatreds. This ideological shapelessness is a product of a number of factors. Nationalism has emerged in very different historical contexts, been shaped by contrasting cultural inheritances, and it has been used to advance a wide variety of political causes and aspirations. However, it also reflects the capacity of nationalism to fuse with and absorb other political doctrines and ideas, thereby creating a series of rival nationalist traditions. The most significant of these traditions are the following:

- liberal nationalism
- conservative nationalism
- expansionist nationalism
- anti-colonial and postcolonial nationalism.

Liberal nationalism

Liberal nationalism is the oldest form of nationalism, dating back to the French Revolution and embodying many of its values. Its ideas spread quickly through much of Europe and were expressed most clearly by Giuseppe Mazzini, often thought of as the 'prophet' of Italian unification. They also influenced the remarkable exploits of Simon Bolivar, who led the Latin American independence movement in the early nineteenth century and expelled the Spanish from much of Hispanic America. Woodrow Wilson's 'Fourteen Points', proposed as the basis for the reconstruction of Europe after the First World War, were also based on liberal nationalist principles. Moreover, many twentieth-century anti-colonial leaders were inspired by liberal ideas, as in the case of Sun Yat-Sen, one of the leaders of China's 1911 Revolution, and Jawaharlal Nehru, the first prime minister of India.

The ideas of liberal nationalism were clearly shaped by J.-J. Rousseau's defence of popular sovereignty, expressed in particular in the notion of the 'general will'. As the nineteenth century progressed, the aspiration for popular self-government was progressively fused with liberal principles. This fusion was brought about by the fact that the multinational empires against which nationalists fought were also autocratic and oppressive. Mazzini, for example, wished the Italian states to unite, but this also entailed throwing off the influence of autocratic Austria. For many European revolutionaries in the mid-nineteenth century, liberalism and nationalism were virtually indistinguishable. Indeed, their nationalist creed was largely forged

Giuseppe Mazzini
(1805–72)

MAZZINI

Italian nationalist. Mazzini, the son of a doctor, was born in Genoa, Italy. He came into contact with revolutionary politics as a member of the patriotic secret society, the Carbonari. During the 1848 revolutions Mazzini helped to liberate Milan from Austrian influence and became head of the short-lived Roman Republic.

Mazzini's nationalism fused a belief in the nation as a distinctive linguistic and cultural community with the principles of liberal republicanism. Above all, Mazzini's was a principled form of nationalism, which treated nations as sublimated individuals endowed with the right to self-government. Mazzini was confident that the assertion of the principle of national self-determination would eventually bring about perpetual peace.

by applying liberal ideas, initially developed in relation to the individual, to the nation and to international politics.

Liberalism was founded on a defence of individual freedom, traditionally expressed in the language of rights. Nationalists believed nations to be sovereign entities, entitled to liberty, and also possessing rights, most importantly the right of self-determination. Liberal nationalism is therefore a liberating force in two senses. First, it opposes all forms of foreign domination and oppression, whether by multinational empires or colonial powers. Second, it stands for the ideal of self-government, reflected in practice in a belief in constitutionalism (see p. 39) and representation. Woodrow Wilson, for example, argued in favour of a Europe composed not only of nation-states, but also one in which political democracy rather than autocracy ruled. For him, only a democratic republic, on the US model, could be a genuine nation-state.

Furthermore, liberal nationalists believe that nations, like individuals, are equal, at least in the sense that they are equally entitled to the right of self-determination. The ultimate goal of liberal nationalism is, therefore, the construction of a world of independent nation-states, not merely the unification or independence of a particular nation. John Stuart Mill (see p. 29) expressed this as the principle that 'the boundaries of government should coincide in the main with those of nationality'. Mazzini formed the clandestine organization 'Young Italy' to promote the idea of a united Italy, but he also founded 'Young Europe in the hope of spreading nationalist ideas throughout the continent. At the Paris Peace Conference, Woodrow Wilson advanced the principle of self-determination not simply because the break-up of the European empire served US national interests, but because he believed that the Poles, Czechs, Hungarians and so on all had the same right to political independence that Americans already enjoyed.

Liberals also believe that the principle of balance or natural harmony applies to the nations of the world, not just to individuals within society. The achievement of national self-determination is a means of establishing a peaceful and stable international order. Wilson believed that the First World War had been caused by an 'old order', dominated by autocratic and mili-taristic empires. Democratic nation-states, on the other hand, would respect the national sovereignty of their neighbours and have no incentive to wage war or subjugate others. For a liberal, nationalism does not divide nations from one another, promoting distrust, rivalry and possibly war. Rather, nationalism is a force that is capable of promoting both unity within each nation and brotherhood amongst all nations on the basis of mutual respect for national rights and characteristics. At heart, liberal-ism looks beyond the nation to the ideas of cosmopoli-tanism (see p. 326) and **internationalism**, as discussed later in the chapter.

Internationalism:
A theory or practice of politics that is based on transnational or global cooperation; the belief that nations are artificial and unwanted formations (see p. 169).

Critics of liberal nationalism have sometimes suggested that its ideas are naive and romantic. Liberal nationalists see the progressive and liberating face of nationalism; their nationalism is rational and tolerant. However, they perhaps ignore the darker face of nation-alism, the irrational bonds or **tribalism** that distinguish 'us' from a foreign and threatening 'them'. Liberals see nationalism as a universal principle, but have less understanding of the emotional power of nationalism, which has, in times of war, persuaded individuals to kill or die for their country, regardless of the justice of their nation's cause. Liberal nationalism is also misguided in its belief that the nation-state is the key to political and international harmony. The mistake of Wilsonian nationalism was the belief that nations live in convenient and discrete geographical areas, and that states can be constructed that coincide with these areas. In practice, all so-called 'nation-states' comprise a range of linguistic, religious, ethnic or regional groups, some of which may also consider themselves to be 'nations'. For example, in 1918 the newly created nation-states of Czechoslovakia and Poland contained a significant number of German speakers, and Czechoslovakia itself was a fusion of two major ethnic groups: the Czechs and the Slovaks. The former Yugoslavia, also created by Versailles, contained a bewildering variety of ethnic groups – Serbs, Croats,

Tribalism: Group behaviour character-ized by insularity and exclusivity, typically fuelled by hostility towards rival groups.

TENSIONS WITHIN
NATIONALISM (2)

LIBERAL NATIONALISM	v.	EXPANSIONIST NATIONALISM
national self-determination	←→	national chauvinism
inclusive	←→	exclusive
voluntaristic	←→	organic
progressive	←→	reactionary
rational/principled	←→	emotional/instinctive
human rights	←→	national interest
equal nations	←→	hierarchy of nations
constitutionalism	←→	authoritarianism
ethnic/cultural pluralism	←→	ethnic/cultural purity
cosmopolitanism	←→	imperialism/militarism
collective security	←→	power politics
supranationalism	←→	international anarchy

Slovenes, Bosnians, Albanians and so on – which have subsequently realized their aspiration for nationhood. In fact, the ideal of a politically unified and culturally homogeneous nation-state can only be achieved by a policy of forcible deportation of minority groups and an outright ban on immigration.

Conservative nationalism

In the early nineteenth century, conservatives regarded nationalism as a radical and dangerous force, a threat to order and political stability. However, as the century progressed, conservative statesmen such as Disraeli, Bismarck and even Tsar Alexander III became increasingly sympathetic towards nationalism, seeing it as a natural ally in maintaining social order and defending traditional institutions. In the modern period, nationalism has become an article of faith for most conservatives. In the UK, for example, this has been expressed in the Conservative Party's antipathy towards European integration. In the USA, George W. Bush used the so-called 'war on terror' to link military assertiveness to a defence of national values and demonstration of national character.

Conservative nationalism tends to develop in established nation-states, rather than ones that are in the process of nation building. Conservatives care less for the principled nationalism of universal self-determination and more about the promise of social cohesion and public order embodied in the sentiment of national patriotism. For conservatives, society is organic: they believe that nations emerge naturally from the desire of human beings to live with others who possess the same views, habits and appearance as themselves. Human beings are thought to be limited and imperfect creatures, who seek meaning and security within the national community. Therefore, the principal goal of conservative nationalism is to maintain national unity by fostering patriotic loyalty and 'pride in one's country', especially in the face of the divisive idea of class solidarity preached by socialists. Indeed, by incorporating the working class into the nation, conservatives have often seen nationalism as the antidote to social revolution. Charles de Gaulle, French president, 1959–69, harnessed nationalism to the conservative cause in France with particular skill. De Gaulle appealed to national pride by pursuing an independent, even anti-American defence and foreign policy, and by attempting to restore order and authority to social life and build up a powerful state. In some respects, **Thatcherism** in the UK amounted to a British form of Gaullism, in that it fused an appeal based upon nationalism, or at least national independence within Europe, with the promise of strong government and firm leadership.

Thatcherism: The free-market/strong state ideological stance associated with Margaret Thatcher; the UK version of the new right political project.

The conservative character of nationalism is maintained by an appeal to tradition and history; nationalism becomes thereby a defence for traditional institutions and a traditional way of life. Conservative nationalism is essentially nostalgic and backward-looking, reflecting on a past age of national glory or triumph. This is evident in the widespread tendency to use ritual and commemoration to present past military victories as defining moments in a nation's history. It is also apparent in the use of traditional institutions as symbols of national identity. This occurs in the case of British, or, more accurately, English nationalism, which is closely linked to the institution of monarchy. Britain (plus Northern Ireland) is the United Kingdom, its national anthem is 'God Save the Queen', and the royal family plays a prominent role in national celebrations such as Armistice Day, and on state occasions such as the opening of Parliament. Conservative nationalism is particularly prominent when the sense of national identity is felt to be threatened or in danger of being lost. The issues of immigration and **supranationalism** have therefore helped to keep this

Supranationalism: The ability of bodies with transnational or global jurisdictions to impose their will on nation-states.

form of nationalism alive in many modern states. Conservative reservations about immigration stem from the belief that cultural diversity leads to instability and conflict. As stable and successful societies must be based on shared values and a common culture, immigration, particularly from societies with different religious and other traditions, should either be firmly restricted or minority ethnic groups should be encouraged to assimilate into the culture of the 'host' society. Conservative nationalists are also concerned about the threat that supranational bodies, such as the EU, pose to national identity and so to the cultural bonds of society. This is expressed in the UK in the form of Conservative Party 'Euroscepticism', with similar views being expressed in continental Europe by a variety of far right groups such as the French National Front. Eurosceptics not only defend sovereign national institutions and a distinctive national currency on the grounds that they are vital symbols of national identity, but also warn that the 'European project' is fatally misconceived because a stable political union cannot be forged out of such national, language and cultural diversity.

Although conservative politicians and parties have derived considerable political benefit from their appeal to nationalism, opponents have sometimes pointed out that their ideas are based on misguided assumptions. In the first place, conservative nationalism can be seen as a form of elite manipulation. The 'nation' is invented and certainly defined by political leaders who may use it for their own purposes. This is most evident in times of war or international crisis when the nation is mobilized to fight for the 'fatherland' by emotional appeals to patriotic duty. Furthermore, conservative nationalism may also serve to promote intolerance and bigotry. By insisting on the maintenance of cultural purity and established traditions, conservatives may portray immigrants, or foreigners in general, as a threat, and in the process promote, or at least legitimize, racialist and xenophobic fears.

Expansionist nationalism

In many countries the dominant image of nationalism is one of aggression and **militarism**, quite the opposite of a principled belief in national self-determination. The aggressive face of nationalism became apparent in the late nineteenth century as European powers indulged in a 'scramble for Africa' in the name of national glory and their 'place in the sun'. The imperialism of the late nineteenth century differed from earlier periods of colonial expansion in that it was supported by a climate of popular nationalism: national prestige was increasingly linked to the possession of an empire and each colonial victory was

Militarism: The achievement of ends by military means, or the extension of military ideas, values and practices to civilian society.

Jingoism: A mood of nationalist enthusiasm and public celebration provoked by military expansion or imperial conquest.

greeted by demonstrations of public approval. In the UK, a new word, **jingoism**, was coined to describe this mood of popular nationalism. In the early twentieth century, the growing rivalry of the European powers divided the continent into two armed camps, the Triple Entente, comprising the UK, France and Russia, and the Triple Alliance, containing Germany, Austria and Italy. When world war eventually broke out in August 1914, after a prolonged arms race and a succession of international crises, it provoked public rejoicing in all the major cities of Europe. Aggressive and expansionist nationalism reached its high point in the inter-war period when the authoritarian or fascist regimes of Japan, Italy and Germany embarked on policies of imperial expansion and world domination, eventually leading to war in 1939.

What distinguished this form of nationalism from earlier liberal nationalism was its chauvinism, a term derived from the name of Nicolas Chauvin, a French soldier who had been fanatically devoted to Napoleon I. Nations are not thought to be equal in their right to self-determination; rather, some nations are believed to possess characteristics or qualities that make them superior to others. Such ideas were clearly evident in European **imperialism**, which was justified by an ideology of racial and cultural superiority. In nineteenth-century Europe it was widely believed that the 'white' peoples of Europe and America were intellectually and morally superior to the 'black', 'brown' and 'yellow' peoples of Africa and Asia. Indeed, Europeans portrayed imperialism as a moral duty: colonial peoples were the 'white man's burden'. Imperialism supposedly brought the benefits of civilization, and in particular Christianity, to the less fortunate and less sophisticated peoples of the world.

Imperialism: The extension of control by one country over another, whether by overt political means or through economic domination.

Pan-nationalism: A style of nationalism that is dedicated to unifying a disparate people either through expansionism or political solidarity ('pan' means all or every).

More particular varieties of national chauvinism have developed in the form of **pan-nationalism**. In Russia this took the form of pan-Slavism, sometimes called Slavophile nationalism, which was particularly strong in the late nineteenth and early twentieth centuries. The Russians are Slavs, and enjoy linguistic and cultural links with other Slavic peoples in eastern and south-eastern Europe. Pan-Slavism was defined by the goal of Slavic unity, which the Russians believed to be their historic mission. In the years before 1914, such ideas brought Russia into growing conflict with Austro-Hungary for control of the Balkans. The chauvinistic character of pan-Slavism derived from the belief that the Russians are the natural leaders of the Slavic people, and that the Slavs are culturally and spiritually superior to the peoples of central or western Europe. Pan-Slavism is therefore both anti-western and anti-liberal. Forms of pan-Slavism have been re-awakened since 1991 and the collapse of communist rule in Russia.

Traditional German nationalism also exhibited a marked chauvinism, which was born out of defeat in the Napoleonic Wars. Writers such as Fichte and Jahn reacted strongly against France and the ideals of its revolution, emphasizing instead the uniqueness of German culture and its language, and the racial purity of its people. After unification in 1871, German nationalism developed a pronounced chauvinistic character with the emergence of pressure groups such as the Pan-German League and the Navy League, which campaigned for closer ties with German-speaking Austria and for a German empire, Germany's 'place in the sun'. Pan-Germanism was an expansionist and aggressive form of nationalism that envisaged the creation of a German-dominated Europe. German chauvinism found its highest expression in the **racialist** and anti-Semitic (see p. 223) doctrines developed by the Nazis. The Nazis adopted the expansionist goals of pan-Germanism with enthusiasm, but justified them in the language of biology rather than politics. This is examined more fully in Chapter 7, in connection with racialism.

Racialism: A belief that racial divisions are politically significant, either because races should live apart or because they possess different qualities and are thus suited to different social roles (see p. 221).

National chauvinism breeds from a feeling of intense, even hysterical nationalist enthusiasm. The individual as a separate, rational being is swept away on a tide of patriotic emotion, expressed in the desire for aggression, expansion and war. The right-wing French nationalist Charles Maurras (1868–1952) called such intense patriotism 'integral nationalism': individuals and independent groups lose their identity within an all-powerful 'nation', which has an existence and meaning beyond the life of any single individual. Such militant nationalism is often accompanied by militarism. Military glory and conquest are the ultimate evidence of national greatness and have been capable of generating intense feelings of nationalist commitment. The civilian population is, in effect, militarized: it is infected by the martial values of absolute loyalty, complete dedication and willing self-sacrifice. When the honour or integrity of the nation is in question, the lives of ordinary citizens become unimportant. Such emotional intensity was amply demonstrated in August 1914, and perhaps also underlies the emotional power of *jihad* (crudely defined as 'holy war') from the viewpoint of militant Islamic groups.

National chauvinism has a particularly strong appeal for the isolated and powerless, for whom nationalism offers the prospect of security, self-respect and pride. Militant or integral nationalism requires a heightened sense of belonging to a distinct national group. Such intense nationalist feeling is often stimulated by 'negative integration', the portrayal of another nation or race as a threat or an enemy. In the face of the enemy, the nation draws together and experiences an intensified sense of its own identity and importance. National chauvinism therefore breeds from a clear distinction between 'them' and 'us'. There has to be a 'them' to deride or hate in order to forge a sense of 'us'. In politics, national chauvinism has commonly been reflected in racialist ideologies, which divide the world into an 'in group' and an 'out group', in which the 'out group' becomes a scapegoat for all the misfortunes and frustrations suffered by the 'in group'. It is therefore no coincidence that chauvinistic political creeds are a breeding ground for racialist ideas. Both pan-Slavism and pan-Germanism, for example, have been characterized by virulent anti-Semitism.

Anti-colonial and postcolonial nationalism

Nationalism may have been born in Europe, but it became a worldwide phenomenon thanks to imperialism. The experience of colonial rule helped to forge a sense of nationhood and a desire for 'national liberation' amongst the peoples of Asia and Africa, and gave rise to a specifically anti-colonial form of nationalism. During the twentieth century, the political geography of much of the world was transformed by anti-colonialism. Although Versailles applied the principle of self-determination to Europe, it was conveniently ignored in other parts of the world, where German colonies were simply transferred to UK and French control. However, during the inter-war period independence movements increasingly threatened the overstretched empires of the UK and France. The final collapse of the European empires came after the Second World War. In some cases, a combination of mounting nationalist pressure and declining domestic economic performance persuaded colonial powers to depart relatively peacefully, as occurred in India in 1947 and in Malaysia in 1957. However, decolonization in the post-1945 period was often characterized by revolution, and sometimes periods of armed struggle. This occurred, for instance, in the case of China, 1937–45 (against Japan), Algeria, 1954–62 (against France), and Vietnam, 1946–54 (against France) and 1964–75 (against USA).

In a sense, the colonizing Europeans had taken with them the seed of their own destruction: the doctrine of nationalism. For example, it is notable that many of the leaders of independence or liberation movements were western educated. It is therefore not surprising that anti-colonial movements sometimes articulated their goals in the language of liberal nationalism, reminiscent of Mazzini or Woodrow Wilson. However, emergent African and Asian nations were in a very different position from the newly created European states of the nineteenth and early twentieth centuries. For these African and Asian nations, the quest for political independence was closely related to their awareness of economic under-development and their subordination to the industrialized states of Europe and North America. Anti-colonialism thus came to express the desire for national liberation in both political and economic terms, and this has left its mark on the form of nationalism practised in the developing world. Most of the leaders of Asian and African anti-colonial movements were attracted to some form of socialism, ranging from the moderate and peaceful ideas represented by Gandhi and Nehru in India, to the revolutionary Marxism espoused by Mao Zedong in China, Ho Chi Minh in Vietnam and Fidel Castro in Cuba. On the surface, as is discussed later, socialism is more clearly related to internationalism than to nationalism. Socialist ideas have, nevertheless, appealed powerfully to nationalists in the developing world. In the first place, socialism embodies the values of community and cooperation that were already well-established in traditional, preindustrial societies. More importantly, socialism, and in particular Marxism, provided an analysis of inequality and exploitation through which the colonial experience could be understood and colonial rule challenged.

During the 1960s and 1970s in particular, developing-world nationalists were drawn to revolutionary Marxism, influenced by the belief that colonialism is in practice an extended form of class oppression. Lenin (see p. 125) had earlier provided the basis for such a view by portraying imperialism as essentially an economic phenomenon, a quest for profit by capitalist countries seeking investment opportunities, cheap labour and raw materials, and secure markets (Lenin, [1916] 1970). The class struggle thus became a colonial struggle against exploitation and oppression. As a result, the overthrow of colonial rule implied not only political independence, but also a social revolution offering the prospect of both political and economic emancipation.

In some cases, developing-world regimes have openly embraced Marxist-Leninist principles. On achieving independence, China, North Korea, Vietnam and Cambodia moved swiftly to seize foreign assets and nationalize economic resources. They founded one-party states and centrally planned economies, closely following the Soviet model. In other cases, states in Africa and the Middle East have developed a less ideological form of nationalistic socialism, as has been evident in Algeria, Libya, Zambia, Iraq and South Yemen. The 'socialism' proclaimed in such countries usually took the form of an appeal to a unifying national cause or interest, in most cases economic or social development, as in the case of so-called 'African socialism', embraced, for instance, by Tanzania, Zimbabwe and Angola. African socialism is not based on Soviet-style state socialism or western social democracy, but rather is founded on traditional communitarian values and the desire to subordinate divisive tribal rivalries to the overriding need for economic progress.

The postcolonial period has thrown up quite different forms of nationalism, however. With the authority of socialism and especially the attraction of Marxism–Leninism, declining significantly since the 1970s, nation building in the postcolonial period has increasingly been shaped more by the rejection of western ideas and culture than by the attempt to reapply them. If the West is regarded as the source of oppression and exploitation, postcolonial nationalism must seek an anti-western voice. In part, this has been a reaction against the dominance of western, and increasingly US, culture and economic power in much of the developing world. The principal vehicle for expressing such views has been religious fundamentalism, notably political Islam, which is discussed in Chapter 10.

Beyond nationalism

A variety of political creeds can be said to look beyond the nation. This applies to any doctrine or ideology that propounds a transnational view of political identity. Such ideas are expressed either through internationalism or through cosmopolitanism (see p. 326). In international politics, such thinking has been advanced via the 'idealist' tradition, which is characterized by a belief in universal morality and the prospect of global peace and cooperation. The German philosopher Immanuel Kant (1724 –1804) is often seen as the father of this tradition, his *Towards Perpetual Peace* ([1795] 1991) having envisaged a kind of 'league of nations' based on the belief that reason and morality combine to dictate that 'There should be no war'. As far as the major ideologies are concerned, this vision has been most clearly associated with liberalism and socialism, each of which has developed a particular brand of internationalism.

Liberal internationalism

There are, broadly, two bases of liberal internationalism. The first is a fear of an international 'state of nature'. Liberals have long accepted that national self-determination is a mixed blessing. While it preserves self-government and forbids foreign control, it also creates a world of sovereign nation-states in which each nation has the freedom to pursue its own interests, possibly at the expense of other nations. Liberal nationalists have certainly accepted that constitutionalism and democracy reduce the tendency towards mili-

INTERNATIONALISM

Internationalism is the theory or practice of politics based on transnational or global cooperation. It is rooted in universalist assumptions about human nature that put it at odds with political nationalism, the latter emphasizing the degree to which political identity is shaped by nationality. However, internationalism is compatible with nationalism in the sense that it calls for cooperation or solidarity *between* or *among* preexisting nations, rather than for the removal or abandonment of national identities altogether. Internationalism thus differs from cosmopolitanism (see p. 326), the latter implying the displacement of national allegiances by global allegiances. 'Weak' forms of internationalism can be seen in doctrines such as feminism, racialism and religious fundamentalism, which hold that national ties are secondary to other political bonds. 'Strong' forms of internationalism have usually drawn on the universalist ideas of either liberalism or socialism.

tarism and war, but when sovereign nations operate within conditions of 'international anarchy', self-restraint alone may not be sufficient to ensure enduring peace. Liberals have generally proposed two means of preventing a recourse to conquest and plunder. The first is national interdependence, aimed at promoting mutual understanding and cooperation. This is why liberals have traditionally supported the policy of **free trade**: economic interdependence means that the material cost of international conflict is so great that warfare becomes virtually unthinkable. For the nineteenth-century 'Manchester liberals' in the UK, Richard Cobden (1804–65) and John Bright (1811–89), not only would free trade promote prosperity by allowing countries to specialize in producing what they are best suited to produce, but it would also draw people of different races, creeds and languages together into what Cobden described as 'the bonds of eternal peace'.

Free trade: A system of trading between states that is unrestricted by tariffs or other forms of protectionism.

Liberals have also proposed that national ambition should be checked by the construction of supranational bodies capable of bringing order to an otherwise lawless international scene. This argument draws on precisely the same logic as social contract theory: government is the solution to the problem of disorder. This explains Woodrow Wilson's support for the first, if flawed, experiment in world government, the League of Nations, set up in 1919, and far wider support for its successor, the United Nations, founded by the San Francisco Conference of 1945. Liberals have looked to these bodies to establish a law-governed state system to make possible the peaceful resolution of international conflicts. However, liberals also recognize that law must be enforced, and hence have usually endorsed the principle of collective security, the idea that aggression can best be resisted by united action by a number of states. This sympathy for supranationalism is also evident in the liberal attitude towards bodies such as the European Union.

The second basis for liberal internationalism stems from an overriding commitment to the individual and the principle of individualism (see p. 28). This implies that all human beings, regardless of race, creed, social background and nationality, are of equal moral worth. While liberals endorse the idea of national self-determination, by no means do they believe that it entitles nations to treat their people however they choose. Respect for the rights and liberties of the individual in that sense outranks the claims of national sovereignty. Liberal internationalism is thus characterized not so much by a desire to supersede the nation as a political formation, but rather by the demand that nations conform to a higher morality embodied in the doctrine of human rights. As liberals believe that these rights are universally applicable and lay down the minimum conditions for a truly human existence, they should clearly also constitute the basis of international law. Such beliefs have led to the drawing up of documents such as the UN Declaration of Human Rights in 1948 and the European Convention on Human Rights and Fundamental Freedoms in 1956. They also imply support for an international rule of law, enforced through institutions such as the International Court of Justice and the International Criminal Court.

Socialist internationalism

Socialists are more likely than liberals to reject nationalism in principle, believing both that it breeds resentment and conflict, and that it has an implicitly right-wing character. Although this has not prevented modern socialists, as rulers and aspiring rulers, from reaching an accommodation with the nation-state, it has inclined them, at least in rhetoric, to treat internationalism as an article of faith, if not as a core value. This has been clearest in relation to the Marxist tradition. Marxism has traditionally embraced a form of proletarian internationalism, rooted in the idea that class solidarity is more powerful and politically significant than national identity. In the Communist Manifesto, Marx (see p. 121) wrote:

> The working men have no country. We cannot take from them what they have not got. Since the proletariat must first of all acquire politi-

Leon Trotsky
(1879–1940)

Russian Marxist, political thinker and revolutionary. An early critic of Lenin and leader of the 1905 St Petersburg Soviet, Trotsky joined the Bolsheviks in 1917, becoming commissar for foreign affairs and later commissar for war. Outmanoeuvred by Stalin after Lenin's death, he was banished from the Soviet Union in 1929 and assassinated in Mexico in 1940 on Stalin's orders.

Trotsky's theoretical contribution to Marxism centres on the theory of permanent revolution, which suggested that socialism could be established in Russia without the need for the bourgeois stage of development. Trotskyism is usually associated with an unwavering commitment to internationalism and to an anti-Stalinism that highlights the dangers of bureaucratization, as outlined in *The Revolution Betrayed* (1937).

cal supremacy, must rise to be the leading class of the nation, must constitute itself the nation, it is, so far, itself national, though not in the bourgeois sense of the word. (Marx and Engels, [1848] 1968)

Marx did not envisage that the working class would be national 'in the bourgeois sense of the word', by which he meant that, in recognizing the brotherhood of all proletarians, it would transcend what Engels called 'national egoism'. The *Communist Manifesto* expresses this graphically in its famous final words: 'Working men of all countries, unite!' Socialism therefore has an intrinsically international character. Not only does proletarian class solidarity inevitably cut across national borders, but, as Marx pointed out, the emergence of world markets had turned capitalism into an international system that could only be challenged by a genuinely international movement. This is why Marx helped to found the International Workingmen's Association, the so-called First International, in 1864. A Second or 'Socialist' International was set up in 1889 and revived in 1951. A Third International or 'Comintern' was formed by Lenin in 1919, while a rival Fourth International was set up in 1936 by Leon Trotsky, an arch critic of Stalin's policy of 'Socialism in One Country'.

However, socialists have seldom seen proletarian internationalism as an end in itself. Their aim has not been to replace a world divided on national lines by one divided on class lines, but rather – through an international class struggle – to establish harmony and cooperation amongst all the world's peoples. Socialist internationalism is therefore ultimately based on a belief in a common humanity. This is the idea that humankind is bound together by mutual sympathy, compassion and love, based on the belief that what human beings share with one another is greater than what divides them. From this perspective, socialists may reject nationalism not only as a species of bourgeois ideology, which conceals the contradictions on which capitalism and all other class societies are based, but also because it encourages people to deny their common humanity. Internationalism, for a socialist, may thus imply not merely cooperation amongst nations within a framework of international law, but the more radical and utopian goal of the dissolution of the nation and the recognition that there is but one world and one people.

Nationalism in the twenty-first century

Few political ideologies have been forced to endure prophecies of their imminent demise for as long as nationalism. As early as 1848, Marx proclaimed that 'National differences and antagonisms between peoples are daily more and more vanishing'. Similarly, the death of nationalism as the project of nation-building was widely proclaimed after the First World War, following the reconstruction of Europe according to the principle of national self-determination and, after the Second World War, as a result of decolonization in Africa, Asia and elsewhere. Once a world of nation-states had been constructed, what further role would there be for nationalism? Moreover, as the twentieth century progressed, it appeared that the nation had been made redundant by the progressive internationalization of political and economic life. International organizations – from the United Nations to the European Union and from the World Trade Organization to the International Monetary Fund – have come to dominate world politics, leaving fewer and fewer decisions in the hands of individual nations. What role would there be for nations in a globalized world?

Globalization has had a far-reaching impact on both the nation-state and political doctrines rooted in the idea of national distinctiveness. It has, for instance, led to the emergence of an integrated global economy, meaning that material prosperity is often more determined by the investment decisions of transnational corporations than it is by the actions of national governments. In cultural terms, with the growth of air travel, foreign tourism, satellite television and the internet, globalization means the spread of a market-driven society, sometimes seen as the 'McDonaldization' of the world. Can nations any longer be regarded as meaningful entities when people in different parts of the world watch the same films and television programmes, eat the same food, enjoy the same sports and so on? Given the remorseless nature of such developments, surely the twenty-first century is going to witness the final eclipse of political nationalism.

Nevertheless, at least two factors point to the continued political significance of the nation. First, there is evidence that precisely by weakening traditional civil and national bonds, globalization may fuel the emergence of ethnically based and sometimes aggressive forms of nationalism. If the conventional nation-state is no longer capable of generating meaningful collective identities, 'particularisms' based on region, religion, ethnicity or race may develop to take its place. This has already occurred most dramatically in an upsurge of ethnic conflict in many parts of the former Soviet bloc, particularly in the former Yugoslavia, but is also evident in the centrifugal nationalisms that have taken root in states such as the UK, Spain, Italy and Belgium.

Second, globalization may invest the national project with a new meaning and significance, that of mapping out a future for nations in an increasingly globalized and interdependent world. In this sense, globalization may not so much make nations irrelevant as force them to reinvent themselves, continuing to provide societies with a source of social cohesion and identity but within an increasingly fluid and competitive context. In their different ways, states such as Singapore, Malaysia, Australia, New Zealand and Canada have undergone such a process of self-affirmation, as they have attempted to refashion their national identities by fusing elements from their past with an essentially future-looking orientation.

Questions for discussion

→ Do nations develop 'naturally', or are they, in some sense, manufactured?

→ Why have nations and states often been confused?

→ How does nationalism differ from racialism?

→ In what sense is liberal nationalism principled?

→ Why have liberals viewed nationalism as the antidote to war?

→ Are all conservatives nationalist? If so, why?

→ Why has nationalism so often been associated with expansionism, conquest and war?

→ Why and how has developing-world nationalism differed from nationalism in the developed world?

→ Has globalization made nationalism irrelevant?

Further reading

Brown, D., *Contemporary Nationalism: Civic, Ethnocultural and Multicultural Politics* (London:Routledge: 2000). A clear and stimulating account of differing approaches to nationalism and of the contrasting forms of modern nationalist politics.

Hearn, J., *Rethinking Nationalism: A Critical Introduction* (Basingstoke and New York: Palgrave Macmillan, 2006). An innovative and wide-ranging study of nationalism that critically reviews approaches to the nature and origins of nationalism.

Hobsbawm, E. J., *Nations and Nationalism since 1780: Programme, Myth and Reality* (Cambridge and New York: Cambridge University Press, 1990). A good and accessible introduction to the subject.

Hutchinson, J. and Smith, A. D. (eds), *Nationalism* (Oxford and New York: Oxford University Press, 1994). A wide-ranging and useful collection of readings that examine debates on the nature, development and significance of nationalism.

Özkirmli, U., *Contemporary Debates on Nationalism: A Critical Engagement* (Basingstoke and New York: Palgrave Macmillan, 2005). A clear and genuinely international account of classical and modern contributions to debates about nationalism.

Smith, A. D., *Nationalism: Theory, Ideology, History* (Cambridge and Malden, MA: Polity Press, 2001). A clear and incisive introduction to the subject of nationalism and its varying manifestations.

Spencer, P. and Wollman, H., *Nationalism: A Critical Introduction* (London and Thousand Oaks, CA: Sage, 2002). A very useful survey of classical and contemporary approaches to nationalism that addresses all the key issues, theories and debates.

CHAPTER 6

ANARCHISM

PREVIEW

The word 'anarchy' comes from Greek and literally means 'without rule'. The term 'anarchism' has been in use since the French Revolution, and was initially employed in a critical or negative sense to imply a breakdown of civilized or predictable order. In everyday language, anarchy implies chaos and disorder. Needless to say, anarchists themselves fiercely reject such associations. It was not until Pierre-Joseph Proudhon proudly declared in *What is Property?* ([1840] 1970), 'I am an anarchist', that the word was clearly associated with a positive and systematic set of political ideas.

Anarchist ideology is defined by the central belief that political authority in all its forms, and especially in the form of the state, is both evil and unnecessary. Anarchists therefore look to the creation of a stateless society though the abolition of law and government. In their view, the state is evil because, as a repository of sovereign, compulsory and coercive authority, it is an offence against the principles of freedom and equality. The core value of anarchism is thus unrestricted personal autonomy. Anarchists believe that the state is unnecessary because order and social harmony can arise naturally and spontaneously, and do not have to be imposed 'from above' through government. This draws attention to the utopian character of anarchist thought, notably reflected in highly optimistic assumptions about human nature. However, anarchism draws from two quite different ideological traditions: liberalism and socialism. This has resulted in rival individualist and collectivist forms of anarchism. Although both accept the goal of statelessness, they advance very different models of the future anarchist society.

Origins and development

Anarchist ideas have sometimes been traced back to Taoist or Buddhist ideas, to the Stoics and Cynics of Ancient Greece, or to the Diggers of the English Civil War. However, the first, and in a sense classic, statement of anarchist principles was produced by William Godwin (see p. 181) in his *Enquiry Concerning Political Justice* ([1793] 1971), although Godwin never described himself as an anarchist. During the nineteenth century, anarchism was a significant component of a broad but growing socialist movement. In 1864, Proudhon's (see p. 188) followers joined with Marx's (see p. 121) to set up the International Workingmen's Association, or First International. The International collapsed in 1871 because of growing antagonism between Marxists and anarchists led by Michael Bakunin (see p. 185). In the late nineteenth century, anarchists sought mass support amongst the landless peasants of Russia and southern Europe and, more successfully, through anarcho-syndicalism, amongst the industrial working classes.

Syndicalism was popular in France, Italy and Spain, and helped to make anarchism a genuine mass movement in the early twentieth century. The powerful CGT union in France was dominated by anarchists before 1914, as was the CNT in Spain, which claimed a membership of over two million during the Civil War. Anarcho-syndicalist movements also emerged in Latin America in the early twentieth century, especially in Argentina and Uruguay, and syndicalist ideas influenced the Mexican Revolution, led by Emiliano Zapata. However, the spread of authoritarianism and political repression gradually undermined anarchism in both Europe and Latin America. The victory of General Franco in the Spanish Civil War (1936–9) brought an end to anarchism as a mass movement. The CNT was suppressed and anarchists, along with left-wingers in general, were persecuted. The influence of anarchism was also undermined by the success of Lenin and the Bolsheviks in 1917, and thus by the growing prestige of communism within the socialist and revolutionary movements.

> **Syndicalism**: A form of revolutionary trade unionism that is based on a crude notion of class war and emphasizes the use of direct action and the general strike.

Anarchism is unusual amongst political ideologies in that it has never succeeded in winning power, at least at the national level. No society or nation has been modelled according to anarchist principles. Hence, it is tempting to regard anarchism as an ideology of less significance than, say, liberalism, socialism, conservatism or fascism, each of which has proved itself capable of achieving power and reshaping societies. The nearest anarchists have come to winning power was during the Spanish Civil War, when they briefly controlled parts of eastern Spain and set up workers' and peasants' collectives throughout Catalonia. Consequently, anarchists have looked to historical societies that reflect their principles, such as the cities of Ancient Greece or medieval Europe, or to traditional peasant communes such as the Russian *mir*. Anarchists have also stressed the non-hierarchic and egalitarian nature of many traditional societies – for instance, the Nuer in Africa – and supported experiments in small-scale, communal living within western society.

Anarchism's appeal as a political movement has been restricted by both its ends and its means. The goal of anarchism, the overthrow of the state and dismantling of all forms of political authority, is widely considered to be unrealistic, if not impossible. Most, indeed, view the notion of a stateless society as, at best, a utopian dream. In terms of means, anarchists reject as corrupt, and corrupting, the conventional means of exercising political influence: forming political parties, standing for elections, seeking public office and so on. As a result, they have deprived themselves of the advantages of political organization and strategic planning, often placing their faith instead in mass spontaneity and a popular thirst for freedom. Nevertheless, anarchism refuses to die. Precisely because of its uncompromising attitude to authority and political activism, it has an enduring, and often strong, moral appeal, particularly to the young. This can be seen, for example, in the prominence of anarchist ideas, slogans and groups within the emergent anti-capitalist or anti-globalization movement.

Core themes – against the state

The defining feature of anarchism is its opposition to the state and the accompanying institutions of government and law. Anarchists have a preference for a stateless society in which free individuals manage their affairs by voluntary agreement, without compulsion or coercion. However, the ideological character of anarchism is blurred by two factors. First, anarchism is, arguably, stronger on moral assertion than on analysis and explanation. As anarchism is based on the assumption that human beings are, at heart, moral creatures, instinctively drawn to freedom and **autonomy**, its energies have often been more directed towards awakening these moral instincts than to analyzing the system of state oppression and explaining how it can or should be challenged. Second, anarchism is, in a sense, less a unified and coherent ideology in its own right, and more a point of overlap between two rival ideologies – liberalism and socialism – the point at which both ideologies reach anti-statist conclusions. This is illustrated in Figure 6.1. Anarchism thus has a dual character: it can be

Autonomy: Literally, self-government; the ability to control one's own destiny by virtue of enjoying independence from external influences.

interpreted as either a form of 'ultra-liberalism', which resembles extreme liberal individualism, or as a form of 'ultra-socialism', which resembles extreme socialist collectivism. Nevertheless, anarchism is justified in being treated as a separate ideology, in that its supporters, despite drawing on very different political traditions, are united by a series of broader principles and positions. The most significant of these are the following:

- anti-statism
- natural order
- anti-clericalism
- economic freedom

Figure 6.1
The nature
of anarchism

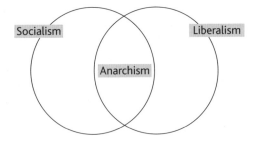

Anti-statism

Sébastien Faure, in *Encyclopédie anarchiste*, defined anarchism as 'the negation of the principle of Authority'. The anarchist case against authority is simple and clear: authority is an offence against the principles of freedom and equality. Anarchism is unique in that it endorses the principles of absolute freedom and unrestrained political equality. In this light, authority, based as it is on political inequality and the alleged right of one person to influence the behaviour of others, enslaves, oppresses and limits human life. It damages and corrupts both those who are subject to authority and those who are in authority. Since human beings are free and autonomous creatures, to be subject to authority means to be diminished, to have one s essential nature suppressed and thereby succumb to debilitating dependency. To be in authority, even the so-called expert authority of doctors and teachers, which flows from the unequal distribution of knowledge in society, is to acquire an appetite for prestige, control and eventually domination. Authority therefore gives rise to a 'psychology of power', based on a pattern of 'dominance and submission', a society in which, according to the US anarchist and social critic Paul Goodman (1911–72), 'many are ruthless and most live in fear' (1977).

THE STATE

LIBERALS see the state as a neutral arbiter amongst the competing interests and groups in society, a vital guarantee of social order. While classical liberals treat the state as a necessary evil and extol the virtues of a minimal or nightwatchman state, modern liberals recognize the state's positive role in widening freedom and promoting equal opportunities.

CONSERVATIVES link the state to the need to provide authority and discipline and to protect society from chaos and disorder, hence their traditional preference for a strong state. However, whereas traditional conservatives support a pragmatic balance between the state and civil society, neoliberals have called for the state to be 'rolled back', as it threatens economic prosperity and is driven, essentially, by bureaucratic self-interest.

SOCIALISTS have adopted contrasting views of the state. Marxists have stressed the link between the state and the class system, seeing it either as an instrument of class rule or as a means of ameliorating class tensions. Other socialists, however, regard the state as an embodiment of the common good, and thus approve of interventionism in either its social-democratic or state-collectivist form.

ANARCHISTS reject the state outright, believing it to be an unnecessary evil. The sovereign, compulsory and coercive authority of the state is seen as nothing less than legalized oppression operating in the interests of the powerful, propertied and privileged. As the state is inherently evil and oppressive, all states have the same essential character.

FASCISTS, particularly in the Italian tradition, see the state as a supreme ethical ideal, reflecting the undifferentiated interests of the national community, hence their belief in totalitarianism (see p. 217). The Nazis, however, saw the state more as a vessel that contains, or tool that serves, the race or nation.

FEMINISTS have viewed the state as an instrument of male power, the patriarchal state serving to exclude women from, or subordinate them within, the public or 'political' sphere of life. Liberal feminists nevertheless regard the state as an instrument of reform that is susceptible to electoral and other pressures.

FUNDAMENTALISTS have adopted a broadly positive attitude towards the state, seeing it as a means of bringing about social, moral and cultural renewal. The fundamentalist state is therefore regarded as a political manifestation of religious authority and wisdom.

In practice, the anarchist critique of authority usually focuses on *political* authority, especially when it is backed up by the machinery of the modern state. Anarchism is defined by its radical rejection of state power, a stance that sets anarchism apart from all other political ideologies (with the exception of Marxism). The flavour of this anarchist critique of law and government is conveyed by one of Proudhon's famous diatribes:

> To be governed is to be watched over, inspected, spied on, directed, legislated, regimented, closed in, indoctrinated, preached at, controlled, assessed, evaluated, censored, commanded; all by creatures that have neither the right, nor the wisdom, nor the virtue. (Quoted in Marshall, 1993, p. 245)

The state is a sovereign body that exercises supreme authority over all individuals and associations living within a defined geographical area. Anarchists emphasize that the authority of the state is absolute and unlimited: law can restrict public behaviour, limit political activity, regulate economic life, interfere with private morality and thinking, and so on. The authority of the state is also compulsory. Anarchists reject the liberal notion that political authority arises from voluntary agreement, through some form of 'social contract', and argue instead that individuals become subject to state authority either by being born in a particular country or through conquest. Furthermore, the state is a coercive body, whose laws must be obeyed because they are backed up by the threat of punishment. For the Russian-born US anarchist Emma Goldman (1869–1940), government was symbolized by 'the club, the gun, the handcuff, or the prison'. The state can deprive individuals of their property, their liberty and ultimately, through capital punishment, their lives. The state is also exploitative, in that it robs individuals of their property through a system of taxation, once again backed up by the force of law and the possibility of punishment. Anarchists often argue that the state acts in alliance with the wealthy and privileged, and therefore serves to oppress the poor and weak. Finally, the state is destructive. 'War', as the US anarchist Randolph Bourne (1886–1918) suggested, 'is the health of the State' (1977). Individuals are required to fight, kill and die in wars that are invariably precipitated by a quest for territorial expansion, plunder or national glory by one state at the expense of others.

The basis of this critique of the state lies in the anarchist view of human nature. Although anarchists subscribe to a highly optimistic, if not utopian, view of human potential, they are also deeply pessimistic about the corrupting influence of political authority and economic inequality. Human beings can be either 'good' or 'evil' depending on the political and social circumstances in which they live. People who would otherwise be cooperative, sympathetic and sociable, become nothing less than oppressive tyrants when raised up above others by power, privilege or wealth. In other words, anarchists replace the liberal warning that 'power tends to corrupt and absolute power corrupts absolutely' (Lord Acton, 1956) with the more radical and alarming warning that power in any shape or form will corrupt absolutely. The state, as a repository of sovereign, compulsory and coercive authority, is therefore nothing less than a concentrated form of evil. The anarchist theory of the state has nevertheless also attracted criticism. Quite apart from concerns about the theory of human nature on which it is based, the assumption that state oppression stems from the corruption of individuals by their political and social circumstances is circular, in that it is unable to explain how political authority arose in the first place.

Natural order

Anarchists not only regard the state as evil, but also believe it to be unnecessary. William Godwin sought to demonstrate this by, in effect, turning the most celebrated justification for the state – social contract theory – on its head. The social contract arguments of Hobbes (see p. 72) and Locke (see p. 37) suggest that a stateless society, the 'state of nature', amounts to a civil war of each against all, making orderly and stable life impossible. The

William Godwin
(1756–1836)

GODWIN

UK philosopher and novelist. Godwin was a Presbyterian minister who lost his faith and eventually became a professional writer, *Caleb Williams* (1794) being his most successful novel. He led an intellectual circle that included his wife, Mary Wollstonecraft (see p. 243) and a group of aspiring writers, among whom were Wordsworth and Shelley, his son-in-law.

Godwin's political reputation was established by *Enquiry Concerning Political Justice* ([1773] 1971) which, by developing a thorough-going critique of authoritarianism, constituted the first full exposition of anarchist beliefs. Godwin developed an extreme form of liberal rationalism that amounted to an argument for human perfectibility based on education and social conditioning. Though an individualist, Godwin believed that humans are capable of genuinely disinterested benevolence.

UTOPIANISM

A utopia (from the Greek *outopia*, meaning 'nowhere', or *eutopia*, meaning 'good place') is literally an ideal or perfect society. Although utopias of various kinds can be envisaged, most are characterized by the abolition of want, the absence of conflict and the avoidance of oppression and violence. Utopianism is a style of political theorizing that develops a critique of the existing order by constructing a model of an ideal or perfect alternative. Good examples are anarchism and Marxism. Utopian theories are usually based on assumptions about the unlimited possibilities of human self-development. However, utopianism is often used as a pejorative term to imply deluded or fanciful thinking, a belief in an unrealistic and unachievable goal.

source of such strife lies in human nature, which according to Hobbes and Locke is essentially selfish, greedy and potentially aggressive. Only a sovereign state can restrain such impulses and guarantee social order. In short, order is impossible without law. Godwin, in contrast, suggested that human beings are essentially rational creatures, inclined by education and enlightened judgement to live in accordance with truth and universal moral laws. He thus believed that people have a natural propensity to organize their own lives in a harmonious and peaceful fashion. Indeed, in his view it is the corrupting influence of government and unnatural laws, rather than any 'original sin' in human beings, that creates injustice, greed and aggression. Government, in other words, is not the solution to the problem of order, but its cause. Anarchists have often sympathized with the famous opening words of Jean-Jacques Rousseau's (see p. 153) *Social Contract* ([1762] 1913), 'Man was born free, yet everywhere he is in chains.'

At the heart of anarchism lies an unashamed utopianism, a belief in the natural goodness, or at least potential goodness, of humankind. From this perspective, social order arises naturally and spontaneously; it does not require the machinery of 'law and order'. This is why anarchist conclusions have only been reached by political thinkers whose views of human nature are sufficiently optimistic to sustain the notions of natural order and spontaneous harmony. For example, collectivist anarchists stressed the human capacity for sociable and cooperative behaviour, while individualist anarchists highlight the importance of enlightened human reason. Not uncommonly, this potential for spontaneous harmony within human nature is linked to the belief that nature itself, and indeed the universe, are biased in favour of natural order. Anarchists have thus sometimes been drawn to the

ideas of non-western religions such as Buddhism and Taoism, which emphasize interdependence and oneness. The most influential modern version of
such ideas is found in the notion of ecology, particular the 'social ecology'
of thinkers such as Murray Bookchin (see p. 275). Social ecology is
discussed in Chapter 9 in relation to eco-anarchism.

However, anarchism is not simply based on a belief in human 'goodness'.
In the first place, anarchist theories of human nature have often been
complex, and have acknowledged that rival potentialities reside within the
human soul. For instance, in their different ways, Proudhon, Bakunin and
Kropotkin (see p. 191) accepted that human beings could be selfish and
competitive as well as sociable and cooperative (Morland, 1997). Although
the human 'core may be morally and intellectually enlightened, a capacity
for corruption lurks within each and every individual. Second, anarchists
have paid as much attention to social institutions as they have to human
nature. They regard human nature as 'plastic', in the sense that it is shaped
by the social, political and economic circumstances within which people
live. Just as law, government and the state breed a domination/subordination
complex, other social institutions nurture respect, cooperation and spontaneous harmony. Collectivist anarchists thus endorse common ownership or
mutualist institutions, while individualist anarchists have supported the
market. Nevertheless, the belief in a stable and peaceful yet stateless society
has usually been viewed as the weakest and most contentious aspect of anarchist theory. Opponents of anarchism have argued that, however socially
enlightened institutions may be, if selfish or negative impulses are basic to
human nature and not merely evidence of corruption, the prospect of natural
order is nothing more than a utopian dream.

Anti-clericalism

Although the state has been the principal target of anarchist hostility, the
same criticisms apply to any other form of compulsory authority. Indeed,
anarchists have sometimes expressed as much bitterness towards the church
as they have towards the state, particularly in the nineteenth century. This
perhaps explains why anarchism has prospered in countries with strong religious traditions, such as Catholic Spain, France, Italy and the countries of
Latin America, where it has helped to articulate anti-clerical sentiments.

Anarchist objections to organized religion serve to highlight broader criticisms of authority in general. Religion, for example, has often been seen as
the source of authority itself. The idea of God represents the notion of a
'supreme being' who commands ultimate and unquestionable authority. For
anarchists such as Proudhon and Bakunin, an anarchist political philosophy

had to be based on the rejection of Christianity because only then could human beings be regarded as free and independent. Moreover, anarchists have suspected that religious and political authority usually work hand in hand. Bakunin proclaimed that 'The abolition of the Church and the State must be the first and indispensable condition of the true liberation of society'. Anarchists view religion as one of the pillars of the state: it propagates an ideology of obedience and submission to both spiritual leaders and earthly rulers. As the Bible says, 'give unto Caesar that which is Caesar's'. Earthly rulers have often looked to religion to legitimize their power, most obviously in the doctrine of the divine right of kings.

Finally, religion seeks to impose a set of moral principles on the individual, and to establish a code of acceptable behaviour. Religious belief requires conformity to standards of 'good' and 'evil', which are defined and policed by figures of religious authority such as priests, imams or rabbis. The individual is thus robbed of moral autonomy and the capacity to make ethical judgements. Nevertheless, anarchists do not reject the religious impulse altogether. There is a clear mystical strain within anarchism.

Millenarianism:
A belief in a thousand-year period of divine rule; political millenarianism offers the prospect of a sudden and complete emancipation from misery and oppression.

Anarchists can be said to hold an essentially spiritual conception of human nature, a utopian belief in the virtually unlimited possibilities of human self-development and in the bonds that unite humanity, and indeed all living things. Early anarchists were sometimes influenced by **millenarianism**; indeed, anarchism has often been portrayed as a form of political millenarianism. Modern anarchists have often been attracted to religions such as Taoism and Zen Buddhism, which offer the prospect of personal insight and preach the values of toleration, respect and natural harmony.

Economic freedom

Anarchists have rarely seen the overthrow of the state as an end in itself, but have also been interested in challenging the structures of social and economic life. Bakunin (1973) argued that 'political power and wealth are inseparable'. In the nineteenth century, anarchists usually worked within the working-class movement and subscribed to a broadly socialist philosophy. Capitalism was understood in class terms: a 'ruling class' exploits and oppresses 'the masses'. However, this 'ruling class' was not, in line with Marxism, interpreted in narrow economic terms, but was seen to encompass all those who command wealth, power or privilege in society. It therefore included kings and princes, politicians and state officials, judges and police officers, and bishops and priests, as well as industrialists and bankers.

Michael Bakunin
(1814 –76)

BAKUNIN

Russian anarchist and revolutionary. Bakunin was born into a prosperous aristocratic family. He renounced a military career and, after philosophical studies, was drawn into political activism by the 1848 revolutions. By the 1860s, he had renounced Slav nationalism for anarchism and spent the rest of his life as an agitator and propagandist, famous for his interest in secret societies and his endless appetite for political intrigue.

Bakunin's anarchism was based on a belief in human sociability, expressed in the desire for freedom within a community of equals and in the 'sacred instinct of revolt'. He embraced a view of collectivism as self-governing communities of free individuals, which put him at odds with Marx and his followers. However, Bakunin's real importance is more as the founder of the historical anarchist movement than as an original thinker or an anarchist theoretician.

Bakunin thus argued that in every developed society three social groups can be identified: a vast majority who are exploited; a minority who are exploited but also exploit others in equal measure; and 'the supreme governing estate', a small minority of 'exploiters and oppressors pure and simple'. Hence, nineteenth-century anarchists identified themselves with the poor and oppressed and sought to carry out a social revolution in the name of the 'exploited masses', in which both capitalism and the state would be swept away.

However, it is the economic structure of life that most keenly exposes tensions within anarchism. Although many anarchists acknowledge a kinship with socialism, based on a common distaste for property and inequality, others have defended property rights and even revered competitive capitalism. This highlights the distinction between the two major anarchist traditions, one of which is collectivist and the other individualist. Collectivist anarchists advocate an economy based on cooperation and collective ownership, while individualist anarchists support the market and private property.

Despite such fundamental differences, anarchists nevertheless agree about their distaste for the economic systems that dominated much of the twentieth century. All anarchists oppose the 'managed capitalism' that flourished in western countries after 1945. Collectivist anarchists argue that state intervention merely props up a system of class exploitation and gives capitalism a human face. Individualist anarchists suggest that intervention distorts the competitive market and creates economies dominated by both public and private monopolies. Anarchists have been even more united in their disapproval of Soviet-style 'state socialism'. Individualist anarchists object to the violation of property rights and individual freedom that, they argue, occurs in a planned economy. Collectivist anarchists argue that 'state socialism' is a contradiction in terms, in that the state merely replaces the capitalist class as the main source of exploitation. Anarchists of all kinds have a preference for an economy in which free individuals manage their own affairs without the need for state ownership or regulation. However, this has allowed them to endorse a number of quite different economic systems, ranging from 'anarcho-communism' to 'anarcho-capitalism'.

Collectivist anarchism

The philosophical roots of collectivist anarchism lie in socialism rather than liberalism. Anarchist conclusions can be reached by pushing socialist collectivism to its limits. Collectivism (see p. 104) is, in essence, the belief that human beings are social animals, better suited to working together for the common good than striving for individual self-interest. Collectivist anarchism, sometimes called social anarchism, stresses the human capacity for social solidarity, or what Kropotkin termed 'mutual aid'. As pointed out earlier, this does not amount to a naïve belief in 'natural goodness', but rather highlights the potential for goodness that resides within all human beings. Human beings are, at heart, sociable, gregarious and cooperative creatures. In this light, the natural and proper relationship between and amongst people is one of sympathy, affection and harmony. When people are linked together by the recognition of a common humanity, they have no need to be regulated or controlled by government: as Bakunin (1973) proclaimed, 'Social solidarity is the first human law; freedom is the second law'. Not only is government unnecessary but, in replacing freedom with oppression, it also makes social solidarity impossible.

Philosophical and ideological overlaps between anarchism and socialism, particularly Marxist socialism, are evident in the fact that anarchists have often worked within a broad revolutionary socialist movement. For example, the First International, 1864–72, was set up by supporters of Proudhon and Marx. A number of clear theoretical parallels can be identified between collectivist anarchism and Marxism. Both fundamentally reject capitalism, regarding it as a system of class exploitation and structural injustice. Both have endorsed revolution as the preferred means of bringing about political change. Both exhibit a preference for the collective ownership of wealth and the communal organization of social life. Both believe that a fully communist society would be anarchic, expressed by Marx in the theory of the 'withering away' of the state. Both, therefore, agree that human beings have the ultimate capacity to order their affairs without the need for political authority.

Nevertheless, anarchism and socialism diverge at a number of points. This occurs most clearly in relation to parliamentary socialism. Anarchists, dismiss parliamentary socialism as a contradiction in terms. Not only is it impossible to reform or 'humanize' capitalism through the corrupt and corrupting mechanisms of government, but also any expansion in the role and responsibilities of the state can only serve to entrench oppression, albeit in the name of equality and social justice. The bitterest disagreement between collectivist anarchists and Marxists centres on their rival conceptions of the transition from capitalism to communism. Marxists have called for a revolutionary 'dictatorship of the proletariat'. This proletarian state will nevertheless 'wither away' as capitalist class antagonisms abate. In this view, state power is nothing but a reflection of the class system, the state being, in essence, an instrument of class oppression. Anarchists, on the other hand, regard the state as evil and oppressive in its own right: it is, by its very nature, a corrupt and corrupting body. They therefore draw no distinction between bourgeois states and proletarian states. Genuine revolution, for an anarchist, requires not only the overthrow of capitalism but also the immediate and final overthrow of state power. The state cannot be allowed to 'wither away'; it must be abolished.

Mutualism

The anarchist belief in social solidarity has been used to justify various forms of cooperative behaviour. At one extreme, it has led to a belief in pure communism, but it has also generated the more modest ideas of **mutualism**, associated with Pierre-Joseph Proudhon. In a sense, Proudhon's libertarian socialism stands between the individualist and collectivist traditions of anarchism, Proudhon's ideas sharing much in common with those of US individualists such as Josiah Warren (1798–1874). In *What is Property?*, Proudhon came up with the famous statement that 'Property is theft', and condemned a system of economic exploitation based on the accumulation of capital. Nevertheless, unlike Marx, Proudhon was not opposed to all forms of private property, distinguishing between property and what he called 'possessions'. In particular, he admired the independence and initiative of smallholding peasants, craftsmen and artisans. Proudhon

Mutualism: A system of fair and equitable exchange, in which individuals or groups bargain with one another, trading goods and services without profiteering or exploitation.

Pierre-Joseph Proudhon
(1809–65)

PROUDHON

French anarchist. Proudhon was a largely self-educated printer, who was drawn into radical politics in Lyons before settling in Paris in 1847. As a member of the 1848 Constituent Assembly, Proudhon famously voted against the constitution 'because it was a constitution'. He was later imprisoned for three years, after which, disillusioned with active politics, he concentrated on writing and theorizing.

Proudhon's best-known work, *What is Property?* ([1840] 1970) attacked both traditional property rights and communism, and argued instead for mutualism, a cooperative productive system geared towards need rather than profit and organized within self-governing communities. Nevertheless, towards the end of his life, Proudhon sought an alliance with the labour movement, and in *The Federal Principle* (1863) acknowledged the need for a minimal state to 'set things in motion'.

therefore sought, through mutualism, to establish a system of property ownership that would avoid exploitation and promote social harmony. Social interaction in such a system would be voluntary, mutually beneficial and harmonious, thus requiring no regulation or interference by government. Proudhon's followers tried to put these ideas into practice by setting up mutual credit banks in France and Switzerland, which provided cheap loans for investors and charged a rate of interest only high enough to cover the cost of running the bank, but not so high that it made a profit. Proudhon's own views were largely founded on his admiration for small communities of peasants or craftsmen, notably the watchmakers of Switzerland, who had traditionally managed their affairs on the basis of mutual cooperation.

Anarcho-syndicalism

Although mutualism and anarcho-communism exerted significant influence within the broader socialist movement in the late nineteenth and early twentieth centuries, anarchism only developed into a mass movement in its own right in the form of anarcho-syndicalism. Syndicalism is a form of revolutionary trade unionism, drawing its name from the French word *syndicat*, meaning union or group. Syndicalism emerged first in France, and was embraced by the powerful CGT union in the period before 1914. Syndicalist ideas spread to Italy, Latin America, the USA and, most significantly, Spain, where the country's largest union, the CNT, supported them.

Syndicalist theory drew on socialist ideas and advanced a crude notion of class war. Workers and peasants were seen to constitute an oppressed class, and industrialists, landlords, politicians, judges and the police were portrayed as exploiters. Workers could defend themselves by organizing syndicates or unions, based on particular crafts, industries or professions. In the short term, these syndicates could act as conventional trade unions, raising wages, shortening hours and improving working conditions. However, syndicalists were also revolutionaries, who looked forward to the overthrow of capitalism and the seizure of power by the workers. In *Reflections on Violence* ([1908] 1950), Georges Sorel (1847–1922), the influential French syndicalist theorist, argued that such a revolution would come about through a general strike, a 'revolution of empty hands'. Sorel believed that the general strike was a 'myth', a symbol of working-class power, capable of inspiring popular revolt.

Although syndicalist theory was at times unsystematic and confused, it nevertheless exerted a strong attraction for anarchists who wished to spread their ideas among the masses. As anarchists entered the syndicalist movement, they developed the distinctive ideas of anarcho-syndicalism. Two features of syndicalism inspired particular anarchist enthusiasm. First, syndicalists rejected conventional politics as corrupting and pointless. Working-class power, they believed, should be exerted through direct action, boycotts, sabotage and strikes, and ultimately a general strike. Second, anarchists saw the syndicate as a model for the decentralized, non-hierarchic society of the future. Syndicates typically exhibited a high degree of grassroots democracy and formed federations with other syndicates, either in the same area or in the same industry.

Although anarcho-syndicalism enjoyed genuine mass support, at least until the Spanish Civil War, it failed to achieve its revolutionary objectives. Beyond the rather vague idea of the general strike, anarcho-syndicalism did not develop a clear political strategy or a theory of revolution, relying instead on the hope of a spontaneous uprising of the exploited and oppressed. Other anarchists have criticized syndicalism for concentrating too narrowly on short-term trade union goals and, therefore, for leading anarchism away from revolution and towards reformism.

Anarcho-communism

In its most radical form, a belief in social solidarity leads in the direction of collectivism and full **communism**. Sociable and gregarious human beings

Communism:
The principle of the common ownership of wealth; communism is often used more broadly to refer to movements or regimes that are based on Marxist principles.

should lead a shared and communal existence. For example, labour is a social experience, people work in common with fellow human beings and the wealth they produce should therefore be owned in common by the community, rather than by any single individual. In this sense, all forms of private property are theft: they represent the exploitation of workers, who alone create wealth, by employers who merely own it. Furthermore, private property encourages selfishness and, particularly offensive to the anarchist, promotes conflict and social disharmony. Inequality in the ownership of wealth fosters greed, envy and resentment, and therefore breeds crime and disorder.

Anarcho-communism is rooted in highly optimistic beliefs about the human capacity for cooperation, most famously expressed by Peter Kropotkin's theory of 'mutual aid'. Kropotkin attempted to provide a biological foundation for social solidarity by a re-examination of Darwin's theory of evolution. Whereas social thinkers such as Herbert Spencer (1820–1903) had used Darwinism to support the idea that humankind is naturally competitive and aggressive, Kropotkin argued that species are successful precisely because they manage to harness collective energies though cooperation. The process of evolution thus strengthens sociability and favours cooperation over competition. Successful species, such as the human species, must, Kropotkin concluded, have a strong propensity for mutual aid. Kropotkin argued that while mutual aid had flourished in, for example, the city-states of Ancient Greece and Medieval Europe, it had been subverted by competitive capitalism, threatening the further evolution of the human species.

Although Proudhon had warned that communism could only be brought about by an authoritarian state, anarcho-communists such as Kropotkin and Malatesta (1853–1932) argued that true communism requires the abolition of the state. Anarcho-communists admire small, self-managing communities along the lines of the medieval city-state or the peasant commune. Kropotkin envisaged that an anarchic society would consist of a collection of largely self-sufficient communes, each owning its wealth in common. From the anarcho-communist perspective, the communal organization of social and economic life has three key advantages. First, as communes are based on the

Direct democracy:
Popular self-government, characterized by the direct and continuous participation of citizens in the tasks of government.

principles of sharing and collective endeavour, they strengthen the bonds of compassion and solidarity, and help to keep greed and selfishness at bay. Second, within communes decisions are made through a process of participatory or **direct democracy**, which guarantees a high level of popular participation and political equality. Popular self-government is the only form of government

Peter Kropotkin
(1842–1921)

Russian geographer and anarchist theorist. The son of a noble family who first entered the service of Tsar Alexander II, Kropotkin encountered anarchist ideas whilst working in the Jura region on the French–Swiss border. After imprisonment in St Petersburg in 1874, he travelled widely in Europe, returning to Russia after the 1917 Revolution.

Kropotkin's anarchism was imbued with the scientific spirit and based upon a theory of evolution that provided an alternative to Darwin's. By seeing mutual aid as the principal means of human and animal development, he claimed to provide an empirical basis for both anarchism and communism. Kropotkin's major works include *Mutual Aid* (1897), *Fields, Factories and Workshops* (1901) and *The Conquest of Bread* (1906).

that would be acceptable to anarchists. Third, communes are small-scale or 'human-scale' communities, which allow people to manage their own affairs through face-to-face interaction. In the anarchist view, centralization is always associated with depersonalized and bureaucratic social processes.

Individualist anarchism

The philosophical basis of individualist anarchism lies in the liberal idea of the sovereign individual. In many ways, anarchist conclusions are reached by pushing liberal individualism (see p. 28) to its logical extreme. For example, William Godwin's anarchism amounts to a form of extreme classical liberalism. At the heart of liberalism is a belief in the primacy of the individual and the central importance of individual freedom. In the classical liberal view, freedom is negative: it consists in the absence of external constraints on the individual. When individualism is taken to its extreme, it therefore implies individual sovereignty: the idea that absolute and unlimited authority resides within each human being. From this perspective, any constraint on the individual is evil; but when this constraint is imposed by the state, by definition a sovereign, compulsory and coercive body, it amounts to an absolute evil. Quite simply, the individual cannot be sovereign in a society ruled by law and government. Individualism and the state are thus irreconcilable principles.

Although these arguments are liberal in inspiration, significant differences exist between liberalism and individualist anarchism. First, while liberals accept the importance of individual liberty, they do not believe this can be guaranteed in a stateless society. Classical liberals argue that a minimal or 'nightwatchman' state is necessary to prevent self-seeking individuals from abusing one another by theft, intimidation, violence or even murder. Law therefore exists to protect freedom, rather than constrain it. Modern liberals take this argument further, and defend the state intervention on the grounds that it enlarges positive freedom. Anarchists, in contrast, believe that individuals can conduct themselves peacefully, harmoniously and prosperously without the need for government to 'police' society and protect them from their fellow human beings. Anarchists differ from liberals because they believe that free individuals can live and work together constructively because they are rational and moral creatures. Reason dictates that where conflict exists it should be resolved by arbitration or debate, and not by violence.

Second, liberals believe that government power can be 'tamed' or controlled by the development of constitutional and representative institutions. Constitutions claim to protect the individual by limiting the power of government and creating checks and balances amongst its various institutions. Regular elections are designed to force government to be accountable to the general public, or at least a majority of the electorate. Anarchists dismiss the idea of limited, constitutional or representative government. They regard **constitutionalism** and democracy as simply façades, behind which naked political oppression operates. All laws infringe individual liberty, whether the government that enacts them is constitutional or arbitrary, democratic or dictatorial. In other words, all states are an offence against individual liberty.

Constitutionalism: The belief that government power should be exercised within a framework of rules (a constitution) that define the duties, powers and functions of government institutions and the rights of the individual (see p. 39).

Egoism

The boldest statement of anarchist convictions built on the idea of the sovereign individual is found in Max Stirner's *The Ego and His Own* ([1845] 1971). Like Marx, the German philosopher Stirner (1806–56) was deeply influenced by ideas of Hegel (1770–1831), but the two arrived at fundamentally different conclusions. Stirner's theories represent an extreme form of individualism. The term 'egoism' can have two meanings. It can suggest that individuals are essentially concerned about their ego or 'self', that they are self-interested or self-seeking, an assumption that would be accepted by thinkers such as Hobbes or Locke. Self-interested-ness, however, can generate conflict amongst individuals and justify the existence of a state, which would be needed to restrain each individual from harming or abusing others.

In Stirner's view, egoism is a philosophy that places the individual self at the centre of the moral universe. The individual, from this perspective, should simply act as he or she chooses, without any consideration for laws, social conventions, religious or moral principles. Such a position amounts to a form of nihilism, literally a belief in nothing. This is a position that clearly points in the direction of both atheism and an extreme form of individualist anarchism. However, as Stirner's anarchism also dramatically turned its back on the principles of the Enlightenment and contained few proposals about how order could be maintained in a stateless society, it had relatively little impact on the emerging anarchist movement. His ideas nevertheless influenced Nietzsche and twentieth-century existentialism.

Libertarianism

The individualist argument was more fully developed in the USA by liber-tarian thinkers such as Henry David Thoreau (1817–62), Lysander Spooner (1808–87), Benjamin Tucker (1854–1939) and Josiah Warren. Thoreau's quest for spiritual truth and self-reliance led him to flee from civilized life and live for several years in virtual solitude, close to nature, an experience described in *Walden* ([1854] 1983). In his most political work, *Civil Disobedience* ([1849] 1983), Thoreau approved of Jefferson's liberal motto, 'That government is best which governs least', but adapted it to conform with his own anarchist sentiment: 'That government is best which governs not at all'. For Thoreau, individualism leads in the direction of civil disobe-dience: the individual has to be faithful to his or her conscience and do only what each believes to be right, regardless of the demands of society or the laws made by government. Thoreau's anarchism places individual conscience above the demands of political obligation. In Thoreau's case, this led him to disobey a US government he thought to be acting immorally in both upholding slavery and waging war against other countries.

Libertarianism:
A belief that the individual should enjoy the widest possible realm of freedom; libertarianism implies the removal of both external and internal constraints upon the individual.

Benjamin Tucker took **libertarianism** (see p. 86) further by considering how autonomous individuals could live and work with one another without the danger of conflict or disorder. Two possible solutions to this problem are available to the individualist. The first emphasizes human rationality, and suggests that when conflicts or disagreements develop they can be resolved by reasoned discussion. This, for example, was the position adopted by Godwin, who believed that truth will always tend to displace falsehood. The second solution is to find some sort of mechanism through which the independent actions of free individuals could be brought into harmony with one another. Extreme individualists such as Warren and Tucker believed that this could be achieved through a system of market exchange. Warren thought that individuals have a sovereign right to the property they themselves produce, but are also forced by economic logic to work with others in order to gain the advantages of the division of labour. He suggested that this could be achieved by a system of 'labour-for-labour' exchange, and set up 'time stores' through which one person's labour could be exchanged for a promise to return labour in kind. Tucker argued that 'Genuine anarchism is consistent Manchesterism', referring to the nineteenth-century free-trade, free-market principles of Richard Cobden and John Bright (see Nozick, 1974).

Anarcho-capitalism

The revival of interest in free-market economics in the late twentieth century led to increasingly radical political conclusions. New right conservatives, attracted to classical economics, wished to 'get government off the back of business' and allow the economy to be disciplined by market forces, rather than managed by an interventionist state. Right-wing libertarians such as Robert Nozick (see p. 92) revived the idea of a minimal state, whose principal function is to protect individual rights. Other thinkers, for instance Ayn Rand (1905–82), Murray Rothbard (1926–95) and David Friedman, have pushed free-market ideas to their limit and developed a form of anarcho-capitalism. They have argued that government can be abolished and be replaced by unregulated market competition. Property should be owned by sovereign individuals, who may choose, if they wish, to enter into voluntary contracts with others in the pursuit of self-interest. The individual thus remains free and the market, beyond the control of any single individual or group, regulates all social interaction.

Anarcho-capitalists go well beyond the ideas of free-market liberalism. Liberals believe that the market is an effective and efficient mechanism for delivering most goods, but argue that it also has its limits. Some services, such as the maintenance of domestic order, the enforcement of contracts and protection against external attack, are 'public goods', which must be provided by the state because they cannot be supplied through market competition. Anarcho-capitalists, however, believe that the market can

TENSIONS WITHIN
ANARCHISM

INDIVIDUALIST ANARCHISM	v.	COLLECTIVIST ANARCHISM
ultra-liberalism	←→	ultra-socialism
extreme individualism	←→	extreme collectivism
sovereign individual	←→	common humanity
civil disobedience	←→	social revolution
atomism	←→	class politics
egoism	←→	cooperation/mutualism
contractual obligation	←→	social duty
market mechanism	←→	communal organization
private property	←→	common ownership
anarcho-capitalism	←→	anarcho-communism

satisfy all human wants. For example, Rothbard (1978) recognized that in an anarchist society individuals will seek protection from one another, but argued that such protection can be delivered competitively by privately owned 'protection associations' and 'private courts', without the need for a police force or a state court system.

Indeed, according to anarcho-capitalists, profit-making protection agencies would offer a better service than the present police force because competition would provide consumers with a choice, forcing agencies to be cheap, efficient and responsive to consumer needs. Similarly, private courts would be forced to develop a reputation for fairness in order to attract custom from individuals wishing to resolve a conflict. Most importantly, unlike the authority of public bodies, the contracts thus made with private agencies would be entirely voluntary, regulated only by impersonal market forces. Radical though such proposals may sound, the policy of privatization has already made substantial advances in many western countries. In the USA, several states already use private prisons, and experiments with private courts and arbitration services are well established. In the UK, private prisons and the use of private protection agencies have become commonplace, and schemes such as 'Neighbourhood Watch' have helped to transfer responsibility for public order from the police to the community.

Roads to anarchy

Anarchists have been more successful in describing their ideals in books and pamphlets than they have been at putting them into practice. Quite commonly, anarchists have turned away from active politics, concentrating instead on writing or on experiments in communal or cooperative living. Anarchists have not only been apolitical, turning away from political life, but also positively antipolitical, repelled by the conventional processes and machinery of politics. The problem confronting anarchism is that if the state is regarded as evil and oppressive, any attempt to win government power or even influence government must be corrupting and unhealthy. For example, electoral politics is based on a model of representative democracy, which anarchists firmly reject. Political power is always oppressive, regardless of whether it is acquired through the ballot box or at the point of a gun. Similarly, anarchists are disenchanted by political parties, both parliamentary and revolutionary parties, because they are bureaucratic and hierarchic organizations. The idea of an anarchist government, an anarchist political party, or an anarchist politician is therefore a contradiction in terms. As there is no conventional 'road to anarchy', anarchists have been forced to explore less orthodox means of political activism.

Revolutionary violence

In the nineteenth century, anarchist leaders tried to rouse the 'oppressed masses' to insurrection and revolt. Michael Bakunin, for example, led a conspiratorial brotherhood, the Alliance for Social Democracy, and took part in anarchist risings in France and Italy. Other anarchists, for example Malatesta in Italy, the Russian Populists and Zapata's revolutionaries in Mexico, worked for a peasant revolution. However, anarchist risings ultimately failed, partly because they were based on a belief in spontaneous revolt rather than careful organization. By the end of the nineteenth century, many anarchists had turned their attention to the revolutionary potential of the syndicalist movement, and, during the twentieth century, anarchism increasingly lost support to the better organized and more tightly disciplined communist movement.

Terrorism: The use of violence to induce a climate of fear or terror in order to further political ends; a clearly pejorative and usually subjective term (see p. 293).

Nevertheless, some anarchists continued to place particular emphasis on the revolutionary potential of terrorism and violence. Anarchist violence has been prominent in two periods in particular, in the late nineteenth century, reaching its peak in the 1890s, and again in the 1970s. Anarchists have employed **terrorism** or 'clandestine violence', often involving bombings or assassinations, designed to create an atmosphere of terror or apprehension. Amongst its victims were Tsar Alexander II, King Humbert of Italy, Empress Elizabeth of Austria and Presidents Carnot of France and McKinley of the USA. The typical anarchist terrorist was either a single individual working alone, such as Emile Henry, who was guillotined in 1894 after placing a bomb in the Café Terminus in Paris, or clandestine groups such as the People's Will in Russia, which assassinated Alexander II. In the 1970s, anarchist violence was undertaken by groups such as Baader–Meinhof in West Germany, the Italian Red Brigades, the Japanese Red Army and the Angry Brigade in the UK.

The anarchist case for the use of violence has been distinctive, in that bombings and assassinations have been thought to be just and fair in themselves and not merely a way of exerting political influence. In the anarchist view, violence is a form of revenge or retribution. Violence originates in oppression and exploitation, perpetrated by politicians, industrialists, judges and the police against the working masses. Anarchist violence merely mirrors the everyday violence of society, and directs it towards those who are really guilty. It is therefore a form of 'revolutionary justice'. Violence is also seen as a way of demoralizing the ruling classes, encouraging them to loosen their grip on power and privilege. In addition, violence is a way of raising political consciousness and stimulating the masses to revolt. Russian populists believed violence to be a form of 'propaganda by the deed', a demonstration that the ruling class is weak and defenceless, which, they hoped, would stimulate popular insurrection amongst the peasants.

However, in practice, anarchist violence has been counterproductive at best. Far from awakening the masses to the reality of their oppression, political violence has normally provoked public horror and outrage. There is little doubt that the association between anarchism and violence has damaged the popular appeal of the ideology. Furthermore, violence seems an unpromising way of persuading the ruling class to relinquish power. Violence and coercion challenge the state on the territory on which its superiority is most clearly overwhelming. Terrorist attacks in both the 1890s and the 1970s merely encouraged the state to expand and strengthen its repressive machinery, usually with the backing of public opinion.

Direct action

Short of a revolutionary assault on existing society, anarchists have often employed tactics of **direct action**. Direct action may range from passive resistance to terrorism. Anarcho-syndicalists, for example, refused to engage in conventional, representative politics, preferring instead to exert direct

Direct action: Political action taken outside the constitutional and legal framework; direct action may range from passive resistance to terrorism.

pressure on employers by boycotting their products, sabotaging machinery and organizing strike action. The modern anti-globalization or anti-corporate movement, influenced by anarchism, has also employed strategies of mass popular protest and direct political engagement. From the anarchist point of view, direct action has two advantages. The first is that it is uncontaminated by the processes of government and the machinery of the state. Political discontent and opposition can therefore be expressed openly and honestly; oppositional forces are not diverted in a constitutional direction and cannot be 'managed' by professional politicians.

The second strength of direct action is that it is a form of popular political activism that can be organized on the basis of decentralization and participatory decision-making. This is sometimes seen as the 'new politics', which turns away from established parties, interest groups and representative processes towards a more innovative and theatrical form of protest politics. The clear impact of anarchism can be seen in the tendency of so-called 'new' social movements (such as the feminist, environmental, gay rights and anti-globalization movements) to engage in this form of 'anti-political' politics. Nevertheless, direct action also has its drawbacks. Notably, it may damage public support by leaving political groups and movements that employ it open to the charge of 'irresponsibility' or 'extremism'. Moreover, although direct action attracts media and public attention, it may restrict political influence because it defines the group or movement as a political 'outsider' that is unable to gain access to the process of public policy-making.

Non-violence

In practice, most anarchists see violence as tactically misguided, while others, following Godwin and Proudhon, regard it as abhorrent in principle. These latter anarchists have often been attracted to the principles of non-

Pacifism: The principled rejection of war and all forms of violence as fundamentally evil.

violence and **pacifism** developed by the Russian novelist Leo Tolstoy (1828–1910) and Mahatma Gandhi (see p. 315). Although neither of them can properly be classified as anarchists, both, in different ways, expressed ideas that were sympathetic to anarchism. In his political writings, Tolstoy developed the image of a corrupt and false modern civilization. He suggested that salvation could be achieved by living according to religious principles and returning to a simple, rural existence, based on the traditional life-style of the Russian peasantry. For Tolstoy (1937), Christian respect for life required that 'no person would employ violence against anyone, and under no consideration'. Gandhi campaigned against racial discrimination and led the movement for India's independence from the UK, eventually granted in 1947. His political method was based upon the idea of *satyagraha*, or non-violent resistance, influenced both by the teachings of Tolstoy and Hindu religious principles.

The principle of non-violence has appealed to anarchists for two reasons. First, it reflects a respect for human beings as moral and autonomous creatures. The optimistic anarchist view of human nature thus dictates that other people are treated with compassion and respect. Second, non-violence was attractive as a political strategy. To refrain from the use of force, especially when subjected to intimidation and provocation, demonstrates the strength and moral purity of one's convictions. However, the anarchists who have been attracted to the principles of pacifism and non-violence have tended to shy away from mass political activism, preferring instead to build model communities that reflect the principles of cooperation and mutual respect. They hope that anarchist ideas will be spread not by political campaigns and demonstrations, but through the stark contrast between the peacefulness and contentment enjoyed within such communities, and the 'quiet desperation', in Thoreau's words, that typifies life in conventional society.

Anarchism in the twenty-first century

It would be easy to dismiss the whole idea of anarchism in the twenty-first century as a mere fantasy. After all, anarchism cannot be said to have existed as a significant political movement since the early twentieth century, and even then it failed to provide the basis for political reconstruction in any major society. However, the enduring significance of anarchism is perhaps less that it has provided an ideological basis for acquiring and retaining political power, and more that it has challenged, and thereby fertilized, other political creeds. Anarchists have highlighted the coercive and destructive nature of political power and, in so doing, have countered statist tendencies within other ideologies, notably liberalism, socialism and conservatism. In fact, in this sense, anarchism has had a growing influence on modern political thought. Both the new left and the new right, for instance, have exhibited libertarian tendencies, which bear the imprint of anarchist ideas. The new left encompassed a broad range of movements that were prominent in the 1960s and early 1970s, including student activism, anti-colonialism, feminism and environmentalism. The unifying theme within the new left was the goal of 'liberation', understood to mean personal fulfilment, and it endorsed an activist style of politics that was based on popular protest and direct action, clearly influenced by anarchism. The new right also empha- sizes the importance of individual freedom, but believes that this can only be guaranteed by market competition. Anarcho-capitalists have sought to high- light what they see as the evils of state intervention, and have been promi- nent in the rediscovery of free-market economics.

Does this mean that anarchism in the twenty-first century is destined to be nothing more than a pool of ideas from which other political thinkers and traditions can draw at will? Is anarchism now only of philosophical impor- tance? A more optimistic picture of anarchism's future can be painted. In some respects, the continuing practical significance of anarchism is merely concealed by its increasingly diverse character. In addition to, and in some ways in place of, established political and class struggles, anarchists have

Consumerism: A psychic and social phenomenon whereby personal happiness is equated with the consumption of material possessions

come to address issues such as pollution and environ- mental destruction, **consumerism**, urban development, gender relations and global inequality. Many of these concerns, indeed, are expressed by modern social move- ments such as the anti-capitalist or anti-globalization movement, which, though a broad coalition of ideologi- cal forces, has marked anarchist features. For example, Noam Chomsky, the most important theoretical influence on the anti-globalization movement, developed his ideas on the basis of anarchist assumptions. To argue that anarchism is irrelevant because it has long since ceased to be a mass move-

Noam Chomsky (born 1928)

US linguistic theorist and radical intellectual. Chomsky's *Syntactic Structures* (1957) revolutionized the study of linguistics through the theory of transformational grammar, which proposes that humans have an innate capacity to acquire language. Chomsky's political radi- calism is grounded in anarchist beliefs, in particular in a faith in the moral sensibilities of private citizens and a distrust of all human insti- tutions. His critique of arbitrary authority is most clearly articulated through his criticism of US foreign policy as neo-colonialist and mili- taristic, developed in over 30 books, including *American Power and the New Mandarins* (1969), *New Military Humanism* (1999) and *9/11* (2003). His attack on US democracy places considerable emphasis on the capacity of the media to manipulate ordinary citizens, as argued in *Manufacturing Consent* (with Edward Herman, 1988). Chomsky is the USA's most prominent political dissident.

ment in its own right is perhaps to miss the point. As the world becomes increasingly complex and fragmented, it might be that it is mass politics itself that is dead. From this perspective, anarchism, by virtue of its association with values such as individualism, participation, decentralization and equality, may be better equipped than many other political creeds to respond to the challenges of postmodernity.

Questions for discussion

→ Why do anarchists view the state as evil and oppressive?

→ How and why is anarchism linked to utopianism?

→ How convincing is the anarchist theory of human nature?

→ Is collectivist anarchism simply an extreme form of socialism?

→ How do anarcho-communists and Marxists agree, and over what do they disagree?

→ How do individualist anarchists reconcile egoism with statelessness?

→ Is anarcho-communism merely free-market liberalism taken to its logical conclusion?

→ Why have anarchist ideas been attractive to modern social movements?

→ How has anarchism influenced the analysis of international politics?

Further reading

Carter, A., *The Political Theory of Anarchism* (London: Routledge & Kegan Paul, 1971). A useful and straightforward examination of the anarchist ideas that contrasts anarchism with more orthodox political theory.

Marshall, P., *Demanding the Impossible: A History of Anarchism* (London: Fontana, 1993). A very comprehensive, authoritative and engagingly enthusiastic account of the full range of anarchist theories and beliefs.

Miller, D., *Anarchism* (London: Dent, 1984). An excellent and insightful introduction to anarchist ideas and theories.

Purkis, J. and Bowen, J., *Twenty-first Century Anarchism: Unorthodox Ideas for a New Millennium* (London: Cassell, 1997). An interesting collection of essays that consider anarchist ideas and actions in the late twentieth century.

Roussopoulos, D. (ed.), *The Anarchist Papers* (New York and London: Black Rose Books, 2002). A collection of articles by anarchist thinkers that reflects the range of modern anarchist concerns.

Wolff, R. P., *In Defence of Anarchism*, 2nd edn (Berkeley, CA: University of California Press, 1998). A classic modern examination of the philosophical basis of anarchist thought that responds to the main criticisms of anarchism.

Woodcock, G., Anarchism: *A History of Libertarian Ideas and Movements* (Harmondsworth and New York: Penguin, 1962). For some time the standard work on anarchism as an idea and movement; authoritative and still worth consulting.

CHAPTER 7

FASCISM

The term 'fascism' derives from the Italian word *fasces*, meaning a bundle of rods with an axe-blade protruding that signified the authority of magistrates in Imperial Rome. By the 1890s, the word *fascia* was being used in Italy to refer to a political group or band, usually of revolutionary socialists. It was not until Mussolini employed the term to describe the paramilitary armed squads he formed during and after the First World War that *fascismo* acquired a clearly ideological meaning.

The defining theme of fascism is the idea of an organically unified national community, embodied in a belief in 'strength through unity'. The individual, in a literal sense, is nothing; individual identity must be entirely absorbed into the community or social group. The fascist ideal is that of the 'new man', a hero, motivated by duty, honour and self-sacrifice, prepared to dedicate his life to the glory of his nation or race, and to give unquestioning obedience to a supreme leader. In many ways, fascism constitutes a revolt against the ideas and values that dominated western political thought from the French Revolution onwards; in the words of the Italian fascists' slogan: '1789 is dead'. Values such as rationalism, progress, freedom and equality were thus overturned in the name of struggle, leadership, power, heroism and war. Fascism thus has a strong 'anti-character': it is anti-rational, anti-liberal, anti-conservative, anti-capitalist, anti-bourgeois, anti-communist and so on. Fascism has nevertheless been a complex historical phenomenon, encompassing, many argue, two distinct traditions. Italian fascism was essentially an extreme form of statism that was based on absolute loyalty towards a 'totalitarian' state. In contrast, German fascism, or Nazism, was founded on racial theories, which portrayed the Aryan people as a 'master race' and advanced a virulent form of anti-Semitism.

Origins and development

Whereas liberalism, conservatism and socialism are nineteenth-century ideologies, fascism is a child of the twentieth century, some would say specifically of the period between the two world wars. Indeed, fascism emerged very much as a revolt against modernity, against the ideas and values of the Enlightenment and the political creeds that it spawned. The Nazis in Germany, for instance, proclaimed that '1789 is Abolished'. In Fascist Italy slogans such as 'Believe, Obey, Fight' and 'Order, Authority, Justice' replaced the more familiar principles of the French Revolution, 'Liberty, Equality and Fraternity'. Fascism came not only as a 'bolt from the blue', as O'Sullivan (1983) put it, but also attempted to make the political world anew, quite literally to root out and destroy the inheritance of conventional political thought.

Although the major ideas and doctrines of fascism can be traced back to the nineteenth century, they were fused together and shaped by the First World War and its aftermath, in particular by a potent mixture of war and revolution. Fascism emerged most dramatically in Italy and Germany. In Italy, a Fascist Party was formed in 1919, its leader, Benito Mussolini (see p. 218), was appointed prime minister in 1922, and by 1926 a one-party fascist state had been established. The National Socialist German Workers' Party, known as the Nazis, was also formed in 1919, and, under the leadership of Adolf Hitler (see p. 210), it consciously adopted the style of Mussolini's Fascists. Hitler was appointed German chancellor in 1933 and, in little over a year, had turned Germany into a Nazi dictatorship. During the same period, democracy collapsed or was overthrown in much of Europe, often being supplanted by right-wing, authoritarian or openly fascist regimes, especially in eastern Europe. Regimes that bear some relationship to fascism have also developed outside Europe, notably in the 1930s in Imperial Japan and in Argentina under Perón (1945–55).

The origins and meaning of fascism have provoked considerable historical interest and often fierce disagreements. No single factor can, on its own, account for the rise of fascism; rather, fascism emerged out of a complex range of historical forces that were present during the inter-war period. In the first place, democratic government had only recently been established in many parts of Europe, and democratic political values had not replaced older, autocratic ones. Moreover, democratic governments, representing a coalition of interests or parties, often appeared weak and unstable when confronted by economic or political crises. In this context, the prospect of strong leadership brought about by personal rule cast a powerful appeal. Second, European society had been disrupted by the experience of industrialization, which had particularly threatened a lower middle class of shop-keepers, small businessmen, farmers and craftsmen, who were squeezed between the growing might of big business, on the one hand, and the rising power of organized labour, on the other. Fascist movements drew their membership and support largely from such lower middle-class elements. In a sense, fascism was an 'extremism of the centre' (Lipset, 1983), a revolt of the lower middle classes, a fact that helps to explain the hostility of fascism to both capitalism and communism.

Third, the period after the First World War was deeply affected by the Russian Revolution and the fear amongst the propertied classes that social revolution was about to spread throughout Europe. Fascist groups undoubtedly drew both financial and political support from business interests. As a result, Marxist historians have interpreted fascism as a form of counter-revolution, an attempt by the bourgeoisie to cling on to power by lending support to fascist dictators. Fourth, the world economic crisis of the 1930s often provided a final blow to already fragile democracies. Rising unemployment and economic failure produced an atmosphere of crisis and pessimism that could be exploited by political extremists and demagogues. Finally, the First World War had failed to resolve international conflicts and rivalries, leaving a bitter inheritance of frustrated nationalism and the desire for revenge. Nationalist tensions were strongest in those 'have not' nations that had either, like Germany, been defeated in war, or had been deeply disappointed by the terms of the Versailles peace settlement; for example, Italy and Japan. In addition, the experience of war itself had generated a particularly militant form of nationalism and imbued it with militaristic values.

Fascist regimes were not overthrown by popular revolt or protest but by defeat in the Second World War. Since 1945, fascist movements have achieved only marginal success, encouraging some to believe that fascism was a specifically inter-war phenomenon, linked to the unique combination of historical circumstances that characterized that period (Nolte, 1965). Others, however, regard fascism as an ever-present danger, seeing its roots in human psychology, or as Erich Fromm (1984) called it, 'the fear of freedom'. Modern civilization has produced greater individual freedom but, with it, the danger of isolation and insecurity. At times of crisis, individuals may therefore flee from freedom, seeking security in submission to an all-powerful leader or a totalitarian state. Political instability or an economic crisis could therefore produce conditions in which fascism could revive. Fears, for example, have been expressed about the growth of neofascism in parts of eastern Europe following the collapse of communist rule (1989–91). Similarly, the pressures generated by economic and cultural globalization and increasing transnational population movements have created opportunities for extreme nationalist or fascist-style political activism. As the combination of economic crisis, political instability and frustrated nationalism has provided fertile ground for fascist movements in the past, it would be foolish to discount the possibility of a resurgence of fascism in the future. The prospects for fascism in the twenty-first century are discussed in the final section of the chapter.

Core themes – strength through unity

Fascism is a difficult ideology to analyse, for at least two reasons. First, it is sometimes doubted if fascism can be regarded, in any meaningful sense, as an ideology. Lacking a rational and coherent core, fascism appears to be, as Hugh Trevor-Roper put it, 'an ill-assorted hodge-podge of ideas' (Woolf, 1981). Hitler, for instance, preferred to describe his ideas as a *Weltanschauung*, or 'world view', rather than a systematic ideology. In this sense, a world view is a complete, almost religious, set of attitudes that demand commitment and faith, rather than invite reasoned analysis and debate. Fascists were drawn to ideas and theories less because they helped to make sense of the world, in rational terms, but more because they had the capacity to stimulate political activism. Fascism may thus be better described as a political movement or even political religion, rather than an ideology.

Second, so complex has fascism been as a historical phenomenon that it has been difficult to identify its core principles or a 'fascist minimum', sometimes seen as generic fascism. Where does fascism begin and where does it end? Which movements and regimes can be classified as genuinely fascist? Doubt, for instance, has been cast on whether Imperial Japan, Vichy France, Franco's Spain, Perón's Argentina and even Hitler's Germany can be classified as fascist. Controversy surrounds the relationship between modern radical right groups, such as the *Front National* in France and the British National Party in the UK, and fascism: are these groups 'fascist', 'neofascist', 'post-fascist', 'extreme nationalist' or whatever? Among the attempts to define the ideological core of fascism have been Ernst Nolte's (1965) theory that it is a 'resistance to transcendence', A. J. Gregor's (1969) belief that it looks to construct 'the total charismatic community', Roger Griffin's (1993) assertion that it constitutes 'palingenetic ultranationalism' (palingenesis meaning rebirth) and Roger Eatwell's (1996) assertion that it is a 'holistic-national radical Third Way'. While each of these undoubtedly highlights an important feature of fascism, it is difficult to accept that any single-sentence formula can sum up a phenomenon as resolutely shapeless as fascist ideology. Perhaps the best we can hope to do is to identify a collection of themes that, when taken together, constitute fascism's structural core. The most significant of these include the following:

- anti-rationalism
- struggle
- leadership and elitism
- socialism
- ultranationalism

Anti-rationalism

Although fascist political movements were born out of the upheavals that accompanied the First World War, they drew on ideas and theories that had been circulating since the late nineteenth century. Amongst the most significant of these were anti-rationalism and the growth of counter-Enlightenment thinking generally. The Enlightenment, based on the ideas of universal reason, natural goodness and inevitable progress, was committed to liberating humankind from the darkness of irrationalism and superstition. In the late nineteenth century, however, thinkers had started to highlight the limits of human reason and draw attention to other, perhaps more powerful, drives and impulses. For instance, Friedrich Nietzsche proposed that human beings are motivated by powerful emotions, their 'will' rather than the rational mind, and in particular by what he called the 'will to power'. In *Reflections on Violence* ([1908] 1950), the French syndicalist Georges Sorel (1847–1922) highlighted the importance of '**political myths**', and especially the 'myth of the general strike, which are not passive descriptions of political reality but 'expressions of the will' that engaged the emotions and provoked action. Henri Bergson (1859–1941), the French philosopher, advanced the theory of **vitalism**. This suggests that the purpose of human existence is therefore to give expression to the life force, rather than to allow it to be confined or corrupted by the tyranny of cold reason or soulless calculation.

Political myth: A belief that has the capacity to provoke political action by virtue of its emotional power rather than through an appeal to reason.

Vitalism: The theory that living organisms derive their characteristic properties from a universal 'life-force'; vitalism implies an emphasis upon instinct and impulse rather than intellect and reason.

Although anti-rationalism does not necessarily have a right-wing or proto-fascist character, fascism gave political expression to the most radical and extreme forms of counter-Enlightenment thinking. Anti-rationalism has influenced fascism in a number of ways. In the first place, it gave fascism a marked anti-intellectualism, reflected in a tendency to despise abstract thinking and revere action. For example, Mussolini's favourite slogans included 'Action not Talk' and 'Inactivity is Death'. Intellectual life was devalued, even despised: it is cold, dry and lifeless. Fascism, instead,

Friedrich Nietzsche (1844–1900)

German philosopher. A professor of Greek at Basel at the age of twenty-five, Nietzsche abandoned philology and, influenced by the ideas of Schopenhauer (1788–1860), he attempted to develop a critique of traditional religious and philosophical thought. Deteriorating health and growing insanity after 1889 brought him under the control of his sister, Elizabeth, who edited and distorted his writings.

Nietzsche's complex and ambitious work stressed the importance of will, especially the 'will to power', and anticipated modern existentialism in emphasizing that people create their own world and make their own values – 'God is dead'. A fierce critic of Christianity and an opponent of egalitarianism and nationalism, his ideas have influenced anarchism and feminism as well as fascism. Nietzsche's best known writings include *Thus Spoke Zarathustra* (1883–84), *Beyond Good and Evil* (1886) and *On the Genealogy of Morals* (1887).

addresses the soul, the emotions and the instincts. Its ideas possess little coherence or rigour, but seek to exert a mythic appeal. Its major ideologists, in particular Hitler and Mussolini, were essentially propagandists, interested in ideas and theories very largely because of their power to elicit an emotional response and spur the masses into action. Fascism thus practises the 'politics of the will'.

Second, the rejection of the Enlightenment gave fascism a predominantly negative or destructive character. Fascists, in other words, have often been clearer about what they oppose than what they support. Fascism thus appears to be 'anti-philosophy' – it is anti-rational, anti-liberal, anti-conservative, anti-capitalist, anti-bourgeois, anti-communist and so on. In this light, some have portrayed fascism as an example of **nihilism**. Nazism, in particular, has been described as a 'revolution of nihilism'. However, fascism is not merely the negation of established beliefs and principles. Rather, it is an attempt to reverse the heritage of the Enlightenment. It represents the darker underside of the western political tradition, the central and enduring values of which were not abandoned but rather transformed or turned upside-down. For example, in fascism, 'freedom' came to mean unquestioning submission, 'democracy' was equated with absolute dictator-

Nihilism: Literally a belief in nothing, the rejection of all moral and political principles; nihilism is sometimes, but not necessarily, associated with destruction and the use of violence.

ship, and 'progress' implied constant struggle and war. Moreover, despite an undoubted inclination towards nihilism, war and even death, fascism saw itself as a creative force, a means of constructing a new civilization through 'creative destruction'. Indeed, this conjunction of birth and death, creation and destruction, can be seen as one of the characteristic features of the fascist world view.

Third, by abandoning the standard of universal reason, fascism has placed its faith entirely in history, culture and the idea of organic community. Such a community is shaped not by the calculations and interests of rational individuals but by innate loyalties and emotional bonds forged by a common past. In fascism, this idea of organic unity is taken to its extreme. The national community, or as the Nazis called it, the *Volksgemeinschaft*, was viewed as an indivisible whole, all rivalries and conflicts being subordinated to a higher, collective purpose. The strength of the nation or race is therefore a reflection of its moral and cultural unity. This prospect of unqualified social cohesion was expressed in the Nazi slogan, 'Strength through Unity.' The revolution that fascists sought was thus 'revolution of the spirit', aimed at creating a new type of human being (always understood in male terms). This was the 'new man' or 'fascist man', a hero, motivated by duty, honour and self-sacrifice, and prepared to dissolve his personality in that of the social whole.

Struggle

The ideas that the UK biologist Charles Darwin (1809–82) developed in *The Origin of Species* ([1859] 1972), popularly known as the theory of '**natural selection**', had a profound effect not only on the natural sciences, but also, by the end of the nineteenth century, on social and political thought. The notion that human existence is based on competition or struggle was particularly attractive in the period of intensifying international rivalry that eventually led to war in 1914. Social Darwinism also had a considerable impact on emerging fascism. In the first place, fascists regarded struggle as the natural and inevitable condition of both social and international life. Only competition and conflict guarantee human progress and ensure that the fittest and strongest will prosper. As Hitler told German officer cadets in 1944, 'Victory is to the strong and the weak must go to the wall.' If the testing ground of human existence is competition and struggle, then the ultimate test is war, which Hitler described as 'an unalterable law of the whole of life'. Fascism is perhaps unique amongst political ideologies in regarding war as good in

Natural selection: The theory that species go through a process of random mutations that fits some to survive (and possibly thrive) while others become extinct.

Adolf Hitler
(1889–1945)

German Nazi dictator. The son of an Austrian customs official, Hitler joined the German Worker's Party (later the NSDAP or Nazis) in 1919, becoming its leader in 1921. He became chancellor in 1933 and declared himself *Führer* (Leader) of Germany the following year. His regime was marked by relentless military expansionism and the attempt to exterminate European Jewry.

By no means an original thinker, in *Mein Kampf* (My Struggle) (1925) Hitler nevertheless drew together expansionist German nationalism, racial **anti-Semitism** and a belief in relentless struggle into a near-systematic Nazi programme. The central feature of his world view was a theory of history that highlighted the endless battle between the Germans and the Jews, respectively representing the forces of good and evil.

Anti-Semitism: Prejudice or hatred towards Jews; anti-Semitism may take religious, economic or racial forms (see p. 223).

itself, a view reflected in Mussolini's belief that 'War is to men what maternity is to women.'

Darwinian thought also invested fascism with a distinctive set of political values, which equate 'goodness' with strength, and 'evil' with weakness. In contrast to traditional humanist or religious values, such as caring, sympathy and compassion, fascists respect a very different set of martial values: loyalty, duty, obedience and self-sacrifice. When the victory of the strong is glorified, power and strength are worshipped for their own sake. Similarly, weakness is despised and the elimination of the weak and inadequate is positively welcomed: they must be sacrificed for the common good, just as the survival of a species is more important than the life of any single member of that species. Weakness and disability must therefore not be tolerated; they should be removed.

Eugenics: The theory or practice of selective breeding, achieved either by promoting procreation amongst 'fit' members of a species or by preventing procreation by the 'unfit'.

This was most graphically illustrated by the programme of **eugenics**, introduced by the Nazis in Germany, whereby mentally and physically handicapped people were first forcibly sterilized and then, between 1939 and 1941, systematically murdered. The attempt by the Nazis to exterminate European Jewry from 1941 onwards was, in this sense, an example of racial eugenics. Finally, fascism's conception of life as an 'unending struggle' gave it a restless and expansionist character. National qualities can only be cultivated through conflict and demonstrated by conquest and victory. This was clearly reflected in Hitler's foreign policy goals, as outlined in *Mein Kampf* ([1925] 1969): '*Lebensraum* [living space] in the East', and the ultimate prospect of world domination. Once in power in 1933, Hitler embarked on a programme of rearmament in preparation for expansion in the late 1930s. Austria was annexed in the *Anschluss* of 1938; Czechoslovakia was dismembered in the spring of 1939; and Poland invaded in September 1939, provoking war with the UK and France. In 1941, Hitler launched Operation Barbarossa, the invasion of the Soviet Union. Even when facing imminent defeat in 1945, Hitler did not abandon social Darwinism, but declared that the German nation had failed him and gave orders, never fully carried out, for a fight to the death and, in effect, the annihilation of Germany.

Leadership and elitism

Fascism also stands apart from conventional political thought in its radical rejection of equality. Fascism is deeply elitist and fiercely patriarchal; its ideas were founded on the belief that absolute leadership and **elitism** are

Elitism: A belief in rule by an elite or minority; elite rule may be thought to be desirable (the elite having superior talents or skills) or inevitable, (egalitarianism simply being impractical).

natural and desirable. Human beings are born with radically different abilities and attributes, a fact that emerges as those with the rare quality of leadership rise, through struggle, above those capable only of following. Fascists believe that society is composed, broadly, of three kinds of people. First and most importantly, there is a supreme, all-seeing leader who possesses unrivalled authority. Second, there is a 'warrior' elite, exclusively male and distinguished, unlike traditional elites, by its heroism, vision and the capacity for self-sacrifice. In Germany, this role was ascribed to the SS, which originated as a bodyguard but developed during Nazi rule into a state within a state. Third, there are the masses, who are weak, inert and ignorant, and whose destiny is unquestioning obedience. Such a pessimistic view of the capabilities of ordinary people puts fascism starkly at odds with the ideas of liberal democracy. Nevertheless, the idea of supreme leadership was also associated with a distinctively fascist, if inverted, notion of democratic rule. The fascist approach to leadership, especially in Nazi Germany, was crucially influenced by Friedrich Nietzsche's idea of the *Übermensch*, the 'over-man' or 'superman', a supremely gifted or powerful individual. Most fully developed in *Thus Spoke Zarathustra* ([1884] 1961), Nietzsche portrayed the 'superman as an individual who rises above the 'herd instinct' of conventional morality and lives according to his own will and desires. Fascists, however, turned the

AUTHORITY

LIBERALS believe that authority arises 'from below' through the consent of the governed. Though a requirement of orderly existence, authority is rational, purposeful and limited, a view reflected in a preference for legal-rational authority and public accountability.

CONSERVATIVES see authority as arising from natural necessity, being exercised 'from above' by virtue of the unequal distribution of experience, social position and wisdom. Authority is beneficial as well as necessary, in that it fosters respect and loyalty, and promotes social cohesion.

SOCIALISTS, typically, are suspicious of authority, which is regarded as implicitly oppressive and generally linked to the interests of the powerful and privileged. Socialist societies have nevertheless endorsed the authority of the collective body, however expressed, as a means of checking individualism and greed.

ANARCHISTS view all forms of authority as unnecessary and destructive, equating authority with oppression and exploitation. Since there is no distinction between authority and naked power, all checks on authority and all forms of accountability are entirely bogus.

FASCISTS regard authority as a manifestation of personal leadership or charisma, a quality possessed by unusually gifted (if not unique) individuals. Such charismatic authority is, and should be, absolute and unquestionable, and is thus implicitly, and possibly explicitly, totalitarian in character.

RELIGIOUS FUNDAMENTALISTS see authority as a reflection of unequal access to religious wisdom, authority being, at heart, an essentially moral quality possessed by enlightened individuals. Since such authority has a charismatic character, it is difficult to challenge or reconcile it with constitutionalism (see p. 39).

superman ideal into a theory of supreme and unquestionable political leadership. Fascist leaders styled themselves simply as 'the Leader' – Mussolini proclaimed himself to be *Il Duce*, while Hitler adopted the title *Der Führer* – precisely in order to emancipate themselves from any constitutionally defined notion of leadership. In this way, leadership became exclusively an expression of **charismatic** authority emanating from the leader himself. While constitutional, or, in Max Weber s term, legal-rational authority operates within a framework of laws or rules,

Charisma: Charm or personal power; the ability to inspire loyalty, emotional dependence or even devotion in others.

charismatic authority is potentially unlimited. As the leader was viewed as a uniquely gifted individual, his authority was absolute. At the Nuremburg Rallies, the Nazi faithful thus chanted 'Adolf Hitler is Germany, Germany is Adolf Hitler.' In Italy, the principle that 'Mussolini is always right' became the core of fascist dogma.

The 'leader principle' (in German, the *Führerprinzip*), the principle that all authority emanates from the leader personally, thus became the guiding principle of the fascist state. Intermediate institutions such as elections, parliaments and parties were either abolished or weakened to prevent them from challenging or distorting the leader's will. This principle of absolute leadership was underpinned by the belief that the leader possesses a monopoly of ideological wisdom: the leader, and the leader alone, defines the destiny of his people, their 'real' will, their **general will**. A Nietzscheian theory of leadership thus coincided with a Rousseauian belief in a single, indivisible public interest. In this light, a genuine democracy is an absolute dictatorship, absolutism and popular sovereignty being fused into a form of **totalitarian democracy** (Talmon, 1952). The role of the leader is to awaken the people to their destiny, to transform an inert mass into a powerful and irresistible force. Fascist regimes therefore exhibited populist-mobilizing features that set them clearly apart from traditional dictatorships. Whereas traditional dictatorships aimed to exclude the masses from politics, totalitarian dictatorships set out to recruit them into the values and goals of the regime through constant propaganda and political agitation. In the case of fascist regimes, this was reflected in the widespread use of plebiscites, rallies and popular demonstrations.

General will: The genuine interests of a collective body, equivalent to the common good; the will of all provided each person acts selflessly.

Totalitarian democracy: An absolute dictatorship that masquerades as a democracy, typically based on the leader's claim to a monopoly of ideological wisdom.

Socialism

At times, both Mussolini and Hitler portrayed their ideas as forms of 'socialism'. Mussolini had previously been an influential member of the Italian Socialist Party and editor of its newspaper, Avanti, while the Nazi Party espoused a philosophy it called 'national socialism'. To some extent, undoubtedly, this represented a cynical attempt to elicit support from urban workers. Nevertheless, despite obvious ideological rivalry between fascism and socialism, fascists did have an affinity for certain socialist ideas and positions. In the first place, lower middle-class fascist activists had a profound distaste for large-scale capitalism, reflected in a resentment towards big business and financial institutions. For instance, small shop-keepers were under threat from the growth of departmental stores, the small-holding peasantry was losing out to large-scale farming, and small businesses were increasingly in hock to the banks. Socialist or 'leftist' ideas were therefore prominent in German grassroots organizations such as the SA, or Brownshirts, which recruited significantly from amongst the lower middle classes. Second, fascism, like socialism, subscribes to collectivism, putting it at odds with the 'bourgeois' values of capitalism. Fascism places the community above the individual; Nazi coins, for example, bore the inscription 'Common Good before Private Good'. Capitalism, on the other hand, is based on the pursuit of self-interest and therefore threatens to under-mine the cohesion of the nation or race. Fascists also despise the material-ism that capitalism fosters: the desire for wealth or profit runs counter to the idealistic vision of national regeneration or world conquest that inspires fascists.

Third, fascist regimes often practised socialist-style economic policies designed to regulate or control capitalism. Capitalism was thus subordinated to the ideological objectives of the fascist state. As Oswald Mosley, leader of the British Union of Fascists, put it, 'Capitalism is a system by which capital uses the nation for its own purposes. Fascism is a system by which the nation uses capital for its own purposes.' Both the Italian and German regimes tried to bend big business to their political ends by policies of nationalization and state regulation. For example, after 1939, German capi-talism was reorganized under Hermann Göring's Four Year Plan, deliber-ately modelled upon the Soviet idea of Five Year Plans.

However, the notion of fascist socialism has severe limitations. For instance, 'leftist' elements within fascist movements, such as the SA in Germany and Sorelian revolutionary syndicalists in Italy, were quickly marginalized once fascist parties gained power, in the hope of cultivating the support of big business. This occurred most dramatically in Nazi Germany, through the purge of the SA and the murder of its leader, Ernst Rohm, in the 'Night of the Long Knives' in 1934. Marxists have thus argued that the purpose of fascism was to salvage capitalism rather than to subvert it. Moreover, fascist ideas about the organization of economic life were, at best, vague and sometimes inconsistent; pragmatism not ideology determined fascist economic policy. Finally, anti-communism was more prominent within fascism than anti-capitalism. A core objective of fascism was to seduce the working class away from Marxism and Bolshevism, which preached the insidious, even traitorous, idea of international working-class solidarity and upheld the misguided values of cooperation and equality. Fascists were dedicated to national unity and integration, and so wanted the allegiances of race and nation to be stronger than those of social class.

Ultranationalism

Fascism embraced an extreme version of chauvinistic and expansionist nationalism. This tradition regarded nations not as equal and interdependent entities, but as rivals in a struggle for dominance. Fascist nationalism did not preach respect for distinctive cultures or national traditions, but asserted the superiority of one nation over all others. In the explicitly racial nationalism of Nazism this was reflected in the ideas of Aryanism, the belief that the German people are a 'master race'. Between the wars, such militant nationalism was fuelled by an inheritance of bitterness and frustration, which resulted from the First World War and its aftermath.

Integral nationalism: An intense, even hysterical, form of nationalist enthusiasm, in which individual identity is absorbed within the national community.

Fascism seeks to promote more than mere patriotism, the love of one's country; it wishes to establish an intense and militant sense of national identity, which Charles Maurras (1868–1952), the leader of *Action Française*, called '**integral nationalism**'. Fascism embodies a sense of messianic or fanatical mission: the prospect of national regeneration and the rebirth of national pride. Indeed, the popular appeal that fascism has exerted has largely been based on the promise of national greatness. According to Griffin (1993), the mythic core of generic fascism is the conjunction of the ideas of 'palingenesis', or recurrent rebirth, and 'populist ultranationalism'. All fascist movements therefore highlight the moral bankruptcy and cultural decadence of modern society, but proclaim the possibility of rejuvenation, offering the image of the nation 'rising phoenix-like from the ashes'. Fascism thus fuses myths about a glorious past with the image of a future characterized by renewal and reawakening, hence the idea of the 'new' man. In Italy, this was reflected in attempts to recapture the glories of Imperial Rome; in Germany, the Nazi regime was portrayed as the 'Third Reich', in succession to Charlemagne's 'First Reich' and Bismarck's 'Second Reich'.

However, in practice, national regeneration invariably meant the assertion of power over other nations through expansionism, war and conquest. Influenced by social Darwinism and a belief in national and sometimes racial superiority, fascist nationalism became inextricably linked to militarism and imperialism. Nazi Germany looked to construct a 'Greater Germany' and build an empire stretching into the Soviet Union – '*Lebensraum* in the East'. Fascist Italy sought to found an African empire though the invasion of Abyssinia in 1934. Imperial Japan occupied Manchuria in 1931 in order to found a 'co-prosperity' sphere in a new Japanese-led Asia. These empires were to be **autarkic**, based on strict self-suffi-

Autarky: Economic self-sufficiency, brought about either through expansionism aimed at securing markets and sources of raw materials or by withdrawal from the international economy.

ciency. In the fascist view, economic strength is based on the capacity of the nation to rely solely on resources and energies it directly controls. Conquest and expansionism are therefore a means of gaining economic security as well as national greatness. National regeneration and economic progress are therefore intimately tied up with military power.

Fascism and the state

Although it is possible to identify a common set of fascist values and principles, Fascist Italy and Nazi Germany nevertheless represented different versions of fascism and were inspired by distinctive and sometimes rival beliefs. Fascist regimes and movements have therefore corresponded to one of two major traditions. One, following Italian Fascism, emphasizes the ideal of an all-powerful or totalitarian state, in the form of extreme **statism**. The other, reflected in German Nazism or national socialism, stresses the importance of **race** and racialism.

Statism: A belief that the state is the most appropriate means of resolving problems and of guaranteeing economic and social development.

The totalitarian ideal

Totalitarianism is a controversial concept. The height of its popularity came during the Cold War period, when it was used to draw attention to parallels between fascist and communist regimes, highlighting the brutal features of both. As such, it became a vehicle for expressing anti-communist views and, in particular, hostility towards the Soviet Union. Nevertheless, totalitarianism remains a useful concept for the analysis of fascism. Generic fascism tends towards totalitarianism in at least three respects. First, the extreme collectivism that lies at the heart of fascist ideology, the goal of the creation of 'fascist man' – loyal dedicated and utterly obedient – effectively obliterates the distinction between 'public' and 'private' existence. The good of the collective body, the nation or the race, is placed firmly before the good of the individual: collective egoism consumes individual egoism. Second, as the fascist leader principle invests the leader with unlimited authority, it violates the liberal idea of a distinction between the state and civil society. An unmediated relationship between the leader and his people implies active participation and total commitment on the part of citizens; in effect, the politicization of the masses.

Race: A collection of people who share a common genetic inheritance and are thus distinguished from others by biological factors.

TOTALITARIANISM

Totalitarianism is an all-encompassing system of political rule that is typically established by pervasive ideological manipulation and open terror and brutality. It differs from autocracy, authoritarianism and traditional dictatorship in that it seeks 'total power' through the politicization of every aspect of social and personal existence. Totalitarianism thus implies the outright abolition of civil society: the abolition of 'the private'. Fascism and communism have sometimes been seen as left- and right-wing forms of totalitarianism, based on their rejection of toleration, pluralism and the open society. However, radical thinkers such as Marcuse (see p. 128) have claimed that liberal democracies also exhibit totalitarian features.

Monism: A belief in only one theory or value; monism is reflected politically in enforced obedience to a unitary power and is thus implicitly totalitarian.

Third, the **monistic** belief in a single value system, and a single source of truth, places fascism firmly at odds with the notions of pluralism (see p. 325) and civil liberty. However, the idea of an all-powerful state has particular significance for Italian fascism.

The essence of Italian fascism was a form of state worship. In a formula regularly repeated by Mussolini, the idealist philosopher Giovanni Gentile (1875–1944) proclaimed: 'Everything for the state; nothing against the state; nothing outside the state.' The individual's political obligations are thus absolute and all-encompassing. Nothing less than unquestioning obedience and constant devotion are required of the citizen. This fascist theory of the state has sometimes been associated with the ideas of the German philosopher Hegel (1770–1831). Hegel portrayed the state as an ethical idea, reflecting the altruism and mutual sympathy of its members. In this view, the state is capable of motivating and inspiring individuals to act in the common interest, and Hegel thus believed that higher levels of civilization would only be achieved as the state itself developed and expanded. Hegel's political philosophy therefore amounted to an uncritical reverence of the state, expressed in practice in firm admiration for the autocratic Prussian state of his day.

In contrast, the Nazis did not venerate the state as such, but viewed it as a means to an end. Hitler, for instance, described the state as a mere 'vessel', implying that creative power derives not from the state but from the race, the German people. However, there is little doubt that the Hitler regime came closer to realizing the totalitarian ideal in practice than did the Mussolini regime. Although it seethed with institutional and personal rivalries, the Nazi

Benito Mussolini
▬ (1883–1945)

MUSSOLINI

Italian Fascist dictator. A teacher and journalist in his early life, Mussolini became a leading member of the Socialist Party before being expelled in 1914 for supporting intervention in the First World War. He founded the Fascist Party in 1919, was appointed prime minister in 1922, and within three years had established a one-party Fascist state.

Mussolini liked to portray himself as the founder of fascism, though his speeches and writings were often prepared for him by scholars. Basic to his political philosophy was the belief that human existence is only meaningful if it is sustained and determined by the community. This, however, required that the state be recognized as 'the universal ethical will', a notion embodied in totalitarianism. Outside the state, 'no human or spiritual values can exist, much less have value'.

state was brutally effective in suppressing political opposition, and succeeded in extending political control over the media, art and culture, education and youth organizations. On the other hand, despite its formal commitment to totalitarianism, the Italian state operated, in some ways, like a traditional or personalized dictatorship rather than a totalitarian dictatorship. For example, the Italian monarchy survived throughout the fascist period; many local political leaders, especially in the south, continued in power; and the Catholic Church retained its privileges and independence throughout the fascist period.

Corporatism

Although fascists revere the state, this does not extend to an attempt to collectivize economic life. Fascist economic thought is seldom systematic, reflecting the fact that fascists seek to transform human consciousness rather than social structures. Its distinguishing feature is the idea of corporatism, which Mussolini proclaimed to be the 'third way' between capitalism and socialism, a common theme in fascist thought that was embraced by Mosley in the UK and Perón in Argentina. Corporatism opposes both the free market and central planning: the former leads to the unrestrained pursuit of profit by individuals, while the latter is linked to the divisive idea of class war. In contrast, corporatism is based on the belief that business and labour are bound together in an organic and spiritually unified whole. This holistic vision was based on the

CORPORATISM

Corporatism, in its broadest sense, is a means of incorporating organized interests into the processes of government. There are two faces of corporatism. *Authoritarian* corporatism (closely associated with Fascist Italy) is an ideology and an economic form. As an ideology, it offers an alternative to capitalism and socialism based on holism and group integration. As an economic form, it is characterized by the extension of direct political control over industry and organized labour. *Liberal* corporatism ('neo-corporatism' or 'societal' corporatism) refers to a tendency found in mature liberal democracies for organized interests to be granted privileged and institutional access to policy formulation. In contrast to its authoritarian variant, liberal corporatism strengths groups rather than government.

assumption that social classes do not conflict with one another, but can work in harmony for the common good and the national interest. Such a view was influenced by traditional Catholic social thought, which, in contrast to the Protestant stress on the value of individual hard work, emphasizes that social classes are held together by duty and mutual obligations.

Social harmony between business and labour offers the prospect of both moral and economic regeneration. However, class relations have to be mediated by the state, which is responsible for ensuring that the national interest takes precedence over narrow sectional interests. Twenty-two corporations were set up in Italy in 1927, each representing employers, workers and the government. These corporations were charged with overseeing the development of all the major industries in Italy. The 'corporate state' reached its peak in 1939, when a Chamber of Fasces and Corporations was created to replace the Italian parliament. Nevertheless, there was a clear divide between corporatist theory and the reality of economic policy in Fascist Italy. The 'corporate state' was little more than an ideological slogan, corporatism in practice amounting to little more than an instrument through which the fascist state controlled major economic interests. Working-class organizations were smashed and private business was intimidated.

Modernization

The state also exerted a powerful attraction for Mussolini and Italian fascists because they saw it as an agent of modernization. Italy was less industrialized than many of its European neighbours, notably the UK, France and Germany, and many fascists equated national revival with economic modernization. All forms of fascism tend to be backward- looking, high-lighting the glories of a lost era of national greatness; in Mussolini's case, Imperial Rome. However, Italian fascism was also distinctively forward-looking, extolling the virtues of modern technology and industrial life and looking to construct an advanced industrial society. This tendency within Italian fascism is often linked to the influence of **futurism**, led by Filippo Marinetti (1876–1944). After 1922, Marinetti and other leading futurists were absorbed into fascism, bring with them a belief in dynamism, a cult of the machine and a rejection of the past. For Mussolini, the attraction of an all-powerful state was, in part, that it would help Italy break with backwardness and tradition, and become an future-orientated industrialized country.

Futurism: An early twentieth-century movement in the arts that glorified factories, machinery and industrial life generally.

Fascism and racialism

Not all forms of fascism involve overt racialism, and not all racialists are necessarily fascists. Italian fascism, for example, was based primarily on the supremacy of the fascist state over the individual and on submission to the will of Mussolini. It was therefore a **voluntaristic** form of fascism, in that, at least in theory, it could embrace all people regardless of race, colour or, indeed, country of birth. When Mussolini passed anti-Semitic laws after 1937, he did so largely to placate Hitler and the Germans, rather than for any ideological purpose. Nevertheless, fascism has often coincided with, and bred from, racialist ideas. Indeed, some argue that its emphasis on militant nationalism means that all forms of fascism are either hospitable to racialism, or harbour implicit or explicit racialist doctrines (Griffin, 1993). Nowhere has this link between race and fascism been so evident as in Nazi Germany, where official ideology at times amounted to little more than hysterical, pseudo-scientific anti-Semitism.

Voluntarism: A theory that empahasizes free will and personal commitment, rather than any form of determinism.

The politics of race

The term 'race' implies that there are meaningful biological or genetic differences amongst human beings. While it may be possible to drop a national identity and assume another by a process of 'naturalization', it is impossible to change one's race, determined as it is at birth, indeed before birth, by the racial identity of one's parents. The symbols of race – skin tone, hair colour, physiognomy and blood – are thus fixed and unchangeable. The

RACIALISM

Racialism is, broadly, the belief that political or social conclusions can be drawn from the idea that humankind is divided into biologically distinct 'races'. Racialist theories are thus based on two assumptions. The first is that there are fundamental genetic, or species-type, differences amongst the peoples of the world. The second is that these genetic divisions are reflected in cultural, intellectual and/or moral differences, making them politically or socially significant. Political racialism is manifest in calls for racial segregation (for instance, apartheid) and in doctrines of 'blood' superiority or inferiority (for example, Aryanism or anti-Semitism). 'Racialism' and 'racism' are often used interchangeably, but the latter is better used to refer to prejudice or hostility towards people because of their racial origin, whether or not this is linked to a developed racial theory.

use of racial terms and categories became commonplace in the West during the nineteenth century as imperialism brought the predominantly 'white' European races into increasingly close contact with the 'black', 'brown' and 'yellow' races of Africa and Asia.

However, racial categories largely reflect cultural stereotypes and enjoy little, if any, scientific foundation. The broadest racial classifications, for example those based upon skin colour – white, brown, yellow and so on – are at best misleading and at worst simply arbitrary. More detailed and ambitious racial theories, such as those of the Nazis, simply produced anomalies, the most glaring of which was perhaps that Adolf Hitler himself certainly did not fit the racial stereotype of the tall, broad-shouldered, blond-haired, blue-eyed Aryan commonly described in Nazi literature.

The core assumption of racialism is that political and social conclusions can be drawn from the idea that there are innate or fundamental differences between the races of the world. At heart, genetics determines politics: racialist political theories can be traced back to biological assumptions, as is illustrated in Figure 7.1. A form of implicit racialism has been associated with conservative nationalism. This is based on the belief that stable and successful societies must be bound together by a common culture and shared values. For example, Enoch Powell in the UK in the 1960s and Jean-Marie Le Pen in France since the 1980s have argued against 'non-white' immigration into their countries on the grounds that the distinctive traditions and culture of the 'white' host community would be threatened.

However, more systematic and developed forms of racialism are based on explicit assumptions about the nature, capacities and destinies of different racial groups. In many cases, these assumptions have had a religious basis.

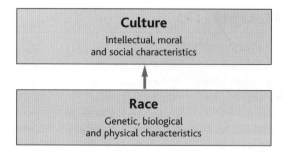

Figure 7.1
The nature of racialism

For example, nineteenth-century European imperialism was justified, in part, by the alleged superiority of the Christian peoples of Europe over the 'heathen' peoples of Africa and Asia. Biblical justification was also offered for doctrines of racial segregation preached by the Ku Klux Klan, formed in the USA after the American civil war, and by the founders of the apartheid system (apartheid meaning 'apartness' in Afrikaans), which operated in South Africa from the 1940s until 1993. In Nazi Germany, however, racialism was rooted in biological, and therefore quasi-scientific, assumptions. Biologically based racial theories, as opposed to those that are linked to culture or religion, are particularly militant and radical because they make claims about the essential and inescapable nature of a people that are supposedly backed up by the certainty and objectivity of scientific belief.

Nazi race theories

Nazi ideology was fashioned out of a combination of racial anti-Semitism and social Darwinism. Anti-Semitism had been a force in European politics, especially in eastern Europe, since the dawn of the Christian era. Its origins were largely theological: the Jews were responsible for the death of Christ, and in refusing to convert to Christianity they were both denying the divinity of·Jesus and endangering their own immortal souls. The association between the Jews and evil was therefore not a creation of the Nazis, but dated back to the Christian Middle Ages, a period when the Jews were first confined in ghettoes and excluded from respectable society. However, anti-Semitism intensified in the late nineteenth century. As nationalism and imperialism spread throughout Europe, Jews were subject to increasing persecution in many countries. In France, this led to the celebrated Dreyfus affair, 1894–1906; in Russia, it was reflected in a series of pogroms carried out against the Jews by the government of Alexander III.

The character of anti-Semitism also changed during the nineteenth century. The growth of a 'science of race', which applied pseudo-scientific ideas to social and political issues, led to the Jews being thought of as a race rather

ANTI-SEMITISM

By tradition, Semites are descendants of Shem, son of Noah, and include most of the peoples of the Middle East. Anti-Semitism refers specifically to prejudice against or hatred towards the Jews. In its earliest systematic form, anti-Semitism had a religious character, reflecting the hostility of Christians towards the Jews, based on their complicity in the murder of Jesus and their refusal to acknowledge him as the Son of God. Economic anti-Semitism developed from the Middle Ages onwards, expressing a distaste for the Jews as money-lenders and traders. The nineteenth century saw the birth of racial anti-Semitism in the works of Wagner and H. S. Chamberlain, who condemned the Jewish peoples as fundamentally evil and destructive. Such ideas provided the ideological basis for German Nazism and found their most grotesque expression in the Holocaust.

than a religious, economic or cultural group. Thereafter, the Jews were defined inescapably by biological factors such as hair colour, facial characteristics and blood. Anti-Semitism was therefore elaborated into a racial theory, which assigned to the Jews a pernicious and degrading racial stereotype. The first attempt to develop a scientific theory of racialism was undertaken by the French social theorist Joseph-Arthur Gobineau (1816–82), whose *Essay on the Inequality of the Human Races* ([1854] 1970) claimed to be a 'science of history'. Gobineau argued that there is a hierarchy of races, with very different qualities and characteristics. The most developed and creative race is the 'white peoples' whose highest element Gobineau referred to as the 'Aryans'. The Jews, on the other hand, were thought to be fundamentally uncreative. Unlike the Nazis, however, Gobineau was a pessimistic racialist, believing that by his day intermarriage had progressed so far that the glorious civilization built by the Aryans had already been corrupted beyond repair.

The doctrine of racial anti-Semitism entered Germany through Gobineau's writing and took the form of Aryanism, a belief in the biological superiority of the Aryan peoples. These ideas were taken up by the composer Richard Wagner and his UK-born son-in-law, H. S. Chamberlain (1855–1929), whose *Foundations of the Nineteenth Century* ([1899] 1913) had an enormous impact on Hitler and the Nazis. Chamberlain defined the highest race more narrowly as the 'Teutons', clearly understood to mean the German peoples. All cultural development was ascribed to the German way of life, while the Jews were described as 'physically, spiritually and morally degenerate'. Chamberlain presented history as a confrontation between the Teutons and the Jews, and therefore prepared the ground for Nazi race theory, which portrayed the Jews as a universal scapegoat for all of Germany's misfortunes. The Nazis blamed the Jews for Germany's defeat in 1918; they were responsible for its humiliation at Versailles; they were behind the financial power of the banks and big business that enslaved the lower middle classes; and their influence was exerted through the working-class movement and the threat of social revolution. In Hitler's view, the Jews were responsible for an international conspiracy of capitalists and communists, whose prime objective was to weaken and overthrow the German nation.

Nazism, or national socialism, portrayed the world in pseudo-religious, pseudo-scientific terms as a struggle for dominance between the Germans and the Jews, representing, respectively, the forces of 'good' and 'evil'. Hitler himself divided the races of the world into three categories. The first, the Aryans, were the *Herrenvolk*, the 'master race'; Hitler described the Aryans as the 'founders of culture' and literally believed them to be responsible for all creativity, whether in art, music, literature, philosophy or political thought. Second, there were the 'bearers of culture', peoples who were able to utilize the ideas and inventions of the German people, but were themselves incapable of creativity. At the bottom, were the Jews, who Hitler described as the 'destroyers of culture', pitted in an unending struggle against the noble and creative Aryans.

Manichaeanism:
A third-century Persian religion that presented the world in terms of conflict between light and darkness, and good and evil.

Hitler's **Manichaean** world view was therefore dominated by the idea of conflict between good and evil, reflected in a racial struggle between the Germans and the Jews, a conflict that could only end in either Aryan world domination (and the elimination of the Jews) or the final victory of the Jews (and the destruction of Germany).

This ideology took Hitler and the Nazis in appalling and tragic directions. In the first place Aryanism, the conviction that the Aryans are a uniquely creative 'master race', dictated a policy of expansionism and war. If the Germans are racially superior, other races are biologically relegated to an inferior and subservient position. Nazi ideology therefore dictated an aggressive foreign policy in pursuit of a racial empire and, ultimately, world domination. Second, the Nazis believed that Germany could never be secure so long as its arch-enemies, the Jews, continued to exist. The Jews had to be persecuted, indeed they deserved to be persecuted, because they represented evil. The Nuremburg Laws, passed in 1935, prohibited both marriage and sexual relations between Germans and Jews. After *Kristallnacht* ('The Night of Broken Glass') in 1938, Jewish people were effectively excluded from the economy. However, Nazi race theories drove Hitler from a policy of persecution to one of terror and, eventually, genocide and racial extermination. In 1941, with a world war still to be won, the Nazi regime embarked on what it called the 'final solution', an attempt to exterminate the Jewish population of Europe in an unparalleled process of mass murder, which led to the death of some six million Jewish people.

Peasant ideology

A further difference between the Italian and German brands of fascism is that the latter advanced a distinctively anti-modern philosophy. While Italian fascism was eager to portray itself as a modernizing force and to embrace the benefits of industry and technology, Nazism reviled much of modern civilization as decadent and corrupt. This particularly applied in the case of urbanization and industrialization. In the Nazi view, the Germans are in truth a peasant people, ideally suited to a simple existence lived close to the land and ennobled by physical labour. However, life in overcrowded, stultifying and unhealthy cities had undermined the German spirit and threatened to weaken the racial stock. Such fears were expressed in the 'Blood and Soil' ideas of the Nazi Peasant Leader Walter Darré. They also explain why the Nazis extolled the virtues of *Kultur*, which embodied the folk traditions and craft skills of the German peoples, over the essentially empty products of western civilization. This peasant ideology had important implications for foreign policy. In particular, it helped to fuel expansionist tendencies by strengthening the attraction of *Lebensraum*. Only through territorial expansion could overcrowded Germany acquire the space to allow its people to resume their proper, peasant existence.

This policy was based on a deep contradiction, however. War and military expansion, even when justified by reference to a peasant ideology, cannot but be pursued through the techniques and processes of a modern industrial

TENSIONS WITHIN
FASCISM

FASCISM	v.	NAZISM
state worship	←→	state as vessel
chauvinist nationalism	←→	extreme racialism
voluntarism	←→	essentialism
national greatness	←→	biological superiority
organic unity	←→	racial purity/eugenics
pragmatic anti-Semitism	←→	genocidal anti-Semitism
futurism/modernism	←→	peasant ideology
corporatism	←→	war economy
colonial expansion	←→	world domination

society. The central ideological goals of the Nazi regime were conquest and empire, and these dictated the expansion of the industrial base and the development of the technology of warfare. Far from returning the German people to the land, the Hitler period witnessed rapid industrialization and the growth of large towns and cities so despised by the Nazis. Peasant ideology thus proved to be little more than rhetoric. Militarism also brought about significant cultural shifts. While Nazi art remained fixated with simplistic images of small-town and rural life, propaganda constantly bombarded the German people with images of modern technology, from the Stuka dive-bomber and Panzer tank to the V-1 and V-2 rockets.

Fascism in the twenty-first century

Some commentators have argued that fascism, properly understood, did not survive into the second half of the twentieth century, still less could it continue into the twenty-first century. In the classic analysis by Ernst Nolte (1965), for instance, fascism is seen as a historically specific revolt against modernization, linked to the desire to preserve the cultural and spiritual unity of traditional society. Since this moment in the modernization process has passed, all references to fascism should be made in the past tense. Hitler's suicide in the Fuhrer bunker in April 1945, as the Soviet Red Army approached the gates of Berlin, may therefore have marked the *Götterdämmerung* of fascism, its 'twilight of the gods'. Such interpretations, however, have been far less easy to advance in view of the revival of fascism or at least fascist-type movements in the late twentieth century, although these movements have adopted very different strategies and styles.

In some respects, the historical circumstances since the late twentieth century bear out some of the lessons of the inter-war period, namely, that fascism breeds from conditions of crisis, uncertainty and disorder. Steady economic growth and political stability in the early post-1945 period had proved a very effective antidote to the politics of hatred and resentment so often associated with the extreme right. However, uncertainty in the world economy and growing disillusionment with the capacity of established parties to tackle political and social problems have opened up opportunities for right-wing extremism, usually drawing on fears associated with immigration and the weakening of national identity. The end of the Cold War and the advance of globalization have, in some ways, strengthened these factors. The end of communist rule in eastern Europe allowed long-suppressed national rivalries and racial hatreds to re-emerge, giving rise, particularly in the former Yugoslavia, to forms of extreme nationalism that have exhibited fascist-type features. Globalization, for its part, has contributed to the growth of insular, ethnically or racially based forms of nationalism by weakening the nation-state and so undermining civic forms of nationalism. Some, for instance, have drawn parallels between the rise of religious fundamentalism (examined in Chapter 10) and the rise of fascism, even seeing militant Islam as a form of 'Islamo-fascism'.

On the other hand, although far right and anti-immigration groups have taken up themes that are reminiscent of 'classical' fascism, the circumstances that have shaped them and the challenges which they confront are very different from those found during the post-First World War period. For instance, instead of building on a heritage of European imperialism, the modern far right is operating in a context of post-colonialization. Multiculturalism (see Chapter 11) has also advanced so far in many western societies that the prospect of creating ethnically or racially pure 'national communities' appears to be entirely unrealistic. Similarly, traditional class divisions, so influential in shaping the character and success of inter-war fascism, have given way to the more complex and pluralized 'post-industrial' social formations. Finally, economic globalization acts as a powerful constraint on the growth of classical fascist movements. So long as global capitalism continues to weaken the significance of national borders, the idea of national rebirth brought about through war, expansionism and autarky will appear to belong, firmly, to a bygone age.

However, what kind of fascism do modern fascist-type parties and groups espouse? While certain, often underground, groups still endorse a militant or revolutionary fascism that proudly harks back to Hitler or Mussolini, most of the larger parties and movements claim either to have broken ideologically with their past or deny that they are or ever have been fascist. For want of a better term, the latter can be classified as 'neofascist'. The principal way in which groups such as the French National Front, the Freedom Party in Austria, the British National Party, the *Alleanza Nazionale* in Italy and anti-immigration groups in the Netherlands, Belgium and Denmark claim to differ from fascism is in their acceptance of political pluralism and electoral democracy. In other words, 'democratic fascism' is fascism divorced from principles such as absolute leadership, totalitarianism and overt racialism. In some respects, this form of fascism may be well positioned to prosper in the twenty-first century. For one thing, in reaching an accommodation with liberal democracy it appears to have buried its past and is no longer tainted with the barbarism of the Hitler and Mussolini period. For another, it still possesses the ability to advance a politics of organic unity and social cohesion in the event of the twenty-first century bringing economic crises and further political instability. Such a form of politics appears to be particularly attractive when the prospect of strong government is embodied in a charismatic leader, as cases such as Le Pen, Joerg Haider in Austria and Pim Fortuyn in the Netherlands appear to demonstrate.

Evaluating the prospects for neofascism, however, requires that two possibilities are examined. The first is that it is questionable whether fascism can remain true to established fascist principles whilst at the same time moving towards an accommodation with liberalism. The emphasis on the organic unity of the national community gives fascism a distinctly anti-liberal emphasis and puts it at odds with ideas such as pluralism, tolerance, individualism and pacifism. This creates the possibility, perhaps parallel to the development of democratic socialism, that the struggle for electoral viability will gradually force 'democratic' fascist parties progressively to abandon their traditional values and beliefs. Democracy will thus prevail over fascism. The second possibility is that the fascist accommodation with liberal democracy is essentially tactical. This implies that the genuine spirit of fascism lives on and is only being concealed by neofascists for the purpose of gaining respectability and winning power. This, after all, is the time-honoured strategy of fascism. Hitler and the Nazis, for example, continued to proclaim their support for parliamentary democracy right up to the time that they gained power in 1933. Whether neofascist parties and movements are using democracy merely as a tactical device will only be revealed if they are similarly successful.

Questions for discussion

→ Was fascism merely a product of the specific historical circumstances of the inter-war period?

→ How has anti-rationalism shaped fascist ideology?

→ Why do fascists value struggle and war?

→ How can the fascist leader principle be viewed as a form of democracy?

→ Is fascism simply an extreme form of nationalism?

→ To what extent can fascism be viewed as a blend of nationalism and socialism?

→ How and why is fascism linked to totalitarianism?

→ Are all fascists racialists, or only some?

→ Is fascism dead?

Further reading

Eatwell, R., *Fascism: A History* (London: Vintage, 1996). A thorough, learned and accessible history of fascism that takes ideology to be important; covers both inter-war and postwar fascisms.

Griffin, R. (ed.), *Fascism* (Oxford and New York: Oxford University Press, 1995). An excellent and wide-ranging reader on fascism that documents fascist views and interpretations of them.

Griffin, R., *International Fascism: Theories, Causes and the New Consensus* (London: Arnold and New York: Oxford University Press, 1998). A collection of essays that examine contrasting interpretations of fascism but arrive at a 'state of the art' theory.

Kallis, A. A. (ed.), *The Fascist Reader* (London and New York: Routledge, 2003). A wide-ranging introduction to the complex manifestations of fascism and to classic and modern interpretations.

Laqueur, W. (ed.), *Fascism: A Reader's Guide* (Harmondsworth: Penguin, 1979). An important collection of studies of various aspects of fascism by noted authorities.

Neocleous, M., *Fascism* (Milton Keynes: Open University Press, 1997). A short and accessible overview of fascism that situates it within the contradictions of modernity and capitalism.

Passmore, K., *Fascism: A Very Short Introduction* (Oxford and New York: Oxford University Press, 2002). A lucid and stimulating introduction to the nature and causes of fascism.

CHAPTER 8

FEMINISM

PREVIEW

As a political term, 'feminism' was a twentieth-century invention and has only been a familiar part of everyday language since the 1960s. ('Feminist' was first used in the nineteenth century as a medical term to describe either the feminization of men or the masculinization of women.) In modern usage, feminism is invariably linked to the women's movement and the attempt to advance the social role of women.

Feminist ideology is defined by two basic beliefs: that women are disadvantaged because of their sex; and that this disadvantage can and should be overthrown. In this way, feminists have highlighted what they see as a political relationship between the sexes, the supremacy of men and the subjection of women in most, if not all, societies. In viewing gender divisions as 'political', feminists challenged a 'mobilization of bias' that has traditionally operated within political thought, by which generations of male thinkers, unwilling to examine the privileges and power their sex had enjoyed, had succeeded in keeping the role of women off the political agenda.

Nevertheless, feminism has also been characterized by a diversity of views and political positions. The women's movement, for instance, has pursued goals that range from the achievement of female suffrage and an increase in the number of women in elite positions in public life, to the legalization of abortion, and the ending of female circumcision. Similarly, feminists have embraced both revolutionary and reformist political strategies, and feminist theory has both drawn on established political traditions and values, notably liberalism and socialism, and, in the form of radical feminism, rejected conventional political ideas and concepts.

Origins and development

Although the term 'feminism' may be of recent origin, feminist views have been expressed in many different cultures and can be traced back as far as the ancient civilizations of Greece and China. Christine de Pisan's *Book of the City of Ladies*, published in Italy in 1405, foreshadowed many of the ideas of modern feminism in recording the deeds of famous women of the past and advocating women's right to education and political influence. Nevertheless, it was not until the nineteenth century that an organized women's movement developed. The first text of modern feminism is usually taken to be Mary Wollstonecraft's (see p. 343) *Vindication of the Rights of Women* ([1792] 1967), written against the backdrop of the French Revolution. By the mid-nineteenth century, the women's movement had acquired a central focus: the campaign for female suffrage, the right to vote, which drew inspiration from the progressive extension of the franchise to men. This period is usually referred to as the 'first wave' of feminism, and was characterized by the demand that women should enjoy the same legal and political rights as men. Female suffrage was its principal goal because it was believed that if women could vote, all other forms of sexual discrimination or prejudice would quickly disappear.

The women's movement was strongest in those countries where political democracy was most advanced; women demanded rights that in many cases were already enjoyed by their husbands and sons. In the USA, a women's movement emerged during the 1840s, inspired in part by the campaign to abolish slavery. The famous Seneca Falls convention, held in 1848, marked the birth of the US women's rights movement. It adopted a Declaration of Sentiments, written by Elizabeth Cady Stanton (1815–1902), which deliberately drew on the language and principles of the Declaration of Independence and called, amongst other things, for female suffrage. The National Women's Suffrage Association, led by Stanton and Susan B. Anthony (1820–1906), was set up in 1869 and merged with the more conservative American Women's Suffrage Association in 1890. Similar movements developed in other western countries. In the UK, an organized movement developed during the 1850s and, in 1867, the House of Commons defeated the first attempt to introduce female suffrage, an amendment to the Second Reform Act proposed by John Stuart Mill (see p. 29). The UK suffrage movement adopted increasingly militant tactics after the formation in 1903 of the Women's Social and Political Union, led by Emmeline Pankhurst (1858–1928) and her daughter Christabel (1880–1958). From their underground base in Paris, the Pankhursts coordinated a campaign of direct action in which 'suffragettes' carried out wholesale attacks on property and mounted a series of well-publicized public demonstrations.

'First-wave' feminism ended with the achievement of female suffrage, introduced first in New Zealand in 1893. The Nineteenth Amendment of the US Constitution granted the vote to American women in 1920. The franchise was extended to women in the UK in 1918, but they did not achieve equal voting rights with men for a further decade. Ironically, in many ways, winning the right to vote weakened and undermined the women's movement. The struggle for female suffrage had united and inspired the movement, giving it a clear goal and a coherent structure. Furthermore, many activists naïvely believed that in winning suffrage rights, women had achieved full emancipation. It was not until the 1960s that the women's movement was regenerated with the emergence of feminism's 'second wave'.

The publication in 1963 of Betty Friedan's *The Feminine Mystique* did much to relaunch feminist thought. Friedan set out to explore what she called 'the problem with no name', the frustration and unhappiness many women experienced as a result of being confined to the roles of housewife and mother. 'Second-wave' feminism acknowledged that the achievement of political and legal rights had not solved the 'women's question'. Indeed, feminist ideas and arguments became increasingly radical, and at times revolutionary. Books such as Kate Millett's *Sexual Politics* (1970) and Germaine Greer's *The Female Eunuch* (1970) pushed back the borders of what had previously been considered to be 'political' by focusing attention on the personal, psychological and sexual aspects of female oppression. The goal of 'second-wave' feminism was not merely political emancipation but 'women's liberation', reflected in the ideas of the growing Women's Liberation Movement. Such a goal could not be achieved by political reforms or legal changes alone, but demanded, modern feminists argued, a more far-reaching and perhaps revolutionary process of social change.

Since the first flowering of radical feminist thought in the late 1960s and early 1970s, feminism has developed into a distinctive and established ideology, whose ideas and values challenge the most basic assumptions of conventional political thought. Feminism has succeeded in establishing **gender** and gender perspectives as important themes in a range of academic disciplines, and in raising consciousness about gender issues in public life in general. By the 1990s, feminist organizations existed in all western countries and most parts of the developing world. However, two processes have accompanied these developments. The first is a process of deradicalization, whereby there has been a retreat from the sometimes uncompromising positions that characterized feminism in the early 1970s. This has led to the popularity of the idea of 'post-feminism', which suggests

Gender: A social and cultural distinction between males and females, as opposed to sex, which refers to biological and therefore ineradicable differences between men and women.

Betty Friedan
(1921–2006)

US feminist and political activist, sometimes seen as the 'mother' of women's liberation. Friedan's *The Feminine Mystique* (1963) is often credited with having stimulated the emergence of 'second-wave' feminism. In 1966, she helped found the National Organization of Women (NOW) and became its first president.

Friedan attacked the cultural myths that sustained female domesticity, highlighting the sense of frustration and despair that afflicted suburban American women confined to the role of housewife and mother. She aimed at broadening educational and career opportunities for women, and has been criticized by radical feminists for focusing on the needs of middle-class women and ignoring patriarchal structures in the 'private' sphere. In *The Second Stage* (1983), Friedan drew attention to the danger that the pursuit of 'personhood' might encourage women to deny the importance of children, the home and the family.

Radical feminism: A form of feminism that holds gender divisions to be the most politically significant of social cleavages, and believes that they are rooted in the structures of domestic life.

that, as feminist goals have been largely achieved, the women's movement has moved 'beyond feminism'. The second process is one of fragmentation. Instead of simply losing its radical or critical edge, feminist thinking has gone through a process of radical diversification, making it difficult, and perhaps impossible, any longer to identify 'common ground' within feminism. In addition to the 'core' feminist traditions – liberal, socialist/Marxist and **radical feminism** – must now be added postmodern feminism, psychoanalytical feminism, black feminism, lesbian feminism and so on.

Core themes – the politics of the personal

Until the 1960s, the idea that feminism should be regarded as an ideology in its own right would have been highly questionable. Feminism would, more likely, have been viewed as a sub-set of liberalism and socialism, the point at which the basic values and theories of these two ideologies can be applied to gender issues. The rise of radical feminism changed this, in that radical feminists proclaimed the central political importance of gender divisions, something that no conventional ideology could accept. Conventional ideologies were therefore viewed as inadequate vehicles for advancing the social role of women, and even, at times, criticized for harbouring patriarchal attitudes and assumptions. However, the emergent ideology of feminism was a cross-cutting ideology, encompassing, from the outset, three broad traditions: liberal feminism, Marxist or socialist feminism and radical feminism. In addition, the 'core' feminist traditions each contain rival tendencies and have spawned hybrid or 'dual-system' feminisms (such as the attempt to blend radical feminism with certain Marxist ideas), and new feminist traditions have emerged, particularly since the 1980s. It is thus easy to dismiss feminism as hopelessly fragmented, to argue that feminism is characterized more by disagreement than by agreement. A range of 'common ground' themes can nevertheless be identified within feminism. The most important of these are the following:

- the public/private divide
- patriarchy
- sex and gender
- equality and difference.

The public/private divide

Traditional notions of what is 'political' locate politics in the arena of public rather than private life. Politics has usually been understood as an activity that takes place within a 'public sphere' of government institutions, political parties, pressure groups and public debate. Family life and personal relationships have normally been thought to be part of a 'private sphere', and therefore to be 'non-political'. Modern feminists, on the other hand, insist that politics is an activity that takes place within all social groups and is not merely confined to the affairs of government or other public bodies. Politics exists whenever and wherever social conflict is found. Millett (1970), for example, defined politics as 'power-structured relationships, arrangements whereby one group of persons is controlled by another'. The relationship between government and its citizens is therefore clearly political, but so is the relationship between employers and workers within a firm, and also relationships in the family, between husbands and wives, and between parents and children.

The definition of what is 'political' is not merely of academic interest. Feminists argue that sexual inequality has been preserved precisely because the sexual division of labour that runs through society has been thought of as 'natural' rather than 'political'. Traditionally, the public sphere of life, encompassing politics, work, art and literature, has been the preserve of men, while women have been confined to an essentially private existence, centred on the family and domestic responsibilities, as is illusrated in Figure 8.1. If politics takes place only within the public sphere, the role of women and the question of sexual equality are issues of little or no political importance. Women, restricted to the private role of housewife and mother, are in effect excluded from politics.

Feminists have therefore sought to challenge the divide between 'public man' and 'private woman'. However, they have not always agreed about what it means to break down the public/private divide, about how it can be achieved, or about how far it is desirable. Radical feminists have been the keenest opponents of the idea that politics stops at the front door, proclaiming, instead, that 'the personal is the political'. Female oppression is thus thought to operate in all walks of life and in many respects originates in the family itself. Radical feminists have therefore been concerned to analyse what can be called 'the politics of everyday life'. This includes the process of conditioning in the family, the distribution of housework and other domestic responsibilities, and the politics of personal and sexual conduct. For some feminists, breaking down the public/private divide implies transferring the responsibilities of private life to the state or other public bodies. For example, the burden of child-rearing on women could be relieved by more generous welfare support for families or the provision of nursery schools or crèches at work. Although liberal feminists object to restrictions on women's access to the public sphere of education, work and political life, they also warn against the dangers of politicizing the private sphere, which, according to liberal theory, is a realm of personal choice and individual freedom.

Patriarchy

Feminists believe that gender, like social class, race or religion, is a politically significant social cleavage. Indeed, radical feminists argue that gender

Figure 8.1
The sexual division of labour

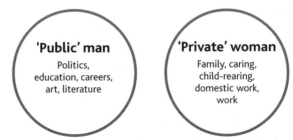

'Public' man
Politics, education, careers, art, literature

'Private' woman
Family, caring, child-rearing, domestic work, work

is the deepest and most politically important of social divisions. Feminists have therefore advanced a theory of 'sexual politics', in much the same way that socialists have preached the idea of 'class politics'. They also refer to 'sexism' as a form of oppression, drawing a conscious parallel with 'racism' or racial oppression. However, conventional political theory has traditionally ignored sexual oppression and failed to recognize gender as a politically significant category. As a result, feminists have been forced to develop new concepts and theories to convey the idea that society is based on a system of sexual inequality and oppression.

Patriarchy: Literally, rule by the father; often more generally to describe the dominance of men and subordination of women in society at large.

Feminists use the concept of '**patriarchy**' to describe the power relationship between men and women. The term literally means 'rule by the father' (*pater* meaning father in Latin). Some feminists employ patriarchy only in this specific and limited sense, to describe the structure of the family and the dominance of the husband-father within it, preferring to use broader terms such as 'male supremacy' or 'male dominance' to describe gender relations in society at large. However, feminists believe that the dominance of the father within the family symbolizes male supremacy in all other institutions. Many would argue, moreover, that the patriarchal family lies at the heart of a systematic process of male domination, in that it reproduces male dominance in all other walks of life: in education, at work and in politics. Patriarchy is therefore commonly used in a broader sense to mean quite simply 'rule by men', both within the family and outside. Millett (1970), for instance described 'patriarchal government' as an institution whereby 'that half of the populace which is female is controlled by that half which is male'. She suggested that patriarchy contains two principles: 'male shall dominate female, elder male shall dominate younger'. A patriarchy is therefore a hierarchic society, characterized by both sexual and generational oppression.

The concept of patriarchy is, nevertheless, broad. Feminists may believe that men have dominated women in all societies, but accept that the form and degree of oppression have varied considerably in different cultures and at different times. At least in western countries, the social position of women significantly improved during the twentieth century as a result of the achievement of the vote and broader access to education, changes in marriage and divorce law, the legalization of abortion and so on. However, in parts of the developing world, patriarchy still assumes a cruel, even gruesome form: 80 million women, mainly in Africa, are subject to the practice of circumcision; bride murders still occur in India, and the persistence of the dowry system ensures that female children are often unwanted and sometimes allowed to die.

Feminists do not have a single or simple analysis of patriarchy, however. Liberal feminists, to the extent that they use the term, use it to draw attention to the unequal distribution to rights and entitlements in society at large. The face of patriarchy they highlight is therefore the under-representation of women in senior positions in politics, business, the professions and public life. Socialist feminists tend to emphasize the economic aspects of patriarchy. In their view, patriarchy operates in tandem with capitalism, gender subordination and class inequality being interlinked systems of oppression. Some socialist feminists, indeed, reject the term altogether, on the grounds that gender inequality is merely a consequence of the class system: capitalism, not patriarchy, is the issue. Radical feminists on the other hand place considerable stress on patriarchy. They see it as a systematic, institutionalized and pervasive form of male power that is rooted in the family. Patriarchy thus expresses the belief that the pattern of male domination and female subordination that characterizes society at large is, essentially, a reflection of the power structures that operate within domestic life.

Sex and gender

The most common of all anti-feminist arguments, often associated with conservatives, asserts that gender divisions in society are 'natural': women and men merely fulfil the social roles that nature designed them for. A woman's physical and anatomical make-up thus suits her to a subordinate and domestic role in society; in short, 'biology is destiny'. The biological factor that is most frequently linked to women's social position is their capacity to bear children. Without doubt, childbearing is unique to the female sex, together with the fact that women menstruate and have the capacity to suckle babies. However, in no way do such biological facts necessarily disadvantage women nor determine their social destiny. Women may be mothers, but they need not accept the responsibilities of motherhood: nurturing, educating and raising children by devoting themselves to home and family. The link between childbearing and child-rearing is cultural rather than biological: women are expected to stay at home, bring up their children and look after the house because of the structure of traditional family life. Domestic responsibilities could be undertaken by the husband, or they could be shared equally between husband and wife in so-called 'symmetrical families'. Moreover, child-rearing could be carried out by the community or the state, or it could be undertaken by relatives, as in 'extended' families.

Feminists have traditionally challenged the idea that biology is destiny by drawing a sharp distinction between sex and gender. 'Sex', in this sense, refers to biological differences between females and males; these differences are natural and therefore are unalterable. The most important sex differences are those that are linked to reproduction. 'Gender', on the other hand, is a cultural term; it refers to the different roles that society ascribes to men and women. Gender differences are typically imposed through contrasting stereotypes of 'masculinity' and 'femininity'. As Simone de Beauvoir (see p. 247) pointed out, 'Women are made, they are not born'. Patriarchal ideas blur the distinction between sex and gender, and assume that all social distinctions between men and women are rooted in biology or anatomy. Feminists, in contrast, usually deny that there is a necessary or logical link between sex and gender, and emphasize that gender differences are socially, or even politically, constructed.

Most feminists believe that sex differences between men and women are relatively minor and neither explain nor justify gender distinctions. As a result, human nature is thought to be **androgynous**. All human beings, regardless of sex, possess the genetic inheritance of a mother and a father, and therefore embody a blend of both female and male attributes or traits. Such a view accepts that sex differences are biological facts of life but insists that they have no social, political or economic significance. Women and men should not be judged by their sex, but as individuals, as 'persons'. The goal of feminism is therefore the achievement of genderless 'personhood'. Establishing a concept of gender that is divorced from biological sex had crucial significance for feminist theory. Not only did it highlight the possibility of social change – socially constructed identities can be reconstructed or even demolished – but it also drew attention to the processes through which women had been 'engendered' and therefore oppressed.

> **Androgyny**: The possession of both male and female characteristics; used to imply that human beings are sexless 'persons' in the sense that sex is irrelevant to their social role or political status.

Although most feminists have regarded the sex/gender distinction as empowering, others have attacked it. These attacks have been launched from two main directions. The first, advanced by so-called 'difference feminists', suggests that there are essential differences between women and men. From this **'essentialist'** perspective, social and cultural characteristics are seen to reflect deeper biological differences. The second attack on the sex/gender distinction challenges the categories themselves. Postmodern feminists have questioned whether 'sex' is as clear-cut a biological distinction as is usually assumed. For example, the features of 'biological womanhood' do not apply to many who are classified as women: some women cannot bear children, some women are not sexually attracted to men, and so on. If there is a biology–culture

> **Essentialism**: The belief that biological factors are crucial in determining psychological and behavioural traits.

GENDER

LIBERALS have traditionally regarded differences between women and men as being of entirely private or personal significance. In public and political life, all people are considered as individuals, gender being as irrelevant as ethnicity or social class. In this sense, individualism is 'gender-blind'.

CONSERVATIVES have traditionally emphasised the social and political significance of gender divisions, arguing that they imply that the sexual division of labour between women and men is natural and inevitable. Gender is thus one of the factors that gives society its organic and hierarchical character.

SOCIALISTS like liberals, have rarely treated gender as a politically significant category. When gender divisions are significant it is usually because they reflect and are sustained by deeper economic and class inequalities.

FASCISTS view gender as a fundamental division within humankind. Men naturally monopolize leadership and decision-making, while women are suited to an entirely domestic, supportive and subordinate role.

FEMINISTS usually see gender as a cultural or political distinction, in contrast to biological and ineradicable sexual differences. Gender divisions are therefore a manifestation of male power. Difference feminists may, nevertheless, believe that gender differences reflect a psycho-biological gulf between female and male attributes and sensibilities.

RELIGIOUS FUNDAMENTALISTS usually regard gender as a God-given division, and thus as one that is crucial to social and political organization. Patriarchal structures and the leadership of males therefore tend to be regarded as natural and desirable.

continuum rather than a fixed biological/cultural divide, the categories 'female' and 'male' become more or less arbitrary, and the concepts of sex and gender become hopelessly entangled.

Equality and difference

Although the goal of feminism is the overthrow of patriarchy and the ending of sexist oppression, feminists have sometimes been uncertain about what this means in practice and how it can be brought about. Traditionally, women have demanded equality with men, even to the extent that feminism is often characterized as a movement for the achievement of sexual equality. However, the issue of equality has also exposed major faultlines within feminism: feminists have embraced contrasting notions of equality and some have entirely rejected equality in favour of the idea of difference. Liberal feminists champion legal and political equality with men. They have supported an equal rights agenda, which would enable women to compete in public life on equal terms with men, regardless of sex. Equality thus means equal access to the public realm. Socialist feminists, in contrast, argue that equal rights may be meaningless unless women also enjoy social equality. Equality, in this sense, has to apply in terms of economic power, and so must address issues such as the ownership of wealth, pay differentials and the distinction between waged and unwaged labour. Radical feminists, for their part, are primarily concerned about equality in family and personal life. Equality must therefore operate, for example, in terms of childcare and other domestic responsibilities, the control of one's own body, and sexual expression and fulfilment.

Despite tensions between them, these egalitarian positions are united in viewing gender differences in a negative light. Egalitarian forms of feminism link 'difference' to patriarchy, seeing it as a manifestation of oppression or subordination. From this viewpoint, the feminist project is defined by the desire to liberate women from 'difference'. However, other feminists champion difference rather than equality. Difference feminists regard the very notion of equality as either misguided or simply undesirable. To want to be equal to a man implies that women are 'male identified', in that they define their goals in terms of what men are or what men have. The demand for equality therefore embodies a desire to be 'like men'. Although feminists seek to overthrow patriarchy, many warn against the danger of modelling themselves on men, which would require them, for example, to adopt the competitive and aggressive behaviour that characterizes male society. For many feminists, liberation means achieving fulfilment as women; in other words, being 'woman identified'.

Difference feminists thus subscribe to a 'pro-woman' position, which holds that sex differences do have political and social importance. This is based on the essentialist belief that women and men are fundamentally different at a psycho-biological level. The aggressive and competitive nature of men and the creative and empathetic character of women are thought to reflect deeper hormonal and other genetic differences, rather than simply the structure of society. To idealize androgyny or personhood and ignore sex differences is therefore a mistake. Women should recognize and celebrate the distinctive characteristics of the female sex; they should seek liberation not as sexless 'persons' but as developed and fulfilled women. In the form

TENSIONS WITHIN
FEMINISM (1)

EGALITARIAN FEMINISM	v.	DIFFERENCE FEMINISM
androgyny	←→	essentialism
personhood	←→	sisterhood
human rights	←→	women's rights
gender equality	←→	sexual liberation
reduce difference	←→	celebrate difference
sex/gender divide	←→	sex equals gender
transcend biology	←→	embrace biology
pro-human	←→	pro-woman
men are redeemable	←→	men are 'the problem'
engagement with men	←→	feminist separatism

of cultural feminism, this has lead to an emphasis on women's crafts, art and literature, and on experiences that are unique to women and promote a sense of 'sisterhood', such as childbirth, motherhood and menstruation.

Sex and politics

Feminism is a cross-cutting ideology. The rival traditions of feminism have largely emerged out of established ideologies or theories, most obviously liberalism and socialism, but also, more recently, ideas such as postmodernism (see p. 62) and psychoanalysis. Such ideologies and theories have served as vehicles for advancing the social role of women because they are generally sympathetic towards equality. Hierarchical or elitist ideologies or theories, in contrast, are more commonly associated with anti-feminism. For instance, traditional conservatism holds that the patriarchal structure of society and the sexual division of labour between 'public' man and 'private' woman is natural and inevitable. Women are born to be housewives and mothers, and rebellion against this fate is both pointless and wrong. At best, conservatives can argue that they support sexual equality on the ground that women's family responsibilities are every bit as important as men's public duties. Men and women are therefore 'equal but different'.

Forms of reactionary feminism have also developed in certain circumstances. This has occurred when the traditional status and position of women has been threatened by rapid social or cultural change. So-called Islamic feminism has this character. In Islamic states, such as Iran, Pakistan and Sudan, the imposition of *shari'a* law and the return to traditional moral and religious principles have sometimes been portrayed as a means of enhancing the status of women, threatened by the spread of western attitudes and values. From this perspective, the veil and other dress codes, and the exclusion of women from public life, have been viewed by some Muslim women as symbols of liberation. Iran is a particularly complex example of this, in that the reimposition of traditionalist values and female dress codes since the 1979 Islamic Revolution has gone hand in hand with, for instance, a dramatic increase in female participation in higher education. However, from the perspective of conventional feminism, reactionary feminism is simply a contradiction in terms, reflecting the misguided belief that the traditional public/private divide genuinely afforded women status and protection. Indeed, it provides evidence of the ideological power of patriarchy, through its capacity to recruit women into their own oppression. The major traditions within feminism are the following:

- liberal feminism
- socialist feminism
- radical feminism
- new feminist traditions.

Liberal feminism

Early feminism, particularly the 'first wave' of the women's movement, was deeply influenced by the ideas and values of liberalism. The first major feminist text, Wollstonecraft's *A Vindication of the Rights of Women* ([1792] 1967), argued that women should be entitled to the same rights and privileges as men on the ground that they are 'human beings'. She claimed that the 'distinction of sex' would become unimportant in political and social life if women gained access to education and were regarded as rational creatures in their own right. John Stuart Mill's *On the Subjection of Women* ([1869] 1970), written in collaboration with Harriet Taylor, proposed that society should be organized according to the principle of 'reason' and that 'accidents of birth' such as sex should be irrelevant. Women would therefore be entitled to the rights and liberties enjoyed by men and, in particular, the right to vote.

'Second-wave' feminism also has a significant liberal component. Liberal feminism has dominated the women's movement in the USA; for instance,

Mary Wollstonecraft (1759–97)

UK social theorist and feminist. Drawn into radical politics by the French Revolution, Wollstonecraft was part of a creative and intellectual circle that included her husband, the anarchist William Godwin (see p. 181). She died giving birth to her daughter Mary, who later married the poet Shelley and wrote *Frankenstein*.

Wollstonecraft's feminism drew on an Enlightenment liberal belief in reason and a radical humanist commitment to equality. In *A Vindication of the Rights of Women* (1792), she stressed the equal rights of women, especially in education, on the basis of the notion of 'personhood'. However, her work developed a more complex analysis of women as the objects and subjects of desire, and also presented the domestic sphere as a model of community and social order.

the publication of Betty Friedan's *The Feminine Mystique* marked the resurgence of feminist thought in the 1960s. The 'feminine mystique' to which Friedan referred is the cultural myth that women seek security and fulfilment in domestic life and 'feminine' behaviour, a myth that serves to discourage women from entering employment politics and public life in general. She highlighted what she called 'the problem with no name', by which she meant the sense of despair and deep unhappiness many women experience because they are confined to a domestic existence unable to gain fulfilment in a career or through political life. In 1966, Friedan helped to found and became the first leader of the National Organization of Women (NOW), which has developed into a powerful pressure group and the largest women's organization in the world.

The philosophical basis of liberal feminism lies in the principle of **individualism**, the belief that the human individual is all important and therefore that all individuals are of equal moral worth. Individuals are entitled to equal treatment, regardless of their sex, race, colour, creed or religion. If individuals are to be judged, it should be on rational grounds, on the content of their character, their talents, or their personal worth. Liberals express this belief in the demand for equal rights: all individuals are entitled to participate in, or gain access to, public or political life. Any form of discrimination against women in this respect should clearly be prohibited. Wollstonecraft, for example, insisted that education, in her day the province of men, should be

Individualism:
A belief in the central importance of the human individual as opposed to social groups or collective bodies (see p. 28).

opened up to women. J. S. Mill argued in favour of equal citizenship and political rights. Indeed, the entire suffrage movement was based on liberal individualism and the conviction that female emancipation would be brought about once women enjoyed equal voting rights with men. Liberal feminist groups therefore aim to break down the remaining legal and social pressures that restrict women from pursuing careers and being politically active. They seek, in particular, to increase the representation of women in senior positions in public and political life.

Liberal feminism is essentially reformist: it seeks to open up public life to equal competition between women and men, rather than to challenge what many feminists see as the patriarchal structure of society itself. In particular, liberal feminists generally do not wish to abolish the distinction between the public and private spheres of life. Reform is necessary, they argue, but only to ensure the establishment of equal rights in the public sphere: the right to education, the right to vote, the right to pursue a career and so on. Significant reforms have undoubtedly been achieved in the industrialized West, notably the extension of the franchise, the 'liberalization' of divorce law and abortion, equal pay and so forth. Nevertheless, far less attention has been given to the private sphere, the sexual division of labour and distribution of power within the family.

Liberal feminists have usually assumed that men and women have different natures and inclinations, and therefore accept that, at least in part, women's leaning towards family and domestic life is influenced by natural impulses and so reflects a willing choice. This certainly applied in the case of nineteenth-century feminists, who regarded the traditional structure of family life as 'natural', but it is also evident in the work of modern liberal feminists such as Friedan. In *The Second Stage* (1983) Friedan discussed the problem of reconciling the achievement of 'personhood', made possible by opening up broader opportunities for women in work and public life, with the need for love, represented by children, home and the family. Friedan's emphasis on the continuing and central importance of the family in women's life has been criticized by more radical feminists as contributing to a 'mystique of motherhood'.

Finally, the demand for equal rights, which lies at the core of liberal feminism, has principally attracted those women whose education and social backgrounds equip them to take advantage of wider educational and career opportunities. For example, nineteenth-century feminists and the leaders of the suffrage movement were usually educated, middle-class women who had the opportunity to benefit from the right to vote, pursue a career or enter public life. The demand for equal rights assumes that all women would have the opportunity to take advantage of, for example, better educational and economic opportunities. In reality, women are judged not only by their talents and abilities, but also by social and economic factors. If emancipation simply means the achievement of equal rights and opportunities for women and men other forms of social disadvantage – for example, those linked to social class and race – are ignored. Liberal feminism may therefore reflect the interests of white, middle-class women in developed societies but fail to address the problems of working-class women black women and women in the developing world.

Socialist feminism

Although some early feminists subscribed to socialist ideas, socialist feminism only became prominent in the second half of the twentieth century. In contrast to their liberal counterparts, socialist feminists have not believed that women simply face political or legal disadvantages that can be remedied by equal legal rights or the achievement of equal opportunities. Rather, they argue that the relationship between the sexes is rooted in the social and economic structure itself, and that nothing short of profound social change, some would say a social revolution, can offer women the prospect of genuine emancipation.

The central theme of socialist feminism is that patriarchy can only be understood in the light of social and economic factors. The classic statement of this argument was developed in Friedrich Engels' *The Origins of the Family, Private Property and the State* ([1884] 1976). Engels (see p. 124), suggested that the position of women in society had fundamentally changed with the development of capitalism and the institution of private property. In pre-capitalist societies, family life had been communistic, and 'mother right' – the inheritance of property and social position through the female line – was widely observed. Capitalism, however, being based on the ownership of private property by men, had overthrown 'mother right' and brought about what Engels called 'the world historical defeat of the female sex'. Like many subsequent socialist feminists, Engels believed that female oppression operates through the institution of the family. The 'bourgeois family' is patriarchal and oppressive because men wish to ensure that their property will be passed on only to *their* sons. Men achieve undisputed paternity by insisting on monogamous marriage, a restriction that is rigorously applied to wives, depriving them of other sexual partners but, as Engels noted, is routinely ignored by their husbands. Women are compensated for this repression by the development of a 'cult of femininity', which extols the attractions of romantic love but, in reality, is an organized hypocrisy designed to protect male privileges and property. Other socialist feminists have proposed that the traditional, patriarchal family should be replaced by a system of communal living and 'free love', as advocated by early utopian socialists such as Charles Fourier (1772–1837) and Owen (1771–1858).

Most socialist feminists agree that the confinement of women to a domestic sphere of housework and motherhood serves the economic interests of capitalism. Some have argued that women constitute a 'reserve army of labour', which can be recruited into the workforce when there is a need to increase production, but easily shed and returned to domestic life during a depression, without imposing a burden on employers or the state. At the same time, women's domestic labour is vital to the health and efficiency of the economy. In bearing and rearing children, women are producing the next generation of capitalist workers. Similarly, in their role as housewives, women relieve men of the burden of housework and child-rearing, allowing them to concentrate their time and energy on paid and productive employment. The traditional family provides the worker with a powerful incentive to find and keep a job because he has a wife and children to support. The family also provides male workers with a necessary cushion against the alienation and frustrations of life as 'wage slaves'. Male 'breadwinners' enjoy high status within the family and are relieved of the burden of 'trivial' domestic labour.

Although socialist feminists agree that the 'women's question' cannot be separated from social and economic life, they are profoundly divided about the nature of that link. Gender divisions clearly cut across class cleavages, creating tension within socialist feminist analysis about the relative importance of gender and social class, and raising particularly difficult questions for Marxist feminists. Orthodox Marxists insist on the primacy of class politics over sexual politics. This suggests that class exploitation is a deeper and more significant process than sexual oppression. It also suggests that women's emancipation will be a by-product of a social revolution in which capitalism is overthrown and replaced by socialism. Women seeking liberation should therefore recognize that the 'class war' is more important than the 'sex war'. Such an analysis suggests that feminists should devote their energies to the labour movement rather than support a separate and divisive women's movement.

However, modern socialist feminists have found it increasingly difficult to accept the primacy of class politics over sexual politics. In part, this was a consequence of the disappointing progress made by women in state-socialist societies such as the Soviet Union, suggesting that socialism does not, in itself, end patriarchy. For modern socialist feminists, sexual oppression is every bit as important as class exploitation. Many of them subscribe to modern Marxism, which accepts the interplay of economic, social, political and cultural forces in society. They therefore refuse to analyse the position of women in simple economic terms and have, instead, given attention to the cultural and ideological roots of patriarchy. For example, Juliet Mitchell (1971), suggested that women fulfil four social functions: (1) they are members of the workforce and are active in production; (2) they bear children and thus reproduce the human species; (3) they are responsible for socializing children; and (4) they are sex objects. From this perspective, liberation requires that women achieve emancipation in each of these areas, and not merely that the capitalist class system is replaced by socialism.

Radical feminism

One of the distinctive features of 'second-wave' feminism is that many feminist writers moved beyond the perspectives of existing political ideologies. Gender differences in society were regarded for the first time as important in themselves, needing to be understood in their own terms. Liberal and socialist ideas had already been adapted to throw light on the position of women in society, but neither acknowledged that gender is the most fundamental of all social divisions. During the 1960s and 1970s, however, the feminist movement sought to uncover the influence of patriarchy not only in politics, public life and the economy, but in all aspects of social, personal and sexual existence. This trend was evident in the pioneering work of

Simone de Beauvoir (1906–86)

French novelist, playwright and social critic. De Beauvoir taught philosophy at the Sorbonne from 1931 to 1943, and later became an independent writer and social theorist. She was a long-time companion of Jean-Paul Sartre (1905–80). *The Second Sex* (1949) had a massive influence on the feminist movement by effectively reopening the issue of gender politics and foreshadowing some of the themes later developed by radical feminists. De Beauvoir insisted that women's position was determined by social and not natural factors, and developed a complex critique of patriarchal culture. Her work highlights the extent to which the masculine is represented as the positive or the norm, while the feminine is portrayed as the 'other'. Such 'otherness' fundamentally limits women's freedom and prevents them from expressing their full humanity. De Beauvoir placed her faith in rationality and critical analysis as the means of exposing this process and of giving women responsibility for their own lives.

Simone de Beauvoir, and was developed by early radical feminists such as Eva Figes, Germaine Greer and Kate Millett.

Figes's *Patriarchal Attitudes* (1970) drew attention not to the more familiar legal or social disadvantages suffered by women, but to the fact that patriarchal values and beliefs pervade the culture, philosophy, morality and religion of society. In all walks of life and learning, women are portrayed as inferior and subordinate to men, a stereotype of 'femininity' being imposed on women by men. In *The Female Eunuch* (1970), Greer suggested that women are conditioned to a passive sexual role, which has repressed their true sexuality as well as the more active and adventurous side of their personalities. In effect, women have been 'castrated' and turned into sexless objects by the cultural stereotype of the 'eternal feminine'. In *Sexual Politics* (1970) Millett described patriarchy as a 'social constant' running through all political, social and economic structures and found in every historical and contemporary society, as well as in all major religions. The different roles of men and women have their origin in a process of 'conditioning': from a very early age boys and girls are encouraged to conform to very specific gender identities. This process takes place largely within the family – 'patriarchy's chief institution' – but it is also evident in literature, art, public life and the economy. Millett proposed that patriarchy should be challenged through a process of **'consciousness raising'**, an idea influenced by the Black Power movement of the 1960s and early 1970s.

Consciousness raising: Strategies to remodel social identity and challenge cultural inferiority by an emphasis on pride, self-worth and self-assertion.

The central feature of radical feminism is the belief that sexual oppression is the most fundamental feature of society and that other forms of injustice – class exploitation, racial hatred and so on – are merely secondary. Gender is thought to be the deepest social cleavage and the most politically significant; more important, for example, than social class, race or nation. Radical feminists have therefore insisted that society be understood as 'patriarchal' to highlight the central role of sex oppression. Patriarchy thus refers to a systematic, institutionalized and pervasive process of gender oppression.

For most radical feminists, patriarchy is a system of politico-cultural oppression, whose origins lie in the structure of family, domestic and personal life. Female liberation thus requires a sexual revolution in which these structures are overthrown and replaced. Such a goal is based on the assumption that human nature is essentially androgynous. However, radical feminism encompasses a number of divergent elements, some of which emphasize the fundamental and unalterable difference between women and men. An example of this is the 'pro-woman' position, particularly strong in France and the USA. This position extols the positive virtues of fertility and motherhood. Women should not try to be 'more like men'. Instead, they should recognize

TENSIONS WITHIN
FEMINISM (2)

LIBERAL FEMINISM	v.	RADICAL FEMINISM
female emancipation	←→	women's liberation
gender inequality	←→	patriarchy
individualism	←→	sisterhood
conventional politics	←→	the personal is political
public/private divide	←→	transform private realm
access to public realm	←→	gender equality
equal rights/opportunities	←→	sexual politics
reform/gradualism	←→	revolutionary change
political activism	←→	consciousness raising

and embrace their sisterhood, the bonds that link them to all other women. The pro-woman position therefore accepts that women's attitudes and values are different from men's, but implies that in certain respects women are superior, possessing the qualities of creativity, sensitivity and caring, which men can never fully appreciate or develop. Such ideas have been associated in particular with ecofeminism, which is examined in Chapter 9.

The acceptance of unalterable differences between men and women has led some feminists towards cultural feminism, a retreat from the corrupting and aggressive male world of political activism into an apolitical, woman-centred culture and life-style. Conversely, other feminists have become politically assertive and even revolutionary. If sex differences are natural, then the roots of patriarchy lie within the male sex itself. 'All men' are physically and psychologically disposed to oppress 'all women'; in other words, 'men are the enemy'. This clearly leads in the direction of feminist separatism. Men constitute an oppressive 'sex-class' dedicated to aggression, domination and destruction; the female 'sex-class' is therefore the 'universal victim'. For example, Susan Brownmiller's *Against Our Will* (1975) emphasized that men dominate women through a process of physical and sexual abuse. Men have created an 'ideology of rape', which amounts to a 'conscious process of intimidation by which all men keep all women in a state of fear'. Brownmiller argued that men rape because they can, because they have the 'biological capacity to rape', and that even men who do not rape nevertheless benefit from the fear and anxiety that rape provokes amongst all women.

Feminists who have pursued this line of argument also believe that it has profound implications for women's personal and sexual conduct. Sexual equality and harmony is impossible because all relationships between men and women must involve oppression. Heterosexual women are therefore thought to be 'male identified', incapable of fully realizing their true nature and becoming 'woman identified'. This has led to the development of political lesbianism, which holds that sexual preferences are an issue of crucial political importance for women. Only women who remain celibate or choose lesbianism can regard themselves as 'woman-identified women'. In the slogan attributed to Ti-Grace Atkinson: 'feminism is the theory; lesbianism is the practice' (Charvet, 1982). However, the issues of separatism and lesbianism have deeply divided the women's movement. The majority of feminists see such uncompromising positions as a distorted reflection of the misogyny, or woman-hating, that pervades traditional male society. Instead, they remain faithful to the goal of sexual equality and the belief that it is possible to establish harmony between women and men in a non-sexist society. Hence, they believe that sexual preferences are strictly a matter of personal choice and not a question of political commitment.

New feminist traditions

Since the 1960s, it has become increasingly difficult to analyze feminism simply in terms of the threefold division into liberal, socialist and radical traditions. Divisions within the 'core' traditions have sometimes deepened, and, on other occasions, divisions between the traditions have been blurred. New forms of feminism have also emerged. Although these new feminisms draw on a wide variety of influences, they reflect a common interest in the issue of difference and, in particular, the desire to apply difference to women and not merely to the relationship between men and women. These new feminist traditions include psychoanalytical feminism, postmodern feminism and black feminism. Feminists such as de Beauvoir, Friedan and Millett had been fiercely critical of psychoanalysis in general and Sigmund Freud (1856–1939) in particular, seeing theories such as 'penis envy' and the 'castration complex' as evidence of flagrant misogyny. However, starting with Juliet Mitchell's pioneering *Psychoanalysis and Feminism* (1975), feminists have come to terms with Freud's work, particularly as developed by thinkers such as Jacques Lacan (1901–81). From this perspective, the attraction of psychoanalysis is that it cast light on the psychological processes through which sexual difference is constructed and maintained.

Postmodern or poststructural feminists have taken issue with forms of feminism, such as cultural feminism, which proclaim that there are essential differences between women and men. In their view, there is no such thing as a fixed female identity, the notion of 'woman' being nothing more than a fiction. However, in calling the male/female divide into question, postmodern feminism perhaps fatally compromises the very idea of a women's movement. Black feminism has challenged the tendency within feminism to ignore racial differences and to suggest that women endure a common oppression by virtue of their sex. Particularly strong in the USA, black feminism portrays sexism and racism as interlinked systems of oppression and highlights the particular and complex range of gender, racial and economic disadvantages that confront 'women of colour'.

Feminism in the twenty-first century

In some respects, feminist theory reached a high-point of creativity and radicalism in the late 1960s and early 1970s. Since that time, the women's movement appears to have undergone a decline and it has become fashionable to discuss the emergence of 'post-feminism'. Without doubt, feminism has confronted a number of difficulties. In the first place, the women's movement has become increasingly fragmented and incoherent; indeed, some, as pointed out above, question whether the notion of a women's movement is any longer meaningful. Although united by a common desire to advance the role of women, feminists disagree about how this can be achieved, and about what it means in practice. Divisions have long existed – between reformists and revolutionaries, between radical and socialist feminists, and over highly controversial issues such as separatism and lesbianism. However, these have now proliferated, with divisions emerging over issues such as prostitution, pornography and censorship, abortion, motherhood, race and ethnicity, the welfare state, and so on. Nevertheless, such a broad range of concerns and interests may be more an indication of feminism's strength than a source of feminist weakness. Indeed, it may merely serve to highlight the fact that feminism has developed from a political movement into a political ideology that, like other ideologies, encompasses a range of often-competing traditions.

A further problem is that, particularly since the 1980s, feminism has operated in a hostile political environment. In Islamic countries, the advance of fundamentalism was reflected in pressure for the exclusion of women from politics and public life, the abolition of their legal rights and a return to the veil. A conservative backlash against feminism was also evident in the industrialized West. Both the Thatcher and the Reagan administrations in the 1980s, for instance, were openly anti-feminist in their call for the restoration of 'family values', and in their emphasis on women's traditional role as mothers and housewives. The new right tried to reassert 'pro-family' patriarchal values and ideas, not only because they are seen to be 'natural' but also because they are viewed as a guarantee of social order and stability. For example, the rise in crime and vandalism amongst young people was blamed upon working mothers, and in both the USA and the UK single mothers were demonized for threatening the traditional family and increasing the welfare burden. These are examples of what Susan Faludi referred to in *Backlash* (1991) as the 'blame it on feminism' syndrome. At the same time, however, such anti-feminism also paid the women's movement a backhanded compliment. The attempt to reassert conventional social and religious values reflected the success of feminism in encouraging women to question established attitudes and rethink traditional sex roles.

Feminism in the twenty-first century also faces the problem that many of its original goals have been achieved or are being achieved, which is the basis of the post-feminism critique. Just as the right to vote was won in the early years of the twentieth century, so 'second-wave' feminism successfully campaigned in many countries for the legalization of abortion, equal pay legislation, anti-discrimination laws, and wider access to education and political and professional life. Some have even suggested the victory of feminism can be seen in the emergence of a new breed of man, no longer the chauvinist bigot of old, but the 'new man', who has come to terms with the 'feminine' elements of his make-up and is prepared to share domestic and family responsibilities within the 'symmetrical family'. The so-called men's movement has, in fact, argued that matters have gone further still, that men have become the victims of gender politics and are no longer its beneficiaries. Feminism, in short, has simply gone 'too far'. Confronted by the decline of traditional 'male' occupations, faced with growing competition from women in the workplace and at home, and deprived of their status as 'breadwinners', there is a danger that men, particularly young men, will retreat into a culture of non-achievement, unable to cope with a future that is female.

In the face of these challenges, the women's movement has certainly undergone a process of de-radicalization. The militant and revolutionary wing of the movement has been increasingly marginalized, and feminist literature reflects clear evidence of revisionism. Friedan's *The Second Stage* (1983) and Greer's *Sex and Destiny* (1985) both celebrated the importance of childbearing and motherhood, and drew criticism from more radical feminists for lending support to traditional gender stereotypes. Moreover, new feminist thinkers are generally more iconoclastic and less politically radical than their counterparts in the 1960s and 1970s. For instance, Camille Paglia (1990) attacked the image of women as 'victims', and insisted on the need for women to take greater responsibility for their own sexual and personal conduct.

The central illusion of post-feminism is that the most obvious forms of sexist oppression have been overcome, and therefore that society is no longer patriarchal. Without doubt, an increasing number of women go out to work, in many western countries a clear majority of married women. However, despite anxiety about male non-achievement, it is still women who are predominantly employed in poorly paid, low-status and often part-time jobs. Women also have less control of their own bodies than men, thanks to still-powerful stereotypes of femininity and beauty, and continue to play a subordinate role within marriage and to be under-represented in positions of power within society. In *The Whole Woman* (1999), Greer attacked the notion that women are 'having it all', arguing that they have abandoned the goal of liberation and settled for a phoney equality that amounts to assimilation, becoming more like men. This highlights the capacity of patriarchy to reproduce itself generation after generation, subordinating women by creating bogus forms of emancipation. Quite simply, feminism will survive as long as patriarchy persists. However, feminism's chief challenge in the twenty-first century is to establish a viable and coherent 'third wave' that is capable of making sense of the changing nature of gender relations and of exploding the myth of post-feminism.

Questions for discussion

→ How have feminists challenged conventional notions of politics?

→ Why has the distinction between sex and gender been so important to feminist analysis?

→ What role does patriarchy play in feminist theory?

→ Why do some feminists reject the goal of gender equality?

→ To what extent is feminism compatible with liberalism?

→ In what sense is radical feminism revolutionary?

→ Is feminist socialism a contradiction in terms?

→ Are the differences within feminism greater than the similarities?

→ Have the core liberal, socialist and radical feminist traditions been exhausted?

Further reading

Beasley, C., *What is Feminism?* (London: Sage, 1999). A useful examination of the nature of feminism that considers modern developments within feminist theory.

Bryson, V., *Feminist Political Theory: An Introduction*, 2nd edn (Basingstoke and New York: Palgrave Macmillan, 2003). A thorough and accessible introduction to the development and range of feminist theories.

Coole, D., *Women in Political Theory: From Ancient Misogyny to Contemporary Feminism*, 2nd edn (Hemel Hempstead: Harvester Wheatsheaf, 1993). A fascinating account of attitudes to women in western political thought that highlights the different forms that misogyny has taken.

Elshtain, J. B., *Public Man, Private Woman: Women in Social and Political Thought* (Oxford: Martin Robertson, and Princeton, NJ: Princeton University Press, 1981). A critical examination, from a feminist perspective, of the notions of public and private as they appear in the theories of major western thinkers.

Freedman, J., *Feminism* (Buckingham and Philadelphia, PA: Open University Press, 2001). A clear, short and up-to-date introduction to some of the major debates in feminist theory and practice.

Schneir, M., *The Vintage Book of Feminism: The Essential Writings of the Contemporary Women's Movement* (London: Vintage, 1995). A useful and comprehensive collection of writings from major contemporary feminist theorists.

Squires, J., *Gender in Political Theory* (Cambridge and Malden, MA: Polity Press, 1999). A thoughtful and wide-ranging account of the main issues within feminist political theory.

CHAPTER 9

ECOLOGISM

The term 'ecology' was coined by the German zoologist Ernst Haeckel in 1866. Derived from the Greek *oikos*, meaning household or habitat, he used it to refer to 'the investigations of the total relations of the animal both to its organic and its inorganic environment'. Since the early years of the twentieth century, ecology has been recognized as a branch of biology that studies the relationship amongst living organisms and their environment. It has, however, increasingly been converted into a political term by the use made of it, especially since the 1960s, by the growing green movement.

As a political ideology, ecologism is based on the belief that nature is an interconnected whole, embracing humans and non-humans, as well as the inanimate world. Ecologists therefore adopt an ecocentric or biocentric perspective that accords priority to nature or the planet, and thus differs from the anthropocentric, or human-centred, perspectives of conventional ideological traditions. Nevertheless, there are different strains and tendencies within ecologism. Some ecologists are committed to 'shallow' ecology (sometimes viewed as environmentalism, rather than ecologism), which attempts to harness the lessons of ecology to human ends and needs, and embraces a moderate or reformist approach to environmental change. 'Deep' ecologists, on the other hand, completely reject any lingering belief that the human species is in some way superior to, or more important than, any other species. Moreover, ecologism has drawn from a variety of other ideologies, notably socialism, anarchism, feminism, fascism and conservatism, creating a series of sub-traditions such as eco-socialism and ecofeminism. Each of these offers a different analysis of the origins of the contemporary ecological crisis, a different set of remedies, and a different model of the ecologically viable society of the future.

Origins and development

Although modern environmental or green politics did not emerge until the 1960s, ecological ideas can be traced back to much earlier times. Many have suggested that the principles of contemporary ecologism owe much to ancient pagan religions, which stressed the concept of an Earth Mother, and also to eastern religions such as Hinduism, Buddhism and Taoism. However, to a large extent, ecologism was, and remains, a reaction against the process of industrialization. This was evident in the nineteenth century, when the spread of urban and industrial life created a profound nostalgia for an idealized rural existence, as conveyed by novelists such as Thomas Hardy and political thinkers such as the UK libertarian socialist William Morris (1834–96) and Peter Kropotkin (see p. 191). This reaction was often strongest in those countries that had experienced the most rapid and dramatic process of industrialization. For example, Germany's rapid industrialization in the nineteenth century deeply scarred its political culture, creating powerful myths about the purity and dignity of peasant life, and giving rise to a strong 'back to nature' movement amongst German youth. Such romantic **pastoralism** was to be exploited in the twentieth century by nationalists and fascists.

Pastoralism: A belief in the virtues of rural existence: simplicity, community and a closeness to nature, in contrast to the allegedly corrupting influence of urban and industrialized life.

The growth of ecologism since the late twentieth century has been provoked by the further and more intense advance of industrialization and urbanization, linked to the emergence of post-material sensibilities amongst young people in particular. Environmental concern has become more acute because of the fear that economic growth is endangering both the survival of the human race and the very planet it lives on. Such anxieties have been expressed in a growing body of literature. Rachel Carson's *The Silent Spring* (1962), a critique of the damage done to wildlife and the human world by the increased use of pesticides and other agricultural chemicals, is often considered to have been the first book to draw attention to a developing ecological crisis. Other important early works included Ehrlich and Harriman's *How to be a Survivor* (1971), Goldsmith et al.'s *Blueprint for Survival* (1972), the unofficial UN report *Only One Earth* (1972) and the Club of Rome's *The Limits to Growth* (1972). At the same time, a new generation of activist pressure groups have developed – ranging from Greenpeace and Friends of the Earth to animal liberation activists and so-called 'eco-warrior' groups – campaigning on issues such as the dangers of pollution, the dwindling reserves of fossil fuels, deforestation and animal experiments. Together with established and much larger groups, such as the Worldwide Fund for Nature, this has led to the emergence of a well-publicized and increasingly powerful environmental movement. From the 1980s onwards, environmental questions have been kept high on the political agenda by green parties, which now exist in most industrialized countries, often modelling themselves on the pioneering efforts of the German Greens.

Environmental issues have also become an increasingly major focus of international concern and activity. Indeed, the environmental crisis could arguably be regarded as *the* global political issue, both because of the far-reaching nature of its implications and because of its intrinsically **transnational** character. The UN Conference on the Human Environment, held in Stockholm in 1972, was the first attempt to establish an international framework to promote a coordinated approach to environmental problems. The idea of 'sustainable development' was advanced in the 1987 Brundtland Report, a product of the work of the UN World Commission on Environment and Development, and by the Rio 'Earth Summit' in 1992. However, the most prominent global environmental issue is 'climate change', which most scientists now accept is a consequence of global warming resulting from the emission of so-called 'greenhouse' gases, such as carbon dioxide. The 1997 Kyoto Protocol established a legally binding commitment by developed states to limit such emissions in a phased process. Nevertheless, despite growing evidence of global warming, concerted and effective action in this area has been difficult to bring about.

Transnationalism: Processes and developments that transcend national and state boundaries and thus have a cross-border character; transnationalism fuels globalization.

Core themes – return to nature

Ecologism stands apart from traditional political creeds because it starts from an examination of what they ignore: the interrelationships that bind humans to all living organisms and, more broadly, to the 'web of life' (Capra, 1997). Traditional ideologies commit, ecologists believe, the sad, even comic, mistake of believing that humans are the centrepiece of existence. David Ehrenfeld (1978) called this the 'arrogance of **humanism**'. Instead of preserving and respecting the Earth and the diverse species that live on it, humans have sought to become, in the words of John Locke (see p. 37), 'the masters and possessors of nature'. Ecologism therefore represents a new style of politics, whose central vision is of nature as a network of precious but fragile relationships between living species – including the human species – and the natural envi-

Humanism: A philosophy that gives moral priority to the achievement of human needs and ends.

ronment. Humankind no longer occupies centre stage, but is regarded as an inseparable part of nature. In order to give expression to this vision, ecologists have been forced to search for new concepts and ideas in the realm of science or rediscover ancient ones from the realms of religion and mythology. The central themes of ecologism are the following:

- ecology
- holism
- sustainability
- environmental ethics
- self-actualization.

Ecology

The central principle of all forms of green thought is **ecology**. Ecology developed as a distinct branch of biology through a growing recognition that

Ecology: The study of the relationship between living organisms and the environment; ecology stresses the network of relationships that sustains all forms of life.

plants and animals are sustained by self-regulating natural systems – ecosystems – composed of both living and non-living elements. Simple examples of an ecosystem are a field, a forest or, as illustrated in Figure 9.1, a pond. All ecosystems tend towards a state of harmony or equilibrium through a system of self-regulation. Biologists refer to this as homeostasis. Food and other resources are recycled, and the population size of animals, insects and plants adjusts naturally to the available food supply.

However, such ecosystems are not 'closed' or entirely self-sustaining: each interreacts with other ecosystems. A lake may constitute an ecosystem, but it also needs to be fed with fresh water from tributaries, and receive warmth

Figure 9.1
A pond as an ecosystem

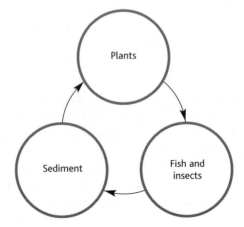

NATURE

LIBERALS see nature as a resource to satisfy human needs, and thus rarely question human dominion over it. Lacking value in itself, nature is invested with value only when it is transformed by human labour, or when it is harnessed to human ends.

CONSERVATIVES often portray nature as threatening, even cruel, characterized by an amoral struggle and harshness that also shapes human existence. Humans may be seen as part of nature within a 'great chain of being', their superiority nevertheless being enshrined in their status as custodians of nature.

SOCIALISTS, like liberals, have viewed and treated nature as merely a resource. However, a romantic or pastoral tradition within socialism has also extolled the beauty, harmony and richness of nature, and looks to human fulfilment through a closeness to nature.

ANARCHISTS have often embraced a view of nature that stresses unregulated harmony and growth. Nature therefore offers a model of simplicity and balance, which humans would be wise to apply to social organization in the form of social ecology.

FASCISTS have often adopted a dark and mystical view of nature that stresses the power of instinct and primal life forces, nature being able to purge humans of their decadent intellectualism. Nature is characterized by brutal struggle and cyclical regeneration.

FEMINISTS generally hold nature to be creative and benign. By virtue of their fertility and disposition to nurture, women are often thought to be close to nature and in tune with natural forces, while men, creatures of culture, are out of step or in conflict with nature.

ECOLOGISTS, particularly deep ecologists, regard nature as an interconnected whole, embracing humans and non-humans as well as the inanimate world. Nature is sometimes seen as a source of knowledge and 'right living', human fulfilment coming from a closeness to and respect for nature, not from the attempt to dominate it.

RELIGIOUS FUNDAMENTALISTS view nature as an expression of divine creation: what is 'natural' is thus God-given. While this may imply a duty of respect towards nature, it may also suggest that nature was created specifically to satisfy human ends.

and energy from the sun. In turn, the lake provides water and food for species living along its shores, including human communities. The natural world is therefore made up of a complex web of ecosystems, the largest of which is the global ecosystem, commonly called the 'ecosphere' or 'biosphere'.

The development of scientific ecology radically altered our understanding of the natural world and of the place of human beings within it. Ecology conflicts quite dramatically with the notion of humankind as 'the master' of nature, and instead suggests that a delicate network of interrelationships that had hitherto been ignored sustains each human community, indeed the entire human species. Ecologists argue that humankind currently faces the prospect of environmental disaster precisely because, in its passionate but blinkered pursuit of material wealth, it has upset the 'balance of nature' and endangered the very ecosystems that make human life possible. This has happened in a broad variety of ways. These include the exponential growth in the world's human population; the depletion of finite and irreplaceable fuel resources such as coal, oil and natural gas; the eradication of tropical rain forests that help clean the air and regulate the Earth's climate; the pollution of rivers, lakes and forests and the air itself; the use of chemical, hormonal and other additives to foodstuffs; and the threat to biodiversity that has resulted from the thousandfold increase in species extinction that has coincided with the dominance of the human species.

Ecologism provides a radically different vision of nature and the place of human beings within it, one that favours **ecocentrism** and challenges **anthropocentrism**. However, green or environmental thinkers have applied ecological ideas in different ways, and sometimes drawn quite different conclusions. The most important distinction in the environmental movement is between what the Norwegian philosopher Arne Naess (born 1912) termed '**shallow ecology**' and '**deep ecology**'. The 'shallow' perspective accepts the lessons of ecology but harnesses them to human needs and ends. In other words, it preaches that if we conserve and cherish the natural world, it will continue to sustain human life. This view is reflected in a particular concern with issues such as controlling population growth,

Ecocentrism: A theoretical orientation that gives priority to the maintenance of ecological balance rather than the achievement of human ends.

Anthropocentrism: A belief that human needs and interests are of overriding moral and philosophical importance; the opposite of ecocentrism.

Shallow ecology: A green ideological perspective that harnesses the lessons of ecology to human needs and ends, and is associated with values such as sustainability and conservation.

Deep ecology: A green ideological perspective that rejects anthropocentrism and gives priority to the maintenance of nature, and is associated with values such as biocentric equality, diversity and decentralization.

Environmentalism:
A belief in the political importance of the natural environment; often used (in contrast to ecologism) to denote a reformism approach to nature that reflects human needs and concerns.

cutting back on the use of finite, non-renewable resources and reducing pollution. While some regard such a stance as a form of 'weak ecologism', others classify it as **environmentalism** to distinguish it more clearly from ecologism.

'Deep' ecologists dismiss 'shallow' ecologism as a thinly concealed form of anthropocentrism, arguing that its central objective is to maintain the health and prosperity of people who live in developed countries. The 'deep' perspective advances a form of 'strong' ecologism that completely rejects any lingering belief that the human species is in some way superior to, or more important than, any other species, or indeed nature itself. It is based on the more challenging idea that the purpose of human life is to help sustain nature, and not the other way around. What Naess (1989) called 'ecosophy' thus represents a fundamentally new world view based on philosophical ecology, as well as an entirely novel moral vision. For their part, shallow ecologists, or, as they prefer, 'humanist' ecologists, criticize deep ecology for subscribing to 'irrational' or mystical doctrines and for advocating starkly unrealistic solutions that are, in any event, unlikely to have a wide appeal to human populations. The alternative idea of '**social ecology**' is considered later in the chapter in connection with eco-anarchism.

Social ecology: The theory that human society operates according to ecological principles, implying a belief in natural harmony and the need for a balance between humankind and nature.

TENSIONS WITHIN
ECOLOGISM

'DEEP' ECOLOGISM	v.	'SHALLOW' ECOLOGISM
ecologism	←→	environmentalism
ecocentrism	←→	'light' anthropocentricism
mysticism	←→	science
nature	←→	humankind
radical holism	←→	reluctant holism
value-in-nature	←→	instrumental value
biocentric equality	←→	conserve non-human
nature animal rights	←→	animal welfare
anti-growth	←→	sustainable growth
ecological consciousness	←→	personal development

Holism

Traditional political ideologies have typically assumed that human beings are the masters of the natural world, and have therefore regarded nature as little more than an economic resource. In that sense, they have been part of the problem and not part of the solution. In *The Turning Point* (1982), Fritjof Capra traced the origin of such ideas to the scientists and philosophers, such as René Descartes (1596–1650) and Isaac Newton (1642–1727). The world had previously been seen as organic; however, these seventeenth-century philosophers portrayed it as a machine, whose parts could be analysed and understood through the newly discovered scientific method. Science enabled remarkable advances to be made in human knowledge and provided the basis for the development of modern industry and technology. So impressive were the fruits of science, that intellectual inquiry in the modern world has come to be dominated by **scientism**. However, Capra argued that orthodox science, what he referred to as the 'Cartesian–Newtonian paradigm', amounts to the philosophical basis of the contemporary environmental crisis. Science treats nature as a machine, implying that, like any other machine, it can be tinkered with, repaired, improved on or even replaced. If human beings are to learn that they are part of the natural world rather than its masters, Capra suggested that this fixation with the 'Newtonian world-machine' must be overthrown and replaced by a new paradigm.

Scientism: The belief that scientific method is the only value-free and objective means of establishing truth, and is applicable to all fields of learning.

In searching for this new paradigm, ecological thinkers have been attracted to a variety of ideas and theories, drawn from both modern science and ancient myths and religions. However, the unifying theme amongst these ideas is the notion of **holism**. The term 'holism' was coined in 1926 by Jan Smuts, a Boer general and twice prime minister of South Africa. He used it to describe the idea that the natural world could only be understood as a whole and not through its individual parts. Smuts believed that science commits the sin of reductionism: it reduces everything it studies to separate parts and tries to understand each part in itself. In contrast, holism suggests that each part only has meaning in relation to other parts, and ultimately in relation to the whole. For example, a holistic approach to medicine would consider not just physical ailments but would see these as a manifestation of imbalances within the patient as a whole, taking account of psychological, emotional, social and environmental factors.

Holism: A belief that the whole is more important than its parts; holism implies that understanding is gained by studying relationships among the parts.

Although many ecologists criticize science, others have suggested that modern science may offer a new paradigm for human thought. Capra, for example, argued that the Cartesian–Newtonian view of the world has now been abandoned by many scientists, particularly by physicists like himself. During the twentieth century, with the development of 'new physics', physics moved a long way beyond the mechanistic and reductionist ideas of Newton. The breakthrough was achieved at the beginning of the twentieth century by the German-born US physicist Albert Einstein (1879–1955), whose theory of relativity fundamentally challenged the traditional concepts of time and space. Einstein's work was taken further by quantum theory, developed by physicists such as Niels Bohr (1885–1952) and Verner Heisenberg (1901–76). In quantum theory the physical world is understood not as a collection of individual molecules, atoms or even particles, but as a system, or, more accurately, a network of systems. A systems view of the world concentrates not on individual building blocks, but on the principles of organization within the system. It therefore stresses the relationships within the system and the integration of its various elements within the whole. Such a view has very radical implications. Objective knowledge, for example, is impossible because the very act of observing alters what is being observed. The scientist is not separate from his or her experiment but is intrinsically related to it; subject and object are therefore one. This led Heisenberg, for instance, to advance his 'uncertainty principle', which acknowledges the impact the observer always has on what is observed.

An alternative and particularly fertile source of new concepts and theories has been religion. In *The Tao of Physics* (1975), Capra drew attention to important parallels between the ideas of modern physics and those of eastern mysticism. He argued that religions such as Hinduism, Taoism and Buddhism, particularly Zen Buddhism, have long preached the unity or oneness of all things, a discovery that western science only made in the twentieth century. Many in the green movement have been attracted by eastern mysticism, seeing in it both a philosophy that gives expression to ecological wisdom and a way of life that encourages compassion for fellow human beings, other species and the natural world. Other writers believe that ecological principles are embodied in monotheistic religions such as Christianity, Judaism and Islam, which regard both humankind and nature as products of divine creation. In such circumstances, human beings are viewed as God's stewards on Earth, being invested thereby with a duty to cherish and preserve the planet.

However, perhaps the most influential concepts for modern greens have been developed by looking back to pre-Christian spiritual ideas. Primitive religions often drew no distinction between human and other forms of life, and, for that matter, little distinction between living and non-living objects. All things are alive, stones, rivers, mountains and even the Earth itself, often conceived of as 'Mother Earth'. The idea of an Earth Mother has been

James Lovelock
(born 1919)

LOVELOCK

Canadian atmospheric chemist, inventor and environmental theorist. An independent scientist who lives in Cornwall, Lovelock cooperated with NASA in their space programme, advising on ways of looking for life on Mars.

Lovelock's influence on the green movement stems from his portrayal of the Earth's biosphere as a complex, self-regulating, living 'being', which he named Gaia (at the suggestion of the novelist William Golding). Although the Gaia hypothesis extends the ecological idea by applying it to the Earth as an ecosystem and offers a holistic approach to nature, Lovelock supports technology and industrialization and is an opponent of 'back to nature' mysticism and ideas such as Earth worship. His major writings include *Gaia: A New Look at Life on Earth* (1979) and *The Ages of Gaia: A Biography of Our Living Earth* (1989).

particularly important for ecologists trying to articulate a new relationship between human beings and the natural world, especially so for those sympathetic to ecofeminism, examined later in the chapter. James Lovelock developed the idea that the planet itself is alive and gave it the name 'Gaia', after the Greek goddess of the Earth. According to the **Gaia hypothesis**, the 'Earth's biosphere, atmosphere, oceans and soil' exhibit precisely the kind of self-regulating behaviour that characterizes other forms of life. Gaia has maintained 'homeostasis', a state of dynamic balance, despite major changes that have taken place in the solar system. The most dramatic evidence for this is the fact that although the sun has warmed up by more than 25 per cent since life began, the temperature on Earth and the composition of its atmosphere have remained virtually unchanged.

Gaia hypothesis: The theory that the Earth is best understood as a living entity that acts to maintain its own existence.

The idea of Gaia has developed into an 'ecological ideology' that conveys the powerful message that human beings must respect the health of the planet, and act to conserve its beauty and resources. It also contains a revolutionary vision of the relationship between the animate and inanimate world. However, the Gaia philosophy does not always correspond to the concerns of the environmental movement. Shallow ecologists have typically wished to change policies and attitudes in order to ensure the continued survival of the human species. Gaia, on the other hand, is non-human, and the Gaia theory suggests that the health of the planet matters more than that of any individual species presently living on it. Lovelock has suggested that those species that have prospered have been ones that have helped Gaia to regulate its own existence, while any species that poses a threat to the delicate balance of Gaia, as humans currently do, is likely to be extinguished. Lovelock has also been strongly committed to science, and, contrary to the views of many in the environmental movement, has stressed the importance of nuclear power in providing a solution to the environmental crisis.

Sustainability

Ecologists argue that the ingrained assumption of conventional political creeds, articulated by virtually all mainstream political parties (so-called 'grey parties'), is that human life has unlimited possibilities for material growth and prosperity. Indeed, green thinkers commonly lump capitalism and socialism together, and portray them both as examples of 'industrialism'. A particularly influential metaphor for the environmental movement has been the idea of 'spaceship Earth', because this emphasizes the notion of limited and exhaustible wealth. The idea that Earth should be thought of as a spaceship was first suggested by Kenneth Boulding (1966). Boulding argued that human beings have traditionally acted as though they live in a 'cowboy economy', an economy with unlimited opportunities, like the American West during the frontier period. He suggested that this encourages, as it did in the American West, 'reckless, exploitative, and violent behaviour'. However, as a spaceship is a capsule, it is a 'closed' system.

INDUSTRIALISM

The term 'industrialism', as used by environmental theorists, relates to a 'super-ideology' that encompasses capitalism and socialism, left-wing and right-wing thought. As an economic system, industrialism is characterized by large-scale production, the accumulation of capital and relentless growth. As a philosophy, it is dedicated to materialism, utilitarian values, absolute faith in science and a worship of technology. Many ecologists thus see industrialism as 'the problem'. Ecosocialists, however, blame capitalism rather than industrialism (which ignores important issues such as the role of ownership, profit and the market), while ecofeminists argue that industrialism has its origins in patriarchy.

'Open' systems receive energy or inputs from outside; for example, all ecosystems on Earth – ponds, forests, lakes and seas – are sustained by the sun. However, 'closed' systems, as the Earth itself becomes when it is thought of as a spaceship, show evidence of '**entropy**'. All 'closed' systems tend to decay or disintegrate because they are not sustained by external inputs. Ultimately, however wisely and carefully human beings behave, the Earth, the sun, and indeed all planets and stars, will be exhausted and die. When the 'entropy law' is applied to social and economic issues it produces very radical conclusions.

Entropy: A tendency towards decay or disintegration, exhibited by all 'closed' systems.

No issue reflects the law of entropy more clearly than the 'energy crisis'. Industrialization and mass affluence have been made possible by the exploitation of coal, gas and oil reserves, providing fuel for power stations, factories, motor cars, aeroplanes and so on. These fuels are fossil fuels, formed by the decomposition or compaction of organisms that died in prehistoric times. They are also non-renewable: once used up they cannot be replaced. In *Small is Beautiful* (1973), E. F. Schumacher argued that human beings have made the mistake of regarding energy as an 'income' that is being constantly topped-up each week or each month, rather than as 'natural capital' that they are forced to live off. This mistake has allowed energy demands to soar, especially in the industrialized West, at a time when finite fuel resources are close to depletion and very unlikely to last to the end of the present century. As the spaceship draws to the close of the 'fossil-fuel age', it approaches disintegration because, as yet, there are no alternative sources of energy to compensate for the loss of coal, oil and gas.

Not only have humans failed to recognize that they live within the constraints of a 'closed' ecosystem, but they have also been unwisely cavalier in plundering its resources. Garrett Hardin (1968) developed a particularly influential model to explain why over-exploitation of environmental resources has occurred, in the form of the 'tragedy of the commons'. The notion of the 'tragedy of the commons' demonstrates the environmental vulnerability that arises from people having open access to collective resources. Common land or common fishery stocks encourage individuals to act in rationally self-interested ways, each exploiting the resources available to satisfy their needs and the needs of their families and communities. However, the collective impact of such behaviour may be devastating, as the vital resources on which all depend become depleted or despoiled. Rational individual behaviour may therefore be self-defeating and result in 'irrational' ends. The parable of the 'tragedy of the commons' sheds light on the behaviour of individuals within the community, the actions of groups within society, and also the strategies adopted by states within the international or global system. However, the parable also highlights why it is often so diffi-

Fritz (Ernst Friedrich) Schumacher (1911–77)

German-born UK economist and environmental theorist. Schumacher moved to Britain in 1930 as an Oxford Rhodes scholar, going on to gain practical experience in business, farming and journalism, before re-entering academic life. He was an economic adviser to the British Control Commission in Germany (1946–50) and the National Coal Board (1950–70).

Schumacher's seminal *Small is Beautiful: A Study of Economics as if People Mattered* (1973) championed the cause of human-scale production, and advanced a 'Buddhist' economic philosophy (economics 'as if people mattered') that stresses the importance of morality and 'right livelihood'. Though an opponent of industrial giantism, Schumacher believed in 'appropriate' scale production, and was a keen advocate of 'intermediate' technology.

cult to tackle environmental problems at any level. Any viable solution to the environmental crisis must offer a means of dealing with the 'tragedy of the commons'.

Nevertheless, ecological economics is not only about warnings and threats, it is also about solutions. Entropy may be an inevitable process; however, its effects can be slowed down or delayed considerably if governments and private citizens respect ecological principles. Ecologists argue that the human species will only survive and prosper if it recognizes that it is merely one element of a complex biosphere, and that only a healthy, balanced biosphere will sustain human life. Policies and actions must therefore be judged by the principle of **'sustainability'**. Sustainability sets clear limits on human ambitions and material dreams because it requires that production does as little damage as possible to the fragile global ecosystem. For example, a sustainable energy policy must be based on a dramatic reduction in the use of fossil fuels and a search for alternative, renewable energy sources such as solar energy, wind power and wave power. These are by their very nature sustainable and can be treated as 'income' rather than 'natural capital'.

Sustainability, however, requires not merely the implementation of government controls or tax regimes to ensure a more enlightened use of natural resources, but, at a deeper level, the adoption of an alternative

Sustainability: The capacity of a system to maintain its health and continue in existence over a period of time.

approach to economic activity. This is precisely what Schumacher (1973) sought to offer in his idea of 'Buddhist economics'. For Schumacher, Buddhist economics is based on the principle of 'right livelihood' and stands in stark contrast to conventional economic theories, which assume that individuals are nothing more than 'utility maximizers'. Buddhists believe that, in addition to generating goods and services, production facilitates personal growth by developing skills and talents, and helps to overcome egocentredness by forging social bonds and encouraging people to work together. Such a view moves economics a long way from its present obsession with wealth creation, an obsession that, ecologists believe, has paid little regard to either nature or the spiritual quality of human life.

There is considerable debate about what this implies in practice. So-called 'light' greens, referred to in Germany as the *Realos* (realists), approve of the idea of 'sustainable growth': in effect, getting richer but at a slower pace. This holds that the desire for material prosperity can be balanced against its environmental costs. One way in which this could be achieved would be through changes to the tax system, either to penalize and discourage pollution or to reduce the use of finite resources. However, 'dark' greens, in Germany the *Fundis* (fundamentalists), argue that such views are simply not radical enough. From their perspective, the notion of sustainable growth simply pays lip service to environmental fears whilst allowing human beings to carry on as if nothing is wrong. If, as the dark greens insist, the origin of the ecological crisis lies in materialism, consumerism and a fixation with economic growth, the solution lies in 'zero growth' and the construction of a 'post-industrial age' in which people live in small rural communities and rely on craft skills. This means a fundamental and comprehensive rejection of industry and modern technology, literally a 'return to nature'.

Environmental ethics

Ecological politics, in all its forms, is concerned with extending moral thinking in a number of novel directions. This is because conventional ethical systems are clearly anthropocentric, orientated around the pleasure, needs and interests of human beings. In such philosophies, the non-human world is invested with value only to the extent that it satisfies human ends. One ethical issue that even humanist or 'shallow' ecologists extensively grapple with is the question of our moral obligations towards future generations. It is in the nature of environmental matters that many of the consequences of our actions will not be felt until decades or even centuries to come. For instance, why worry about the accummulation of nuclear waste if the generations that will have to deal with it have yet to be born? Clearly, a concern with our own interests and perhaps those of our immediate family and friends only stretches a little way into the future. Ecologists are therefore forced to extend the notion of human interests to encompass the human species as a whole, making no distinction between the present generation and future generations, the living and the still to be born. Such 'futurity' may be justified in different ways. Ecoconservatives, for instance, may link it to tradition and continuity, to the notion that the present generation is merely the 'custodian' of the wealth that has been generated by past generations and so should conserve it for the benefit of future generations. Ecosocialists, on the other hand, may hold that a concern for future generations merely reflects the fact that compassion and a love for humanity extend through time, just as they cut across national, ethnic, gender and other boundaries.

An alternative approach to environmental ethics involves applying moral standards and values developed in relation to human beings to other species and organisms. The most familiar attempt to do this is in the form of 'animal rights'. Peter Singer's (1975) case for animal welfare had considerable impact on the growing animal liberation movement. Singer argued that an altruistic concern for the well-being of other species derives from the fact that, as sentient beings, they are capable of suffering. Drawing on utilitarianism, he pointed out that animals, like humans, have an interest in avoiding physical pain, and he therefore condemned any attempt to place the interests of humans above those of animals as '**speciesism**'. However, altruistic concern for other species does not imply equal treatment. Singer's argument does not apply to non-sentient life forms such as trees, rocks and rivers. Moreover the moral imperative is the avoidance of suffering, with special consideration being given to more developed and self-aware animals, notably to the great apes. On the other hand, Singer's argument implies that a reduced moral consideration should be given to human foetuses and mentally impaired people who have no capacity for suffering (Singer, 1993).

Speciesism:
A belief in the superiority of one species over other species, through the denial of their moral significance.

Nevertheless, the moral stance of 'deep' ecology goes much further, in particular by suggesting that nature has value in its own right; that is, intrinsic value. From this perspective, environmental ethics have nothing to do with human-instrumentality and cannot be articulated simply through the extension of human values to the non-human world. Goodin (1992), for instance, attempted to develop a 'green theory of value', which holds that resources should be valued precisely because they result from natural processes rather than from human activities. However, since this value stems from the fact that the natural landscape helps people to see 'some sense and pattern in their lives' and to appreciate 'something larger' than themselves, it embodies a residual humanism that fails to satisfy some deep ecologists. A classic statement of their more radical position is articulated in Aldo Leopold's *Sand County Almanac* ([1948] 1968) in the form of the 'land ethic': 'A thing is right when it tends to preserve the integrity, stability and beauty of the biotic community. It is wrong when it tends otherwise.' Nature itself is thus portrayed as an ethical community, meaning that human beings are nothing more than 'plain citizens' who have no more rights and are no more deserving of respect than any other member of the community. Such a moral stance implies '**biocentric equality**'. Arne Naess (1989) expressed this as an 'equal right to live and bloom'. Such a moral position also implies support for 'bio-diversity', on the grounds that the wider the range of diversity within the biotic community, the healthier and more stable that community will be.

Biocentric equality: The principle that all organisms and entities in the ecosphere are of equal moral worth, each of them being part of an interrelated whole.

Self-actualization

Since one of the consistent themes of ecologism is a rejection of human self-interestedness and material greed, it has sought to develop an alternative philosophy that links personal fulfilment to a balance with nature. The growth of concern about environmental issues since the 1960s is commonly associated with the phenomenon of **postmaterialism** (Inglehart, 1977). The idea of postmaterialism is loosely based on Abraham Maslow's (1908–70) 'hierarchy of needs', which places the need for esteem and **self-actualization** above material or economic needs. This implies that while conditions of material scarcity breed egoistical and acquisitive attitudes, conditions of widespread prosperity allow individuals to express more interest in postmaterial or 'quality of life' issues. These are typically concerned with morality, political justice and personal fulfilment, and include gender equality, world peace, racial harmony, ecology and animal rights. In this sense, ecologism can be seen as one of the 'new' social movements that sprang up in the second half of the twentieth century, broadly committed to a new left agenda that rejected the hierarchical, materialist and patriarchal values of conventional society.

Postmaterialism: The theory that as material affluence spreads,'quality of life' issues and concerns tend to displace economic ones.

Self-actualization: Personal fulfilment brought about by the refinement of sensibilities; self-actualization is usually linked to the transcendence of egoism and materialism.

However, to a greater extent than any of the other new social movements, ecologism has indulged in radical and innovative thinking about the nature of human sensibilities and self-realization. All ecologists, for example, would have some sympathy with the view that human development has become dangerously unbalanced: human beings are blessed with massive know-how and material wealth, but possess precious little 'know-why'. Humankind has acquired the ability to fulfil its material ambitions, but not the wisdom to question whether these ambitions are sensible, or even sane. As Schumacher (1973) warned, 'Man is now too clever to survive without wisdom.' However, some shallow or humanistic ecologists have serious misgivings when this quest for wisdom draws ecologism into the realms of religious mysticism or New Age ideas. Many greens, particularly those who subscribe to deep ecology, have nevertheless embraced world views that are quite different from those that have traditionally dominated political thought in the developed West. This, they argue, is the basis of the 'paradigm shift' that ecologism aims to bring about, and without which it is doomed to repeat the mistakes of the 'old' politics because it cannot move beyond its concepts and assumptions.

Deep ecologists are usually happy to acknowledge that there is, in a sense, a spiritual dimension to their view of politics. A closeness to nature is not merely a theoretical stance or an ethical position; it is, at heart, a human experience, the achievement of 'environmental consciousness' or the 'ecological self'. The Australian philosopher Warwick Fox (1990) claimed to go beyond deep ecology in embracing 'transpersonal ecology', the essence of which is the realization that 'things are', that human beings and all other entities are part of a single unfolding reality. For Naess, self-realization is attained through a broader and deeper 'identification with others'. Such ideas have often been shaped by eastern religions, most profoundly by Buddhism, which has been portrayed as an ecological philosophy in its own right. One of the key doctrines of Buddhism is the idea of 'no self', the notion that the individual ego is a myth or delusion, and that awakening or enlightenment involves transcending the self and recognizing that each person is linked to all other living things, and indeed to the universe itself. This can be developed into a kind of holistic individualism, in which freedom comes to be equated with the experience of 'being' and the realization of organic wholeness. Such ideas were advanced by the German psychoanalyst and social philosopher Eric Fromm (1900–80) in *To Have or To Be* (1979). Fromm portrayed 'having' as an attitude of mind that seeks fulfilment in acquisition and control, and is clearly reflected in consumerism and the materialistic society. In contrast, 'being' derives satisfaction from experience and sharing, and leads to personal growth and spiritual awareness.

Nature and politics

Deep ecologists typically dismiss conventional political creeds as merely different versions of anthropocentricism, each embodying an anti-nature bias. They claim to have developed an entirely new ideological paradigm (although many reject the term 'ideology' because of its association with human-centred thinking), developed through the radical application of ecological and holistic principles. Nevertheless, other ecological or environmental thinkers have drawn inspiration, to a greater or lesser extent, from established political traditions. Such a stance is based on the belief that these traditions contain values and doctrines that are capable of accommodating a positive view of non-human nature, and of shedding light on why the ecological crisis has come about and how it can be tackled. In this sense, ecologism, like nationalism and feminism, can be regarded as a cross-cutting ideology. At different times, conservatives, fascists, socialists, anarchists, feminists and liberals have claimed a special sympathy with the environment. However, they have enlisted ecological ideas in support of very different political goals. The most significant sub-traditions within ecologism are the following:

- right-wing ecologism
- ecosocialism
- eco-anarchism
- ecofeminism.

Right-wing ecologism

The earliest manifestations of political ecology had an essentially right-wing orientation (Bramwell, 1989). This was most dramatically demonstrated by the emergence of a form of fascist ecologism during the Nazi period in Germany. Its principal exponent was Walter Darré, who was minister of agriculture under Hitler, 1933–42, and also held the post of Nazi peasant leader. The experience of rapid industrialization in late nineteenth-century Germany had created a strong 'back to the land' movement, which was especially attractive to students and young people. The German Youth Movement developed out of the *Wandervoegel*, bands of German students who took to the forests and mountains to escape from the alienation of urban life. Darré's own ideas were a mixture of Nordic racialism (see p. 231) and the idealization of peasant or rural life, fused into an agrarian philosophy of 'Blood and Soil' that overlapped at several points with national socialism. As peasant leader, Darré was responsible for introducing the hereditary farm law, which gave owners of small and medium-size farms complete security of tenure, and also for setting up the National Food

Estate to market agricultural produce with the intention of keeping food prices high and maintaining rural prosperity. Despite his links with the Nazis, Darré's ideas have much in common with the modern green movement. In the first place, he was convinced that only a life lived close to nature and on the land could be truly fulfilling, and he therefore wished to recreate a peasant Germany. Such ideas have been echoed by modern ecologists such as Edward Goldsmith (1988). Moreover, Darré became a powerful advocate of organic farming, which uses only natural fertilizers such as animal manure. Darré believed in an organic cycle of animal–soil–food–humans, which he discovered in the works of the Austrian philosopher and educationalist Rudolph Steiner (1861–1925) and the anthroposophy movement. Organic farming reflects ecological principles and has become a major plank in the idea of environmentally friendly agriculture. During the Third Reich, Darré's peasant ideology helped the Nazis to secure committed support in the German countryside. However, in practice, the Nazi regime did little to fulfil Darré's dreams of a sturdy, peasant Germany. Despite Hitler's attachment to the idea of 'Blood and Soil', his obsession with military expansion intensified the process of industrialization in Germany and brought poverty to the countryside.

On the 'soft' right, conservatives have also evinced a sympathy for environmental issues. This has been done on two grounds. First, ecoconservatism has drawn from a romantic and nostalgic attachment to a rural way of life threatened by the growth of towns and cities. It is clearly a reaction against industrialization and the idea of 'progress'. It does not envisage the construction of a post-industrial society, founded on the principles of cooperation and ecology, but a return to, or the maintenance of, a more familiar pre-industrial one. Such environmental sensibilities typically focus on the issue of conservation and upon attempts to protect the natural heritage – woodlands, forests and so on – as well as the architectural and social heritage. The conservation of nature is therefore linked to a defence of traditional values and institutions. Second, conservatives have advocated market-based solutions to environmental problems, even espousing the idea of 'green capitalism'. Market-based environmental solutions include the adoption of tax structures that incentivize eco-friendly individual and corporate behaviour, and emissions trading schemes such as those proposed by the Kyoto Protocol. Capitalism's green credentials are based on both its willingness to respond to more ecologically aware consumers by producing new goods and technology, and its recognition that long-term corporate profitability can only be ensured in a context of sustainable development.

Ecosocialism

There is a distinct socialist strand within the green movement, which has been particularly pronounced amongst the German Greens, many of whose leaders have been former members of far-left groups. Ecosocialism has drawn from the pastoral socialism of thinkers such as William Morris, who extolled the virtues of small-scale craft communities living close to nature. However, it has more usually been associated with Marxism. For example, Rudolph Bahro (1982), a leading German ecosocialist, argued that the root cause of the environmental crisis is capitalism. The natural world has been despoiled by industrialization, but this is merely a consequence of capitalism's relentless search for profit. Capitalism is thus characterized not only by class conflict, but also by the destruction of the natural environment. Both human labour and the natural world are exploited because they are treated simply as economic resources. Any attempt to improve the environment must therefore involve a radical process of social change, some would say a social revolution.

The core theme of ecosocialism is the idea that capitalism is the enemy of the environment, whilst socialism is its friend. However, as with socialist feminism, such a formula embodies tension between two elements, this time between 'red' and 'green' priorities. If environmental catastrophe is nothing more than a by-product of capitalism, environmental problems are best tackled by abolishing capitalism, or at least taming it. Therefore, ecologists should not form separate green parties or set up narrow environmental organizations, but work within the larger socialist movement and address the real issue: the economic system. On the other hand, socialism has also been seen as another 'pro-production' political creed: it espouses exploiting the wealth of the planet, albeit for the good of humanity, rather than just the capitalist class. Socialist parties have been slow to adopt environmental policies because they, like other 'grey' parties, continue to base their electoral appeal on the promise of economic growth. As a result, ecologists have often been reluctant to subordinate the green to the red, hence the proclamation by the German Greens that they are 'neither left nor right'. Indeed, ecosocialists such as Bahro (1984) have come to the conclusion that the ecological crisis is so pressing that it must take precedence over the class struggle.

Ecosocialists argue that socialism is naturally ecological. If wealth is owned in common it will be used in the interests of all, which means in the long-term interests of humanity. However, it is unlikely that ecological problems can be solved simply by a change in the ownership of wealth. This was abundantly demonstrated by the experience of state socialism in the Soviet Union and eastern Europe, which produced some of the world's most intractable environmental problems. Examples of this include the Aral Sea in Central Asia, once the fourth biggest lake in the world, which has shrunk to half its original size as a result of the re-routing two rivers, and the Chernobyl nuclear explosion in the Ukraine in 1986.

Eco-anarchism

Perhaps the ideology that has the best claim to being environmentally sensitive is anarchism. Some months before the publication of Rachel Carson's *The Silent Spring*, Murray Bookchin brought out *Our Synthetic Environment* ([1962] 1975). Many in the green movement also acknowledge a debt to nineteenth-century anarcho-communists, particularly Peter Kropotkin. Bookchin (1977) suggested that there is a clear correspondence between the ideas of anarchism and the principles of ecology, articulated in the idea of 'social ecology', the belief that ecological balance is the surest foundation for social stability. Anarchists believe in a stateless society, in which harmony develops out of mutual respect and social solidarity amongst human beings. The richness of such a society is founded on its variety and diversity. Ecologists also believe that balance or harmony spontaneously develops within nature, in the form of ecosystems, and that these, like anarchist communities, require no external authority or control. The anarchist rejection of government within human society thus parallels the ecologists'

Murray Bookchin
(1921–2006)

US anarchist social philosopher and environmental thinker. Bookchin was a radical activist in the American labour movement of the 1930s, and was one of the very earliest social thinkers to take environmental issues seriously. He was professor emeritus of the Institute of Social Ecology in Vermont.

Bookchin's contribution to anarchism is linked to an emphasis on the potential for non-hierarchic cooperation within conditions of post-scarcity, and on ways of promoting decentralization and community within modern societies. As the leading proponent of 'social ecology', he argued that ecological principles can be applied to social organization and suggested that the environmental crisis is a result of the breakdown of the organic fabric of both society and nature. Bookchin's major works include *Post-Scarcity Anarchism* (1971), *The Ecology of Freedom* (1982) and *Remaking Society* (1989).

warnings about human 'rule' within the natural world. Bookchin therefore likened an anarchist community to an ecosystem, and suggested that both are distinguished by respect for the principles of diversity, balance and harmony.

Anarchists have also advocated the construction of decentralized societies, organized as a collection of communes or villages. Life in such communities would be lived close to nature, each community attempting to achieve a high degree of self-sufficiency. Such communities would be economically diverse; they would produce food and a wide range of goods and services, and therefore contain agriculture, craftwork and small-scale industry. Self-sufficiency would make each community dependent on its natural environment, spontaneously generating an understanding of organic relationships and ecology. In Bookchin's view, decentralization would lead to 'a more intelligent and more loving use of the environment'.

Without doubt, the conception that many ecologists have of a postindustrial society has been influenced by the writings of Kropotkin and William Morris. The green movement has also adopted ideas such as decentralization, participatory democracy and direct action from anarchist thought. However, even when anarchism is embraced as providing a vision of an ecologically sound future, it is seldom accepted as a means of getting there. Anarchists believe that progress will only be possible when government and all forms of political authority are overthrown. In contrast, many in the green movement see government as an agency through which collective action can be organized and, therefore, as the most likely means through which the environmental crisis can be addressed, at least in the short term. They fear that dismantling or even weakening government may simply give free rein to those forces that generated industrialization and blighted the natural environment in the first place.

Ecofeminism

The idea that feminism offers a distinctive and valuable approach to green issues has grown to such a point that ecofeminism has developed into one of the major philosophical schools of environmentalist thought. Its basic theme is that ecological destruction has its origins in **patriarchy**: nature is under threat not from humankind but from men and the institutions of male power. Feminists who adopt an androgynous or sexless view of human nature argue that patriarchy has distorted the instincts and sensibilities of men by divorcing them from the 'private' world of nurturing, home making and

Patriarchy: Literally, rule by the father; patriarchy is often taken more generally to describe the dominance of men and the subordination of women in society at large.

personal relationships. The sexual division of labour thus inclines men to subordinate both women and nature, seeing themselves as 'masters' of both. From this point of view, ecofeminism can be classified as a particular form of social ecology. However, many ecofeminists subscribe to essentialism, in that their theories are based on the belief that there are fundamental and ineradicable differences between women and men.

Such a position is adopted, for instance, by Mary Daly in *Gyn/Ecology* (1979). Daly argued that women would liberate themselves from patriarchal culture if they aligned themselves with 'female nature'. The notion of an intrinsic link between women and nature is not a new one. Pre-Christian religions and 'primitive' cultures often portrayed the Earth or natural forces as a goddess, an idea resurrected in the Gaia hypothesis. Modern ecofeminists, however, highlight the biological basis for women's closeness to nature, in particular the fact that they bear children and suckle babies. The fact that women cannot live separate from natural rhythms and processes in turn structures their politico-cultural orientation. Traditional 'female' values therefore include reciprocity, cooperation and nurturing, values that have a 'soft' or ecological character. The idea that nature is a resource to be exploited or a force to be subdued is more abhorrent to women than men, because they recognize that nature operates in and through them, and intuitively sense that personal fulfilment stems from acting with nature rather than against it. The overthrow of patriarchy therefore promises to bring with it an entirely new relationship between human society and the natural world.

If there is an essential or 'natural' bond between women and nature, the relationship between men and nature is quite different. While women are creatures of nature, men are creatures of culture: their world is synthetic or man-made, a product of human ingenuity rather than natural creativity. In the male world, then, intellect is ranked above intuition, materialism is valued over spirituality, and mechanical relationships are emphasized over holistic ones. In politico-cultural terms, this is reflected in a belief in self-striving, competition and hierarchy. The implications of this for the natural world are clear. Patriarchy, in this view, establishes the supremacy of culture over nature, the latter being nothing more than a force to be subdued, exploited or risen above. Ecological destruction and gender inequality are therefore part of the same process in which 'cultured' men rule over 'natural' women.

Ecologism in the twenty-first century

The prospects for ecologism in the twenty-first century would appear to be firmly linked to the state of the environmental crisis and the general level of understanding about environmental issues and problems. As evidence of the blighting of nature accumulates – through climate change resulting from global warming, reduced levels of male fertility caused by pollution, the eradication of animal and plant species, and so on – the search for an alternative to growth-obsessed industrialism will surely intensify. The fluctuating fortunes of green parties and single-issue environmentalist groups provide no reliable indication of the strength of ecological ideas and values. One of the problems confronting green parties is that their mainstream and much larger rivals have taken up 'eco-friendly' positions that were once exclusively theirs. Similarly, the membership and activist base of single-issue environmental groups does not reflect the number of 'fellow-travellers' in society at large, nor the wider adoption of ecological practices such as recycling and the use of organic foods. It is also notable that environmental groups and ecological activists have been prominent within the emergent anti-globalization movement. From this perspective, humankind will have little choice in the twenty-first century but to reverse the policies and practices that have brought both the human species and the natural world close to destruction.

A number of problems confront ecological theory, however. In the first place, it is difficult to see how ecologism can become a genuinely global ideology. As far as developing-world states are concerned, its strictures appear to deny them the opportunity to catch up with the West. Western states developed through large-scale industrialization, the exploitation of finite resources and a willingness to pollute the natural world, practices they now seek to deny to the developing world. For example, economic development in China resulted in the commissioning, on average, of one new coal-fuelled power station every week during 2006, resulting in eight of the ten most polluted cities being in China. However, the industrialized West is no more likely than the developing world fully to adopt ecological priorities, as this would mean that it, as the major consumer of energy and resources, would have to forgo the prosperity it already enjoys. This is evident in the reluctance of states such as the USA and Australia to sign up to the Kyoto Protocol.

Second, industrialism and its underpinning values, such as competitive individualism and consumerism, have become more deeply entrenched as a result of economic globalization. Globalization, in this sense, can be seen as a form of hyper-industrialism. The link between ecologism and the anti-globalization movement, in other words, is no coincidence. Third, difficulties surround the anti-growth message of ecologism. The politics of zero or even sustainable growth may be so electorally unattractive to populations that it proves to be democratically impossible. Fourth, greenism may simply be an urban fad, a form of post-industrial romanticism. This suggests that environmental awareness is merely a temporary reaction to industrial progress and is likely to be restricted to the young and the materially affluent.

Perhaps the most daunting challenge facing ecologism is the very scale of the changes it calls for. Ecologism, at least in the guise of deep ecology, is more radical than socialism, fascism, feminism or any of the other political creeds examined in this book. It does not merely demand the transformation of the economic system or the reordering of power relations within the political system; it seeks to establish nothing less than a new mode of being, a different way of experiencing and understanding existence. What is more, its theories, values and sensibilities are entirely at odds with those that have traditionally dominated industrialized societies. The problem of ecologism is, therefore, that it is based on a philosophy that is deeply alien to the culture that it must influence if it is to be successful. However, this may also be the source of its appeal.

Questions for discussion

→ How does an ecocentric perspective challenge conventional approaches to politics?

→ Is 'shallow' ecologism a contradiction in terms?

→ Why have ecologists been ambivalent about science?

→ What are the features of a sustainable economy?

→ How has ecological politics extended moral thinking?

→ To what extent have ecologists rethought the nature of human fulfilment?

→ Which political ideologies are most compatible with ecologism, and why?

→ Which ideologies are least compatible with ecologism, and why?

→ Can ecological politics ever be electorally and politically viable?

Further reading

Baxter, B., *Ecologism: An Introduction* (Edinburgh: Edinburgh University Press, 1999). A clear and comprehensive survey of the main components of ecologism that considers its moral, political and economic implications.

Bramwell, A., *Ecology in the Twentieth Century: A History* (New Haven, CT and London: Yale University Press, 1989). A highly influential study of the intellectual and political history of the ecological movement; detailed and provocative.

Capra, F., *The Web of Life: A New Synthesis of Mind and Matter* (London: Flamingo, 1997). A bold attempt to develop a new foundation for ecological politics that uses deep ecology as its theoretical paradigm.

Dobson, A., *Green Political Thought*, 4th edn (London: Routledge, 2007). An accessible and very useful account of the ideas behind green politics; sometimes seen as the classic text on the subject.

Dobson, A., *The Green Reader* (London: André Deutsch, 1991). An excellent collection of short extracts from important texts by ecological thinkers; a good basis for further reading.

Eckersley, R., *Environmentalism and Political Theory: Towards an Ecocentric Approach* (London: UCL Press, 1992). A detailed and comprehensive examination of the impact of environmentalist ideas on contemporary political thought.

Marshall, P., *Nature's Web: Rethinking Our Place on Earth* (London: Cassell, 1995). A history of ecological ideas that serves as a compendium of the various approaches to nature in different periods and from different cultures.

CHAPTER 10

RELIGIOUS FUNDAMENTALISM

The word 'fundamentalism' derives from the Latin *fundamentum*, meaning base. The term was first used in debates within American Protestantism in the early twentieth century. Between 1910 and 1915, evangelical Protestants published a series of pamphlets entitled *The Fundamentals*, upholding the inerrancy, or literal truth, of the Bible in the face of 'modern' interpretations of Christianity.

The term 'fundamentalism' is highly controversial. It is commonly associated with inflexibility, dogmatism and authoritarianism. As a result, many of those who are classified as fundamentalists reject the term as simplistic or demeaning, preferring instead to describe themselves as 'traditionalists', 'conservatives', 'evangelicals', 'revivalists' and so forth. However, unlike alternative terms, fundamentalism has the advantage of conveying the idea of a religio-political movement or project, rather than simply the assertion of the literal truth of sacred texts (although this remains a feature of certain forms of fundamentalism). Religious fundamentalism is thus characterized by a rejection of the distinction between religion and politics. Politics, in effect, *is* religion. This implies that religious principles are not restricted to personal or 'private' life, but are seen as the organizing principles of 'public' existence, including law, social conduct and the economy as well as politics. As such, fundamentalist tendencies can be identified in all the world's major religions – Christianity, Islam, Hinduism, Judaism, Buddhism and Sikhism. Nevertheless, although some forms of religious fundamentalism co-exist with pluralism (for example, Christian fundamentalism in the USA and Jewish fundamentalism in Israel), because their goals are limited and specific, other forms of religious fundamentalism are revolutionary (notably Islamic fundamentalism), in that they aim to construct a theocracy, in which the state is reconstructed on the basis of religious principles, and political position is linked to one's place within a religious hierarchy.

PREVIEW

Origins and development

Despite its backward-looking emphasis and evident anti-modernism, religious **fundamentalism** is very much a creature of the modern world.

Fundamentalism:
A belief in the original or most basic principles of a creed, often associated with fierce commitment and sometimes reflected in fanatical zeal (see p. 288).

Indeed, most commentators treat it as a distinctively modern phenomenon and deny that it has historical parallels. Possible exceptions to this include the German preacher and Anabaptist, Thomas Müntzer (1489–1525), who led the Peasants' War, and the French Protestant reformer, Jean Calvin (1509–64), who founded a theocracy in Geneva that allowed him to control almost all the city's affairs. Similarly, the Puritans played a major role in initiating the English Revolution of the seventeenth century, and demonstrated their 'this-worldly' concern to establish a new political and social system by sailing to North America to found a New England.

The upsurge in religious fundamentalism in the final decades of the twentieth century has confounded advocates of the so-called **secularization** thesis: this is the belief that modernization is invariably accompanied by the victory of reason over religion and the displacement of spiritual values by secular ones. In many parts of the world, religious movements have gained a renewed potency. Moreover, in its fundamentalist guise, this religious revivalism has assumed an overtly political form. This became evident in the 1970s within Islam, and was most dramatically demonstrated by the 1979 Islamic Revolution in Iran.

Secularization:
The spread of worldly or rationalist ideas and values in the place of religious or sacred ones.

During the 1980s, however, it became clear that this was not an exclusively Islamic development, as fundamentalist movements emerged within Christianity, particularly in the form of the so-called new Christian right in the USA, and within Hinduism and Sikhism in India.

It is difficult to generalize about the causes of the fundamentalist upsurge that has occurred since the late twentieth century because, in different parts of the world, it has taken different doctrinal forms and displayed contrasting ideological features. What is clear, nevertheless, is that fundamentalism arises in deeply troubled societies, particularly societies afflicted by an actual or perceived crisis of identity. Ruthven (2004) thus emphasized that fundamentalism is driven by a 'search for meaning' in a world of growing doubt and uncertainty. A variety of developments have helped to generate such doubt and uncertainty. Perhaps the most influential, if still deeply controversial, theory explaining the emergence of religious fundamentalism is Samuel Huntington's (1996) notion of a 'clash of civilizations'. This thesis links the emergence of 'civilizational' conflict to changes in world order, particularly the end of the ideological battle between capitalism and communism. As ideological allegiances fade and economic identities become less distinct, people seek meaning in their distinctive culture and the larger civilization within which it is embedded. The most controversial aspect of Huntington's thesis is the idea that a world of growing cultural difference will be characterized by antagonism and conflict, civilizational differences being irreconcilable. Nevertheless, supporters of the thesis have argued that the advent of global terrorism is best explained in civilizational terms; in particular, as a manifestation of the conflict between Islam and the West. However, others have suggested that such developments are not so much evidence of a clash between rival civilizations as evidence of conflict between rival fundamentalist trends within each civilization. The so-called 'war on terror' has, for instance, been interpreted as a 'clash of fundamentalisms' (Ali, 2003).

Amongst the other factors that have contributed to such crises, three are particularly relevant to religious fundamentalism: secularization, postcolonialism and globalization. Secularization has contributed to a decline of traditional religion and a weakening of what is seen as the 'moral fabric' of society. In that sense, fundamentalism represents a moral protest against decadence and hypocrisy; it aims to restore 'rightful' order and re-establish the link between the human world and the divine. Such moral conservatism has been very evident in the new Christian right in the USA, and has been an important component of Islamic fundamentalism in countries such as Iran, Egypt, Turkey, Pakistan and Afghanistan. The impact of postcolonialism helps to explain why, although fundamentalism can be found across the globe, its most potent and influential manifestations have been found in the developing world. Postcolonial societies have grappled with a series of acute problems. For instance, colonial rule invariably devalued and often suppressed indigenous cultures, meaning that postcolonial societies inherited a weakened sense of identity, compounded by a debilitating attachment to western values and institutions, particularly among elite groups. Political independence also failed to bring about social emancipation; rather, traditional imperialism was replaced by neocolonialism, ensuring continuing global inequality and a subordination to western powers and interests. In such circumstances, religious fundamentalism has been attractive both because it offers the prospect of a non-western, and often specifically anti-western, political identity, and because, particularly since the decline of revolutionary socialism in the 1970s, it articulates the aspirations of the urban poor and the lower middle classes.

Finally, fundamentalism has drawn strength from the advance of globalization. Globalization has undermined the capacity of 'civic' nationalism to establish secure and stable political identities. Religion has therefore tended to replace the nation as the principal source of collective identity, meaning that fundamentalism has emerged as a sub-variety of ethnic nationalism. This has been particularly significant in parts of the world where national identity has been challenged or threatened. Fundamentalism as ethnic mobilization can, for instance, be seen in the militant Buddhism of the Sinhalese in Sri Lanka, in the Jewish settler movement in Israel, in Hindu and Sikh extremism in India, and in the resistance of Ulster Protestants to a united Ireland.

Core themes – back to basics

Religious fundamentalism is an untypical political ideology. Not only does it draw inspiration from sacred, spiritual or 'other-worldly' matters, but it also cuts across a variety of, or perhaps all, religions, regardless of their doctrinal and structural differences. To study religious fundamentalism as a single, coherent entity is to treat as secondary the substantial differences that divide the religions of the world – whether they believe in a single god, many small gods or no god at all; whether they have a holy book, a variety of scriptures or place faith in an oral tradition; how they view morality and social conduct, and so forth. Moreover, while some fundamentalisms have been associated with violence and anti-constitutional political action, others have supported law-abiding and peaceful behaviour.

Such differences draw attention to the fact that religious fundamentalism is essentially a *style* of political thought rather than a substantive collection of political ideas and values. To the extent that religious fundamentalism's central or core themes can be identified, they follow from its tendency to recognize certain principles as essential or unchallengeable 'truths', regardless of their content. This, in turn, implies that religion has a profoundly '*this*-worldly' orientation; indeed that it is the very stuff of politics itself. As a programme for the comprehensive restructuring of society on religious lines and according to religious principles, fundamentalism deserves to be classified as an ideology in its own right. Nevertheless, it is difficult to deny that in certain cases fundamentalism constitutes a form of religious nationalism. However, at least in its more radical forms, religious fundamentalism goes well beyond the reassertion of national or ethnic distinctiveness, and in the case of Islam in particular it has a marked transnational dimension. The characteristic themes of religious fundamentalism are the following:

- religion and politics
- the fundamentalist impulse
- anti-modernism
- militancy.

Religion and politics

The core theme of fundamentalism is a rejection of the distinction between religion and politics. In effect, in Khomeini's words, 'Politics is religion.' Religion may be the basis of politics, but what is religion? In its most general sense a religion is an organized community of people bound together by a shared body of beliefs concerning some kind of transcendent reality, usually expressed in a set of approved activities and practices. What 'transcendent' means here is difficult to define, for it may refer to anything from a supreme being, a creator God, to the experience of personal liberation, as in the Buddhist concept of nirvana, the 'extinction' of the personal self.

The impact of religion on political life has progressively been restricted by the spread of liberal culture and ideas, a process that has been particularly prominent in the industrialized **West**. Nevertheless, liberal **secularism** is by no means an anti-religious tendency. Rather, it is concerned to establish a 'proper' sphere and role for religion. A key feature of liberal culture is the so-called public/private divide. This establishes a strict separation between a public sphere of life regulated by collective rules and subject to political authority, and a private sphere in which people are free to do as they like. The great virtue of this distinction, from a liberal perspective, is that it guarantees individual liberty by constraining government's ability to interfere in personal or private affairs. However, it also has important implications for religion, which is fenced into a private arena, leaving public life to be organized on a strictly secular basis. In bringing about the 'privatization of religion', secularism has extended the public/private divide into a distinction between politics and religion. The clearest manifestation of this is the separation of church and state, which is constitutionally enshrined in the USA and elsewhere, and is widely accepted amongst liberal democracies.

West, the: The parts of the world that are distinguished culturally by common Greco-Roman and Christian roots, socially by the dominance of industrial capitalism, and politically by the prevalence of liberal democracy.

Secularism: A belief that religion should not intrude into secular (worldly) affairs, usually reflected in the desire to separate church from state.

Much of the spirit of religious fundamentalism is captured in its rejection of the public/private divide. On one level, fundamentalism is a manifestation of the politics of identity. The expansion of a public realm organized on a secular and rationalistic basis has gradually weakened traditional social norms, textures and values and has left many bereft of identity, or, as Eric Hobsbawm (1994) put it, 'orphans' in the modern world. The intensity and zeal that typically characterizes fundamentalism establishes religion as the primary collective identity, giving its members and supporters a rootedness and sense of belonging that they would otherwise lack. More significantly,

PERSPECTIVES

RELIGION

LIBERALS see religion as a distinct 'private' matter linked to individual choice and personal development. Religious freedom is thus essential to civil liberty and can only be guaranteed by a strict division between religion and politics, and between church and state.

CONSERVATIVES regard religion as a valuable (perhaps essential) source of stability and social cohesion. As it provides society with a set of shared values and the bedrock of a common culture, overlaps between religion and politics, and church and state, are inevitable and desirable.

SOCIALISTS have usually portrayed religion in negative terms, as at best a diversion from the political struggle and at worst a form of ruling-class ideology (leading in some cases to the adoption of state atheism). In emphasizing love and compassion, religion may nevertheless provide socialism with an ethical basis.

ANARCHISTS generally regard religion as an institutionalized source of oppression. Church and state are invariably linked, with religion preaching obedience and submission to earthly rulers while also prescribing a set of authoritative values that rob the individual of moral autonomy.

FASCISTS have sometimes rejected religion on the grounds that it serves as a rival source of allegiance or belief, and that it preaches 'decadent' values such as compassion and human sympathy. Fascism nevertheless seeks to function as a 'political religion', embracing its terminology and internal structure – devotion, sacrifice, spirit, redemption and so on.

RELIGIOUS FUNDAMENTALISTS view religion as a body of 'essen-tial' and unchallengeable principles, which dictate not only personal conduct but also the organization of social, economic and political life. Religion cannot and should not be confined to the 'private' sphere, but finds its highest and proper expression in the politics of popular mobilization and social regeneration.

it is precisely religious fundamentalism's refusal to accept that religion is merely a private or personal matter that establishes its ideological creden-tials. To treat religion only as a personal or spiritual matter is to invite evil and corruption to stalk the public domain, hence the spread of permissive-ness, materialism, corruption, greed, crime and immorality. The fundamen-talist solution is simple: the world must be made anew, existing structures must be replaced with a comprehensive system founded on religious princi-ples and embracing law, politics, society, culture and the economy.

However, the perceived corruption of the secular public realm may give rise to one of two responses. The first, sometimes called 'passive' fundamentalism, takes the route of withdrawal and attempts to construct communities of believers untainted by the larger society. Groups such as the Amish in the USA and the Haredim, the ultra-orthodox Jews of Israel, undoubtedly believe that religion dictates social, economic and political principles, but they are generally more concerned with their own observation of these principles than with the comprehensive regeneration of society. The second response is 'active' fundamentalism, which takes the route of opposition and combat, and which alone should be considered an ideology, on the grounds that only it adopts an overtly political stance. However, the notion of politics that it adopts is a distinctly conventional one. In marked contrast to feminists, who have also challenged the public/private divide, religious fundamentalists view politics in terms of government policy and state action. Far from regarding politics as inherently corrupt, they usually look to seize, or at least exert influence over, the modern state, seeing it as an instrument of moral regeneration. Critics of fundamentalism nevertheless argue that it is precisely this determination to remove the distinction between religion and politics that invests in fundamentalism a tendency towards **totalitarianism**. A state founded on religious principles is, almost by definition, unencumbered by constraints that arise out of the public/private divide. However, the degree to which particular fundamentalisms have succumbed to this totalitarian impulse varies greatly.

Totalitarianism: An all-encompassing process of political rule in which the state penetrates and controls all social institutions, thus abolishing civil society and 'private' life (see p. 217).

The fundamentalist impulse

In its broadest sense, fundamentalism refers to a commitment to ideas and values that are seen as 'basic' or 'foundational'. Since fundamental beliefs are regarded as the core of a theoretical system, as opposed to peripheral and more transitory beliefs, they usually have an enduring and unchanging character, and are linked to the system's original or 'classical' form. Fundamentalism can therefore be seen as the opposite of **relativism**. By this standard, certain political ideologies, notably fascism and communism, can be placed nearer the fundamentalist end of the fundamentalism–relativism spectrum, while liberalism in particular, disposed as it is towards scepticism by its commitment to reason and toleration, can be placed near the relativist end. All ideologies, however, contain elements of fundamentalism. In the sense that

Relativism: A belief that moral or factual statements can only be judged in relation to their contexts, because there are no objective or 'absolute' standards.

FUNDAMENTALISM

Fundamentalism is a style of thought in which certain principles are recognized as essential 'truths' that have unchallengeable and overriding authority, regardless of their content. Substantive fundamentalisms there-fore have little or nothing in common, except that their supporters tend to evince an earnestness or fervour born out of doctrinal certainty. Although it is usually associated with religion and the literal truth of sacred texts, fundamentalism can also be found in political creeds. Even liberal scepticism can be said to incorporate the fundamental belief that all theories should be doubted (apart from its own). Although the term is often used pejoratively to imply inflexibility, dogmatism and authoritarianism, fundamentalism may also give expression to selflessness and a devotion to principle.

fundamentalism implies keeping faith with original or 'classical' ideas, it is also possible to classify some traditions within an ideology as fundamental-ist and others as not. In this respect, fundamentalism is the opposite of revi-sionism. Classical Marxism, which aimed to abolish and replace capitalism, has thus been seen as a form of fundamentalist socialism, while social democracy is portrayed as revisionist socialism by virtue of having modified its opposition to private property, the market, material incentives and so on.

In the case of religious fundamentalism, the 'fundamentals' have usually, but not always, been derived from the content of sacred texts, supported by the assertion of their literal truth. Indeed, scriptural literalism was a central feature of American Protestant fundamentalism, which, for example, has continued to preach creationism or 'creation science', the belief that humankind was created by God, as described in the Book of Genesis, and the outright rejection of the Darwinian theory of evolution. Such tendencies can be found in all three 'religions of the book' – Christianity, Islam and Judaism – each of which possesses sacred texts that have been claimed to express the revealed word of God. Nevertheless, though often related, religious funda-mentalism should not be equated with scriptural literalism. In the first place, all sacred texts contain a complex and diverse range of ideas, doctrines and principles. To treat a sacred text as a political ideology, as a moral and polit-ical programme for the regeneration of society and the mobilization of the masses, it is necessary to extract out its 'fundamentals'. These are a set of simple and clean principles that provide an exact and unambiguous definition of religious identity. In John Garvey's (1993) words, fundamentalism consti-tutes 'a kind of stripped-down religion that travels light and fast'.

Second, in contrast with the ultra-orthodox, whose principal goal is to 'live by the book', fundamentalists have supported an 'activist' reading of texts that enables them to reduce the complexity and profundity of scripture to a theo-political project. In Islam, this is described as 'dynamic interpretation'. Selectivity and interpretation, however, create the problem of how one version of a scripture or doctrine can be upheld over other versions. Fundamentalists have usually resolved this problem by reflecting on *who* is doing the interpreting. In this respect, clerical position and religious office may be of secondary importance; more significantly, the 'true' interpreter must be a person (invariably male) of deep faith and moral purity, as well as an activist whose spiritual insight has been deepened through the experience of struggle. This is why religious fundamentalism is invariably associated with charismatic leadership, which gives it, critics argue, an implicitly authoritarian character.

The great strength of fundamentalism, as demonstrated by the proliferation of fundamentalist movements since the late twentieth century, is its capacity to generate political activism and mobilize the faithful. Fundamentalism thus operates on both psychological and social levels. Psychologically, its appeal is based on its capacity to offer certainty in an uncertain world. Being religious, it addresses some of the deepest and most perplexing problems confronting humankind; being fundamentalist, it provides solutions that are straightforward, practical and above all absolute. Socially, while its appeal has extended to the educated and professional classes, religious fundamentalism has been particularly successful in addressing the aspirations of the economically and politically marginalized. Together with offering a secure identity and the prospect of social order, in the developing world in particular, it has displaced socialism as the creed of political renewal and social justice. However, amongst the limitations of fundamentalism is the fact that its simplicity and stripped-down character prevent it from dealing with complex problems or developing comprehensive solutions.

Anti-modernism

The most prominent feature of religious fundamentalism is that it dramatically turns its back on the modern world. Modernization appears to be equated with decline and decay, typified by the spread of godless secularism, and regeneration can only be brought about by returning to the spirit and traditions of some long-past 'golden age'. Unfortunately, however, this image is simplistic, and in certain respects misleading. Religious fundamentalism is selectively traditional but also selectively modern; a mixture of resentment and envy characterizes its relationship to modernity. One face of fundamentalism is undoubtedly its strident anti-modernism. Its traditionalism is evident in what amounts to a form of moral conservatism. Western societies, having succumbed to the cult of the individual and a passion for personal gratification, are seen as amoral at best and thoroughly degenerate at worst. Permissiveness, adultery, prostitution, homosexuality and pornography are only some of the symptoms of this moral pollution. Nothing less than a moral gulf divides liberal individualism from religious fundamentalism: the former encourages people to make their own moral choices while the latter demands that they conform to a prescribed and divinely ordained moral system. Islamic fundamentalists therefore call for the reintroduction of ancient *shari'a* law and Christian fundamentalists attempt to combat the spread of permissiveness and materialism by a return to 'family' or 'religious' values.

Fundamentalism should not be mistaken for conservatism or traditionalism, however. Despite overlaps between conservatism and fundamentalism and the ease with which they have sometimes constructed alliances, notably in the USA through organizations such as Moral Majority and within the Republican Party, the two differ in terms of both temper and aspirations. Conservatism is modest and cautious, where fundamentalism is strident and passionate; conservatism is disposed to protect elites and defend hierarchy, while fundamentalism embodies populist and egalitarian inclinations; conservatism favours continuity and tradition, while fundamentalism is radical and may be revolutionary. Fundamentalism has little in common with traditionalism, in that it favours 'novel' interpretations of religious teachings and calls for comprehensive social regeneration. There is a closer affinity between fundamentalism and the reactionary radicalism of the new right. Nevertheless, fundamentalism is more clearly reactive than reactionary: behind the rhetoric of moral traditionalism, it is perhaps orientated more towards a purified future than towards an idealized past. The tendency within fundamentalism towards populism, charismatic leadership and psycho-social regeneration has also led some to suggest parallels with fascism. However, this risks ignoring the degree to which fundamentalism is animated by genuinely religious passions.

The clearest evidence that fundamentalists are not just dyed-in-the-wool reactionaries is found in their enthusiasm for particular aspects of modernity. For instance, fundamentalists across the globe have shrewdly exploited the advantages of modern techniques of mass communication, not least in the case of the 'televangelists' of the USA. This contrasts markedly with the revivalist and ultra-orthodox movements that have turned their backs on the 'unredeemed' world. Nevertheless, the fundamentalist accom-

POPULISM

Populism (from the Latin *populus*, meaning 'the people') has been used to describe both distinctive political movements and a particular tradition of political thought. Movements or parties described as populist have been characterized by their claim to support the common people in the face of 'corrupt' economic or political elites. As a political tradition, populism reflects the belief that the instincts and wishes of the people provide the principal legitimate guide to political action. Populist politicians therefore make a direct appeal to the people and claim to give expression to their deepest hopes and fears, all intermediary institutions being distrusted. Although populism may be linked to any cause or ideology, it is often seen as implicitly authoritarian, 'populist' democracy being the enemy of 'pluralist' democracy.

modation with modernity is not merely a cynical or tactical exercise. The willingness to use the internet and other new media, the machinery of the modern state and even accept nuclear weapons suggests sympathy for the spirit of modernity, respect for 'this-worldly' rationalism rather than a descent into 'other-worldly' mysticism. Early interest in Iran, for instance, in the idea of 'Islamic science' quickly gave way to an acceptance of conventional, and therefore western, science. Similarly, the search for 'Islamic economics' soon developed into the application of market principles derived from economic liberalism. Finally, it is significant that fundamentalists advance an essentially modernist view of religion, relying more heavily on 'dynamic' interpretation than on faith in inherited structures and traditions. As Parekh (1994) put it, fundamentalism 'reconstitutes religion within the limits of modernity, even as it copes with modernity within the limits of religion'.

Militancy

While religious fundamentalists have embraced a conventional, state-centred view of politics, they have pursued a highly distinctive style of political activity: one that is vigorous, militant and sometimes violent. Fundamentalists are usually happy to see themselves as militants, in the sense that **militancy** implies passionate and robust commitment. Where does this militancy come from, and what are its implications? Fundamentalist militancy derives from a variety of

Militancy: Heightened or extreme commitment; a level of zeal and passion typically associated with struggle or war.

sources. In the first place, there is a tendency for conflicts involving religion to be intense because religion deals with core values and beliefs. Those who act in the name of religion are often inspired by what they believe to be a divinely ordained purpose, which clearly takes precedence over all other considerations. This perhaps helps to explain why religious wars have been so common throughout history.

A second factor is that fundamentalism in particular is a form of politics of identity: it serves to define who a people are and gives them a collective identity. All forms of politics of identity, whether based on social, national, ethnic or religious distinctiveness, tend to be based on divisions between 'them' and 'us', between an 'out-group' and an 'in-group'. Certainly, religious fundamentalism has been associated with the existence of a hostile and threatening 'other', which serves both to create a heightened sense of collective identity and to strengthen its oppositional and combative character. This demonized 'other' may take various guises, from secularism and permissiveness to rival religions, westernization, the USA, Marxism and imperialism. A third and related factor is that fundamentalists generally possess a Manichaean world view, one that emphasizes conflict between light and darkness, or good and evil. If 'we' are a chosen people acting according to the will of God, 'they' are not merely people with whom we disagree, but a body actively subverting God's purpose on Earth, representing nothing less than the 'forces of darkness'. Political conflict, for fundamentalists, is therefore a battle or war, and ultimately either the believers or the infidels must prevail.

One of the consequences of this militancy is a willingness to engage in extra-legal, anti-constitutional political action. Nonetheless, although God's law outranks human law, fundamentalists do not necessarily disregard the latter, as the new Christian right's firm support for law and order demonstrates. The most controversial issue, however, is the fundamentalist use of violence. While the popular image of fundamentalists as suicide bombers and terrorists is unbalanced and misleading, as it ignores the fact that fundamentalist protest is overwhelmingly peaceful and usually legal, it is impossible to deny a link with terrorism and violence. The most dramatic examples of this were the devastating al-Qaeda terrorist attacks on the World Trade Centre and the Pentagon on September 11, 2001, which resulted in the deaths of some 3,000 people. Other examples include the assassinations of the Egyptian president, Anwar Sadat, by Islamic fundamentalists in 1981, Indian prime minister, Indira Gandhi, by militant Sikhs in 1984, and Israeli prime minister, Yitzak Rabin, by a Jewish fanatic in 1995; and campaigns of terror carried out by Islamist groups such as Hezbollah (Party of Allah) and Hamas. Anti-abortion extremists in the USA have also resorted to bombings and murder.

TERRORISM

Terrorism, in its broadest sense, refers to the use of terror for furthering political ends; it seeks to create a climate of fear and apprehension. The term, nevertheless, is highly controversial. First, the distinction between terrorism and other forms of violence or warfare is blurred by the fact that the latter may also aim to strike fear into the wider population. Second, as the term is highly pejorative, it tends to be used selectively and often subjectively (one person's 'terrorist' is another person's 'freedom fighter'). Third, although terrorism is usually conceived of as an anti-government activity, governments can also use terror against their own or other populations, as in the case of 'state terrorism'.

Millenarianism: A belief in a thousand-year period of divine rule; political millenarianism offers the prospect of a sudden and complete emancipation from misery and oppression

Apocalypticism: A belief in the imminent end of the world (as we know it), often associated with the return of a supreme or god-like figure, denoting final salvation and purification.

The most common fundamentalist justification for such acts is that, as they are intended to eradicate evil, they fulfil the will of God. Islamic suicide bombers, for example, believe that in sacrificing their lives in the cause of Allah they will immediately be dispatched to heaven. The incidence of violence amongst fundamentalist groups is almost certainly increased by a link between fundamentalist belief and **millenarianism**. Other ideologies that have endorsed violence and the use of terror, such as fascism and sometimes anarchism, have been viewed as forms of political millenarianism. However, religion adds an extra dimension to this, in that it creates the heightened expectations and revolutionary fervour of **apocalypticism**.

The family of fundamentalisms

As Marty (1988) pointed out, the various fundamentalisms can be seen to constitute a hypothetical 'family'. Nevertheless, its family members differ from one another in at least three crucial ways. First, they derive from very different religions. Although all religions have spawned fundamentalist or fundamentalist-type movements, certain religions may be more prone than others to fundamentalist developments, or place fewer obstacles in the way of emerging fundamentalism. In this respect, Islam and Protestant Christianity have been seen as most likely to throw up fundamentalist movements, as both are based on a single sacred text and hold that believers have direct access to spiritual wisdom, rather than this being concentrated in the hands of accredited representatives (Parekh, 1994). Second, fundamentalisms emerge in very different societies. The impact and nature of fundamentalist movements is thus conditioned by the social, economic and political structures of the society in which they arise. Third, fundamentalisms differ according to the political causes they are associated with. These broadly fall into three categories. Religious fundamentalism can be used as a means of achieving comprehensive political renewal, which is particularly attractive to marginalized or oppressed peoples; as a way of shoring up an unpopular leader or government by creating a unified political culture; or as a means of strengthening a threatened national or ethnic identity. The main forms of fundamentalism are the following:

- Islamic fundamentalism
- Christian fundamentalism
- other fundamentalisms.

Islamic fundamentalism

Islam is the world's second largest religion and its fastest growing. There are approximately 1.3 billion Muslims in the world today, spread over more than seventy countries. The strength of Islam is concentrated geographically in Asia and Africa; it is estimated, for example, that over half the population of Africa will soon be Muslim. However, it has also spread into Europe and elsewhere. Islam is certainly not, and never has been, just a 'religion'. Rather, it is a complete way of life, with instructions on moral, political and economic behaviour for individuals and nations alike. The 'way of Islam' is based on the teachings of the Prophet Muhammad (*ca.* AD 570–632), as revealed in the Koran, which is regarded by all Muslims as the revealed word of Allah, and the Sunna, or 'beaten path', the traditional customs observed by devout Muslims and said to be based on the Prophet's own life. There are two principal sects within Islam, which developed within fifty years of Muhammad's death in AD 632. The Sunni sect represents the majority of Muslims, while the Shia or Shi'ite sect (sometimes called Shi'ism) contains just over one tenth of Muslims, concentrated in Iran and Iraq.

Fundamentalism in Islam does not mean a belief in the literal truth of the Koran, for this is accepted by all Muslims, and in that sense all Muslims are fundamentalists. Instead, it means an intense and militant faith in Islamic beliefs as the overriding principles of social life and politics, as well as of personal morality. Islamic fundamentalists wish to establish the primacy of religion over politics. In practice, this means the founding of an 'Islamic state', a **theocracy** ruled by spiritual rather than temporal authority, and applying the *shari'a*, divine Islamic law, based on principles expressed in the Koran. The *shari'a* lays down a code for legal and righteous behaviour, including a system of punishment for most crimes as well as rules of personal conduct for both men and women.

Theocracy: Literally, rule by God; the principle that religious authority should prevail over political authority, usually through the domination of church over state.

Although the revival of Islamic fundamentalism can be traced back to the 1920s, and particularly the founding of the Muslim Brotherhood in Egypt in 1928, its most significant development came in 1979 with the popular revolution that brought Ayatollah Khomeini to power and led to Iran declaring itself an 'Islamic Republic'. Since then, Islamists have seized power, usually temporarily, in states such as Sudan, Pakistan, Afghanistan and Somalia. A range of new '*jihadi*' groups have also emerged since the 1990s – the most important of which has been al-Qaeda, led by Osama bin Laden – which have given expression to a particularly militant form of fundamentalism. For these groups, commitment to Islam takes the form of a *jihad* carried out in particular against the USA and Israel (the 'Jewish–Christian crusaders') and for the removal of western influence from the Arab world in general and from Saudi Arabia in particular. However, different explanations have been advanced for the strengthening of Islamic fundamentalism in the modern world. Three broad interpretations can be identified.

Jihad: (*Arabic*) An Islamic term literally meaning 'struggle'; includes the struggle against one's own soul (greater *jihad*) and external, physical effort or even 'holy war' (lesser *jihad*).

First, in line with the 'clash of civilizations' thesis, the source of this militancy has been seen to lie within Islam itself. Such a view implies that there is a basic incompatibility between Islamic values and those of the liberal-democratic West. From this perspective, Islam is inherently totalitarian, in that the goal of constructing an Islamic state based on *shari'a* law is starkly anti-pluralist and irreconcilable with the notion of a public/private divide. In other words, what US neocon theorists have called 'Islamo-fascism' is not a perversion of Islam, but a realization of certain of its core beliefs. However, such a view of Islam seriously misrepresents Islam's central tenets. According to the Prophet Muhammad, for instance, the 'greater *jihad*' is not a political struggle against the infidel, but an inner struggle: the struggle to become a better person through moral and spiritual discipline.

Moreover, such thinking ignores the extent to which Islam has not only drawn on western ideas, including the philosophy of Aristotle, but has also had a significant impact on western, and particularly European, art and culture.

Second, resurgent Islamic fundamentalism has been portrayed as a specific response to a particular historical circumstance. Bernard Lewis (2004), for example, argued that the Muslim world is in crisis largely because of the decline and stagnation of the Middle East and the sense of humiliation that has therefore gripped the Islamic, and more specifically Arab, worlds. This decline stems from the collapse of the once-powerful Ottoman empire and its carve-up by the UK and France after the First World War, as well as the sense of humiliation and powerlessness by the establishment of the state of Israel in 1948, together with the displacement of thousands of Palestinians, and the defeat of Arab forces in a series of wars against Israel in 1948, 1956, 1967 and 1973. Furthermore, the end of colonialism in the post-1945 period brought little benefit to the Arab world, both because Middle Eastern regimes tended to be inefficient and corrupt and because formal colonialism was succeeded by neocolonialism, particularly as US influence in the region expanded. The final historical factor that explains the rise of Islamic fundamentalism is the failure of two western ideas: socialism and secular Arab nationalism. During the 1950s and 1960s, fundamentalism remained on the fringe of Arab politics while Arab leaders looked either to the West, or, after the rise of Gamal Nasser in Egypt, supported some form of Arab socialism. However, the failure of Arab socialism in Egypt and elsewhere to create prosperous and just societies meant that, from the 1970s onwards, fundamentalist ideas and creeds have attracted growing support from amongst the young and the politically committed.

Third, Islamic fundamentalism has been interpreted as a manifestation of a much broader and, arguably, deeper ideological tendency: anti-western-ism. Paul Berman (2003), for example, placed militant Islamism within the context of the totalitarian movements that emerged from the apparent failure of liberal society in the aftermath of the First World War. The significance of the First World War was that it exploded the optimistic belief in progress and the advance of reason, fuelling support for darker anti-liberal movements. In this light, political Islam shares much in common with fascism and communism, in that each of them promises to rid society of corruption and immorality and to make society anew as a 'single blocklike structure, solid and eternal'. Buruma and Margalit (2004) placed Islamic fundamentalism within a larger context of 'occidentalism', a rejection of the cultural and political inheritance of the West, particularly as shaped by the Reformation and the Enlightenment. From this perspective, western society is characterized by individualism, secularism and relativism; it is a mechanical civilization organized around greed and materialism. Occidentalism, or anti-westernism, in contrast, offers the prospect of organic unity, moral certainty and politico-spiritual renewal. Such ideas were first developed in the writings of counter-Enlightenment thinkers in Germany in the early nineteenth century, and they helped to fuel European fascism and Japanese imperialism in the inter-war period. However, in the modern world they are most clearly articulated through the ideas of political Islam.

Varieties of Islamism

However, **Islamism** does not have a single doctrinal or political character. In particular, different forms of Islamic fundamentalism have developed out of

Islamism: The belief that political structures and social conduct should come into line with the religious principles and ideals set out within Islam.

Wahhabism, Shia Islam and moderate or 'liberal' Islam. Wahhabism (or, as some of its supporters prefer, Salafism) is the official version of Islam in Saudi Arabia, the world's first fundamentalist Islamic state. Its origins date back to the eighteenth century and an alliance between supporters of a particularly strict and austere form of Islam and early figures in the Saudi dynasty. Wahhabis seek to restore Islam by purging it of heresies and modern innovations; amongst other things, they ban pictures, photographs, musical instruments, singing, videos and television, and celebrations of Muhammad's birthday. The authority of Wahhabism in the Islamic world expanded as a result of the capture of Mecca and Medina, the chief Muslim holy cities, which fell under Saudi control in 1924, and from the discovery of oil in Arabia in 1958.

Wahhabi ideas and beliefs had a particular impact on the Muslim Brotherhood, which, until the emergence of modern '*jihadi*' groups, was the most important fundamentalist organization within the Islamic world. Founded by Hassan al Banna (1906–49), the Brotherhood sought to revitalize what it believed to be a corrupted Islamic faith and to provide the faithful with a political voice, a party of Islam. The Brotherhood aimed to found an Islamic government that would provide an alternative to both capitalist and socialist forms of development. Such a government would transform the social system by applying Islamic principles to economic and political life as well as personal morality. The Brotherhood spread into Jordan, Sudan and Syria, where it set up branches containing mosques, schools, youth clubs and even business enterprises. It trained young people physically and militarily to prepare them for the coming *jihad*, crudely translated as 'holy war', through which they would achieve their objectives.

The most influential thinker to emerge out of the Muslim Brotherhood was Sayyid Qutb (1906–66), sometimes seen as the father of modern politi-

Ayatollah Ruhollah Khomeini
(1900–89)

KHOMEINI

Iranian cleric and political leader. The son and grandson of Shia clergy, Khomeini received a religious education and was one of the foremost scholars in the major theological centre in Qom until being expelled from Iran in 1964. His return from exile in 1979 sparked the popular revolution that overthrew the shahdom, leaving the Ayatollah (literally, 'gift of Allah') as the supreme leader of the world's first Islamic state until his death.

Although Khomeini raised the idea of Islamic government as early as the 1940s, his notion of institutionalized clerical rule, the basis of an 'Islamic republic', did not emerge until the late 1960s. Khomeini's world view was rooted in a clear division between the oppressed, understood largely as the poor and excluded of the Third World, and the oppressors, seen as the twin Satans: the USA and the Soviet Union, capitalism and communism. Islam thus became a theo-political project aimed at regenerating the Islamic world by ridding it of occupation and corruption from outside.

cal Islam. Qutb's radicalization occurred during a two-year study visit to the USA, which instilled in him a profound distaste for the materialism, immorality and sexual licentiousness he claimed to have encountered. As it developed, Qutb's world view, or Qutbism, as it is sometimes called, highlighted the barbarism and corruption that westernization had inflicted on the world, with a return to strict Islamic practice in all aspects of life offering the only possibility of salvation. However, whereas Osama bin Laden and al-Qaeda were later to use such thinking to justify attacks on the West itself, Qutb's primary targets were the westernized rulers of Egypt and other Muslim states. Nevertheless, Qutb's ideas were perhaps best exemplified by the Taliban regime in Afghanistan, which was established in 1997 but overthrown by US-orchestrated military action in 2001. The Taliban refused to compromise with any ideas, Islamic or otherwise, which departed from their world view. They attempted to root out all forms of 'non-Islamic' corruption and to enforce a harsh and repressive interpretation of *shari'a* law. Women were entirely excluded from education, the economy and from public life in general. Strict censorship was imposed and all forms of music were banned. Taliban rule was highly authoritarian, with political power being concentrated in the hands of a small group of senior Taliban clerics, under the supreme leadership of Mullah Omar.

Shia fundamentalism stems from the quite different temper and doctrinal character of the Shia sect as opposed to the Sunni sect. Sunnis have tended to see Islamic history as a gradual movement away from the ideal community, which existed during the life of Muhammad and his four immediate successors. Shias, though, believe that divine guidance is about to re-emerge into the world with the return of the 'hidden imam', or the arrival of the mahdi, a leader directly guided by God. Shia see history moving towards the goal of an ideal community, not away from it. Such ideas of revival or imminent salvation have given the Shias sect a messianic and emotional quality that is not enjoyed by the traditionally more sober Sunnis. The religious temper of the Shia sect is also different from that of the Sunnis. Shias believe that it is possible for an individual to remove the stains of sin through the experience of suffering and by leading a devout and simple life. The prospect of spiritual salvation has given the Shia sect its characteristic intensity and emotional strength. When such religious zeal has been harnessed to a political goal it has generated fierce commitment and devotion.

The Shia sect has traditionally been more political than the Sunni sect. It has proved especially attractive to the poor and the downtrodden, for whom the re-emergence of divine wisdom into the world has represented the purification of society, the overthrow of injustice and liberation from oppression. In 1979, following a growing wave of popular demonstrations that forced the Shah to flee the country and prepared the way for the return of Ayatollah Khomeini, Iran was declared an Islamic Republic. Power fell into the hands of the Islamic Revolutionary Council, comprising fifteen senior clerics, dominated by Khomeini himself. All legislation passed by the popularly elected Islamic Consultative Assembly has to be ratified by the Council for the Protection of the Constitution, on which sit six religious and six secular lawyers, to ensure that it conforms to Islamic principles. Iran exhibited a fierce religious consciousness, reflected in popular antipathy to the 'Great Satan' (the USA), and the application of strict Islamic principles to social and political life. For example, the wearing of a headscarf and chador, loose-fitting clothes, became obligatory for all women in Iran, Muslims and non-Muslims alike. Restrictions on polygamy were removed, contraception was banned, adultery punished by public flogging or execution, and the death penalty was introduced for homosexuality. Both Iranian politics and society were thoroughly 'Islamized' and Friday prayers in Tehran became an expression of official government policy and a focal point of political life. The religious nationalism generated by the Islamic Revolution reached new heights during the Iran–Iraq war between 1980 and 1988.

However, Iran is a highly complex society, in which radical and reformist and traditionalist and modernizing tendencies are often closely linked. For

example, the end of the Iran–Iraq war and the death of Ayatollah Khomeini
in 1989 appeared to pave the way for more moderate forces to surface within
Iran. This was reflected in the emergence of Hashemi Rafsanjani, speaker of
the Iranian parliament (the Islamic Consultative Assembly), and his election
as president in 1989 marked a more pragmatic and less ideological turn in
Iranian politics. Nevertheless, the election of Mahmoud Ahmadinejad as
president in 2005 signalled a return to conservative politics and the emergence of a form of explicit Khomeinism.

Finally, it would be a mistake to conclude that all forms of Islamism are
militant and revolutionary. By comparison with Christianity, Islam has
generally been tolerant of other religions and rival belief systems, a fact that
may provide the basis for reconciliation between Islamism and political
pluralism. This can most clearly be seen in relation to political developments
in Turkey. The Turkish state, as established in 1923 by Mustafa Kemal
Ataturk, was founded on strict secularism and embraced a determinedly
western model of political and social development. However, political Islam
attracted growing support during the 1990s, particularly in the form of the
Welfare Party and its successor, Virtue, which became the largest party in the
Turkish parliament in 1997. However, military intervention prevented an
Islamacist government from being formed, and the Welfare Party was
disbanded. Its more moderate successor, the Justice and Development Party
(AK), nevertheless won power in 2003, advancing a constitutional form of
Islamism. AK has attempted to balance a moderate conservative politics
based on Islamic values with an acceptance of Turkey's secular democratic
framework. Rather than choosing between East and West, it has tried to
establish a Turkish identity that is confident in being part of both. A key
aspect of this compromise is continuing attempts by Turkey to gain membership of the European Union. What is unclear, however, is whether constitutional Islamism has long-term viability: does an acceptance of human rights
and liberal-democratic principles necessarily mean that politics must be
decoupled from religion?

Christian fundamentalism

With about two billion adherents, Christianity is the world's largest religion.
From its origins in Palestine, it was spread via the Roman Empire throughout Europe and was later exported to the Americas and elsewhere by
European settlers. Despite attempts to extend Christianity further by
conquest and missionary endeavour, by 1900 about 83 per cent of the
world's Christians still lived in the West. However, while during the twentieth century Christian belief declined in the West, especially in Europe,

vigorous growth occurred in the developing world, meaning that the majority of Christians now live in Africa, Asia and Latin America.

Although all Christians acknowledge the authority of the Bible, three main divisions have emerged: the Catholic, Orthodox and Protestant churches. Roman Catholicism is based on the temporal and spiritual leadership of the pope in Rome, seen as unchallengeable since the promulgation of the doctrine of papal infallibility in 1871. Eastern Orthodox Christianity emerged from the split with Rome in 1054 and developed into a number of autonomous churches, the Russian Orthodox Church and the Greek Orthodox Church being the most significant. Protestantism embraces a variety of movements that, during the Reformation of the sixteenth century, rejected Roman authority and established reformed national versions of Christianity. Although there are many doctrinal divisions amongst Protestants, Protestantism tends to be characterized by the belief that the Bible is the sole source of truth and by the idea that it is possible for people to have a direct, personal relationship with God.

Since the Reformation, the political significance of Christianity has declined markedly. The advance of liberal constitutionalism was in part reflected in the separation of church and state, and in the thoroughgoing secularization of political life. Christianity, at least in the developed West, adjusted to these circumstances by increasingly becoming a personal religion, geared more to the spiritual salvation of the individual than to the moral and political regeneration of society. This, in turn, helped to shape the character of Christian fundamentalism since the late twentieth century. Confronted by stable social, economic and political structures, rooted in secular values and goals, fundamentalists have been mainly content to work within a pluralist and constitutional framework. Rather than seeking to establish a theocracy, they have usually campaigned around single issues, or concentrated their attention on moral crusading.

One of the causes that Christian fundamentalism has helped to articulate is ethnic nationalism. This has been evident in Northern Ireland, where an upsurge in evangelical Protestantism has been one of the consequences of 'the troubles' since 1969. Largely expressed through Ian Paisley's breakaway Free Presbyterian Church and organized politically by the Democratic Unionist Party (DUP), Ulster fundamentalism equates the idea of a united Ireland with the victory of Catholicism and Rome. Although Paisley himself has never actively promoted violence, he has warned that, should reunification go ahead, it would lead to armed resistance by the Protestant community. By appealing to working-class Protestants as well as fundamentalists, Paisley and his supporters have succeeded in keeping 'the iron in the soul of Ulster unionism' and blocking political moves that might ultimately lead to the establishment of a united Ireland (Bruce, 1993). However, the theological basis of Paisleyite resistance draws heavily from the USA, the birthplace of evangelical Protestantism and home of the most influential Christian fundamentalist movement, the new Christian right.

The new Christian right

In terms of the number of church-going Christians, the USA is easily the most religious of western countries. About 60 million American citizens claim to have been 'born again', and half of these describe themselves as fundamentalists. This largely reflects the fact that, from its earliest days, America provided a refuge for religious sects and movements wishing to escape from persecution. During the nineteenth century, a fierce battle was fought within American Protestantism between modernists, who adopted a liberal view of the Bible, and conservatives (later 'fundamentalists') who took a literal view of it. Nevertheless, such religious passions and views were largely confined to the private world of the family and the home. Religious groups were rarely drawn into active politics, and when they were, they were rarely successful. The introduction of prohibition, 1920–33, was a notable exception to this. The new Christian right, which emerged in the late 1970s, was therefore a novel development, in that it sought to fuse religion and politics in attempting to 'turn America back to Christ'.

The 'new Christian right' is an umbrella term that describes a broad coalition of groups primarily concerned with moral and social issues and intent on maintaining or restoring what is seen as 'Christian culture'. Two main factors explain its emergence. The first is that in the post-1945 period the USA, as elsewhere, experienced a significant extension of the public sphere. For instance, in the early 1960s the Supreme Court ruled against the use of prayers in American schools (because it was contrary to the First Amendment, which guarantees religious freedom), and, particularly as part of Lyndon Johnson's 'Great Society' initiative, there was a proliferation of welfare, urban development and other programmes. The result of this was that many 'God-fearing' southern conservatives felt that their traditional values and way of life were being threatened, and that the Washington-based liberal establishment was to blame.

The second factor was the increasingly political prominence of groups representing blacks, women and homosexuals, whose advance threatened traditional social structures, particularly in rural and small-town America. As the new Christian right emerged in the 1970s to campaign for the restoration of 'traditional family values', its particular targets thus included 'affirmative action' (positive discrimination in favour of blacks), feminism and the gay rights movement. In the 1980s and 1990s, this politics of morality increasingly coalesced around the anti-abortion issue.

A variety of organizations emerged to articulate these concerns, often mobilized by noted televangelists. These included the Religious Round Table, Christian Voice, American Coalition for Traditional Values and the most influential of all, Moral Majority, formed by Jerry Falwell in 1980. Although Catholics were prominent in the anti-abortion movement, new Christian right groups drew particularly from the ranks of evangelical Protestants, who as 'Bible believers' subscribed to scriptural inerrancy, and often claimed to be 'born again' in the sense that they had undergone a personal experience of conversion to Christ. Divisions nevertheless exist amongst evangelicals; for instance, between those who style themselves as fundamentalists and tend to keep apart from non-believing society, and charismatics or evangelicals, who believe that the Holy Spirit can operate through individuals giving the the gifts of prophecy and healing. Since the 1980s, Moral Majority and other such groups have provided campaign finance and organized voter-registration drives with a view to targeting liberal or 'pro-choice' Democrats, and encouraging Republicans to embrace a new social and moral agenda based on opposition to abortion and calls for the restoration of prayers in US schools. Ronald Reagan's willingness to embrace this agenda in the 1980s meant that the new Christian right became an important component of a new Republican coalition that placed as much emphasis on moral issues as it did on traditional ones such as the economy and foreign policy.

Since the end of the Reagan era, the influence of the new Christian right has fluctuated significantly. Reagan's successor, George Bush Sr, was not 'one of them' (until 1980, for instance, he supported abortion) and also broke his campaign promise not to put up taxes. This prompted the Christian right to put up its own candidate for the presidency, leading to televangelist Pat Robertson's unsuccessful 1992 bid for the Republican nomination. In response to such setbacks, elements of the evangelical movement adopted more militant strategies. The extreme example of this was the emergence of the so-called militias, which claimed to be influenced by shady groups such as the Christian Patriots, and which have resorted to campaigns of terrorism, as exemplified by the Oklahoma bombing in 1995.

However, the Christian right received a major boost from the election of George W. Bush in 2000. Not only were a number of members of Bush's cabinet, including Bush himself and his vice-president, Dick Cheney, 'born again' Christians, but a leading evangelical, John Ashcroft, was appointed attorney general. Fundamentalist influence on the Bush administration has been clearest in relation to foreign policy, particularly in the aftermath of the September 11 terrorist attacks. This was evident in two key ways. First, it was reflected in greater emphasis being placed on humanitarianism and human-rights policies, especially an increase in foreign aid to Africa. Second, it deepened US support for Israel and affected how the Bush administration set out to fight the 'war on terror'. Evangelical Christians have sometimes interpreted the decline and poverty of the Arab world as evidence that God curses those who curse Israel (Mead, 2006). In this light, bolstering the position of Israel in the Middle East became a prime focus of US foreign policy.

Other fundamentalisms

Islam and Protestant Christianity have been distinguished by their capacity to throw up comprehensive programmes of political renewal, albeit with very different characters and ambitions. In most cases, however, other fundamentalist movements have been more narrowly concerned with helping to clarify or redefine national or ethnic identity. In this sense, many fundamentalisms can be seen as sub-varieties of ethnic nationalism. This has usually occurred as a reaction to a change in national identity, occasioned by the growth of rival ethnic or religious groups or actual or threatened territorial changes. The attraction of religion rather than the nation as the principal source of political identity is that it provides a supposedly primordial and seemingly unchangeable basis for the establishment of group membership, which is why it tends to be associated with the emergence of an enclave culture. The fundamentalism of Ulster Protestants – whose religion gives their national identity, their 'Britishness', an ethnic substance – is very different from the fundamentalism of US evangelicals, which has little bearing on their ethnicity. Hindu, Sikh, Jewish and Buddhist fundamentalism also resemble forms of ethnic mobilization.

Hinduism, the principal religion of India, appears on the surface to be relatively inhospitable to fundamentalism. It is the clearest example of an ethnic religion where emphasis is placed on custom and social practice rather than formal texts or doctrines. Nevertheless, a fundamentalist movement emerged out of the struggle for Indian independence, achieved in 1947, although this was modest by comparison with the support for the secular Congress Party. However, it has flourished in India since the decline of Congress and the collapse of the Nehru–Gandhi dynasty in the mid-1980s. Its key goal is to challenge the multicultural, multi-ethnic mosaic of India by making Hinduism the basis of national identity. This is not expressed in demands for the expulsion of 'foreign' religions and culture so much as in a call for the 'Hinduization' of Muslim, Sikh, Jain and other communities. The Bharatiya Janata Party (BJP) has been the largest party in the Indian parliament since 1996, articulating, as it does, the newly prosperous middle class's ambivalence towards modernity and, particularly, its concerns about a weakening of national identity. The more radical World Hindu Council preaches

'India for the Hindus', while its parent body, the RSS, aims to create a 'Greater India', stretching from Burma to Iraq, and to establish India's geo-political dominance across central Asia. The most dramatic demonstration of Hindu militancy came in 1992 with the destruction of the ancient Babri Masjid (mosque) in Ayodhya, believed to have been built on the birthplace of the god Rama. This has led to on-going communal violence between Hindus and Muslims in the state of Gujarat.

Sikh fundamentalism is different, in that it is associated with the struggle to found an independent nation-state, not with the remaking of a national identity within an existing one. As such, it overlaps with the concerns of liberal nationalism, and is distinguished from the latter only by its vision of the nation as an essentially religious entity. Sikh nationalists thus look to establish 'Khalistan', located in present-day Punjab, with Sikhism as the state religion and its government obliged to ensure its unhindered flourishing. Just as Hindu nationalism has a markedly anti-Islamic character, Sikh nationalism is in part defined by its antipathy towards Hinduism. This was evident in the seizing of the Golden Temple in Amritsar in 1982 by the Damdami Taksal, under its militant leader, Jarail Singh Bhindranwale, and in the assassination of Indira Gandhi two years later, following the storming of the temple. The separate upsurges in Hindu, Sikh and Islamic fundamentalism in the Indian subcontinent are undoubtedly interconnected developments. Not only have they created a chain reaction of threats and resentments, but they have also inspired one another by closely linking ethnic identity to religious fervour.

Both Jewish and Buddhist fundamentalisms are also closely linked to the sharpening of ethnic conflict. In contrast with the ultra-orthodox Jews, some of whom have refused to accept Israel as the Jewish state prophesied in the Old Testament, Jewish fundamentalists have transformed Zionism (see p. 306) into a defence of the 'Greater Land of Israel', characterized by territorial aggressiveness. In the case of Israel's best known fundamentalist group, Gushmun Emunim (Bloc of the Faithful), this has been expressed in a campaign to build Jewish settlements in territory occupied in the Six Day War of 1967 and then formally incorporated into Israel. More radical groups such as Katch (Thus) proclaim that Jews and Arabs can never live together and so look to the expulsion of all Arabs from what they see as the 'promised land'. Although small, Israel's collection of ultra-orthodox parties tend to exert disproportional influence because their support is usually necessary for either of the major parties, Likud and Labour, to form a government.

The spread of Buddhist nationalism in Sri Lanka has largely occurred as a result of growing tension between the majority and largely Buddhist Sinhalese population and the minority Tamil community, comprising Hindus, Christians and Muslims. Although on the surface – by virtue of its

ZIONISM

Zionism (*Zion* is Hebrew for the Kingdom of Heaven) is the movement for the establishment of a Jewish homeland, usually seen as located in Palestine. The idea was first advanced in 1897 by Theodore Herzl (1860–1904) at the World Zionist Congress in Basle, as the only means of protecting the Jewish people from persecution. Early Zionists had secularist and nationalistic aspirations, often associated with socialist sympathies. Since the foundation of the state of Israel in 1948, however, Zionism has come to be associated both with the continuing promise of Israel to provide a home for all Jews and with attempts to promote sympathy for Israel and defend it against its enemies. In the latter sense, it has been recruited to the cause of fundamentalism, and, according to Palestinians, it has acquired an expansionist, anti-Arab character.

commitment to individual responsibility, religious toleration and non-violence – Buddhism is the least fundamentalist of the major religions (Dalai Lama, 1996), the Theravada Buddhism of Southern Asia has supported fundamentalist-type developments when nationalism and religious revivalism have been intertwined. In Sri Lanka, the drive for the 'Sinhalization' of national identity, advanced by militant groups such as the People's Liberation Front, has been expressed in the demand that Buddhism be made a state religion. Such pressures, however, merely fuelled Tamil separatism, giving rise to a terrorist campaign by the Tamil Tigers, which commenced in the late 1970s.

Religious fundamentalism in the twenty-first century

Is religious fundamentalism destined to survive throughout the twenty-first century, or will it ultimately be viewed as a temporary phenomenon, linked to the conjunction of particular historical circumstances? The question of the future of fundamentalism raises two starkly different scenarios. The first questions the long-term viability of any religiously based political creed in the modern world, and highlights the particular limitations of fundamentalism as a political project. According to this view, fundamentalist religion is essentially a symptom of the difficult adjustments that modernization brings about, but it is ultimately doomed because it is out of step with the principal thrust of the modernization process. Modernization as westernization is destined to prevail because it is supported by the trend towards economic globalization and the spread of liberal democracy. Religion will therefore be restored to its 'proper' private domain, and public affairs will once again be contested by secular political creeds.

This analysis suggests that the theo-political project that lies at the heart of fundamentalism will gradually fade, with religious groups becoming mere components of broader nationalist movements. The emergence of a western-dominated global system may allow for the survival of civic nationalism, orientated around the goal of self-determination, but it suggests that there is little future for militant ethnic nationalisms, especially when they are based on religious distinctiveness. The limitations of fundamentalism will thus become particularly apparent if fundamentalists succeed in winning power and are confronted with the complex tasks of government. Lacking a clear political programme or a coherent economic philosophy, fundamentalism as an ideology of protest will survive, if it survives at all, only as rhetoric or as the 'founding myth' of a regime.

The rival view holds that religious fundamentalism offers a glimpse of the 'postmodern' future. From this perspective, it is secularism and liberal culture that are in crisis. Their weakness, dramatically exposed by fundamentalism, is their failure to address deeper human needs and their inability to establish authoritative values that give social order a moral foundation. Far from the emerging global system fostering uniformity modelled on western liberal democracy, this view suggests that a more likely scenario is that the twentieth-century battle between capitalism and communism will give way, as Huntington (1996) predicted, to a clash of civilizations. Competing transnational power blocs will emerge, and religion is likely to provide them with a distinctive politico-cultural identity. Fundamentalism, in this version, is seen to have strengths rather than weaknesses. Religious fundamentalists have already demonstrated their adaptability by embracing the weapons and spirit of the modern world, and the very fact that they are not encumbered by tradition but travel 'fast and light' enables them to reinvent their creeds in response to the challenges of postmodernity.

Questions for discussion

→ Do all political ideologies harbour fundamentalist tendencies?

→ Is secularism anti-religious?

→ Is the rise of religious fundamentalism evidence of a 'clash of civilizations'?

→ Is religious fundamentalism necessarily based on a belief in the literal truth of sacred texts?

→ Are religious fundamentalists always anti-modern?

→ Is fundamentalism implicitly totalitarian and prone to violence?

→ To what extent is Islamic fundamentalism a form of anti-westernism?

→ Is religious fundamentalism compatible with constitutionalism and political pluralism?

→ What is the relationship between religious fundamentalism and ethnic nationalism?

Further reading

Ahmed, A. and Donnan, H., *Islam, Globalization and Postmodernity* (London and New York: Routledge, 1994). A useful collection of essays examining both the nature of political Islam and its relationship to modernity.

Ahmed, R., *Jihad: The Rise of Militant Islam in Central Asia* (New Haven, CT: Yale University Press, 2001). A clear and authoritative account of the rise and significance of radical new fundamentalism in various parts of Central Asia.

Bruce, S., *Fundamentalism* (Oxford: Polity Press, 2000). An examination of fundamentalism as a key concept, which portrays it as a symptom of rapid social change but also takes its ideological character seriously.

Burma, I. and Margalit, A., *Occidentalism: A Short History of Anti-Westernism* (London: Atlantic Books, 2004). A succinct and challenging attempt to link modern trends in Islamic fundamentalism to longer-term ideological developments.

Hadden, J. K. and Shupe, A. (eds), *Prophetic Religions and Politics: Religion and Political Order* (New York: Paragon House, 1986). A useful collection of essays by noted sociologists of religion that examines a wide range of movements across the globe.

Marty, M. E. and Appleby, R. S. (eds), *Fundamentalisms and the State: Remaking Polities, Economies, and Militance* (Chicago, IL and London: University of Chicago Press, 1993). Part of the massively comprehensive, authoritative yet accessible six-volume Fundamentalism Project. Other volumes that are of interest include *Fundamentalism Observed* (1991) and *Accounting for Fundamentalisms* (1994).

Parekh, B., 'The Concept of Fundamentalism', in A. Shtromas (ed.), *The End of 'isms'? Reflections on the Fate of Ideological Politics after Communism's Collapse* (Oxford and Cambridge, MA: Blackwell, 1994). A clear and insightful introduction to the nature of fundamentalism and the modernization process.

Ruthven, M., *Fundamentalism: The Search for Meaning* (Oxford and New York: Oxford University Press, 2004). A short and engaging reflection on the meaning of fundamentalism which looks in particular at the relationship between Islam and the West.

CHAPTER 11

MULTICULTURALISM

PREVIEW

Although multicultural societies have long existed – examples including the Ottoman Empire, which reached its peak in the late sixteenth and early seventeenth centuries, and the USA from the early nineteenth century onwards – the term 'multiculturalism' is of relatively recent origin. It was first used in 1965 in Canada to describe a distinctive approach to tackling the issue of cultural diversity. In 1971, multiculturalism, or 'multiculturalism within a bilingual framework', was formally adopted as public policy in Canada, providing the basis for the introduction of the Multiculturalism Act in 1988. Australia also officially declared itself multicultural and committed itself to multiculturalism in the early 1970s. However, the term 'multiculturalism' has only been prominent in wider political debate since the 1990s.

Multiculturalism is more an arena for ideological debate that an ideology in its own right. As an arena for debate, it encompasses a range of views about the implications of growing cultural diversity and, in particular, about how cultural difference can be reconciled with civic unity. Its key theme is therefore diversity within unity. A multiculturalist stance implies a positive endorsement of communal diversity, based on the right of different cultural groups to recognition and respect. In this sense, it acknowledges the importance of beliefs, values and ways of life in establishing a sense of self-worth for individuals and groups alike. Distinctive cultures thus deserve to be protected and strengthened, particularly when they belong to minority or vulnerable groups. However, there are a number of competing models of a multicultural society, which draw on, variously, the ideas of liberalism, pluralism and cosmopolitanism. On the other hand, the multiculturalist stance has also been deeply controversial, and has given rise to a range of objections and criticisms.

Origins and development

Multiculturalism first emerged as a theoretical stance through the activities of the black consciousness movement of the 1960s, primarily in the USA. The origins of black nationalism date back to the early twentieth century and the emergence of a 'back to Africa' movement inspired by figures such as the Jamaican political activist Marcus Garvey (1887–1940). Black politics, however, gained greater prominence in the 1960s with an upsurge in both the reformist and revolutionary wings of the movement. In its reformist guise, the movement took the form of a struggle for civil rights that reached national prominence in the USA under the leadership of Martin Luther King (1929–68). The strategy of non-violent civil disobedience was nevertheless rejected by the Black Power movement, which supported black separatism and, under the leadership of the Black Panther Party, founded in 1966, promoted the use of armed confrontation. Of more enduring significance, however, have been the Black Muslims (now the Nation of Islam), who advocate a separatist creed based on the idea that black Americans are descended from an ancient Muslim tribe. Founded in 1929, the Black Muslims were led for over 40 years by Elijah Mohammad (1897–1975), and they counted amongst the most prominent activists in the 1960s the militant black leader Malcolm X (1925–65).

The late 1960s and early 1970s witnessed growing political assertiveness amongst minority groups, sometimes expressed through **ethnocultural nationalism**, in many parts of western Europe and else-where in North America. This was most evident amongst the French-speaking people of Quebec in Canada, but it was also apparent in the rise of Scottish and Welsh nationalism in the UK, and the growth of separatist movements in Catalonia and the Basque area in Spain, Corsica in France, and Flanders in Belgium. A trend towards ethnic assertiveness was also found amongst the Native Americans in Canada and the USA, the aboriginal peoples in Australia, and the Maoris in New Zealand. The common theme amongst these emergent forms of ethnic politics was a desire to challenge economic and social marginalization, and sometimes racial oppression. In this sense, ethnic politics was a vehicle for political liberation, its enemy being structural disadvantage and ingrained inequality. For blacks in North America and western Europe, for example, the establishment of an ethnic identity provided a means of confronting a dominant white culture that had traditionally emphasized their inferiority and demanded subservience.

Ethnocultural nationalism:
A form of nationalism that is fuelled primarily by a keen sense of ethnic and cultural distinctiveness and the desire to preserve it.

Apart from growing assertiveness amongst established minority groups, multicultural politics has also been strengthened by trends in international migration since 1945 that have significantly widened cultural diversity in many societies. Migration rates rose steeply in the early post-1945 period as western states sought to recruit workers from abroad to help in the process of post-war reconstruction. In many cases, migration routes were shaped by links between European states and their former colonies. Thus, immigrants into the UK in the 1950s and 1960s came mainly from the West Indies and the Indian subcontinent, while immigration in France came largely from Algeria, Morocco and Tunisia. In the case of West Germany, immigrants were *Gastarbeiter* (guest workers), usually recruited from Turkey or Yugoslavia. Immigration into the USA since the 1970s has mainly come from Mexico and other Latin American countries. It is estimated, for instance, that the Latino (or Hispanic) community in the USA will exceed the number of African-Americans by 2010, and that by 2050 about a quarter of the US population will be Latinos.

However, during the 1990s there was a marked intensification of cross-border migration across the globe, creating what some have seen as a 'hyper-mobile planet'. There are two main reasons for this. First, there has been a growing number of refugees, reaching a peak of about 18 million in 1993. This resulted from an upsurge in war, ethnic conflict and political upheaval in the post-Cold War era, in areas ranging from Algeria, Rwanda and Uganda to Bangladesh, Indo-China and Afghanistan. The collapse of communism in Eastern Europe in 1989–91 contributed to this by creating, almost overnight, a new group of migrants as well as by sparking a series of ethnic conflicts, especially in former Yugoslavia. Second, economic global-ization has intensified pressures for international migration in a variety of ways. Migrants have been 'pushed' by the disruption to economic life caused by intensifying international competition, the impact of transnational corporations, and pressures to produce goods for export rather than to satisfy domestic needs. However, they have also been 'pulled' by the development of a 'dual' labour market in many industrialized states, through the growth of a stratum of low-paid, low-skilled and low-status jobs that the domestic population is increasingly unwilling to fill.

By the early 2000s, a growing number of western states, including virtu-ally all of the member states of the European Union, had officially incorpo-rated multiculturalism into public policy. This was in recognition of the fact that multi-ethnic, multi-religious and multicultural trends within modern societies have come to be irreversible. In short: despite the continuing and sometimes increasing prominence of issues such as immigration and asylum, a return to monoculturalism, based on a unifying national culture, is no longer feasible. Indeed, arguably the most pressing ideological issue such societies now confront is how to reconcile cultural diversity with the main-tenance of civic and political cohesion. Nevertheless, an additional factor has pushed multicultural politics further up the political agenda. This is the advent of global terrorism and the launch of the so-called 'war on terror'. The spread of religious fundamentalism (see p. 288), and particularly of militant Islam, to western states has encouraged some to speculate on whether Samuel Huntington's (1996) famous 'clash of civilizations' is happening not just between societies but also *within* them. Whereas supporters of multiculturalism have argued that cultural recognition and minority rights help to keep political extremism at bay, opponents have warned that multicultural politics may provide a cloak for, or even legitimize, political extremism.

Core themes – diversity within unity

The term 'multiculturalism' has been used in a variety of ways, both descriptive and normative. As a descriptive term, it has been taken to refer to cultural diversity that arises from the existence within a society of two or more groups whose beliefs and practices generate a distinctive sense of collective identity. Multiculturalism, in this sense, is invariably reserved for communal diversity that arises from racial, ethnic and language differences. The term can also be used to describe governmental responses to such communal diversity, either in the form of public policy or in the form of institutional design. Multicultural public policies, whether applied in education, health care, housing or other aspects of social policy, are characterised by a formal recognition of the distinctive needs of particular cultural groups and a desire to ensure equality of opportunity between and amongst them.

Consociationalism: A form of power sharing involving a close association amongst a number of parties or political formations, typically used in deeply divided societies.

Multicultural institutional design goes further than this by attempting to fashion the apparatus of government around the ethnic, religious and other divisions in society. In the form of **consociationalism**, it has shaped political practice in states such as the Netherlands, Switzerland and Belgium, and has also been applied to the Northern Ireland Assembly and to the constitutional arrangements for Bosnia-Herzegovina.

As a normative term, multiculturalism implies a positive endorsement, even celebration, of communal diversity, typically based on either the right of different cultural groups to respect and recognition, or to the alleged benefits to the larger society of moral and cultural diversity. However, multiculturalism is more an ideological 'space' than a political ideology in its own right. Instead of advancing a comprehensive world view which maps out an economic, social and political vision of the 'good society', multiculturalism is, rather, an arena within which increasingly important debates about the balance in modern societies between cultural diversity and civic unity are conducted. Nevertheless, a distinctive multiculturalist ideological stance can be identified. The most significant themes within multiculturalism are the following:

■ postcolonialism
■ identity and culture
■ minority rights
■ diversity.

Postcolonialism

The foundations for the ideas of multiculturalism were laid by the postcolonial theories that developed out of the collapse of the European empires in the early post-1945 period. The black nationalism that emerged in the 1960s can be seen as a manifestation of postcolonialism, and multiculturalism itself can be viewed as one of the offshoots of postcolonialism. The significance of postcolonialism was that it sought to challenge and overturn the cultural dimensions of imperial rule by establishing the legitimacy of non-western and sometimes anti-western political ideas and traditions. Postcolonialism has nevertheless taken a variety of forms. For example, Gandhi advanced a political philosophy that fused Indian nationalism with an ethic of non-violence and self-sacrifice that was ultimately rooted in Hinduism. The Martinique-born French revolutionary theorist Franz Fanon (1926–61), however, emphasized links between the anti-colonial struggle and violence. His theory of imperialism emphasized the psychological dimension of colonial subjugation. For Fanon (1965), decolonization was not merely a political process, but one through which a new 'species' of man is created. He argued that only the cathartic experience of violence is powerful enough to bring about this psycho-political regeneration. Edward Said's

Eurocentrism: The application of values and theories drawn from European culture to other groups and peoples, implying a biased or distorted viewpoint.

Orientalism ([1978] 2003) is sometimes seen as the most influential text of postcolonialism. This developed a critique of **Eurocentrism**. Orientalism highlights the extent to which western cultural and political hegemony over the rest of the world, but over the Orient in particular, had been maintained through elaborate stereotypical fictions that belittled and demeaned non-western people and culture. Examples of such stereotypes include ideas such as the 'mysterious East', 'inscrutable Chinese' and 'lustful Turks'.

Postcolonialism made two important contributions to emergent multiculturalism. In the first place, it challenged a predominantly Eurocentric world

Mohandas Karamchand Gandhi (1869–1948)

GANDHI

Indian spiritual and political leader (called Mahatma, 'Great Soul'). A lawyer trained in the UK, Gandhi developed his political philosophy while working in South Africa, where he organized protests against discrimination. After returning to India in 1915, he became the leader of the nationalist movement, campaigning tirelessly for independence, finally achieved in 1947. Gandhi was assassinated in 1948 by a fanatical Hindu, becoming a victim of the ferocious Hindu–Muslim violence which followed independence.

Gandhi's ethic of non-violent resistance, *satyagraha*, reinforced by his ascetic lifestyle, gave the movement for Indian independence enormous moral authority and provided a model for the later civil rights activists, including Martin Luther King. Derived from Hinduism, Gandhi's political philosophy was based on the assumption that the universe is regulated by the primacy of truth, or *satya*. As humankind is 'ultimately one', love, care and a concern for others is the natural basis for human relations. When asked what he thought of western civilization, Gandhi famously responded that it would be a nice idea.

view, in that it attempted to give the developing world a distinctive political voice separate from the universalist pretensions of western ideologies such as liberalism. This not only allowed non-western religions, ideas and philosophies to be taken more seriously, but also encouraged a broader reassessment within political thought. In particular, it allowed western and non-western ideas – for instance, liberal and Islamic political theories – to be considered equally legitimate in articulating the traditions, values and aspirations of their own communities. Second, it highlighted the political importance of culture, by focusing in particular on the cultural legacy of colonial rule. If people are encouraged to view an 'imposed' culture as oppressive and demeaning, they are thereby invited to invite to seek emancipation through the rediscovery of their 'native' culture.

Identity and culture

Multiculturalism is a form of identity politics. Identity politics seeks to advance the interests of particular groups in society, usually in the face of actual or perceived social injustice, by strengthening its members' awareness

COMMUNITARIANISM

Communitarianism is the belief that the self or person is constituted through the community, in the sense that individuals are shaped by the communities to which they belong and thus owe them a debt of respect and consideration – there are no 'unencumbered selves'. Although clearly at odds with liberal individualism, communitarianism nevertheless has a variety of political forms. *Left-wing* communitarianism holds that community demands unrestricted freedom and social equality (for example, anarchism). *Centrist* communitarianism holds that community is grounded in an acknowledgement of reciprocal rights and responsibilities (for example, social democracy/Tory paternalism). *Right-wing* communitarianism holds that community requires respect for authority and established values (for example, the new right).

of their collective identity and common experiences. Identity, in this sense, links the personal to the social, and sees the individual as 'embedded' in a particular cultural, social, institutional or ideological context. As such, multiculturalism is rooted in an essentially communitarian view of human nature, which emphasizes that people cannot be understood 'outside' society but are intrinsically shaped by the social, cultural and other contexts within which they live and develop. Communitarian theorists such as Alistair MacIntyre (1981) and Michael Sandel (1982) have therefore been particularly critical of liberal individualism (see p. 28), seeing it as a cause of rootless atomism. In the case of the Canadian philosopher Charles Taylor (1994), a defence of the 'politics of recognition' has been explicitly constructed on the basis of communitarian assumptions about personal identity.

A particular emphasis within multiculturalism is placed on the role and significance of culture. **Culture**, in its broadest sense, is the way of life of a people. Sociologists and anthropologists tend to distinguish between 'culture' and 'nature', in that the former encompasses that which is passed on from one generation to the next by learning, rather than through biological inheritance. The vital importance of culture, from the multiculturalist perspective, is that it shapes the values, norms and assumptions through which individual identity is formed and the external world becomes meaningful. A pride in one's culture, and especially a public acknowledgement, even celebration, of one's cultural identity, thus gives people a sense of social and historical rootedness. In contrast, a weak or fractured sense of cultural identity leaves people

Culture: Beliefs, values and practices that are passed on from one generation to the next through learning; culture is distinct from nature.

CULTURE

PERSPECTIVES

LIBERALS have sometimes been critical of traditional or 'popular' culture, seeing it as a source of conformism and a violation of individuality. 'High' culture, however, especially in the arts and literature, may nevertheless be viewed as a manifestation of, and stimulus to, individual self-development. Culture is thus valued only when it promotes intellectual development.

CONSERVATIVES place a strong emphasis on culture, emphasizing its benefits in terms of strengthening social cohesion and political unity. Culture, from this perspective, is strongest when it overlaps with tradition and therefore binds one generation to the next. Conservatives support monocultural societies, believing that only a common culture can inculcate the shared values that bind society together.

SOCIALISTS, and particularly Marxists, have viewed culture as part of the ideological and political 'superstructure' that is conditioned by the economic 'base'. In this view, culture is a reflection of the interests of the ruling class, its role being primarily ideological. Culture thus helps to reconcile subordinate classes to their oppression within the capitalist class system.

FASCISTS draw a sharp distinction between rationalist culture, which is a product of the Enlightenment and is shaped by the intellect alone, and organic culture, which embodies the spirit or essence of a people, often grounded in blood. In the latter sense, culture is of profound importance in preserving a distinctive national or racial identity and in generating a unifying political will. Fascists believe in strict and untrammelled monoculturalism.

FEMINISTS have often been critical of culture, believing that, in the form of patriarchal culture, it reflects male interests and values and serves to demean women, reconciling them to a system of gender oppression. Nevertheless, cultural feminists have used culture as a tool of feminism, arguing that, in strengthening distinctive female values and ways of life, it can safeguard the interests of women.

MULTICULTURALISTS view culture as the core feature of personal and social identity, giving people an orientation in the world and strengthening their sense of cultural belonging. They believe that different cultural groups can live peacefully and harmoniously within the same society because the recognition of cultural difference underpins, rather than threatens, social cohesion. However, cultural diversity must in some way, and at some level, be balanced against the need for common civic allegiances.

feeling isolated and confused. In its extreme form, this can result in what has been called 'culturalism', as practised by writers such as the French political philosopher Montesquieu (1689–1775) and the German critic and the 'father' of cultural nationalism Herder (1744–1803), which portrays human beings as culturally defined creatures.

Although modern multiculturalists rarely sympathize with this form of crude cultural determinism, the rise of multiculturalism nevertheless reflects a shift away from universalism to particularism, reflecting an emphasis less on what people share or have in common and more on what is distinctive about the groups to which they belong.

This concern with culture helps to explain the stress within multiculturalism on **ethnicity**, religion and language. Ethnicity is a complex term because it carries both racial and cultural overtones. The members of ethnic groups are often seen, correctly or incorrectly, to have descended from common ancestors, and these groups are therefore thought of as extended kinship groups, in which case they are united by blood. More commonly, though, ethnicity is understood as a form of cultural identity, albeit one that operates at a deep and emotional level. An 'ethnic' culture encompasses values, traditions and practices, but, crucially, it also gives a people a common identity and sense of distinctiveness, usually by focusing on their origins and descent. Religion is particularly important for cultural groups from non-western countries of origin, for whom the influence of secularism has been less pronounced. Indeed, in such cases, religion can sometimes become the defining feature of cultural identity, as has happened for some Muslim groups in western societies. However, for groups such as the Quebeçois in Canada, the Welsh in the UK, the Basques in Spain and France and the Flemish in Belgium, the maintenance of cultural distinctiveness has been closely linked to the preservation of their 'national' language. Language is often an important component of cultural identity both because it helps to keep alive a body of traditional literature as well as myths and legends, and because it helps to shape how the world is viewed and understood.

Ethnicity: A sentiment of loyalty towards a particular population, cultural group, or territorial area; bonds that are cultural rather than racial.

Minority rights

The advance of multiculturalism has gone hand in hand with a willingness to recognize minority rights, sometimes called multicultural rights. The most systematic attempt to identify such rights was undertaken by Will Kymlicka (1995). Kymlicka identified three kinds of minority rights: self-government rights, polyethnic rights and representation rights. Self-government rights belong, Kymlicka argued, to what he called national minorities, peoples who are territorially concentrated, possess a shared language and are characterized by a 'meaningful way of life across the full range of human activities'. Examples would include the Native Americans, the Inuits in Canada, the Maoris in New Zealand and the aboriginal peoples in Australia. In these cases, the right to self-government should involve the devolution of political power, usually through federalism, to political units that are substantially controlled by the members of a national minority, although it may extend to the right of succession and, therefore, to sovereign independence. Polyethnic rights are rights that help ethnic groups and religious minorities, which have developed through immigration, to express and maintain their cultural distinctiveness. This would, for instance, provide the basis for legal exemptions, such as the exemption of Jews and Muslims from animal slaughtering

Positive discrimination: Preferential treatment towards a group designed to compensate its members for past disadvantage or structural inequality.

laws, and the exemption of Muslim girls from school dress codes. Special representation rights attempt to redress the under-representation of minority or disadvantaged groups in education and in senior positions in political and public life. Kymlicka justified reverse or **'positive' discrimination** in such cases, on the grounds that it is the only way of ensuring full and equal participation, which, in turn, guarantees that public policy reflects the interests of all groups and peoples, and not merely those of traditionally dominant groups.

Minority or multicultural rights are distinct from the traditional liberal conception of rights, in that they belong to groups rather than to individuals. This highlights the extent to which multiculturalists subscribe to **collectivism** rather than individualism. Minority rights are also often thought of as 'special' rights. This applies in two senses. First, these rights are specific to

Collectivism: A belief that human ends are best achieved through collaborative or collective effort, highlighting the importance of social groups (see p. 104).

the groups to which they belong, each cultural group having different needs for recognition based on the specific character of its religion, traditions and way of life. For instance, legal exemptions for Sikhs to ride motorcycles without wearing crash helmets, or, perhaps, to wear ceremonial daggers, would be meaningless to other groups. Second, minority rights are 'special' in that

they may specifically set out to advantage certain groups over other groups. This reflects the fact that, although multiculturalism may, in principle treat all cultural groups as equal in their entitlement to recognition and basic rights, it is prepared to violate the principle of formal equality by granting preferential rights to certain groups to compensate them for past injustices or present disadvantages. Multiculturalism, in this sense, sets out to redress social injustice. It has typically discharged its commitment to promote social justice through support for 'positive' discrimination. This has been particularly evident in the USA where the political advancement of African-Americans has, since the 1960s, been associated with so-called 'affirmative action'. For example, in the *Regents of the University of California* v. *Bakke* case (1978), the Supreme Court upheld the principle of reverse discrimination in educational admissions, allowing black students to gain admission to university with lower qualifications than white students.

The issue of minority rights has nevertheless been highly controversial. These controversies have included, first, that because minority rights address the distinctive needs of particular groups, they have sometimes been criticized for blocking integration into the larger society. The issue of the veil, as worn by some Muslim women, has attracted particular attention in this respect. While supporters of the right of Muslim women to wear the veil have argued that it is basic to their cultural identity, critics have objected to it either because it discriminates against women or because the veil is a symbol of separateness. Second, 'positive' discrimination has been criticized, both by members of majority groups, who believe that it amounts to unfair discrimination, and by some members of minority groups, who argue that it is demeaning and possibly counter-productive because it implies that such groups cannot gain advancement through their own efforts.

Third, considerable debate has surrounded the vexed issue of 'offence' and the alleged right not to be offended. This especially concerns religious groups, which consider certain beliefs to be sacred, and therefore particularly deserving of protection. To criticize, insult or even ridicule such beliefs is thus seen as an attack on the group itself, as was evident, for instance, in protests against the publication of Salman Rushdie's *The Satanic Verses* and against allegedly anti-Islamic cartoons published in Denmark in 2006. States such as the UK have, as a result, introduced laws banning expressions of religious hatred. However, such rights have major implications for traditional liberal rights, notably the right to freedom of expression. If freedom of expression means anything, it surely means the right to express views that others find objectionable or offensive. Finally, there is inevitable tension between minority rights and individual rights, in that cultural belonging, particularly when it is based on ethnicity or religion, is usually a product of family and social background, rather than personal choice: most people do not 'join' ethnic or religious groups. Some multiculturalists have gone as far as to question whether people have the right to opt out from 'a culture', or to opt in.

Diversity

Multiculturalism shares much in common with nationalism. Both emphasize the capacity of culture to generate social and political cohesion, and both seek to bring political arrangements into line with patterns of cultural differentiation. Nevertheless, whereas nationalists believe that stable and successful societies are ones in which nationality, in the sense of a shared cultural identity, coincides with citizenship, multiculturalists hold that cultural diversity is compatible with political cohesion. Multiculturalism is characterized by a steadfast refusal to link diversity to conflict or instability. All forms of multiculturalism are based on the assumption that diversity and unity can, and should, be blended with one another: they are not opposing forces. In this sense, multiculturalists accept that people can have multiple identities and multiple loyalties; for instance, to their 'country of origin' and their 'country of settlement'. Indeed, multiculturalists argue that cultural recognition underpins political stability. People become willing and able to participate in society precisely because they have a firm and secure identity rooted in their own culture. From this perspective, the denial of cultural recognition results in isolation and powerlessness, providing a breeding ground for extremism and the politics of hate. For instance, growing support for militant Islam, and other forms of religious fundamentalism (as discussed in Chapter 10), have been interpreted in this light.

Multiculturalists do not just believe that diversity is possible; they believe it is also desirable and should be celebrated. Apart from its benefits to the individual in terms of a stronger sense of cultural identity and belonging, multiculturalists believe that diversity is of value to society at large. This can be seen, in particular, in terms of the vigour and vibrancy of a society in which there are a variety of lifestyles, cultural practices, traditions and beliefs. Multiculturalism, in this sense, parallels ecologism, in drawing links between diversity and systemic health. Cultural diversity is seen to benefit society in just the same way that biodiversity benefits an ecosystem. An additional advantage of diversity is that by promoting cultural exchange between groups that live side by side with one another it fosters cross-cultural tolerance and understanding, and therefore a willingness to respect 'difference'. Diversity, in this sense, is the antidote to social polarization and prejudice. Nevertheless, this may highlight internal tension within multiculturalism itself. On the one hand, multiculturalists emphasize the distinctive and particular nature of cultural groups and the need for individual identity to be firmly embedded in a cultural context. On the other hand, by encouraging cultural exchange and mutual understanding, they risk blurring the contours of group identity and creating a kind of 'pick and mix', melting-pot society in which individuals have a 'shallower' sense of social and historical identity. As people learn more about other cultures, the contours of their 'own' culture, arguably, become blurred.

Multiculturalism and politics

All forms of multiculturalism advance a political vision that claims to reconcile cultural diversity with civic cohesion. However, multiculturalism is not a single doctrine in the sense that there is no settled or agreed view of how multicultural society should operate. Indeed, multiculturalism is another example of a cross-cutting ideology that draws from a range of other political traditions and encompasses a variety of ideological stances. Multiculturalists disagree both about how far they should go in positively endorsing cultural diversity, and about how civic cohesion can best be brought about. In short, there are competing models of multiculturalism, each offering a different view of the proper balance between diversity and unity. The three main models of multiculturalism are the following:

- liberal multiculturalism
- pluralist multiculturalism
- cosmopolitan multiculturalism.

Liberal multiculturalism

There is a complex and, in many ways, ambivalent relationship between liberalism and multiculturalism. As is discussed in greater detail later in the chapter, some view liberalism and multiculturalism as rival political traditions, arguing that multiculturalism threatens cherished liberal values. Since the 1970s, however, liberal thinkers have taken the issue of cultural diversity increasingly seriously, and have developed a form of liberal multiculturalism. Its cornerstone has been a commitment to **toleration** and a desire to uphold freedom of choice in the moral sphere, especially in relation to matters that are of central concern to particular cultural or religious traditions. This has contributed to the idea that liberalism is 'neutral' in relation to the moral, cultural and other choices that citizens make. Liberalism, in this sense, is 'difference-blind': it treats factors such as culture, ethnicity, race, religion and gender as, in effect, irrelevant, because all people should be evaluated as morally autonomous individuals. However, toleration is not morally neutral, and only provides a limited endorsement of cultural diversity. In particular, toleration extends only to views, values and social practices that are themselves tolerant; that is, ideas and actions that are compatible with personal freedom and autonomy. Liberals thus cannot accommodate 'deep diversity'. For example, liberal multiculturalists may be unwilling to endorse practices such as

Toleration:
Forbearance; a willingness to accept views or action with which one is in disagreement (see pp. 34–6).

female circumcision, forced (and possibly arranged) marriages and female dress codes, however much the groups concerned may argue that these are crucial to the maintenance of their cultural identity. The individual's rights, and particularly his or her freedom of choice, must therefore come before the cultural rights of the group.

The second feature of liberal multiculturalism is that it draws an important distinction between 'private' and 'public' life. It sees the former as a realm of freedom, in which people are, or should be, free to express their cultural, religious and language identity, whereas the latter must be characterized by at least a bedrock of shared civic allegiances. Citizenship is thus divorced from cultural identity, making the latter essentially a private matter. Such a stance implies that multiculturalism is compatible with civic nationalism. This can be seen in the so-called 'hyphenated nationality' that operates in the USA, through which people view themselves as African-Americans, Polish-Americans, German-Americans and so forth. In this tradition, inclusion, rather than diversity, is emphasized in the public sphere. The USA, for instance, stresses proficiency in English and a knowledge of US political history as preconditions for gaining citizenship. In the more radical 'republican' multiculturalism that is practised in France, an emphasis on *laïcité*, or secularism, in public life has led to bans on the wearing of the *hijab*, or Muslim headscarf, in schools, and, since 2003, to a ban on all forms of overt religious affiliation in French schools. Some multiculturalists, indeed, view such trends as an attack on multiculturalism itself.

The third and final aspect of liberal multiculturalism is that it regards liberal democracy as the sole legitimate political system. The virtue of liberal democracy is that it alone ensures that government is based on the consent of the people, and that it provides guarantees for personal freedom and toleration. Liberal multiculturalists would therefore oppose calls, for instance, for the establishment of an Islamic state based on the adoption of s*hari'a* law, and may be willing to prohibit groups and movements that campaign for such a political end. Groups are therefore only entitled to toleration and respect, if they, in turn, are prepared to tolerate and respect other groups.

Pluralist multiculturalism

Pluralism provides firmer foundations for a politics of difference than does liberalism. For liberals, as has been seen, diversity is endorsed but only when it is constructed within a framework of toleration and personal autonomy. This is the sense in which liberals 'absolutize' liberalism (Parekh, 2005). The UK philosopher Isaiah Berlin (1909–97) nevertheless went beyond liberal

Value pluralism: The theory that there is no single, overriding conception of the 'good life', but rather a number of competing and equally legitimate conceptions.

toleration in endorsing the idea of **value pluralism**. This holds, in short, that people are bound to disagree about the ultimate ends of life, as it is not possible to demonstrate the superiority of one moral system over another. As values conflict, the human predicament is inevitably characterized by moral conflict. In this view, liberal or western beliefs, such as support for personal freedom, toleration and democracy, have no greater moral authority than illiberal or non-western beliefs. Berlin's (1969) stance implies a form of live-and-let-live multiculturalism, or what has been called the politics of *in*difference. However, as Berlin remained a liberal to the extent that he believed that only within a society that respects individual liberty can value pluralism be contained, he failed to demonstrate how liberal and illiberal cultural beliefs can co-exist harmoniously within the same society. Nevertheless, once liberalism accepts moral pluralism, it is difficult to contain it within a liberal framework. John Gray (1995b), for instance, argued that pluralism implies a 'post-liberal' stance, in which liberal values, institutions and regimes are no longer seen to enjoy a monopoly of legitimacy.

An alternative basis for pluralist multiculturalism has been advanced by Bhikhu Parekh (2005). In Parekh's view, cultural diversity is, at heart, a reflection of the dialectic or interplay between human nature and culture. Although human beings are natural creatures, who possess a common species-derived physical and mental structure, they are also culturally constituted in the sense that their attitudes, behaviour and ways of life are shaped by the groups to which they belong. A recognition of the complexity of human nature, and the fact that any culture expresses only part of what it means to be truly human, therefore provides the basis for a politics of recognition and thus for a viable form of multiculturalism.

Beyond pluralist multiculturalism, a form of 'particularist' multiculturalism can be identified. Particularist multiculturalists stress that cultural diversity takes place within a context of unequal power, in which certain groups have customarily enjoyed advantages and privileges that have been denied to other groups. Particularist multiculturalism is very clearly aligned to the needs and interests of marginalized or disadvantaged groups. The plight of such groups tends to be explained in terms of the corrupt and corrupting nature of western culture, values and lifestyles, which are either believed to be tainted by the inheritance of colonialism and racialism (see p. 221) or associated with 'polluting' ideas such as materialism and permissiveness. In this context, an emphasis on cultural distinctiveness amounts to a form of political resistance, a refusal to succumb to repression or corruption. However, such an emphasis on cultural 'purity', which may extend to an unwillingness to engage in cultural exchange, raises concerns about the

PLURALISM

Pluralism, in its broadest sense, is a belief in or commitment to diversity or multiplicity, the existence of many things. As a descriptive term, pluralism may denote the existence of party competition (*political* pluralism), a multiplicity of ethical values (*moral* or value pluralism), a variety of cultural beliefs (*cultural* pluralism) and so on. As a normative term it suggests that diversity is healthy and desirable, usually because it safeguards individual liberty and promotes debate, argument and understanding. More narrowly, pluralism is a theory of the distribution of political power. As such, it holds that power is widely and evenly dispersed in society, not concentrated in the hands of an elite or ruling class. In this form, pluralism is usually seen as a theory of 'group politics', implying that group access to govern-ment ensures broad democratic responsive-ness.

prospects for civic cohesion: diversity may be stressed at the expense of unity. Particularist multiculturalism may thus be an example of 'plural monoculturalism' (Sen, 2006), rather than a form of multiculturalism.

Cosmopolitan multiculturalism

Cosmopolitanism and multiculturalism can be seen as entirely distinct, even conflicting, ideological traditions. Whereas cosmopolitanism encourages people to adopt a global consciousness that emphasizes that ethical respon-sibility should not be confined by national borders, multiculturalism appears to particularize moral sensibilities, focusing on the specific needs and inter-ests of a distinctive cultural group. However, for theorists such as Jeremy Waldron (1995), multiculturalism can effectively be equated with cosmopolitanism. Cosmopolitan multiculturalists endorse cultural diversity and identity politics, but they view them as essentially transitional states in a larger reconstruction of political sensibilities and priorities. This position celebrates diversity on the ground of what each culture can learn from other cultures, and because of the prospects for personal self-development that are offered by a world of wider cultural opportunities and options. This results in what has been called a pick-and-mix multiculturalism, in which cultural exchange and cultural mixing are positively encouraged. People, for instance, may eat Italian food, practise yoga, enjoy African music and develop an interest in world religions.

Culture, from this perspective, is fluid and responsive to changing social

COSMOPOLITANISM

Cosmopolitanism literally means a belief in a cosmopolis or 'world state'. As such, it implies the obliteration of national identities and the establishment of a common political allegiance, uniting all human beings. The term, however, is usually employed to refer to the more modest goal of peace and harmony amongst nations, founded upon mutual understanding, toleration and, above all, interdependence. Liberal cosmopolitanism has long been associated with support for free trade, based upon the belief that it promotes both international understanding and material prosperity. The cosmopolitan ideal is also promoted by supranational bodies that aim to encourage cooperation amongst nations rather than replace the nation-state.

circumstances and personal needs; it is not fixed and historically embedded, as pluralist or particularist multiculturalists would argue. A multicultural society is thus a 'melting pot' of different ideas, values and traditions, rather than a 'cultural mosaic' of separate ethnic and religious groups. In particular, the cosmopolitan stance positively embraces **hybridity**. The benefit of this form of multiculturalism is that it broadens moral and political sensibilities, ultimately leading to the emergence of a 'one world' perspective. However, multiculturalists from rival traditions criticize the cosmopolitan stance for stressing unity at the expense of diversity. To treat cultural identity as a matter of self-definition, and to encourage hybridity and cultural mixing, is, arguably, to weaken any genuine sense of cultural belonging.

Hybridity: A condition of social and cultural mixing in which people develop multiple identities.

Critiques of multiculturalism

The advance of multicultural ideas and policies has stimulated considerable political controversy. Together with conversion of liberal and other progressive thinkers to the cause of minority rights and cultural recognition, oppositional forces have also emerged. This has been most clearly expressed in the growing significance, since the 1980s, of anti-immigration parties and movements in many parts of the world. Examples of these include the National Front in France, the Freedom Party in Austria, Vlaams Blok in

Belgium, Pim Fortuyn's List in the Netherlands, the One Nation party in Australia and the New Zealand First party. Other examples of a retreat from 'official' multiculturalism can be seen in the prohibition of Muslim head-scarves, and subsequently all overt forms of religious insignia in French schools, and calls in countries such as the Netherlands, the UK and Germany for bans on the wearing of veils by Muslim women in public places. However, ideological opposition to multiculturalism has come from a variety of sources. The most significant of these have been:

- liberalism
- conservatism
- feminism
- social reformism.

While some liberals have sought to embrace wider cultural diversity, others have remained critical of the ideas and implications of multiculturalism. The key theme of liberal criticism is the threat that multiculturalism poses to individualism, reflected in the core multiculturalist assumption that personal identity is embedded in group or social identity. Multiculturalism is therefore, like nationalism and even racialism, just another form of collectivism, and, like all forms of collectivism, it subordinates the rights and needs of the individual to those of the social group. In this sense, it threatens individual freedom and personal self-development. Amartya Sen (2006) developed a particularly sustained attack on what he called the 'soli-taristic' theory which underpins multiculturalism (particularly in its plural-ist and particularist forms), which suggests that human identities are

TENSIONS WITHIN
LIBERALISM

UNIVERSALIST LIBERALISM	v.	PLURALIST LIBERALISM
universal reason	←→	scepticism
search for truth	←→	pursuit of order
fundamental values	←→	value pluralism
liberal toleration	←→	politics of difference
human rights	←→	cultural rights
liberal-democratic culture	←→	multiculturalism
liberal triumphism	←→	plural political forms

formed by membership of a *single* social group. This, Sen argued, leads not only to the 'miniaturization' of humanity, but also makes violence more likely, as people identify only with their own monoculture and fail to recognize the rights and integrity of people from other cultural groups. Multiculturalism thus breeds a kind of 'ghettoization' that diminishes, rather than broadens, cross-cultural understanding. According to Sen, solitaristic thinking is also evident in ideas that emphasize the incompatibility of cultural traditions, such as the 'clash of civilizations' thesis (Huntington, 1996). Even when liberals are sympathetic to multiculturalism they condemn pluralist and especially particularist multiculturalism for endorsing as legitimate ideas, such as the theories of militant Islam, which they view as anti-democratic and oppressive.

Conservatism is the political tradition that most starkly contrasts with multiculturalism. Indeed, most of the anti-immigration nationalist backlash against multiculturalism draws from essentially conservative assumptions. In other cases, it more closely resembles the racial nationalism of fascism, or even Nazi race theory. The chief conservative objection to multiculturalism is that shared values and a common culture are a necessary precondition for a stable and successful society. As discussed in Chapter 5, conservatives thus favour nationalism over multiculturalism. The basis for such a view is the belief that human beings are drawn to others who are similar to themselves. A fear or distrust of strangers or foreigners is therefore 'natural' and unavoidable. From this perspective, multiculturalism is inherently flawed: multicultural societies are inevitably fractured and conflict-ridden societies, in which suspicion, hostility and even violence come to be accepted as facts of life. The multiculturalist image of 'diversity within unity' is thus a myth, a sham exposed by the simple facts of social psychology.

Assimilation: The process through which immigrant communities lose their cultural distinctiveness by adjusting to the values, allegiances and lifestyles of the 'host' society.

The appropriate political responses to the threats embodied in multiculturalism therefore include restrictions on immigration, particularly from parts of the world whose culture is different from the 'host' society, pressures for **assimilation** to ensure that minority ethnic communities are absorbed into the larger 'national' culture, and, in the view of the far right, the repatriation of immigrants to their country of origin. A further aspect of the conservative critique of multiculturalism is a concern about its implications for the majority or 'host' community. In this view, multiculturalism perpetrates a new, albeit 'reverse', set of injustices, by demeaning the culture of majority groups through its alleged association with colonialism and racism, while favouring the interests and culture of minority groups through 'positive' discrimination and the allocation of 'special' rights.

The relationship between feminism and multiculturalism has sometimes been a difficult one. Although forms of Islamic feminism (considered in Chapter 8) have sought to fuse the two traditions, feminists have more commonly raised concerns about some of the implications of multiculturalism. This happens when minority rights and the politics of recognition serve to preserve and legitimize patriarchal and traditional beliefs that systematically disadvantage women (this is an argument that may equally be applied to gays and lesbians). This occurs when cultural practices such as dress codes, family structures and access to elite positions establish structural gender biases. Indeed, some aspects of multiculturalism can be seen as systematic attempts to protect patriarchal power.

Social reformists have advanced a number of criticisms of multiculturalism, linked to its wider failure adequately to address the interests of disadvantaged groups or sections of society. Concerns, for instance, have been raised about the extent to which multiculturalism encourages groups to seek advancement through cultural or ethnic assertiveness, rather than through a struggle for social justice. In that sense, the flaw of multiculturalism is its failure to address issues of class inequality: the 'real' issue confronting minority groups is not their lack of cultural recognition but their lack of economic power and social status. Indeed, as Brian Barry (2002) argued, by virtue of its emphasis on cultural distinctiveness, multiculturalism serves to divide, and therefore weaken, people who have a common economic interest in alleviating poverty and promoting social reform. Similarly, a more acute awareness of cultural difference may weaken support for welfarist and redistributive policies, as it may narrow people's sense of social responsibility (Goodhart, 2004). The existence of a unifying national culture may therefore be a necessary precondition for the politics of social justice.

Multiculturalism in the twenty-first century

In many ways, multiculturalism may turn out to be *the* ideology of the twenty-first century. One of the chief features of globalization has been a substantial increase in geographical, and particularly cross-border, mobility. More and more societies have, as a result, accepted multiculturalism as an irreversible fact of life. Not only is the relatively homogeneous nation-state a receding memory in many parts of the world, but attempts to reconstruct it – through, for example, strict immigration controls, enforced assimilation or pressure for repatriation – increasingly appear, to be politically fanciful. If this is the case, just as nationalism was the major ideological force in world politics during the nineteenth and twentieth centuries, helping to reshape the contours of political authority as well as the relationship between different societies, multiculturalism, its successor, may be the predominant ideological force of the twenty-first century. The major ideological issue for our time, and for succeeding generations, may therefore be the search for ways in which people with different moral values and from different cultural and religious traditions can find a way of living together without civil strife and violence. Multiculturalism is not only the ideology that most squarely addresses this question, but it also offers solutions, albeit tentative ones.

On the other hand, multiculturalism may prove to be a once-fashionable idea whose limitations, even dangers, were quickly exposed. In this view, multiculturalism is a particular response to an undeniable trend towards cultural and moral pluralism in modern societies. However, its long-term viability is more in question. Multicultural solutions may be worse than the diseases they set out to tackle. The flaw of multiculturalism, from this perspective, is the belief that by endorsing diversity people will be drawn together as a collection of mutually respectful and tolerant cultural groups. Instead, diversity may endorse separation and lead to 'ghettoization', as groups become increasingly inward-looking and concerned to protect their 'own' traditions and cultural purity. Multiculturalism may thus encourage people to focus on what divides them rather than on what unites them. If this is the case, the twenty-first century is destined to witness a retreat from multiculturalism, seen as a non-viable means of addressing the undoubted challenge of cultural diversity. However, what will replace multiculturalism?

One possibility is that the failure of multiculturalism will lead to a return to nationalism, whose enduring potency derives from the recognition that, at some level and in some way, political unity always goes hand in hand with cultural cohesion. The strains generated by irreversible trends towards the construction of multi-ethnic, multi-religious and multicultural societies can therefore only be contained by the establishment of a stronger and clearer sense of national identity. The other possibility is that multiculturalism will be superseded by a genuine form of cosmopolitanism. This would require (as some multiculturalists anyway hope) that differences of both culture and nationality are gradually recognized to be of secondary importance as people everywhere come to view themselves as global citizens, united by a common interest in addressing ecological, social and other challenges that are, increasingly, global in nature.

Questions for discussion

→ Is multiculturalism a form of communitarianism?

→ What is the justification for minority or multicultural rights?

→ Is multiculturalism compatible with the idea of individual rights?

→ Why do multiculturalists believe that diversity provides the basis for politically stable?

→ Why have liberals supported diversity, and when do they believe that diversity is 'excessive'?

→ How does pluralism go 'beyond liberalism'?

→ Are western cultures tainted by the inheritance of colonialism and racialism?

→ Can multiculturalism be reconciled with any form of nationalism?

→ Could multiculturalism lead to cosmopolitanism?

Further reading

Barry, B., *Culture and Equality* (Cambridge: Polity Press, 2001). An influential critique of multiculturalism, which examines the social implications of cultural politics.

Carens, J., *Culture, Citizenship and Community* (Oxford and New York: Oxford University Press, 1998). An excellent introduction to the themes and debates that have developed out of multiculturalism.

Gutmann, A. (ed.), *Multiculturalism: Explaining the Politics of Recognition* (Princeton, NJ: Princeton University Press, 1995). A wide-reaching and authoritative set of essays on various aspects of multicultural politics.

Kymlicka, W., *Multicultural Citizenship* (Oxford: Oxford University Press, 1995). A highly influential attempt to reconcile multiculturalism with liberalism by advancing a model of citizenship that is based on the recognition of minority or multicultural rights.

Parekh, B., *Rethinking Multiculturalism: Cultural Diversity and Political Theory*, 2nd edn (Basingstoke and New York: Palgrave Macmillan, 2005). A comprehensive defence of the pluralist perspective on cultural diversity that also discusses the practical problems of multicultural societies.

Said, E., *Orientalism* (Harmondsworth: Penguin, 2003). Regarded by many as the founding text for postcolonialism, the concept of 'orientalism' has had a significant impact on emergent multiculturalist thinking.

Taylor, C., *Multiculturalism and 'The Politics of Recognition'* (Princeton, NJ: Princeton University Press, 1994). This is an expanded version of Taylor's seminal text on the 'politics of recognition', and includes a series of commentaries by theorists sympathetic and less sympathetic to Taylor's position.

CHAPTER 12

CONCLUSION: A POST-IDEOLOGICAL AGE?

PREVIEW

Political ideology has been an essential component of world history for over two hundred years. Ideology sprang out of the upheavals – economic, social and political – through which the modern world took shape, and has been intimately involved in the continuing process of social transformation and political development. Although ideology emerged first in the industrializing West, it has subsequently appeared throughout the globe, creating a worldwide language of political discourse. However, opinion has been deeply divided about the role that ideology has played in human history. Has ideology served the cause of truth, progress and justice, or has it generated distorted and blinkered world views, resulting in intolerance and oppression?

This debate has often been carried out in negative terms, highlighting criticisms of ideology, often by predicting its imminent demise. However, what is remarkable is how many and how varied the obituaries for political ideology have been. The various obituaries have been viewed as different forms of 'endism'. The idea of the 'end of ideology' became fashionable in the 1950s and early 1960, and suggested that politics was no longer concerned with larger normative issues, as technical questions about how to deliver affluence had come to dominate political debate. In the aftermath of the collapse of communism, so-called 'end of history' theorists argued that ideological disagreement had ended in the final victory of western liberal democracy. Alternative forms of endism have highlighted the alleged redundancy of the left/right divide, on which the 'classical' ideological traditions depended, and held that the triumph of rationalism and modern technology has fatally undermined the ideological style of thought. Ideological politics, however, remains stubbornly resistant to being *dis*invented. Indeed, as the principal source of meaning and idealism in politics, ideology is destined to be a continuing and unending process.

Endism

The end of ideology?

The idea of the 'end of ideology' became fashionable in the 1950s and 1960s. The most influential statement of this position was advanced by Daniel Bell (1960). Bell was impressed by the fact that after the Second World War politics in the West was characterized by broad agreement amongst major political parties and the absence of ideological division or debate. Fascism and communism had both lost their appeal, while the remaining parties disagreed only about which of them could best be relied on to deliver economic growth and material prosperity. In effect, economics had triumphed over politics. Politics had been reduced to technical questions about 'how' to deliver affluence, and had ceased to address moral or philosophical questions about the nature of the 'good society'. To all intents and purposes, ideology had become an irrelevance. However, the process to which Bell drew attention was not the 'end of ideology' so much as the emergence of a broad ideological consensus amongst major parties, and therefore the suspension of ideological debate. In the immediate postwar period, representatives of the three

Daniel Bell
(born 1919)

US academic and essayist. As professor of sociology at Harvard University, Bell developed an analysis of modern society that had a broad political as well as an academic impact. In the 1960s, with Irving Kristol, he founded the journal *The Public Interest*, which has attacked the philosophy of 'big' government, and helped to give neoconservatism intellectual credibility in the USA.

In *The End of Ideology* (1960), Bell drew attention to the exhaustion of rationalist approaches to social and political issues, and, in the Afterword to the 1988 edition, he warned against the tyranny of utopian end-states. He also helped to popularize 'post-industrialism', highlighting the emergence of 'information societies' dominated by a new 'knowledge class'. In *The Cultural Contradictions of Capitalism* (1976), Bell analysed the growing tension between the need for rationality and efficiency to sustain production and capitalism's tendency to strengthen values such as 'feeling', personal gratification and self-expression.

major western ideologies – liberalism, socialism and conservatism – came to accept the common goal of managed capitalism. This goal, however, was itself ideological – for example, it reflected an enduring faith in market economics, private property and material incentives, tempered by a belief in social welfare and economic intervention. In effect, an ideology of 'welfare capitalism' or 'social democracy' had triumphed over its rivals, although this triumph proved to be only temporary. The 1960s witnessed the rise of more radical new left ideas, reflected in a revival of interest in Marxist and anarchist thought and the growth of modern ideologies such as feminism and ecologism. The onset of economic recession in the 1970s provoked renewed interest in long-neglected, free-market doctrines and stimulated the development of new right theories, which also challenged the post-1945 consensus. Finally, the 'end of ideology' thesis focused attention exclusively on developments in the industrialized West and ignored the fact that in the 1950s and 1960s communism remained firmly entrenched in the Soviet Union, eastern Europe, China and elsewhere, and that revolutionary political movements were operating in Asia, Africa and parts of Latin America.

The end of history?

A broader perspective was adopted by Francis Fukuyama in his essay 'The End of History' (1989). Unlike Bell, Fukuyama did not suggest that political ideas had become irrelevant, but that one particular set of ideas, western liberalism, had triumphed over all its rivals. Fascism had been defeated in 1945, and Fukuyama clearly believed that the collapse of communist rule in eastern Europe in 1989 marked the passing of Marxism-Leninism as an ideology of world significance. By the 'end of history', Fukuyama meant that the history of ideas had ended, and with it, fundamental ideological debate. Throughout the world there was, he argued, an emerging agreement about the desirability of liberal democracy, in the form of a market or capitalist economy and an open, competitive political system.

Without doubt, the eastern European revolutions of 1989–91 and the dramatic reform of surviving communist regimes such as China profoundly altered the worldwide balance of ideological debate. However, it is far less certain that this process amounted to the 'end of history'. One difficulty with the 'end of history' thesis is that no sooner had it been proclaimed, than new ideological forces rose to the surface. While liberal democracy may have made impressive progress during the twentieth century, as the century drew to a close there was undoubted evidence of the revival of very different ideologies, notably political Islam, whose influence has come to extend from the Muslim countries of Asia and Africa into the former Soviet Union and

PERSPECTIVES

HISTORY

LIBERALS see history as progress, brought about as each generation advances further than the last through the accumulation of knowledge and understanding. Liberals generally believe that this will happen through gradual or incremental reform, not through revolution.

CONSERVATIVES understand history in terms of tradition and continuity, allowing little scope for progress. The lessons of the past provide guidance for present and future conduct. Reactionary conservatives believe that history is marked by decline, and wish to return to an earlier and preferred time.

SOCIALISTS are committed to a progressive view of history, which places heavy emphasis on the scope for social and personal development. Marxists believe that class conflict is the motor of history and that a classless, communist society is history's determinant end-point.

FASCISTS generally view history as a process of degeneration and decay, a decline from a past 'golden age'. They nevertheless subscribe to a cyclical theory of history that holds out the possibility of national rebirth and regeneration, usually through violent struggle and war.

RELIGIOUS FUNDAMENTALISTS have an ambivalent attitude towards history. Although they tend to see the present as morally and spiritually corrupt in comparison with an idealized past, they conceive of social regeneration in modernist terms, thus rejecting conservative traditionalism.

also the industrialized West. It is possible, for example, that the 'death of communism' in the Soviet Union and eastern Europe prepared the way for the revival of nationalism, racialism or religious fundamentalism, rather than led to the final victory of liberal democracy.

Underlying Fukuyama's thesis was the optimistic belief, inherited from classical liberalism, that industrial capitalism offers all members of society the prospect of social mobility and material security, encouraging every citizen to regard it as reasonable and attractive. In other words, it is possible for a broad, even universal, agreement to be achieved about the nature of the 'good society'. This can nevertheless only be achieved if a society can be constructed that is capable both of satisfying the interests of all major social groups and of fulfilling the aspirations of at least a substantial majority of individual citizens. Despite the undoubted vigour and efficiency that the capitalist market has demonstrated, it certainly cannot be said that capitalism has treated all social classes or all individuals alike. Ideological conflict and debate are thus unlikely to have ended in the late twentieth century with the ultimate world-wide triumph of liberalism, any more than they did with the 'inevitable 'victory of socialism so widely predicted at the end of the nineteenth century.

Beyond left and right?

Yet another form of 'endism' is the belief that, as the established features of modern society have crumbled, the political creeds and doctrines that it threw up have been rendered irrelevant. This notion is usually advanced through the idea of postmodernity. Not only have the major ideologies, both left-wing and right-wing, been adapted to the 'postmodern condition', giving rise to 'post-isms' such as post-liberalism, post-Marxism and post-feminism, but, according to postmodern theorists, our way of understanding and interpreting the world has changed, or needs to change. This reflects a shift from modernism to postmodernism (see p. 62). Modernism stemmed largely from Enlightenment ideas and theories, and was expressed politically in ideological traditions that offer rival conceptions of the good life. The clearest examples are liberalism and Marxism. Modernist thought is charac-terized by **foundationalism**. In contrast, postmodernism is anti-foundationalist; the central theme of postmod-ernism was summed up by Jean-François Lyotard (1984) as 'incredulity towards meta-narratives', meta-narratives being universal theories of history that view society as a coherent totality.

Foundationalism: The belief that it is possible to establish objective truths and universal values, usually associated with a strong faith in progress.

However, such tendencies also provide evidence of the decline of the left/right divide, which marks an important transition in ideological politics. The left/right divide helped to structure ideological debate in the nineteenth and twentieth centuries, in that, to a large extent, competing ideological posi-tions and arguments offered different solutions but to essentially the same problem. The problem was the destiny of industrial society, and the various solutions offered ranged from free-market capitalism, on the one hand, to central planning and state collectivization on the other. Ideological debate, then, tended to focus on the desirable balance between the market and the state. Since the 1960s, however, politics has certainly not become less ideo-logical, but ideological developments have become increasingly fragmented. The 'new' ideologies – feminism, ecologism, religious fundamentalism and multiculturalism – have each, in their different ways, opened up new directions for ideological thinking. However, because each, in a sense, has throw up its own ideological discourse, they are not part of a larger discourse, as applied in the earlier period in relation to the clash between capitalism and socialism.

This not only implies that ideological developments have, in effect, gone beyond left and right, but it also has implications for party politics and levels of political engagement. The advantage of the left/right divide from the perspective of mainstream political parties was that it gave the parties ideological roots and a sense of purpose, and it gave their supporters a basis for emotional attachment. The declining relevance of the left/right divide has created the spectre of de-ideologized politics. Having abandoned their traditional 'isms', de-ideologized parties have come to sell political 'products' (leaders or policies), rather than hopes and dreams. Indeed, declining party membership and falling voter turnout in mature democracies may, in part, be a consequence of the failure of mainstream political parties to engage the electorate at a level of moral commitment and passion.

Triumph of reason?

The debate about the replacement of ideology by **rationalism** goes back to the nineteenth century and the firm distinction that Marx (see p. 121) drew

Rationalism: A belief that the world can be understood and explained through the exercise of human reason, based upon assumptions about its rational structure.

Science: A method of acquiring knowledge through a process of careful observation and the testing of hypotheses by reproducible experiments.

between 'ideology' and 'science'. For Marx, ideology was intrinsically false because it serves as a vehicle for advancing class interests. In contrast, he portrayed his own ideas as a form of 'scientific' socialism. **Science**, in this view, provides an objective and value-free method of advancing human knowledge, so releasing humanity from enslavement to irrational beliefs, which includes superstitions, prejudices and, in this case, political ideologies. This, indeed, has proved to be one of the enduring myths of modern times. It has recurred, for instance, in relation to the cultural and intellectual implications of globalization, one of the chief features of the emerging global age being an acceptance of a western model of rationality, reflected, most obviously, in the value placed on technology and technological development. In this sense, ideology may be in the process of being displaced by scientism.

However, science is not the antithesis of ideology, but can perhaps be seen as an ideology in its own right. For example, science has been linked to powerful social forces, in particular those represented by industry and technology. Scientism could therefore be viewed as the ideology of the technocratic elite, its main beneficiary being the transnational corporations that are increasingly responsible for funding scientific and technological developments. Moreover, significant ideological controversy has surrounded the advance of science. This can be seen in the case of some ecologists, who view science and technology as the source of the environmental crisis. Multiculturalists and religious fundamentalists, for their part, have sometimes interpreted rationalism as a form of cultural imperialism, on the ground that it undermines faith-based belief systems and helps to strengthen western and often materialist modes of understanding.

Ideology without end

However, each of these versions of endism has one thing in common: they are conducted within an ongoing framework of ideological thinking. In their different ways, each of them heralds the demise of ideology by highlighting the triumph of a particular ideological tradition, be it welfare capitalism, liberal democracy, postmodernism or scientism. Rather than demonstrating the weakened grasp of ideology, endism in fact shows its remarkable resilience and robustness. Once invented, ideological politics has proved stubbornly resistant to being *dis*invented. However, what is the source of its survival and success? The first answer to this question is undoubtedly its flexibility, the fact that ideological traditions and forms go through a seemingly endless process of redefinition and renewal, and, if necessary, new ideologies emerge as old ones fade or fail. The world of ideologies thus does not stand still, but changes in response to changing social and historical circumstances. The second and deeper explanation is that, as the principal source of meaning and idealism in politics, ideology touches those aspects of politics that no other aspects of politics form reaches. In effect, ideology gives people a reason to believe in something larger than themselves, because people's personal narratives only make sense when they are situated within broader historical narratives. A post-ideological age would therefore be an age without hope, without vision. For this, if for no other reason, political ideology is destined to be a continuing and unending process.

Questions for discussion

→ What were the flaws of the 'end of ideology' thesis?

→ Why have 'end of history' theorists viewed liberal democracy as the final solution to the problem of governance?

→ Could history ever come to an end?

→ Why have postmodernists proclaimed the death of 'meta-narratives'?

→ Is the left/right divide now redundant?

→ Can science be thought of as an ideological tradition?

→ Is ideology a help or a hindrance to a political party?

→ Is ideology really a continuing and unending process?

Further reading

Butler, C., *Postmodernism: A Very Short Introduction* (Oxford and New York: Oxford University, 2002). A lucid and concise introduction to the history and significance of postmodernism.

Freeden, M., *Reassessing Political Ideologies: The Durability of Dissent* (London and New York: Routledge, 2001). A volume of essays that consider and reassess the major ideological traditions in a so-called 'post-ideological' age.

Gray, J., *Endgames: Questions in Late Modern Political Thought* (Cambridge and Malden, MA: Blackwell, 1997). A fascinating and insightful discussion of the condition of the major ideological traditions as they confront the collapse of the 'Enlightenment project'.

Scholte, J. A., *Globalization: An Introduction*, 2nd edn (Basingstoke: Palgrave Macmillan, 2005). A comprehensive and authoritative introduction to globalization and debates about its significance.

Shtromas, A. (ed.), *The End of 'isms'? Reflections on the Fate of Ideological Politics after Communism's Collapse* (Oxford and Cambridge, MA: Blackwell, 1994). A collection of considered and carefully argued essays on the state of and future prospects for the politics of ideology after the collapse of communism.

BIBLIOGRAPHY

Acton, Lord (1956) *Essays on Freedom and Power*. London: Meridian.

Adams, I. (1989) *The Logic of Political Belief: A Philosophical Analysis*. London and New York: Harvester Wheatsheaf.

Adams, I. (2001) *Political Ideology Today*, 2nd edn. Manchester: Manchester University Press.

Adonis, A. and Hames, T. (1994) *A Conservative Revolution? The Thatcher–Reagan Decade in Perspective*. Manchester: Manchester University Press.

Ahmed, A. and Donnan, H. (1994) *Islam, Globalization and Postmodernity*. London and New York: Routledge.

Ahmed, R. (2001) *Jihad: The Rise of Militant Islam in Central Asia*. New Haven, CT: Yale University Press.

Ali, T. (2003) *The Clash of Fundamentalism: Crusades, Jihads and Modernity*. London: Verso.

Anderson, B. (1983) *Imagined Communities: Reflections on the Origins and Spread of Nationalism*. London: Verso.

Arblaster, A. (1984) *The Rise and Decline of Western Liberalism*. Oxford: Basil Blackwell.

Arendt, H. (1951) *The Origins of Totalitarianism*. London: Allen & Unwin.

Aristotle (1962), *The Politics*, trans. T. Sinclair. Harmondsworth: Penguin (Chicago, IL: University of Chicago Press, 1985).

Aughey, A., Jones, G. and Riches, W. T. M. (1992) *The Conservative Political Tradition in Britain and the United States*. London: Pinter.

Bahro, R. (1982) *Socialism and Survival*. London: Heretic Books.

Bahro, R. (1984) *From Red to Green*. London: Verso/New Left Books.

Bakunin, M. (1973) *Selected Writings*, ed. Lehning. London: Cape.

Bakunin, M. (1977) 'Church and State', in G. Woodcock (ed.), *The Anarchist Reader*. London: Fontana.

Ball, T. and Dagger, R. (2002) *Political Ideologies and the Democratic Ideal*, 4th edn. London and New York: Longman.

Baradat, L. P. (2003) *Political Ideologies: Their Origins and Impact*, 8th edn. Upper Saddle River, NJ: Prentice Hall.

Barber, B. (1995) *Jihad vs. the World: How Globalism and Tribalism are Reshaping the World*. New York: Ballantine Books.

Barker, R. (1997) *Political Ideas in Modern Britain: In and After the 20th Century*, 2nd edn. London and New York: Routledge.

Barry, B. (2002) *Culture and Equality*. Cambridge and New York: Polity Press.

Barry, J. (1999) *Rethinking Green Politics*. London and Thousand Oaks, CA: Sage.

Barry, N. (1987) *The New Right*. London: Croom Helm.

Baumann, Z. (1999) *In Search of Politics*. Cambridge and Malden, MA: Polity Press.

Baumann, Z. (2000) *Liquid Modernity*. Cambridge and New York: Polity Press.

Baxter, B. (1999) *Ecologism: An Introduction*. Edinburgh: Edinburgh University Press.

Beasley, C. (1999) *What is Feminism?* London: Sage.

Beauvoir, S. de (1968) *The Second Sex*, trans. H. M. Parshley. New York: Bantam.

Beck, U. (1992) *Risk Society: Towards a New Modernity*. London and New York: Sage.

Bell, D. (1960) *The End of Ideology*. Glencoe, IL: Free Press.

Bellamy, R. (1992) *Liberalism and Modern Society: An Historical Argument*. Cambridge: Polity Press.

Benn, T. (1980) *Arguments for Democracy*. Harmondsworth: Penguin.

Bentham, J. (1970) *Introduction to the Principles of Morals and Legislation*, ed. J. Burns and H. L. A. Hart. London: Athlone Press, and Glencoe, IL: Free Press, 1970.

Berki, R. N. (1975) *Socialism*. London: Dent.

Berlin, I. (1969) 'Two Concepts of Liberty', in *Four Essays on Liberty*. London: Oxford University Press.

Berman, P. (2003) *Terror and Liberalism*. New York: W. W. Norton.

Bernstein, E. (1962) *Evolutionary Socialism*. New York: Schocken.

Blakeley, G. and Bryson, V. (eds) (2002) *Contemporary Political Concepts: A Critical Introduction*. London: Pluto Press.

Bobbio, N. (1996) *Left and Right*. Oxford: Polity Press.

Bobbitt, P. (2002) *The Shield of Achilles*. New York: Knopf and London: Allen Lane.

Boff, L. (2006) *Fundamentalism, Terrorism and the Future of Mumanity*. London: Society for Promoting Christian Knowledge.

Bookchin, M. (1975) *Our Synthetic Environment*. London: Harper & Row.

Bookchin, M. (1977) 'Anarchism and Ecology', in G. Woodcock (ed.), *The Anarchist Reader*. London: Fontana.

Boulding, K. (1966) 'The Economics of the Coming Spaceship Earth', in H. Jarrett (ed.), *Environmental Quality in a Growing Economy*. Baltimore: Johns Hopkins Press.

Bourne, R. (1977) 'War is the Health of the State', in G. Woodcock (ed.), *The Anarchist Reader*. London: Fontana.

Bracher, K. D. (1985) *The Age of Ideologies: A History of Political Thought in the Twentieth Century*. London: Methuen.

Bramwell, A. (1989) *Ecology in the Twentieth Century: A History*. New Haven, CT and London: Yale University Press.

Bramwell, A. (1994) *The Fading of the Greens: The Decline of Environmental Politics in the West*. New Haven, CT and London: Yale University Press.

Brown, D. (2000) *Contemporary Nationalism: Civic, Ethnocultural and Multi-cultural Politics*. London: Routledge.

Brownmiller, S. (1975) *Against Our Will: Men, Women and Rape*. New York: Simon & Schuster.

Bruce, S. (1993) 'Fundamentalism, Ethnicity and Enclave', in M. Marty and R. S.

Appleby (eds), *Fundamentalism and the State*. Chicago, IL and London: Chicago University Press.

Bruce, S. (2000) *Fundamentalism*. Oxford: Polity Press.

Bryson, V. (2003) *Feminist Political Theory: An Introduction*, 2nd edn. Basingstoke and New York: Palgrave Macmillan.

Burke, E. (1968) *Reflections on the Revolution in France*. Harmondsworth: Penguin.

Burke, E. (1975) *On Government, Politics and Society*, ed. B. W. Hill. London: Fontana.

Burnham, J. (1960) *The Managerial Revolution*. Harmondsworth: Penguin and Bloomington: Indiana University Press.

Buruma, I. and Margalit, A. (2004) *Occidentalism: A Short History of Anti-Westernism*. London: Atlantic Books.

Butler, C. (2002) *Postmodernism: A Very Short Introduction*. Oxford and New York: Oxford University Press.

Capra, F. (1975) *The Tao of Physics*. London: Fontana.

Capra, F. (1982) *The Turning Point*. London: Fontana (Boston, MA: Shambhala, 1983).

Capra, F. (1997) *The Web of Life: A New Synthesis of Mind and Matter*. London: Flamingo.

Carson, R. (1962) *The Silent Spring*. Boston, MA: Houghton Mifflin.

Carter, A. (1971) *The Political Theory of Anarchism*. London: Routledge & Kegan Paul.

Castells, M. (2000) *The Rise of the Network Society*. Oxford and Malden, MA: Blackewll.

Cecil, H. (1912) *Conservatism*. London and New York: Home University Library.

Chamberlain, H. S. (1913) *Foundations of the Nineteenth Century*. New York: John Lane.

Charvert, J. (1982) *Feminism*. London: Dent.

Club of Rome. See Meadows *et al.* (1972).

Collins, P. (1993) *Ideology after the Fall of Communism*. London: Bowerdean.

Constant, B. (1988) *Political Writings*. Cambridge: Cambridge University Press.

Conway, D. (1995) *Classical Liberalism: The Unvanquished Ideal*. Basingstoke and New York: Palgrave Macmillan.

Coole, D. (1993) *Women in Political Theory: From Ancient Misogyny to Contemporary Feminism*, 2nd edn. Hemel Hempstead: Harvester Wheatsheaf.

Costa, M. D. and James, S. (1972) *The Power of Women and the Subordination of the Community*. Bristol: Falling Wall Press.

Crewe, I. (1989) 'Values: The Crusade that Failed', in D. Kavanagh and A. Seldon (eds), *The Thatcher Effect*. Oxford: Oxford University Press.

Crick, B. (1962) *A Defence of Politics*. Harmondsworth: Penguin.

Critchley, T. A. (1970) *The Conquest of Violence*. London: Constable.

Crosland, C. A. R. (1956) *The Future of Socialism*. London: Cape (Des Plaines, IL: Greenwood, 1977).

Dahl, R. (1961) *Who Governs? Democracy and Power in an American City*. New Haven, CT: Yale University Press.

Dalai Lama (1996) *The Power of Buddhism*. London: Newleaf.

Daly, H. (1974) 'Steady-state economics vs growthmania: a critique of orthodox conceptions of growth, wants, scarcity and efficiency', in *Policy Sciences*, vol. 5, pp. 149 –67.

Daly, M. (1979) *Gyn/Ecology: The Meta-Ethics of Radical Feminism*. Boston, MA: Beacon Press.

Darwin, C. (1972) *On the Origin of Species*. London: Dent.

Dickinson, G. L. (1916) *The European Anarchy*. London: Allen & Unwin.

Dobson, A. (1991) *The Green Reader*. London: André Deutsch.

Dobson, A. (2007) *Green Political Thought*, 4th edn. London: Routledge.

Downs, A. (1957) *An Economic Theory of Democracy*. New York: Harper & Row.

Eagleton, T. (1991) *Ideology: An Introduction*. London and New York: Verso.

Eatwell, R. (1996) *Fascism: A History*. London: Vintage.

Eatwell, R. and O'Sullivan, N. (eds) (1989) *The Nature of the Right: European and American Politics and Political Thought since 1789*. London: Pinter.

Eatwell, R. and Wright, A. (eds) (1999) *Contemporary Political Ideologies*, 2nd edn. London: Pinter.

Eccleshall, R. *et al.* (2003) *Political Ideologies: An Introduction*, 3rd edn. London and New York: Routledge.

Eckersley, R. (1992) *Environmentalism and Political Theory: Towards an Ecocentric Approach*. London: UCL Press.

Edgar, D. (1988) 'The Free or the Good', in R. Levitas (ed.) *The Ideology of the New Right*. Oxford: Polity Press.

Ehrenfeld, D. (1978) *The Arrogance of Humanism*. Oxford: Oxford University Press.

Ehrlich, P. and Ehrlich, A. (1970) *Population, Resources and Environment: Issues in Human Ecology*. London: W. H. Freeman.

Ehrlich, P. and Harriman, R. (1971) *How to be a Survivor*. London: Pan.

Elshtain, J. B. (1981) *Public Man, Private Woman: Women in Social and Political Thought*. Oxford: Martin Robertson and Princeton, NJ: Princeton University Press.

Engels, F. (1976) *The Origins of the Family, Private Property and the State*. London: Lawrence & Wishart (New York: Pathfinder, 1972).

Etzioni, A. (1995) *The Spirit of Community: Rights, Responsibilities and the Communitarian Agenda*. London: Fontana.

Eysenck, H. (1964) *Sense and Nonsense in Psychology*. Harmondsworth: Penguin.

Faludi, S. (1991) *Backlash: The Undeclared War Against American Women*. New York: Crown.

Fanon, F. (1965) *The Wretched of the Earth*. Harmondsworth: Penguin (New York: Grove-Weidenfeld, 1988).

Faure, S. (1977) 'Anarchy–Anarchist', in G. Woodcock (ed.), *The Anarchist Reader*. London: Fontana.

Festenstein, M. and Kenny, M. (eds) (2005) *Political Ideologies: A Reader and Guide*. Oxford ad New York: Oxford University Press.

Figes, E. (1970) *Patriarchal Attitudes*. Greenwich, CT: Fawcett.

Firestone, S. (1972) *The Dialectic of Sex.* New York: Basic Books.

Foley, M. (1994) (ed.) *Ideas that Shape Politics*. Manchester and New York: Manchester University Press.

Fox, W. (1990) *Towards a Transpersonal Ecology: Developing the Foundations for Environmentalism*. Boston, MA: Shambhala.

Freeden, M. (1996) *Ideologies and Political Theory: A Conceptual Approach*. Oxford and New York: Oxford University Press.

Freeden, M. (2001) *Reassessing Political Ideologies: The Durability of Dissent*. London and New York: Routledge.

Freeden, M. (2004) *Ideology: A Very Short Introduction*. Oxford and New York: Oxford University Press.

Freedman, J. (2001) *Feminism*. Buckingham and Philadelphia, PA: Open University Press.

Friedan, B. (1963) *The Feminine Mystique*. New York: Norton.

Friedan, B. (1983) *The Second Stage*. London: Abacus (New York: Summit, 1981).

Friedman, M. (1962) *Capitalism and Freedom*. Chicago, IL: University of Chicago Press.

Friedman, M. and R. Friedman (1980) *Free to Choose*. Harmondsworth: Penguin (New York: Bantam, 1983).

Friedrich, C. J. and Brzezinski, Z. (1963) *Totalitarian Dictatorships and Autocracy*. New York: Praeger.

Fromm, E. (1979) *To Have or To Be*. London: Abacus.

Fromm, E. (1984) *The Fear of Freedom*. London: Ark.

Fukuyama, F. (1989) 'The End of History', *National Interest*, Summer.

Fukuyama, F. (1992) *The End of History and the Last Man*, Harmondsworth: Penguin.

Galbraith, J. K. (1992) *The Culture of Commitment*. London: Sinclair Stevenson.

Gallie, W. B. (1955 –6) 'Essentially Contested Context', in *Proceedings of the Aristotelian Society*, vol. 56.

Gamble, A. (1994) *The Free Economy and the Strong State*, 2nd edn. Basingstoke: Palgrave Macmillan.

Gandhi, M. (1971) *Selected Writings of Mahatma Gandhi*, ed. R. Duncan. London: Fontana.

Garvey, J. H. (1993) 'Fundamentalism and Politics', in Martin E. Marty and R. Scott Appleby (eds), *Fundamentalisms and the State*. Chicago, IL and London: University of Chicago Press.

Gasset, J. Ortega y (1972) *The Revolt of the Masses*. London: Allen & Unwin.

Gellner, E. (1983) *Nations and Nationalism*. Oxford: Blackwell.

Giddens, A. (1984) *The Constitution of Society*. Cambridge: Polity Press.

Giddens, A. (1994) *Beyond Left and Right: The Future of Radical Politics*. Cambridge: Polity Press.

Giddens, A. (1998) *The Third Way: The Renewal of Social Democracy*. Cambridge: Polity Press.

Giddens, A. (2000) *The Third Way and Its Critics*. Cambridge: Polity Press.

Gilmour, I. (1978) *Inside Right: A Study of Conservatism*. London: Quartet Books.

Gilmour, I. (1992) *Dancing with Dogma: Britain under Thatcherism*. London: Simon & Schuster.

Gobineau, J.-A. (1970) *Gobineau: Selected Political Writings*, ed. M. D. Biddiss. New York: Harper & Row.

Godwin, W. (1971) *Enquiry Concerning Political Justice*, ed. K. C. Carter. Oxford: Oxford University Press.

Goldman, E. (1969) *Anarchism and Other Essays*. New York: Dover.

Goldsmith, E. (1988) *The Great U-Turn: De-industrialising Society*. Bideford: Green Books.

Goldsmith, E. et al. (eds) (1972) *Blueprint for Survival*. Harmondsworth: Penguin.

Goodhart, D. (2004) 'The Discomfort of Strangers', *Prospect*, February 2004.

Goodin, R. E. (1992) *Green Political Theory*. Oxford: Polity Press.

Goodman, P. (1964) *Compulsory Miseducation*. New York: Vintage Books.

Goodman, P. (1977) 'Normal Politics and the Psychology of Power', in G. Woodcock (ed.), *The Anarchist Reader*. London: Fontana.

Goodwin, B. (1997) *Using Political Ideas*, 4th edn. London: John Wiley & Sons.

Gorz, A. (1982) *Farewell to the Working Class*. London: Pluto Press (Boston, MA: South End Press, 1982).

Gould, B. (1985) *Socialism and Freedom*. Basingstoke: Palgrave Macmillan (Wakefield, NH: Longwood, 1986).

Gramsci, A. (1971) *Selections from the Prison Notebooks*, ed. Q. Hoare and G. Nowell-Smith. London: Lawrence & Wishart.

Gray, J. (1995a) *Enlightenment's Wake: Politics and Culture at the Close of the Modern Age*. London: Routledge.

Gray, J. (1995b) *Liberalism*, 2nd edn. Milton Keynes: Open University Press.

Gray, J. (1996) *Post-liberalism: Studies in Political Thought*. London: Routledge.

Gray, J. (1997) *Endgames: Questions in Late Modern Political Thought*. Cambridge and Malden, MA: Blackwell.

Gray, J. (2000) *Two Faces of Liberalism*. Cambridge: Polity Press.

Gray, J. and Willetts, D. (1997) *Is Conservatism Dead?* London: Profile Books.

Green, T. H. (1988) *Works*, ed. R. Nettleship. London: Oxford University Press (New York: AMS Press, 1984).

Greenleaf, W. H. (1983) *The British Political Tradition: The Ideological Heritage*, vol. 2. London: Methuen.

Greer, G. (1970) *The Female Eunuch*. New York: McGraw-Hill.

Greer, G. (1985) *Sex and Destiny*. New York: Harper & Row.

Greer, G. (1999) *The Whole Woman*. London: Doubleday.

Gregor, A. J. (1969) *The Ideology of Fascism*. New York: Free Press.

Griffin, R. (1993) *The Nature of Fascism*. London: Routledge.

Griffin, R. (ed.) (1995) *Fascism*. Oxford and New York: Oxford University Press.

Griffin, R. (ed.) (1998) *International Fascism: Theories, Causes and the New Consensus*. London: Arnold and New York: Oxford University Press.

Gutman, A. (ed.) (1995) *Multiculturalism: Examining the Politics of Recognition*. Princeton, NJ: Princeton University Press.

Hadden, J. K. and Shupe, A. (eds) (1986) *Prophetic Religions and Politics: Religion and Political Order*. New York: Paragon House.

Hall, J. A. (1988) *Liberalism: Politics, Ideology and the Market*. London: Paladin.

Hall, S. and Jacques, M. (eds) (1983) *The Politics of Thatcherism*. London: Lawrence & Wishart.

Hardin, G. (1968) 'The Tragedy of the Commons', *Science*, vol. 162, pp. 1243–8.

Harrington, M. (1993) *Socialism, Past and Future*. London: Pluto Press.

Harvey, D. (2005) *A Brief History of Neoliberalism*. Oxford and New York: Oxford University Press.

Hattersley, R. (1987) *Choose Freedom*. Harmondsworth: Penguin.

Hayek, F. A. von (1944) *The Road to Serfdom*. London: Routledge & Kegan Paul (Chicago, IL: University of Chicago Press, 1956, new edn).

Hayek, F. A. von (1960) *The Constitution of Liberty*. London: Routledge & Kegan Paul.

Hayward, T. (1998) *Political Theory and Ecological Values*. Cambridge: Polity Press.

Hearn, J. (2006) *Rethinking Nationalism: A Critical Inroduction*. Basingstoke and New York: Palgrave Macmillan.

Heath, A., Jowell, R. and Curtice, J. (1985) *How Britain Votes*. Oxford: Pergamon.

Heffernan, R. (2001) *New Labour and Thatcherism*. London: Palgrave.

Hegel, G. W. F. (1942) *The Philosophy of Right*, trans. T. M. Knox. Oxford: Clarendon Press.

Hiro, D. (1988) *Islamic Fundamentalism*. London: Paladin.

Hitler, A. (1969) *Mein Kampf*. London: Hutchinson (Boston, MA: Houghton Mifflin, 1973).

Hobbes, T. (1968) *Leviathan*, ed. C. B. Macpherson. Harmondsworth: Penguin.

Hobhouse, L. T. (1911) *Liberalism*. London: Thornton Butterworth.

Hobsbawm, E. (1983) 'Inventing Tradition', in E. Hobsbawm and T. Ranger (eds), *The Invention of Tradition*. Cambridge: Cambridge University Press.

Hobsbawm, E. (1992) *Nations and Nationalism since 1780: Programme, Myth and Reality*, 2nd edn. Cambridge: Cambridge University Press.

Hobsbawm, E. (1994) *Age of Extremes: The Short Twentieth Century, 1914 –1991*. London: Michael Joseph.

Hobson, J. A. (1902) *Imperialism: A Study*. London: Nisbet.

Hoffman, J. and P. Graham (2006) *Introduction to Political Ideologies*. London: Pearson Education.

Holden, B. (1993) *Understanding Liberal Democracy*, 2nd edn. Hemel Hempstead: Harvester Wheatsheaf.

Honderich, T. (1991) *Conservatism*. Harmondsworth: Penguin.

Huntington, S. (1993) 'The Clash of Civilizations', *Foreign Affairs*, vol. 72, no. 3.

Huntington, S. (1996) *The Clash of Civilizations and the Remaking of World Order*. New York: Simon & Schuster.

Hutchinson, J. and Smith, A. D. (eds) (1994) *Nationalism*. Oxford and New York: Oxford University Press.

Hutton, W. (1995) *The State We're In*. London: Jonathan Cape.

Illich, I. (1973) *Deschooling Society*. Harmondsworth: Penguin (New York: Harper & Row, 1983).

Inglehart, R. (1977) *The Silent Revolution: Changing Values and Political Styles amongst Western Publics*. Princeton, NJ: Princeton University Press.

Jefferson, T. (1972) *Notes on the State of Virginia*. New York: W. W. Norton.

Jefferson, T. (1979) 'The United States Declaration of Independence', in W. Laqueur and B. Rubin (eds), *The Human Rights Reader*. New York: Meridan.

Journal of Political Ideologies. Abingdon, UK and Cambridge, MA: Carfax.

Kallis, A. A. (ed.) (2003) *The Fascist Reader*. London and New York: Routledge.

Kant, I. (1991) *Kant: Political Writings*, ed. Hans Reiss, trans. H. B. Nisbet. Cambridge: Cambridge University Press.

Kautsky, K. (1902) *The Social Revolution*. Chicago: Kerr.

Keynes, J. M. (1963) *The General Theory of Employment, Interest and Money*. London: Macmillan (San Diego: Harcourt Brace Jovanovich, 1965).

Kingdom, J. (1992) *No Such Thing as Society? Individualism and Community*. Buckingham and Philadelphia PA: Open University Press.

Klein, M. (2001) *No Logo*. London: Flamingo.

Kropotkin, P. (1914) *Mutual Aid*. Boston, MA: Porter Sargent.

Kuhn, T. (1962) *The Structure of Scientific Revolutions*. Chicago, IL: Chicago University Press.

Kymlicka, W. (1995) *Multicultural Citizenship*. Oxford: Oxford University Press.

Laclau, E. and Mouffe, C. *Hegemony and Socialist Strategy*. London: Verso.

Lane, D. (1996) *The Rise and Fall of State Socialism*. Oxford: Polity Press.

Laqueur, W. (ed.) (1979) *Fascism: A Reader's Guide*. Harmondsworth: Penguin.

Larrain, J. (1983) *Marxism and Ideology*. Basingstoke: Macmillan.

Leach, R. (2002) *Political Ideology in Britain*. Basingstoke: Palgrave Macmillan.

Lenin, V. I. (1964) *The State and Revolution*. Peking: People's Publishing House.

Lenin, V. I. (1970) *Imperialism, the Highest Stage of Capitalism*. Moscow: Progress Publishers.

Lenin, V. I. (1988) *What is to be Done?* Harmondsworth and New York: Penguin.

Leopold, A. (1968) *Sand County Almanac*. Oxford: Oxford University Press.

Letwin, S. R. (1992) *The Anatomy of Thatcherism*. London: Fontana.

Lewis, B. (2004) *The Crisis of Islam: Holy War and Unholy Terror*. London and New York: Random House.

Lindblom, C. (1977) *Politics and Markets*. New York: Basic Books.

Lipset, S. M. (1983) *Political Man: The Social Bases of Behaviour*. London: Heinemann.

Locke, J. (1962) *Two Treatises of Government*. Cambridge: Cambridge University Press.

Locke, J. (1963) *A Letter Concerning Toleration*. The Hague: Martinus Nijhoff.

Lovelock, J. (1979) *Gaia: A New Look at Life on Earth*. Oxford and New York: Oxford University Press.

Lovelock, J. (1988) 'Man and Gaia', in E. Goldsmith and N. Hilyard (eds), *The Earth Report*. London: Mitchell Beazley.

Lyotard, J. -F. (1984) *The Postmodern Condition: The Power of Knowledge*. Minneapolis: University of Minnesota Press.

MacIntyre, A. (1981) *After Virtue*. London: Duckworth.

Macmillan, H. (1966) *The Middle Way*. London: Macmillan.

Macpherson, C. B. (1973) *Democratic Theory: Essays in Retrieval*. Oxford: Clarendon Press.

Maistre, J. de (1971) *The Works of Joseph de Maistre*, trans. J. Lively. New York: Schocken.

Mannheim, K. (1960) *Ideology and Utopia*. London: Routledge & Kegan Paul.

Manning, D. (1976) *Liberalism*. London: Dent.

Marcuse, H. (1964) *One Dimensional Man: Studies in the Ideology of Advanced Industrial Society*. Boston, MA: Beacon.

Marquand, D. (1988) *The Unprincipled Society*. London: Fontana.

Marquand, D. (1992) *The Progressive Dilemma*. London: Heinemann.

Marquand, D. and Seldon, A. (1996) *The Ideas that Shaped Post-War Britain*. London: Fontana.

Marshall, P. (1993) *Demanding the Impossible: A History of Anarchism*. London: Fontana.

Marshall, P. (1995) *Nature's Web: Rethinking our Place on Earth*. London: Cassell.

Martell, L. (2001) *Social Democracy: Global and National Perspectives*. Basingstoke and New York: Palgrave Macmillan.

Marty, M. E. (1988) 'Fundamentalism as a Social Phenomenon', *Bulletin of the American Academy of Arts and Sciences*, vol. 42, pp. 15–29.

Marty, M. E. and Appleby, R. S. (eds) (1993) *Fundamentalisms and the State: Remaking Polities, Economies, and Militance*. Chicago, IL and London: University of Chicago Press.

Marx, K. and Engels, F. (1968) *Selected Works*. London: Lawrence & Wishart.

Marx, K. and Engels, F. (1970) *The German Ideology*. London: Lawrence & Wishart.

McLellan, D. (1998) *Marxism After Marx*, 3rd edn. Basingstoke: Palgrave Macmillan.

McLellan, D. (1980) *The Thought of Karl Marx*, 2nd edn. London: Macmillan.

McLellan, D. (1995) *Ideology*. 2nd edn. Milton Keynes: Open University Press.

Mead, W. R. (2006) 'God's Country?', *Foreign Affairs*, 85/5.

Meadows, D. H., Meadows, D. L., Randers, D. and Williams, W. (1972) *The Limits to Growth*. London: Pan (New York: New American Library, 1972).

Michels, R. (1958) *Political Parties*. Glencoe, IL: Free Press.

Miliband, R. (1969) *The State in Capitalist Society*. London: Verso (New York: Basic, 1978).

Miliband, R. (1995) *Socialism for a Sceptical Age*. Oxford: Polity.

Mill, J. S. (1970) *On the Subjection of Women*. London: Dent.

Mill, J. S. (1972) *Utilitarianism, On Liberty and Consideration on Representative Government*. London: Dent.

Miller, D. (1984) *Anarchism*. London: Dent.

Millett, K. (1970) *Sexual Politics*. New York: Doubleday.

Mitchell, J. (1971) *Women's Estate*. Harmondsworth: Penguin.

Mitchell, J. (1975) *Psychoanalysis and Feminism*. London: Penguin.

Montesquieu, C. de (1969) *The Spirit of Laws*. Glencoe, IL: Free Press.

More, T. (1965) *Utopia*. Harmondsworth: Penguin (New York: Norton, 1976).

Morland, D. (1997) *Demanding the Impossible: Human Nature and Politics in Nineteenth-Century Social Anarchism*. London and Washington, DC: Cassell.

Mosca, G. (1939) *The Ruling Class*, trans. and ed. A. Livingstone. New York: McGraw-Hill.

Moschonas, G. (2002) *In the Name of Social Democracy – The Great Transformation: 1945 to the Present*. London and New York: Verso.

Murray, C. (1984) *Losing Ground: American Social Policy: 1950–1980*. New York: Basic Books.

Murray, C. and Herrnstein, R. (1995) *The Bell Curve: Intelligence and Class Structure in American Life*. New York: Free Press.

Naess, A. (1973) 'The shallow and the deep, long-range ecology movement: a summary', *Inquiry*, vol. 16.

Naess, A. (1989) *Community and Lifestyle: Outline of an Ecosophy*. Cambridge: Cambridge University Press.

Neocleous, M. (1997) *Fascism*. Milton Keynes: Open University Press.

Nietzsche, F. (1961) *Thus Spoke Zarathustra*, trans. R. J. Hollingdale. Harmondsworth: Penguin (New York: Random, 1982).

Nolte, E. (1965) *Three Faces of Fascism: Action Française, Italian Fascism and National Socialism*. London: Weidenfeld & Nicolson.

Nozick, R. (1974) *Anarchy, State and Utopia*. Oxford: Blackwell (New York: Basic, 1974).

Oakeshott, M. (1962) *Rationalism in Politics and Other Essays*. London: Methuen (New York: Routledge Chapman & Hall, 1981).

Ohmae, K. (1989) *Borderless World: Power and Strategy in the Interlinked Economy* (London: HarperCollins).

O'Sullivan, N. (1976) *Conservatism*. London: Dent and New York: St Martin's Press.

O'Sullivan, N. (1983) *Fascism*. London: Dent.

Özkirmli, V. (2005) *Contemporary Debates on Nationalism: A Critical Engagement*. Basingstoke and New York: Palgrave Macmillan.

Paglia, C. (1990) *Sex, Art and American Culture*. New Haven, CT: Yale University.

Paglia, C. (1992) *Sexual Personae: Art and Decadence from Nefertiti to Emily Dickinson*. Harmondsworth: Penguin.

Parekh, B. (1994) 'The Concept of Fundamentalism', in A. Shtromas (ed.), *The End of 'isms'? Reflections on the Fate of Ideological Politics after Communism's Collapse*. Oxford and Cambridge, MA: Blackwell.

Parekh, B. (2005) *Rethinking Multiculturalism: Cultural Diversity and Political Theory*, 2nd edn. Basingstoke and New York: Palgrave Macmillan.

Pareto, V. (1935) *The Mind and Society*. London: Cape and New York: AMS Press.

Passmore, K. (2002) *Fascism: A Very Short Introduction*. Oxford and New York: Oxford University Press.

Pierson, C. (1995) *Socialism After Communism*. Cambridge: Polity Press.

Plato (1955) *The Republic*, trans. H. D. Lee. Harmondsworth: Penguin (New York: Random, 1983).

Popper, K. (1945) *The Open Society and Its Enemies*. London: Routledge & Kegan Paul.

Popper, K. (1957) *The Poverty of Historicism*. London: Routledge.

Porritt, J. (2005) *Capitalism as if the World Matters*. London: Earthscan.

Poulantzas, N. (1968) *Political Power and Social Class*. London: New Left Books (New York: Routledge Chapman & Hall, 1987).

Proudhon, P. J. (1970) *What is Property?*, trans. B. R. Tucker. New York: Dover.

Purkis, J. and Bowen, J. (1997) *Twenty-First Century Anarchism: Unorthodox Ideas for a New Millennium*. London: Cassell.

Ramsay, M. (1997) *What's Wrong with Liberalism? A Radical Critique of Liberal Political Philosophy*. London: Leicester University Press.

Randall, V. (1987) *Women and Politics: An International Perspective*, 2nd edn. Basingstoke: Palgrave Macmillan.

Rawls, J. (1970) *A Theory of Justice*. Oxford: Oxford University Press (Cambridge, MA: Harvard University Press, 1971).

Rawls, J. (1993) *Political Liberalism*. New York: Colombia University Press.

Regan, T. (1983) *The Case for Animal Rights*. London: Routledge & Kegan Paul.

Roemer, J. (ed.) (1986) *Analytical Marxism*, Cambridge: Cambridge University Press.

Rorty, R. (1989) *Contingency, Irony and Solidarity*. Cambridge: Cambridge University Press.

Rothbard, M. (1978) *For a New Liberty*. New York: Macmillan.

Rousseau, J. -J. (1913) *The Social Contract and Discourse*, ed. G. D. H. Cole. London: Dent (Glencoe, IL: Free Press, 1969).

Roussopoulos, D. (ed.) (2002) *The Anarchist Papers*. New York and London: Black Rose Books.

Ruthven, M. (2004) *Fundamentalism: The Search for Meaning*. Oxford and New York: Oxford University Press.

Said, E. ([1978] 2003) *Orientalism*. Harmondsworth: Penguin.

Sandel, M. (1982) *Liberalism and the Limits of Justice*. Cambridge: Cambridge University Press.

Sassoon, D. (1997) *One Hundred Years of Socialism*. London: Fontana.

Schneir, M. (1995) *The Vintage Book of Feminism: The Essential Writings of the Contemporary Women's Movement*. London: Vintage.

Scholte, J. A. (2005) *Globalization: An Introduction*, 2nd edn. Basingstoke and New York: Palgrave Macmillan.

Schumacher, E. F. (1973) *Small Is Beautiful: A Study of Economics as if People Mattered*. London: Blond & Briggs (New York: Harper & Row, 1989).

Schumpeter, J. (1976) *Capitalism, Socialism and Democracy*. London: Allen & Unwin (Magnolia, MA: Petersmith, 1983).

Schwarzmantel, J. (1991) *Socialism and the Idea of the Nation*. Hemel Hempstead: Harvester Wheatsheaf.

Schwartzmantel, J. (1998) *The Age of Ideology: Political Ideologies from the American Revolution to Post-Modern Times*. Basingstoke: Palgrave Macmillan.

Scruton, R. (2001) *The Meaning of Conservatism*, 3rd edn. Basingstoke: Macmillan.

Seabright, P. (2004) *The Company of Strangers*. Princeton, NJ: Princeton University Press.

Seliger, M. (1976) *Politics and Ideology*. London: Allen & Unwin (Glencoe, IL: Free Press, 1976).

Sen, A. (2006) *Identity and Violence*. London: Penguin.

Shtromas, A. (ed.) (1994) *The End of 'isms'? Reflections on the Fate of Ideological Politics after Communism's Collapse*. Oxford and Cambridge, MA: Blackwell.

Singer, P. (1976) *Animal Liberation*. New York: Jonathan Cape.

Singer, P. (1993) *Practical Ethics*, 2nd edn. Cambridge: Cambridge University Press.

Smart, B. (1993) *Postmodernity*. London and New York: Routledge.

Smiles, S. (1986) *Self-Help*. Harmondsworth: Penguin.

Smith, A. (1976) *An Enquiry into the Nature and Causes of the Wealth of Nations*. Chicago, IL: University of Chicago Press.

Smith, A. D. (1986) *The Ethnic Origins of Nations*. Oxford: Blackwell.

Smith, A. D. (1991) *National Identity*. Harmondsworth: Penguin.

Smith, A. D. (2001) *Nationalism: Theory, Ideology, History*. Cambridge and Malden, MA: Polity Press.

Sorel, G. (1950) *Reflections on Violence*, trans. T. E. Hulme and J. Roth. New York: Macmillan.

Spencer, H. (1940) *The Man versus the State*. London: Watts & Co.

Spencer, H. (1967) *On Social Evolution: Selected Writings*. Chicago, IL: University of Chicago Press.

Spencer, P. and Wollman, H. (2002) *Nationalism: A Critical Introduction*. London and Thousand Oaks, CA: Sage.

Squires, J. (1999) *Gender in Political Theory*. Cambridge and Malden, MA: Polity Press.

Stelzer, I. (ed.) (2004) *Neoconservatism*. London: Atlantic Books.

Stirner, M. (1971) *The Ego and His Own*, ed. J. Carroll. London: Cape.

Sumner, W. (1959) *Folkways*. New York: Doubleday.

Sydie, R. A. (1987) *Natural Women, Cultured Men: A Feminist Perspective on Sociological Theory*. Milton Keynes: Open University Press.

Talmon, J. L. (1952) *The Origins of Totalitarian Democracy*. London: Secker & Warburg.

Tam, H. (1998) *Communitarianism: A New Agenda for Politics and Citizenship*. Basingstoke: Palgrave Macmillan.

Tawney, R. H. (1921) *The Acquisitive Society*. London: Bell (San Diego: Harcourt Brace Jovanovich, 1955).

Tawney, R. H. (1969) *Equality*. London: Allen & Unwin.

Taylor, C. (1994) *Multiculturalism and 'The Politics of Recognition'*. Princeton, NJ: Princeton University Press.

Thoreau, H. D. (1983) *Walden and 'Civil Disobedience'*. Harmondsworth: Penguin.

Tocqueville, A. de (1968) *Democracy in America*. London: Fontana (New York: McGraw, 1981).

Tolstoy, L. (1937) *Recollections and Essays*. Oxford: Oxford University Press.

United Nations (1972). See Ward and Dubois (1972).

United Nations (1980) *Compendium of Statistics: 1977*. New York: United Nations.

Vincent, A. (1995) *Modern Political Ideologies*, 2nd edn. Oxford: Blackwell.

Waldron, J. (1995) 'Minority Cultures and the Cosmopolitan Alternative', in W. Kymlicka (ed.), *The Rights of Minority Cultures*. London and New York: Open University Press.

Ward, B. and Dubois, R. (1972) *Only One Earth*. Harmondsworth: Penguin.

White, S. (ed.) (2001) *New Labour: The Progressive Future?* Basingstoke and New York: Palgrave Macmillan.

Willetts, D. (1992) *Modern Conservatism*. Harmondsworth: Penguin.

Wollstonecraft, M. (1967) *A Vindication of the Rights of Women*, ed. C. W. Hagelman. New York: Norton.

Wolff, R. P. (1998) In Defence of Anarchism, 2nd edn. Berkeley, CA: University of California Press.

Woodcock, G. (1962) *Anarchism: A History of Libertarian Ideas and Movements*. Harmondsworth and New York: Penguin.

Woolf, S. J. (1981) (ed.) *European Fascism*. London: Weidenfeld & Nicolson.

Wright, A. (1996) *Socialisms: Theories and Practices*. Oxford and New York: Oxford University Press.

INDEX

Entries in **bold type** refer to boxed information. Entries in *italics* refer to on-page definitions.

greenhouse effect 257
Greenpeace 256
Greer, Germaine 232, 248, 252, 253
Gregor, A. J. 206
Griffin, Roger 206, 215, 220
Grimm Brothers 156
Gushmun Emunim (Bloc of the Faithful) 305
Gyn/Ecology (Daly, (1979) 277

Haeckel, Ernst 255
Haider, J. 228
Hamas 292
Hardin, Garrett 266
Hardy, Thomas 256
Haredim (ultra-orthodox Jews) 287
Harriman, R. 256
Hayek, Friedrich von 13, 52–3, 89–90, **90**
Hegel, G. W. F. 119, 120, 121, 217
hegemony 7, 95
Heisenberg, Verner 263
Henry, Emile 197
Herder, J. G. 156, 317
Hezbollah 292
hierarchy 76–8, *77*
Hinduism 304
historical materialism 119–20, *119*, 132
history **336**
Hitler, Adolf 2, 81, 204, 206, 208–11, **210**,
    212–13, 217–18, 224
  suicide 226
Ho Chi Minh 167
Hobbes, Thomas 36–7, 46, 71, **72**, 181–2
Hobhouse, L. T. 55
Hobsbawm, Eric 285
Hobson, J. A. 55
holism 262–5, *262*
Horkheimer, Max 127
How to be a Survivor (Ehrlich and Harriman,
    1971) 256
human imperfection 71–4
human nature 28, **73**, 180–3
human rights *46*, 170
  see also natural rights
humanism *130, 257*
Humbert, King (Italy) 197
Hungary 146
Huntington, Samuel 19, 95, 282–3, 307, 313
hybridity *326*
hyphenated nationality 323

ideas 2–4
identity 20, 315–16
identity politics 155–7
ideologies 2–3
  new 17–21, **9**
  particular 8–9
  total 8–9
  versus ideology 4
  see also specific ideologies
ideology 2–21, **11**
  definition 5–6, 10–12

demise of 333–5
versus science 6, 11–13
views of 4–10
see also ideologies
Ideology and Utopia (Mannheim) 8
immigration 94, 162–3, 312
imperialism *164*, 167
independence *154*
India 101, 146, 167, 199, 304–5
individual responsibility 51, 55
individualism **28**, 62, 85, 170, 191–2, *243*
  feminism and 243
  liberal 27–8, 45, 54–5
individualist anarchism 191–5
individuality *55*, 243
  see also individualism
individuals 27–8
Indochina 146, 312
industrialism *11*, **265**, 278
industrialization 24–5, 53, 100, 256, 266
inequality 57–8, 62, 82–3, 106
  sexual 234–5, 236
  see also equality
inflation 90
integral nationalism (Maurras) *215*
inter-war era 9
International Working Men's Association (First
    International) 171, 176, 186
internationalism 95, *160*, 168–72, **169**
  liberal 168–70
  socialist 170–2
Iran 67, 242, 282, 283, 291, 299–300
Iran–Iraq war (1980–8) 299–300
Iraq 95, 167
Islam 63, 131, 148, 282, 294
  see also Islamic fundamentalism; Islamism
Islamic feminism 242
Islamic fundamentalism 290, 294–300
  see also Islam; Islamism
Islamic Revolutionary Council (Iran) 282
Islamism 297
  varieties of 297–300
  see also Islam; Islamic fundamentalism
Islamo-fascism 295
Israel 104, 295, 296, 304, 305
Italian Socialist Party 115, 213
Italy 66, 81, 85, 144, 146, 176
  corporatism 219
  fascist 9, 204, 215, 217–18, 219–20
  unification 80, 144, 158

Jahn, F. L. 165
Japan 25, 67, 146, 204, 206, 215
Jefferson, Thomas 45–6, **47**
Jewish fundamentalism 305
Jews 222–5
  ultra-orthodox 287
  see also anti-Semitism; Israel
jihad (holy war) 165, *295*
jingoism *164*
John Paul II, Pope 131